The Darker Side of Family Communication

LIFESPAN
COMMUNICATION
Children, Families, and Aging

Thomas J. Socha
GENERAL EDITOR

Vol. 5

The Lifespan Communication series
is part of the Peter Lang Media and Communication list.
Every volume is peer reviewed and meets
the highest quality standards for content and production.

PETER LANG
New York • Bern • Frankfurt • Berlin
Brussels • Vienna • Oxford • Warsaw

The Darker Side of Family Communication

The Harmful, the Morally Suspect, and the Socially Inappropriate

Edited by Loreen N. Olson & Mark A. Fine

PETER LANG
New York • Bern • Frankfurt • Berlin
Brussels • Vienna • Oxford • Warsaw

Library of Congress Cataloging-in-Publication Data

The darker side of family communication: the harmful, the morally suspect,
and the socially inappropriate / edited by Loreen N. Olson, Mark A. Fine.
pages cm. — (Lifespan communication: children, families, and aging; v. 5)
Includes bibliographical references and index.
1. Families. 2. Marriage. 3. Parent and child. 4. Interpersonal communication.
I. Olson, Loreen N., editor. II. Fine, Mark A., editor.
HQ503.D37   306.85—dc23   2015035544
ISBN 978-1-4331-2538-6 (hardcover)
ISBN 978-1-4331-2537-9 (paperback)
ISBN 978-1-4539-1743-5 (e-book)
ISSN 2166-6466 (print)
ISSN 2166-6474 (online)

Bibliographic information published by **Die Deutsche Nationalbibliothek.**
Die Deutsche Nationalbibliothek lists this publication in the "Deutsche
Nationalbibliografie"; detailed bibliographic data are available
on the Internet at http://dnb.d-nb.de/.

Cover image ©iStock.com/B_Bort
Cover design by Clear Point Designs

© 2016 Peter Lang Publishing, Inc., New York
29 Broadway, 18th floor, New York, NY 10006
www.peterlang.com

This book is dedicated to our parents
Clifford F. and Bonnie L. Olson

Burrill and Marilynn Fine

Your unconditional love fills our souls.

Table of Contents

Editors

Loreen N. Olson (PhD, University of Nebraska) is an Associate Professor in Communication Studies and an Affiliate Faculty member of the Women & Gender Studies program at the University of North Carolina at Greensboro. She is the immediate past editor of the *Journal of Family Communication*. Loreen also wears other administrative hats such as Director of Graduate Studies, Director of the Program to Advance Community Responses to Violence against Women, and the Coordinator of the Violence Prevention Network of Guilford County. Loreen teaches courses in family and gender communication as well as communication theory and the dark side of family/relational communication. Her research addresses communication issues related to gender, family, intimate partner violence, the dark side of close relationships, the communication of deviance, and the luring communication of child sexual predators. Currently, she and her colleagues are examining the relationships between intimate partner violence and traumatic brain injury. Olson is a past chair of the Family Communication Division of the National Communication Association and co-author of the book titled, *The Dark Side of Family Communication*. Her work has appeared in various journals, including the *Journal of Family Communication, Communication Theory, Communication Monographs, Journal of Applied Communication, Women's Studies in Communication,* and *Trauma, Violence, & Abuse.* When not co-editing books together, Loreen and Mark enjoy spending time with their nine-year-old twins, two older daughters, and three neurotic, but loving dogs.

Mark A. Fine (PhD, The Ohio State University) is Professor and Chair in the Department of Human Development and Family Studies (HDFS) at the University of North Carolina at Greensboro. Previously, Mark was a faculty member in HDFS at the University of Missouri Columbia from 1994–2011, serving as Department Chair from 1994–2002. In addition to being the editor of *Family Relations* and the *Journal of Social and Personal Relationships*, Mark was a member of the NIH-supported Early Head Start Research Consortium from 1995–2005. He is a Fellow of the National Council on Family Relations and serves on the editorial boards of eight peer-reviewed journals in family studies, personal relationships, and human development. His research interests lie in the areas of family transitions, such as divorce and remarriage; early intervention program evaluation; social cognition; and relationship stability. Mark has co-authored books titled *Children of Divorce: Stories of Hope and Loss* (with John Harvey) and *Beyond the Average Divorce* (with David Demo). In addition, he is the co-editor of several books, including the *Handbook of Family Diversity* (with David Demo and Katherine Allen), *The Handbook of Divorce and Relationship Dissolution* (with John Harvey), *Keepin' On: The Everyday Struggles of Young Families in Poverty* (with Jean Ispa and Kathy Thornburg), and *Family Theories: A Content-Based Approach* (with Frank Fincham). He has published almost 200 peer-reviewed journal articles, book chapters, and books. When not working, Mark enjoys spending time with his family, playing tennis, and watching sports.

Series Editor Preface

The darker side of family communication: The harmful, the morally suspect, and the socially inappropriate

THOMAS J. SOCHA
Old Dominion University

The darker side of family communication: The harmful, the morally suspect, and the socially inappropriate, edited by Loreen Olson and Mark Fine, offers a significant addition that seeks to broaden the story of communication in the ever-evolving lives of contemporary families by examining dark communication processes. Since the early days of family communication studies in the 1980s, family communication scholars have labored to develop inclusive ways to think about and conceptualize "families" as well as to study a widening array of family communication processes. For all those who study, teach, and live family communication, this volume adds to our understanding of the rich discursive details of darkside of managing communication complexities, challenges, and opportunities at home. Professors Olson and Fine, together with their highly regarded coauthors, paint a compelling portrait of the current state of dark communication at home that will inform contemporary societal discursive strugles, positive-negative, prosocial-antisocial, within famlies, and will undoubtedly become a much-cited work in family communication.

Like this volume, the book series Lifespan Communication: Children, Families and Aging invites communication scholars to view communication through a panoramic lens—from first words to final conversations—a comprehensive communication vista that brings all children, adolescents, adults, and those in later life as well as lifespan groups such as the family into focus. By viewing communication panoramically it is also my hope that communication scholars and educators will incorporate into their work the widely accepted idea that communication (positive and dark) develops, that is, it has a starting point and a developmental arc, changing as we change over time. And further, that developmental communication arcs are historically contextualized. As infants, we begin our communication education in unique historical and familial contexts that shape our early communication learning as well as the foundations of our communication values. Children born in 2015, for example, will begin their communication learning in a time when humans are seeking to remake themselves to fit a rapidly changing and increasingly complex landscape that features a wider variety of types of family relationships. Of course, adults caring for these children—who could have been born anytime between the 1930s to the late 1990s—have experienced vastly different developmental communication arcs but yet must discursively span the generations, pass along their communication knowledge and values, as well as teach children how to communicate effectively within the current historical context, whether their relationships are grounded in birth or social agreement. Historically contextualized lifespan thinking also raises important new questions such as, what is to be passed along from one generation to the next as "timeless" communication knowledge and practices? Or in contemporary digital parlance, what is to become memetic, that is, analogous to genetic information—what survives to become the communication inheritance of future generations?

It is my hope that *The darker side of family communication: The harmful, the morally suspect, and the socially inappropriate* and all of the books published in the Lifespan Communication: Children, Families, and Aging series will offer the communication field new understandings and deeper appreciation of the complexities of all forms of communication as it develops across the lifespan as well as raise important questions about communication for current and future generations to study.

—Thomas J. Socha

Shining Light ON THE Darkness

A Prologue

LOREEN N. OLSON & MARK A. FINE

Humans share one thing in common: we are all *born* into some form of family. Kinship can be a supporting, loving structure as well as a contested, conflictual terrain. The darker side of family life is the focus of this edited volume titled *The darker side of family communication: The harmful, the morally suspect, and the socially inappropriate.* Yet, as the reader will realize, darkness is only one side of the proverbial coin when it comes to examining such interactions. Instead, the complexity of family life means that there are both bright moments and dark fractures. The primary goal of this book is to advance theory and research by presenting *original, empirical* studies as well as *theoretical* and *methodological* overviews on dark family communication processes, revealing their bright and dark DNA.

SHINING LIGHT ON THE WHY

The current volume extends Olson, Baiocchi-Wagner, Kratzer, and Symonds' (2012) book titled *The Dark Side of Family Communication* in several ways. First, this edited volume advances the earlier work by showcasing current empirical tests of dark family communication processes and discussing in more detail issues related to the methodologies involved in dark research. To that end, this volume is one of the few books to provide advanced theorizing and empirical testing of dark communication processes within and about *families* instead of about relationships in general.

Second, the volume takes an interdisciplinary approach to the study of dark family dynamics. More specifically, the co-editors—Olson and Fine—are family scholars from communication studies and human development and family studies, respectively. Further, the contributors represent additional disciplines, including sociology, psychology, and mass communication. The multidisciplinary approach allows us to see how the same concept—dark family communication—can be viewed from different vantage points while simultaneously building its conceptual muscle. The construct becomes more fully developed when such varied views are brought together to be examined.

Also new to this volume is the inclusion of critical theory and methodology. While several of the disciplines represented in this book have established histories of examining family through a critical, theoretical lens, family *communication* scholars do not. Although the field is in the midst of a sea change, a critical voice is surprisingly absent from (dark) family communication scholarship. Olson (2012) argued elsewhere that "Families are sites of power struggles that contain inequities, hegemonic patterns of discourse that reify dominant belief structures, material realities that constrain communicative interactions, and silenced voices that are in need of being heard" (p. 2). Readers will be exposed to this type of scholarship that challenges the status quo of familial interactions as well as to methodological treatises reviewing the role that critical theories, such as feminism and poststructuralism, can play in furthering our research. Likewise, it is our hope that other disciplines are exposed to how family communication scholars interrogate the symbolic, meaning-making system that is both the product of and the vehicle through which these struggles for legitimacy are enacted, exposed, and challenged.

Finally, we would like for this volume to capture our more current thinking about the definition of dark family communication. Before defining our central construct, it is important to present our thinking on the meaning of *family* itself. We agree with Allen, Fine, and Demo's (2000) definition, which is similar to one proposed by Baxter and Braithwaite (2006), that "a family is characterized by two or more persons related by birth, marriage, adoption or choice. Families are further defined by socioemotional ties and enduring responsibilities, particularly in terms of one or more members' dependence on others for support and nurturance" (p. 1). Building off of this definition of family, we adopt Koerner and Fitzpatrick's (2002) definition of *family communication* as "messages that are intentionally or unintentionally exchanged both within a system of individuals who generate a sense of belonging and collective identity and who experience a shared history and future and between these individuals and outsiders."

Extending Olson and colleagues' (2012) definition of *dark family communication*, we have come to believe that the family context itself needs to be more integrated into conceptions of this construct. It is the family context that sets this type of darkness and communication apart from other interpersonal interactions. In addition, dark *family* communication involves not only the type of messages being sent/received but also the ways in which familial bonds can be harmed, manipulated, or exploited. As such, we propose the following revised definition of dark family communication:

Symbolic exchanges between family members that are viewed through the lens of a family system and that are interpreted by family members and/or others as harmful, socially inappropriate, exploitative, or morally suspect.

SHINING LIGHT ON THE WHAT

Having discussed why we feel this book will make an important contribution to literature on the dark side of family communication, we now want to review the types of scholarship that will help us accomplish that goal. Inspired by Bronfenbrenner's (1976) ecological systems theory, Olson et al.'s (2012) Darkness Model, and our current conceptualization of dark family communication, this volume is organized into four parts. We wish to highlight that the chapters in the first three parts all represent original empirical research. The contributors in these empirical chapters either reported the results of analyses of new data from a single study from their own research or presented an integrative summary of the results from multiple studies that they conducted in their area of interest.

In the first part, titled *Individual Traits, Characteristics, and Behaviors*, the contributors address the most proximal context affecting families—the individuals within the families. Segrin and Arroyo in Chapter 1 report the results of their programmatic line of research into how mental health problems can negatively affect families. In Chapter 2, Miller-Day, Dorros, and Day present findings addressing how parental communication patterns affect their children's levels of depression and suicidality. Duggan and Kilmartin, in Chapter 3, share their findings pertaining to how parents' and siblings' behaviors can exacerbate children's eating disorders. Duggan and Kilmartin's findings are consistent with previous research that has found that control dynamics in families are closely related to the development and/or maintenance of eating disorders, but extend earlier work by examining the role of communication behaviors in the family context. Gibson, Webb, and Joseph, in Chapter 4, address a very timely issue that many parents confront—the decision regarding whether to medicate their children for suspected attention deficit disorder (ADHD). The final and fifth chapter in this section by Beyens and Eggermont considers the effects that children's temperament and maternal well-being have on the extent to which mothers rely on television as a way to soothe their children. As a collection, these five chapters shine light on the effects that challenging individually based biological, genetic, and/or psychological factors have on individuals' interactions with others in the family system. In some instances, the research showed how particular individual characteristics were associated with other family members' use of darker communication. Yet in others, an unhealthy family-based communication pattern was associated with the individual's behavior. While the designs of these studies do not allow us to draw inferences regarding causal relationships between these variables, the message is clear: there is a bidirectional relationship among challenging individual traits, behaviors, and characteristics and unhealthy family communication.

Part II, *Family Interactions and Processes,* contains four chapters that emphasize contexts one level more distal than individuals—dyadic relationships and family dynamics. Buehler, Weymouth, and Zhou, in Chapter 6, present their findings on how marital hostility is linked with parent-adolescent hostility. Their results support the systems theory notion that processes within any particular family dyad will have reverberating effects on other family dyads. Chapter 7, authored by Vangelisti, examines hurt feelings in families, with a particular focus on family dynamics that affect hurt. Lin, Giles, and Soliz (Chapter 8) address how problematic intergenerational communication affects elder abuse and neglect. Their work highlights the unfortunate reality that dark communication affects individuals and families at all stages of the lifespan. Finally, in Chapter 9, Eckstein studied abused romantic partners' preferences for the types of "love communication" they wanted to experience from their abusers. The chapters in this unit reveal that unhealthy communication patterns between family members can have long-terms effects on the individuals and dyads within the family unit and can impact the entire family system.

The three chapters in Part III, *Social, Cultural, and Historical Structures and Processes,* all address the most distal contexts affecting families, or the outermost concentric circle in Bronfenbrenner's ecological systems model—gendered patterns, religious doctrine, and economic instability. Etengoff, in Chapter 10, addresses communication processes involved in the coming-out process in highly religious families. Etengoff's work demonstrates that the already difficult process of revealing that one is gay or lesbian becomes more challenging when it occurs within religious family contexts. Chapter 11, written by Anderson, focuses on a critical issue in any treatment of dark-side communication—family violence. More specifically, she examined the gendered nature of the communication used by domestic violence victims (men and women) filing civil protection orders in an attempt to legally protect themselves from their abusers. The final chapter in this section, Chapter 12, examines another macro-level context facing many American and non-American families—economic pressure. Neppl, Senia, and Donnellan studied the consequences of economic pressure on couple communication, parenting, and children's cognitive development. The three chapters in this section are a sampling of how dark-side communicative processes are intimately affected by the macro-level contexts in which they occur. Whether it be gendered ideologies, religious beliefs, or economic disparities, this research underscores that family dynamics are heavily influenced by the social milieu in which they exist. We hope that these chapters spur future researchers to explore a wider array of intercultural, international, and societal contexts that can impact dark communication.

In Part IV, *Methodological Considerations*, we turn to a discussion of methodological issues related to conducting dark family communication research. Chapter 13, authored by Davis and Afifi, provides an integrative road map describing how future researchers can use postpositivist and interpretive methodological approaches in new and interesting ways (including more critical scholarship). Our final chapter, Chapter 14, by Harter, Thompson, and McKerrow, focuses entirely on how researchers may incorporate a critical lens into their dark family communication scholarship by specifically discussing poststructural feminism and the teachings of Foucault. The book is brought to a conclusion with a brief epilogue written by the Series Editor, Thomas Socha, who reminds us of the importance of seeing the darkness that co-exists with the light.

SHINING LIGHT ON THE HOW

This book would not have been possible without the great contributions of all of these researchers. We are so appreciative of their efforts, in terms of the quality of their scholarship as well as their willingness to be flexible with us as deadlines shifted. We also would like to acknowledge the many people who helped turn the idea for this book into a tangible reality with actual words on pages, binding, and a cover. We sincerely appreciate the early help from Beatrice Rodderick and Melanie Pringle, who assisted with research and organizational matters. We also are thankful for the series editor, Tom Socha. Thanks, Tom, for your speedy e-mail responses and guidance along the way. To Mary Savigar, the Senior Acquisitions Editor, and other folks at Peter Lang—thank you for giving us the opportunity to publish this work and for being so gracious, professional, and understanding along the way. To our youngest children, we say thanks for understanding why our editing duties meant that we could not read a book with you from time to time or go outside and shoot the basketball. Hopefully, you will come to understand the constant struggle parents experience as they navigate the tensions between work and family and appreciate the love and commitment that are integral parts of that struggle. We are thankful to our older girls, who are living successful and happy lives. We are both so proud of all you have accomplished and know there is more to come for both of you.

As we draw this prologue to a close, I (Loreen) would like to express a personal thank you to my mom, Bonnie, whom I lost during the editing of this book. Mom, you taught me how to love at all times, laugh when I felt like it, and be tough when needed. Being your daughter was an honor. I will forever remember the feel of your love and the essence of your being. I love you and miss you. I (Mark) express my deep gratitude and appreciation to my father, Burril, who passed just before work on this book began. My father was a renaissance scholar in the true sense of the word and taught me the importance of written communication. His love of literature (and clear but creative writing) led me to work tirelessly to be the best scholar I could be. Thanks for setting the bar so high, Dad. I miss you a great deal.

REFERENCES

Allen, K. R., Fine, M. A., & Demo, D. H. (2000). An overview of family diversity: Controversies, questions, and values. In D. H. Demo, K. R. Allen, & M. A. Fine (Eds.), *Handbook of family diversity* (pp. 1–14). New York: Oxford University Press.

Baxter, L., & Braithwaite, D. (2006). Metatheory and theory in family communication research. In D. Braithwaite & L. Baxter (Eds.), *Engaging theories in family communication: Multiple perspectives* (pp. 1–15). Thousand Oaks, CA: Sage.

Bronfenbrenner, U. (1977). Toward an experimental ecology of human development. *American Psychologist, 32*, 513–531.

Koerner, A. F., & Fitzpatrick, M. A. (2002). Toward a theory of family communication. *Communication Theory, 12*, 70–91.

Olson, L. N. (2012). Editor introduction: Pushing the boundaries. *Journal of Family Communication, 12*, 1–3.

Olson, L. N., Baiocchi-Wagner, E. A. Wilson-Kratzer, J. M., & Symonds, S. E. (2012). *The dark side of family communication*. Cambridge, MA: Polity Press.

PART ONE

Individual Traits, Characteristics, AND Behaviors

CHAPTER ONE

Mental Health Problems
IN Family Contexts

CHRIS SEGRIN
University of Arizona

ANALISA ARROYO
University of Georgia

Family relationships can be extraordinarily beneficial to health and well-being. For example, people in a quality marriage enjoy better physical health, satisfaction with life, and fewer symptoms of depression than their single counterparts (Holt-Lunstad, Birmingham, & Jones, 2008). Similarly, adolescents who have good relationships with their mothers and fathers and who eat an evening meal with their parents 6 or 7 times a week have significantly lower odds of experiencing poor mental health than their peers who lack these family relationship qualities (Rothon, Goodwin, & Stansfeld, 2012). However, just as family relationships may protect against mental health problems, strained or dysfunctional family relationships are a serious risk factor for mental health problems.

Our aim in this chapter is to review exemplars of family research studies conducted out of our lab that illustrate interpersonal and social psychological mechanisms that connect various family relationships with specific mental health problems. Collectively, these studies show how family relationships affect and are affected by mental health problems. Out of necessity we narrow our discussion to two primary family relationships, marital and parent-child, and several mental health problems, namely depression, loneliness, and anxiety. More comprehensive reviews of family relations and mental health problems can be found in Jacob (1987), Lee and Gotlib (1994), and Segrin (2001).

FAMILY APPROACHES TO MENTAL HEALTH PROBLEMS

The idea that the family context can offer insights into the origin, maintenance, and perhaps even alleviation of mental health problems dates back at least 100 years. For example, Freud discussed the causes and consequences of mental illness with references to "the misfortunes of life from which arise deprivation of love, poverty, family quarrels, ill-judged choice of a partner in marriage, (and) unfavorable social circumstances" (Freud, 1917/1966, p. 432). The psychodynamic theory developed by Freud stressed to the point of overemphasis the importance of early parent-child interactions in determining personality formation and later mental health or illness. Nevertheless, it is clear from this quotation and other statements made by Freud that he had an appreciation for marital and family interactions more generally as potential agents of poor mental health. Throughout the middle part of the 20th century, neo-Freudians such as Karen Horney, Frieda Fromm-Reichmann, and Harry Stack Sullivan further developed and expanded the psychodynamic thesis, emphasizing the role of family and other interpersonal relationships in disruption of mental health (e.g., Fromm-Reichmann, 1960; Sullivan, 1953). Many of their ideas about interpersonal relations and mental health are embedded in modern-day object relations theory (Westen, 1990).

Around the time that the neo-Freudians were expanding and modernizing the psychodynamic paradigm, a group of scholars who were grounded in family systems theory developed models of family interaction and schizophrenia. Perhaps most noteworthy among these models was the hypothesis linking double bind family communication to the onset of schizophrenia (e.g., Bateson, Jackson, Haley, & Weakland, 1956; Watzlawick, Bavelas, & Jackson, 1967). According to these researchers, when parents deliver contradictory messages to their children, thus creating a double bind in which there is no choice for an appropriate response, and there is no opportunity for the child to not respond or to leave the scene, the risk for schizophrenia in the child is elevated. R. D. Laing developed a comparable hypothesis based on family mystification (e.g., Laing, 1967). Laing argued that families develop an internalized system for interacting and relating to each other. He observed that the people with schizophrenia were often caught in a maze of confusion, misunderstanding, and contradictions during family interactions.

Other family interaction constructs that supposedly played a role in schizophrenia, such as family schism (hostile family conflict) and family skew (unbalanced parenting by mothers and fathers), in addition to pseudo-mutuality (the illusion of family harmony when there is none), were also brought to the forefront in the middle of the 20th century (e.g., Lidz, Cornelison, Fleck, & Terry, 1957; Wynne, Ryekof, Day, & Hirsch, 1958). Although few of these early approaches to understanding schizophrenia based on family relations and interactions have stood the test of time, perhaps their most enduring legacy is in drawing attention to family interactions as a mechanism for understanding how and why symptoms of poor mental health can develop.

More recent approaches to family relations and mental health have focused on family-based interventions for a range of mental health problems (e.g., Baucom, Shoham, Mueser, Daiuto, & Stickle, 1998). Family interventions tend to be guided by the assumption that improvement in family relations will minimize stress and enhance psychological functioning for the person afflicted with the mental health problem. This reflects a shift in thinking about family relationships as a primary causal factor to a complicating stressor in the etiology and maintenance of mental health problems. With recent advances in techniques for measuring brain function, genetic contributions, and other biological processes, current approaches to mental health and family sometimes incorporate and integrate biological and family interaction variables (e.g., González-Pinto et al., 2011).

DEPRESSION

Depression is one of the most pervasive mental health problems known to the health sciences, with a lifetime prevalence of 10–18% (Williams et al., 2007). Symptoms of depression include dysphoric mood, diminished interest in many activities, significant weight loss or gain, sleep disturbance, psychomotor agitation or retardation, fatigue, feelings of worthlessness and guilt, difficulty concentrating, and recurrent thoughts of death or suicidal ideation (American Psychiatric Association, 2013). Like most mental health problems, depression can be caused by a variety of factors. However, in virtually all cases, depression has substantial interpersonal implications that can and will change the nature of family interactions. In at least some cases, the nature of these family interactions can influence subsequent symptoms of depression.

Depression and Family Social Support

Social support has remarkable salutary effects on people's physical and mental well-being. The family is a context where social support is generally expected, even and especially when other sources of social support are unavailable. In addition to making people generally feel valued and cared for, social support can help to mitigate the ill effects of stressful events, thus minimizing depressive symptoms when faced with difficulties. In one of our studies of 325 adults ranging in age from 19–85, social support from family members was found to be negatively associated with reported symptoms of depression (Segrin, 2003). This effect was significantly moderated by age in that the association between family social support and lower levels of depression was most prominent in younger adults and much weaker in older adults. So, family social support is clearly beneficial for minimizing depression, but this is especially the case for younger adults more so than older adults. Because the coping skills of young adults are generally not as well developed as the coping skills of older adults, social support from family may be especially important and beneficial to younger adults as they attempt to deal with life's stressors.

More recently, we have found that supportive parent-child interactions may play a role in the intergenerational transmission of mental health problems (Arroyo, Segrin, & Curran, in press). The intergenerational transmission of mental health refers to the fact that parental mental health problems are often passed on to offspring. Although genetic mechanisms immediately come to mind as a plausible explanation for the intergenerational transmission of mental health, other evidence suggests that the social environment plays a role in this effect as well. We explored this possibility in 286 family triads defined as a young adult female, her mother, and the young adult female's sibling (Arroyo et al. in press). In this sample, there was a significant indirect effect of maternal mental health (operationalized as a latent variable comprised of depression, loneliness, and low self-esteem) on the young adult female's mental health (operationalized the same as the mother's mental health). The mediating variable in this indirect effect was maternal care, which was conceptualized as mothers' tendency to express care and involvement versus indifference and rejection. In other words, mothers with poor mental health appear to enact lower levels of warmth and care, and this in turn is associated with lower levels of mental health in their young adult daughters. What is particularly remarkable about this finding is the fact that supportive parental communication was operationalized entirely through siblings', not the young adult females', reports. This rules out the possibility of common method variance or a depressive bias influencing reports of one's own symptoms and maternal support in this indirect effect.

Depression and Family Coping with Major Illness

When a family member has a major illness, the entire family often experiences stress and many of the common psychological problems that follow from it, such as depression and anxiety. There are several theoretical mechanisms that explain why this is the case. First, shared emotional experiences, such as depression, within families can be understood from the perspective of *family systems theory*. The systems theory concepts of interdependence and mutual influence predict that major events such as serious illness affect the larger family or social network, not just the individual (Bertalanffy, 1975; Broderick, 1993). Family systems theory would predict that family and social network members experience distress themselves as a family member becomes more distressed with his or her illness. For such relationships, this has both positive and negative implications (DeVellis, Lewis, &

Sterba, 2003). On the positive side, the interdependence reflected in a communal coping perspective reframes responsibility for support and coping as a shared phenomenon. However, at the same time, the heightened interdependence of a close relationship can increase expectations for support and enhance the transmission of negative affect from one family member to the other.

A second perspective that explains concordant emotional experiences in families is based on the concept of *shared stressors* (e.g., Westman, Keinan, Roziner, & Benyamini, 2008). Major illnesses rarely affect only individuals. Spouses and other family members also experience worry, disruption of daily routines, need for time away from work, financial burdens, etc. that often accompany serious illnesses (Turner-Cobb, Steptoe, Perry, & Axford, 1998; Weihs, Fisher, & Baird, 2002). As family members adjust to these secondary stressors, they often go through the same emotional experiences.

Emotional contagion is a third theoretical explanation for shared affect in families. According to the emotional contagion hypothesis, people "catch" the emotional states of those with whom they interact through largely unconscious interpersonal processes (Hatfield, Cacioppo, & Rapson, 1992, 1994). Emotional contagion theorists observe that people will mimic and synchronize their nonverbal behaviors with those of the people around them. This similarity in behavior is theorized to provide feedback that generates the same emotional experience as those people whose behaviors are being observed and matched. Emotional contagion is thought to be the effect of primitive and often unconscious communication that transpires between people who experience and display emotions. Emotional contagion is a primary element of Coyne's (1976a, 1976b) interactional theory of depression. According to Coyne, the interpersonal behavior of people with depression induces a negative affective state in others. This transmission of negative affect is assumed to prompt other people to reject their depressed partner. In theory, this cycle of interaction sends the affective state of both partners on a downward cascade.

In a series of studies, we have discovered what appears to be clear evidence of an emotional contagion effect in the domain of depression. In one investigation, we followed 48 women with breast cancer and their family partner (67% husbands, 17% daughters, 16% other—including cousins, brothers, etc.) over the course of 10 weeks, during which they participated in three assessments (Segrin et al., 2005). For all participants, slopes were estimated, representing the degree and direction of change in symptoms of depression over the course of the 10-week investigation. The depression slopes for cancer patients were significantly correlated with those of their family partners. This indicates that if the patient was on a downward trajectory in terms of her symptoms of depression, so was her family partner. We replicated this effect in an 8-week longitudinal study on a sample of 70 men with prostate cancer and their supportive partners (Segrin, Badger, & Harrington, 2012). The partners were wives in 83% of the cases and siblings or children in the remaining cases. Specifically, we found that the more depressed partners were at time 2 (controlling for their, and the patient's, levels of depression at time 1), the more depressed the men with prostate cancer were at time 3. A comparable effect was also documented in a study of 80 Latinas with breast cancer and their family partners (Segrin & Badger, 2013). In this investigation the family partners were more heterogeneous than in our past studies (44% spouse/significant other, 15% son or daughter, 13% sibling, 8% mother, and 20% others—including daughters in law, cousins, etc.). However, once again, over the course of 16 weeks there was a substantial association between changes in depression experienced by the breast cancer patient and changes in depression experienced by her family partner.

In our most recent sample of 49 women with breast cancer and their family partners, we measured depression at three points in time over the course of 16 weeks (Segrin & Badger, 2014). Using a modified version of the actor-partner interdependence model, we found that one dyad member's depression at time$_n$ was a significant predictor of the other dyad member's subsequent depression at time$_{n+1}$. This was the case over all three waves of assessment.

Summary

Our research on depression in family contexts has identified several elements of family interaction that can protect against or aggravate symptoms of depression. Social support from the family appears to help minimize the experience of depression, especially in younger adults. Parents who fail to enact supportive communication with their young adult offspring may be putting those offspring at risk for experiencing depression. Additionaly, when families have to cope with major illnesses such as cancer, it appears that depressive symptoms in one family member may be causally linked to those in other family members. Schacter's (1959) classic research on emotion showed that when confronted by a threat, people seek the company of others in large part to evaluate the appropriateness of their own emotional state. This social comparison effect plays a major role in Manstead and Fischer's (2001) social appraisal theory of emotion. According to this perspective, family members look to each other as they appraise the threat posed by something like cancer diagnosis and treatment. If they see others acting depressed, they may become depressed themselves. However, if others are optimistic and composed, they may come to feel the same way.

LONELINESS

Many people tend to equate loneliness with aloneness, solitude, or separation from other people. In contrast, "family" is often associated with images of togetherness.

For these reasons, it is often difficult to comprehend how loneliness could be a feature of some family relationships. In fact, loneliness is a discrepancy between desired and achieved levels and quality of social contact (Peplau, Russell, & Heim, 1979). Accordingly, when relationships, family or otherwise, do not meet people's desires for quality and quantity of contact, they are susceptible to experiencing loneliness. For many years, loneliness was understood and treated as a negative affective state but never given much consideration as a significant mental health problem. To this day, loneliness is not recognized in most major taxonomies of mental health problems but is rather conceptualized as a feature or symptom of other mental health problems. However, recent research has shown that loneliness can have profound implications for health, the experience of stress, and even longevity (Cacioppo et al., 2000). In addition, loneliness is a serious risk factor for depression (Cacioppo, Hawkley, & Thistead, 2010).

Family Social Support and Loneliness

It would be reasonable to assume that social support provided by family members could be a powerful antidote to loneliness. However, particularly in American culture, social support from family members is not associated with loneliness as strongly as social support from friends (Poulin, Deng, Ingersoll, Witt, & Swain, 2012). Also, the benefits of social support from family members, in terms of preventing or alleviating loneliness, may not be consistent over the lifespan. In a survey of 325 adults with a mean age of 46, contact with family members and social support from family members were both negatively associated with reports of loneliness (Segrin, 2003). However, when one looks earlier into the lifespan, during adolescence and young adulthood, social support from family members is sometimes positively associated with loneliness (Eshbaugh, 2010; Jones & Moore, 1990). This is not to suggest that social support from family members is harmful, by causing loneliness. In fact, it may be the case that when family members notice the loneliness of their younger members, they respond by increasing the social support to that young family member. Nevertheless, as young people naturally shift their orientation from family to friends, social support from family members may not be an effective substitute for social support from friends.

Intergenerational Transmission of Loneliness in Families

Loneliness, like many other mental health problems, may cluster in families. In a landmark study of loneliness and social ties, Cacioppo, Fowler, and Christakis (2009) found that loneliness coalesces within social networks. In other words, lonely people tend to be in social networks with other lonely people, and nonlonely people tend to be in social networks with other nonlonely people. What is more, when nonlonely people have lonely people in their social networks, they tend to become lonelier over time.

We have been studying the agglomeration of loneliness in families and have found results consistent with Cacioppo et al.'s study of social networks more generally. In one case, we collected data from 2–4 members of 169 different families from multiple generations (e.g., young adults, sibling, parents, grandparents), measuring loneliness and social support from family and friends (Segrin, Burke, & Dunivan, 2012). The results indicated that family membership was a significant predictor of loneliness. In other words, loneliness (or lack thereof) tends to run in families. Incidentally, this study also revealed that social support from friends has a stronger preventative effect on loneliness than social support from family members. About half of the participants in this investigation, as in the Segrin (2003) study, were middle- or older-aged adults.

Why does loneliness cluster in families? One possibility may be found in the concept of social skills. Social skills deficits are a significant risk factor for the experience of loneliness (Segrin, 1999; Segrin & Flora, 2000). This is because people with poor social skills have difficulties making friends with other people, eliciting social support during times of need, and finding companionship. It turns out that social skills, like many other skills in life, are socially learned and that the family of origin may be the primary context for acquiring social skills. In a study of 255 father-mother-young adult child triads, we found social skills to be strongly and negatively associated with loneliness for all three classes of family members (Burke, Woszidlo, & Segrin, 2013). Furthermore, the loneliness of fathers, but not mothers, was a significant predictor of young adults' social skills. So it appears that a lonely parent may be more likely to raise a child with poor social skills that in turn put the child at risk for experiencing loneliness. A further analysis from this same data set showed that family-wise reports of conflict were significant predictors of loneliness among family members (Burke, Woszidlo, & Segrin, 2012). In addition to the cultivation of poor social skills in families, family conflict may be another culprit in the agglomeration of loneliness within family systems.

Another reason loneliness may be aggregated in families is that families cultivate environments that do not promote adequate social skills and psychological well-being of their children. Cold and maladaptive family environments, for instance, foster components of loneliness (e.g., feeling alienated and disconnected) because family members do not feel supported and free to express their thoughts and feelings in the family (Rokach, 1989). Our research also finds that the family environment is associated with young adults' loneliness (Segrin, Nevarez, Arroyo, & Harwood, 2012). This sample consisted of 111 young adult child-and-parent dyads reporting on their own loneliness, as well as both young adults' and parents' reports of family conversation orientation and family communication satisfaction as indicators of the family environment latent variable. Family conversation orientation reflects the extent to which the family engages in frequent discussion and promotes the free and open expression of ideas and feelings (Ritchie & Fitzpatrick, 1990). We found that not only was there a direct effect of parental loneliness on their young adult child's loneliness (parent loneliness → child loneliness), but there was also an indirect effect through a less open and satisfying family communication environment (parent loneliness → family environment → child loneliness). In fact, parental loneliness and the family environment latent variable collectively explained 18% of the variance in young adult children's loneliness.

Although positive family communication—particularly from parents—shapes the family environment, cultivating supportive environments may be exceptionally difficult for parents with mental health problems. Mental health problems have been shown to degrade parenting practices in terms of low caring, intrusive control, etc. (Lovejoy, Graczyk, O'Hare, & Neuman, 2000), and these compromised parenting behaviors put children at risk for subsequent mental health problems of their own (Jackson, 2006; Wang & Dix, 2013). In our study previously mentioned (Arroyo et al. in press), we found support for the intergenerational transmission of parents' psychosocial well-being to that of their children through perceived maternal care (which was reported by a sibling). We found that mothers with higher levels of loneliness and depression and lower self-esteem were perceived by their children to be less warm. These results suggest that one reason parents and their young adult children might exhibit a resemblance on psychological problems is because of the nature of the family interactions wherein mothers with psychosocial problems may not be able to contribute to a supportive family environment. As such, the aforementioned studies suggest that loneliness appears to cluster within families partly because individuals do not learn proper social skills in family environments in which communication is restricted and less cohesive.

Loneliness and Marriage

It would be difficult to imagine a family relationship more antithetical to the experience of loneliness than marriage. Marriage is expected to bring fulfillment of desires for connection with another person, and yet it is not difficult to find cases of people who are married but still lonely (Rokach, 2012). We suspect that the reasons for this are twofold. First, about half of all marriages will end in divorce, and perhaps even more persevere in a state of significant distress. Second, when marriages are declining but not yet terminated, the state of being married probably prevents many people from seeking a partner who would help alleviate their loneliness. For these two reasons, it is not at all surprising that there are people in the population who are married but still lonely.

Our first investigation of marriage and loneliness stemmed from practical observations we made while working with married prison inmates. Some professed to losing their spouse over the course of their incarceration, while others claimed that they were closer to their spouse than ever before, despite years of physical separation. In this investigation of 96 married prison inmates, who had been separated from their spouses on average 3 years since getting married, there was a significant and positive association between duration of marital separation and loneliness, as one might expect (Segrin & Flora, 2001). However, just like civilians in the community (Flora & Segrin, 2003), it appeared that those with the most positive relational history (i.e., low levels of chaos, a sense of "weness" vs. "separateness," low levels of relationship disappointment, and a tendency to glorify the struggle when describing the difficulties of their marriage) had the highest concurrent marital quality (i.e., satisfaction and commitment). This is highly consequential in that high marital quality was associated with low levels of loneliness for these married prisoners.

Attachment theory has figured prominently in the literature on marital quality, with the guiding hypothesis being that people with insecure attachment styles will experience poor relational quality. Extending this line of reasoning, we further hypothesized that loneliness would be a logical outcome of this poor relational quality, as suggested previously by Gottman (1994). Gottman argued that loneliness was the end of the psychological line in marriage before spouses sought a divorce. An investigation of 225 married couples showed that indeed, both anxious and avoidant attachment predicted lower relational quality (i.e., commitment, marital satisfaction), which in turn predicted higher loneliness (Givertz, Woszidlo, Segrin, & Knutson, 2013). In other words, a problematic attachment style has an indirect effect on loneliness through degraded marital quality.

Commitment to marriage comes in several different varieties. Some spouses are committed because they inherently want their relationship to persevere. This is known as personal commitment. In contrast, some people are committed to their marriage because they have poor alternatives or because they have made irretrievable investments in the marriage that would be lost if they broke it off. This is often referred to as constraint commitment. Not surprisingly, personal commitment is the form of commitment most negatively associated with loneliness (Burke & Segrin, 2014). In contrast, spouses who scored high on constraint commitment reported greater loneliness than those with low levels of constraint commitment. Consequently, the reasons for commitment are of paramount importance for minimizing or exacerbating the experience of loneliness in marriage. This is why Tricia Burke wisely titled Burke and Segrin's (2014) paper "Bonded or Stuck?" Being stuck in a bad marriage is at least as bad, and in some cases probably worse, than not being married at all when it comes to feelings of loneliness.

Summary

Loneliness is a very distressing psychological affliction that is associated with a host of family relations variables. In general, social support from the family seems to protect against the experience of loneliness, but this effect is stronger in younger than older adults, and sometimes is at best a modest alternative to social support from friends. Our research has also shown that loneliness tends to run in families. The strands in the cord connecting loneliness to family life include failure to model and/or develop good social skills, family conflict, a dysfunctional family communication style, and compromised parenting. Loneliness also occurs in some marriages, and this seems to be most common among spouses with a problematic relational history, insecure attachment styles, and low levels of commitment to their marriage. Some of the manifestations of stress associated with loneliness may spill over on other family members in close proximity to the lonely person.

ANXIETY

People with anxiety experience a number of debilitating symptoms that may include fear, restlessness, headaches, nausea, heart palpitations, irritability, difficulty concentrating, muscle tension, sleep difficulties, and a sense of impending trouble. Like depression, anxiety disorders are highly prevalent in the population and, also like depression, anxiety occurs in mild subclinical forms to profoundly debilitating clinical syndromes. The lifetime morbidity risk/12-month prevalence estimates for various anxiety disorders are extraordinarily high: specific phobia 18.4%/12.1%, social phobia 13.0%/7.4%, post-traumatic stress disorder 10.1%/3.7%, panic disorder 6.8%/2.4%, agoraphobia 3.7%/1.7%, and obsessive compulsive disorder 2.7%/1.2% (Kessler, Petukhova, Sampson, Zaslavsky, & Wittchen, 2012). More generally speaking, the lifetime morbid risk of any anxiety disorder is estimated at 41.7%. It is interesting to note that Kessler et al.'s epidemiological research showed that certain anxiety disorders such as phobias and social anxiety disorder have earlier age-to-onset than other anxiety-mood disorders. This at least raises the suggestion that family-of-origin matters may play a more prominent role in these disorders.

Anxiety and Family Coping with Major Illness

As noted earlier, we have been studying quality of life in people coping with cancer diagnosis and treatment and their family supportive partners. This research shows remarkable interdependence in the psychological quality of life of cancer survivors and their partners. We first discovered interdependent anxiety in an investigation of 96 women with breast cancer and their family partners, of whom 77% were spouses/significant others, 17% daughters, and 6% some other relation such as cousin or sister (Segrin, Badger, Dorros, Meek, & Lopez, 2007). We do not limit our inclusion of partners to only spouses/significant others because some women with breast cancer do not have such relations in their social networks, and these are the patients probably most at risk for psychological morbidity. Over the course of 10 weeks, symptoms of anxiety were measured three times in both survivors and their partners. Analyses based on the actor-partner interdependence model revealed that women with breast cancer reported more anxiety to the extent that their partner reported more anxiety at the previous wave of assessment (see Figure 1).

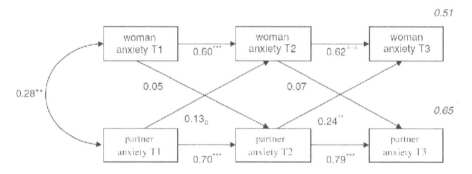

Fig 1. Actor-Partner Interdependence Model for Anxiety in Breast Cancer Survivors and Their Partners.
**$p < .01$. ***$p < .001$. $p = 0.11$. T1 = time 1, T2 = time 2, T3 = time 3. Values in italics are squared multiple correlations (R^2). These findings originally appeared in Segrin, C., Badger, T. A., Dorros, S. M., Meek, P., & Lopez, A. M. (2007). Interdependent anxiety and psychological distress in women with breast cancer and their partners. *Psycho-Oncology, 16*, 634–643. Reprinted with permission of John Wiley and Sons.

The pattern of findings in Figure 2 reveals that even after controlling for initial similarities in anxiety within the dyad and controlling for any actor effects, there were still substantial partner-to-patient partner effects. This effect is reminiscent of a social appraisal mechanism first presented by Schacter (1959). When confronted with a threat, people will often seek the company of others, in part to gauge the nature of the threat and the appropriateness of their emotional reaction to the threat. This concept lies at the core of social appraisal theories of emotion (Manstead & Fischer, 2001). It appears that observing high levels of anxiety in family partners leads women with breast cancer to become more anxious themselves. It is at least possible that the anxiety and worry of the family partner is communicated to the patient via emotional contagion processes. Of course, another way of looking at these findings is to note that a calm and composed partner during this difficult time appears to minimize anxiety in breast cancer patients.

The dyadic interdependence in anxiety was subsequently replicated in a sample of 80 Latinas with breast cancer and their supportive family partners (Segrin & Badger, 2013) and in a sample of 51 mostly Anglo women with breast cancer and their supportive family partners (Segrin & Badger, 2014). In this later investigation, two interesting and significant indirect effects emerged: survivor time 1 anxiety → partner time 2 anxiety → survivor time 3 anxiety and partner time 1 anxiety → survivor time 2 anxiety → partner time 3 anxiety. This is a compelling illustration of mutual influence in the domain of anxiety among dyads coping with cancer diagnosis and treatment.

Men with prostate cancer and their family partners (mostly spouses/significant others) show the same kind of interdependent anxiety as they cope with cancer diagnosis and treatment (Segrin, Badger, & Harrington, 2012). We found, unlike our other samples of breast cancer survivors and their partners, that there was no initial similarity in the anxiety of men with prostate cancer and their partners (see Figure 2). However, men with more anxiety at time 1 had partners with more anxiety at time 2. Then partners' anxiety at time 2 was predictive of even greater anxiety in men at time 3. These results also provide compelling evidence of emotional contagion and indicate that transmission of emotion from one family dyad member to the other is not bound in any way by the sex of either person in the dyad.

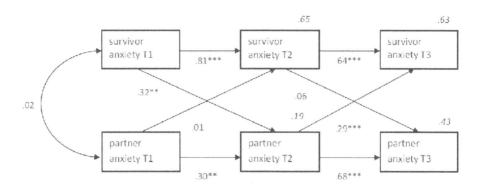

Fig 2. Actor-Partner Interdependence Model for Anxiety in Prostate Cancer Survivors and Their Partners. T1 = time 1, T2 = time 2, T3 = time 3.

**p < .01. ***p < .001. T1 = time 1, T2 = time 2, T3 = time 3. Values in italics are squared multiple correlations (R^2). These findings originally appeared in Segrin, C., Badger, T. A., & Harrington, J. (2012). Interdependent psychological quality of life in dyads adjusting to prostate cancer. *Health Psychology, 31,* 70–79. Reprinted with permission of American Psychological Association.

Intergenerational Transmission of Poor Social Skills and Anxiety

Just as with loneliness, we have found evidence that the acquisition of social skills (or social skills deficits) might be implicated in the family resemblance for anxiety. In a study previously described in the section on loneliness, we surveyed 255 mother-father-adult child triads and found a significant negative association between family members' social skills and their experiences of social anxiety (Burke et al., 2013). Poor social skills were uniformly predictive of high levels of social anxiety, regardless of one's role/position in the family. What is more interesting is that fathers' social skills were predictive of young adult children's social skills, and both mothers' and fathers' social anxiety predicted higher social anxiety in their young adult children. So, like loneliness, social anxiety appears to run in families and the common thread that may link parent and child experiences with social anxiety is poor social skills. Young people who do not acquire effective social skills are clearly at risk for a wide range of psychological problems, and social anxiety is certainly one of them (Segrin, 1996). The fact that fathers' social skills were predictive of young adults' social skills suggests that parental modeling of social skills, or failure to model effective skills, may play a role in young adults' failure to develop good social skills, increasing their risk for social anxiety.

Such results are also found in shyness, which is a less pathogenic form of social anxiety (Bruch, 2001). Similar to social anxiety, shyness affects many people's interactions and relationships (e.g., Arroyo & Harwood, 2011; Kagan & Snidman, 1999; Miller & Coll, 2007) and contributes to significant and recurring problems, such as loneliness and depression (Bruch, 2001; Findlay, Coplan, & Bowker, 2009). Researchers suggest that shy tendencies might be propagated as a result of genetic predispositions, parenting practices, and other factors in the child's social environment (Miller & Coll, 2007). Along these lines, one of our own studies on shyness, social skills, and perceived family communication yielded significant associations between parents' shyness and both the shyness and social skills of their adult children (Arroyo, Nevarez, Segrin, & Harwood, 2012). Parents' shyness also indirectly predicted their adult child's social skills through that child's shyness (parent shyness → adult child shyness → adult child social skills). Just as with many of the other mental health problems, poor social skills consequently contribute to poor communication within the family as well. In the previous study, there was evidence of an indirect effect of parent shyness on perceived family communication through lower adult child's social skills (parent's shyness → child's social skills → perceived family communication), suggesting that shy parents might contribute to less open and satisfying family communication by raising reticent children who are unable to contribute openly to family interactions.

Anxiety in Overparenting

Overparenting, also known as "helicopter parenting" in the popular press, has received a great deal of research attention over the past several years, after many more years of attention in the popular press. Overparenting involves the application of developmentally inappropriate and overcontrolling parenting tactics, usually to late adolescent and young adult children. Parents who regularly engage in this behavior provide excessive advice and direction to their child, try to solve their child's problems, take personal responsibility for their child's mood, try to protect their child from any perceived risk, and engage in extraordinary monitoring and surveillance of their child's activities and whereabouts (Segrin, Givertz, Swiatkowski, & Montgomery, 2015; Segrin, Woszidlo, Givertz, Bauer, & Murphy, 2012). Although overparenting is likely enacted with good intentions, it does not appear to be adaptive to young adults' psychological well-being (LeMoyne & Buchanan, 2011; Segrin, Woszidlo, et al., 2012). Furthermore, there is now evidence to suggest that it may be driven in part by parental anxiety.

Over the past several years, our research team has been attempting to understand two basic questions about overparenting: (1) What drives parents to engage in these behaviors with their young adult children? and (2) What are the potential consequences of being raised in a family environment marked by overparenting? Although the answers to these questions are too numerous to comprehensively review here, relevant to the present discussion, we found evidence that anxiety may be a common element in both parent and child experiences (Segrin, Woszidlo, Givertz, & Montgomery, 2013). In this investigation, we studied 653 parent-young adult child dyads from 32 of the 50 United States. This study revealed that parental anxiety was a significant and proximal predictor of overparenting. But what are these parents anxious about? There is an intriguing possibility that overparenting might be driven by parental worry that their children will not achieve the dreams and ambitions that the parents themselves had never realized. This is suggested by a significant indirect effect of parental regret on enactment of overparenting, through parental anxiety (Segrin et al., 2013). Parents in this investigation completed a measure of their regrets in the following life domains: career, education, parenting, family, finance, leisure, romance, and self. To make sense of this indirect effect, some theoretical background, along with a bit of speculation, may help.

Sociologist Margaret Nelson (2010) noted that professional middle-class parents, who are the most common culprits in overparenting, are often preoccupied with environmental dangers potentially faced by their children. They see excessive monitoring, intensive supervision, protection, and communication with their children as the antidote to these dangers. We took that as a starting point and combined it with the lost opportunity principle of regret (Roese & Summerville, 2005) to understand potential antecedents to overparenting. Roese and Summerville argue that regrets are most powerful when people can see the opportunity for corrective action, but when that window of opportunity is closing or closed (see also Beike, Markman, & Karadogan, 2009). One of the more interesting theoretical accounts of overparenting is premised on the assumption that parents project their own goals onto their children and live vicariously through their children's successes and failures (Munich & Munich, 2009).

What we suspect is going on in the sample of parents in the Segrin et al. (2013) study is something like this: As parents, who were incidentally middle aged, begin to realize that opportunities to achieve certain life goals are foreclosed, they begin to experience anxiety. What does that anxiety concern? One possibility is their child's own possible failure to live up to and achieve that same goal. For example, a parent might have dreamed of becoming a physician. As that parent approaches middle age, it may become apparent that this dream will never become a reality. The parent may therefore shift that dream, driven by narcissistic enmeshment, to the child. The parent may simultaneously become fearful of the child also not achieving this goal, and overparenting thus becomes the remedy that should ensure the child's success. Of course, there is no assurance that the child even wants to pursue the goal, but that is often of little concern to the parent. Without question, a great deal of additional research would be required to verify each of these points, but the significant indirect effect of parental regret on overparenting through parental anxiety suggests that this might be a fruitful direction for future research on overparenting.

It turns out that anxiety is implicated not only in parental enactment of overparenting but also in the children who are the recipients of overparenting. A test of a structural model of parental reports of overparenting and child narcissism, coping, stress, and anxiety revealed some interesting associations that are depicted in Figure 3.

Parental reports of overparenting were associated with higher young adult child reports of narcissism as well as higher young adult child reports of dysfunctional coping strategies such as internalizing and avoidance. The tendency to engage in poor coping strategies was itself predictive of higher stress and higher anxiety in young adult children. It is at least possible that the hyperprotective and involved parenting behavior that comprises overparenting actually leaves children less able to cope with life's stressors effectively because, presumably, someone else always looked after that task for them. An impoverished repertoire of coping strategies could easily contribute to feelings of stress, which may actually be rational, and the attendant anxiety that goes hand in hand with stress. Of course, one has to at least acknowledge the possibility that children displaying high levels of anxiety, stress, and poor coping may actually pull for overparenting from their mothers and fathers. Clearly this is an area in need of carefully controlled long-term longitudinal research in an effort to sort out cause and effect. In the meantime, it is apparent that both parental and child anxiety are key elements of the parent-child transactions referred to as helicopter parenting or overparenting.

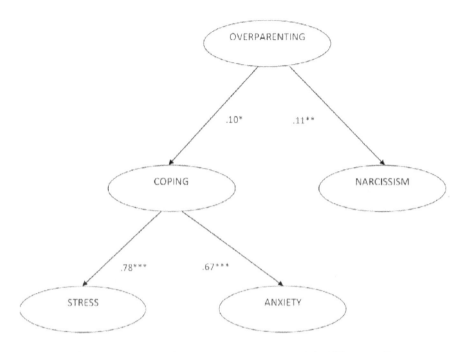

Fig 3. Structural Model of Parental Reports of Overparenting and Child Reports of Narcissism, Coping, Stress, and Anxiety.

*p < .05. **p < .01. ***p < .001. Path coefficients are standardized regression coefficients. Indirect effect of overparenting on stress through coping is β = .08, p = .05, and indirect effect of overparenting on anxiety through coping is β = .06, p = .05. These findings originally appeared in Segrin, C., Woszidlo, A., Givertz, M., & Montgomery, N. (2013). Parent and child traits associated with overparenting. *Journal of Social and Clinical Psychology, 32*, 569–595. Reprinted with permission of Guilford Press.

Summary

Like depression, there is strong evidence for contagious anxiety in families coping with major health threats. One way that families may impart a risk for anxiety in their young adult members is by failing to adequately model and teach good social skills that allow family members to effectively cope with stress. Poor social skills may be one key reason anxiety runs in families (i.e., parents with poor social skills often raise children with poor social skills). Overparenting is another phenomenon that can explain why anxiety sometimes runs in families. Overparenting may be driven in part by anxiety experienced by parents. The heavy-handed and overly directive parenting tactics appear to leave their children with poor coping skills that in turn make these children susceptible to anxiety. Just as with depression and loneliness, anxiety may therefore be viewed not just as an individual problem, but as a family system problem.

SUMMARY AND FUTURE DIRECTIONS

Research on family relations and mental health has revealed a diverse array of pathogenic family interaction processes that appear to generate a risk for mental health problems. Some of the themes that have emerged from this work include a lack of social support, emotional contagion, maladaptive parenting styles, and intergenerational transmission possibly through social learning. These are but a small collection of the family processes that can be disruptive to mental health. The good news with most of these phenomena is that their effects seem to run in both directions. That is to say, for example, that the availability of adequate family social support appears to be as protective as lack of family social support is deleterious to mental health, especially in young family members. One of the major challenges for those in applied settings is finding ways to reverse these deficient family processes, turning impediments to mental health (e.g., contagion of negative affect) into processes that will be a boon to family members' mental health (e.g., contagion of positive affect).

One of the major complications inherent in studying family interactions and mental health is the confounding of genes and environment. In most families, the same parents who create the environment in which the child lives also supply the child's genes. What is more, there is no reason to assume that genetic and psychosocial origins of mental illness are independent of each other. This complication is a major concern, especially in studies of the intergenerational transmission of mental health, in that a large number of mental health problems appear to have some genetic origin or at least contribution (e.g., Boomsma, Willemsen, Dolan, Hawkley, & Cacioppo, 2005; Price, 1994). Disentangling this confound requires sophisticated and often expensive behavioral genetic studies with unique designs based on twins, adopted children, and so forth. Although there are some excellent examples of such studies in the literature (e.g., Silberg, Maes, & Eaves, 2012), these are few and far between. Nevertheless, studies of this sort have great potential to make major contributions to the understanding of families and mental health. Thus, one of the key issues for future research will be determining the extent to which family processes such as emotional contagion, lack of social support, and maladaptive parenting contribute to offspring and other family members' mental health, above and beyond that which can be explained by purely genetic influences.

Almost any theory of family relations and mental health is an inherently developmental theory. In the abstract, something is assumed to transpire within the family environment that, in turn, corrupts the psychological well-being of children living in the family, either concurrently or later on in the future. Such models are well informed by long-term longitudinal data, often collected over the course of decades. Here again, one can find excellent examples of such research in the literature (e.g., Hammen, Hazel, Brennan, & Najman, 2012), but such studies remain scarce. This methodology could be employed to answer vital questions about potentially etiological family interaction processes in the development of mental health problems. For example, to what extent does overparenting during adolescence predict adjustment problems during young adulthood? Does a lack of family social support predict only concurrent or subsequent psychological problems in family members?

Finally, there is still a pressing need for studies that measure what actually transpires in family interactions that are assumed to play an etiologic role in the development of offspring mental health problems. It is often the case that long-term longitudinal data sets that are suitable for exploring the role of early childhood exposure to some pathogenic family interaction pattern in the subsequent development of mental illness are beset by extraordinarily crude measures of "family interaction" or "family relationships," sometimes assessed in only one or two questions. This area of research would benefit extensively from in-depth assessments using a variety of methods (e.g., self-report, observation). In addition, it would be useful to address questions about specific forms of family interaction in the disruption of mental health. For example, what is the role of poor conflict management, verbal aggressiveness, argumentativeness, expression of affection, negative affect reciprocity, poor problem solving, misunderstandings, and expressions of emotional support in creating an environment that is conducive or corrosive to mental health? Prior research on some of these specific process suggests that this line of research has considerable potential (e.g., Mammen, Pilkonis, & Kolko, 2000). It must be acknowledged that these criteria for valuable research on families and mental health (i.e., behavioral genetic studies, long-term longitudinal studies, and in-depth assessment of family interaction) represent something of a holy grail that may be pursued but rarely achieved by the research community. Such research is difficult to conduct owing to its extraordinary expense (complicated by shrinking opportunities for funding), labor intensiveness, and just the sheer amount of time it takes to follow young people into adulthood. Nevertheless, this type of research will have exceptional scientific value in the pursuit of understanding how family relations affect mental health.

REFERENCES

American Psychiatric Association. (2013). *Diagnostic and statistical manual of mental disorders* (5th ed.). Arlington, VA: American Psychiatric Publishing. doi: 10.1176/appi.books.9780890425596

Arroyo, A., & Harwood, J. (2011). Communication competence mediates the link between shyness and relational quality. *Personality and Individual Differences, 50,* 264–267. doi: 10.1016/j.paid.2010.09.041

Arroyo, A., Nevarez, N., Segrin, C., & Harwood, J. (2012). The association between parent and adult child shyness and social skills on their family environment. *Journal of Family Communication, 12,* 249–264. doi: 10.1080/15267431.2012.686941

Arroyo, A., & Segrin, C., & Curran, T. M. (in press). Maternal care and control as mediators in the relationship between mothers' and adult children's psychosocial problems. *Journal of Family Communication*.

Bateson, G., Jackson, D., Haley, J., & Weakland, J. (1956). Toward a theory of schizophrenia. *Behavioral Science, 1*, 252–264. doi: 10.1002/bs.3830010402

Baucom, D. H., Shoham, V., Mueser, K. T., Daiuto, A. D., & Stickle, T. R. (1998). Empirically supported couple and family interventions for marital distress and adult mental health problems. *Journal of Consulting and Clinical Psychology, 66*, 53–88. doi: 10.1037/0022-006X.66.1.53

Beike, D. R., Markman, K. D., & Karadogan, F. (2009). What we regret most are lost opportunities: A theory of regret intensity. *Personality and Social Psychology Bulletin, 35*, 385–397. doi: 10.1177/0146167208328329

Bertalanffy, L., von. (1975). *Perspectives on general systems theory: Scientific-philosophical studies*. New York: George Braziller.

Boomsma, D. I., Willemsen, G., Dolan, C., Hawkley, L. C., & Cacioppo, J. T. (2005). Genetic and environmental contributions to loneliness in adults. *Behavior Genetics, 35*, 745–752.

Broderick, C. B. (1993). *Understanding family processes: Basics of family systems theory*. Newbury Park, CA: Sage. doi: 10.1007/s10519-005-6040-8

Bruch, M. A. (2001). Shyness and social interaction. In W. R. Crozier & L. E. Alden (Eds.), *International handbook of social anxiety: Concepts, research and interventions relating to the self and shyness* (pp. 195–215). Chichester, England: Wiley.

Burke, T. J., & Segrin, C. (2014). Bonded or stuck? Effects of personal and constraint commitment on loneliness and stress. *Personality and Individual Differences, 64*, 101–106. doi: 10.1016/j.paid.2014.02.027

Burke, T. J., Woszidlo, A., & Segrin, C. (2012). Social skills, family conflict, and loneliness in families. *Communication Reports, 25*, 75–87. doi: 10.1080/08934215.2012.719461

Burke, T. J., Woszidlo, A., & Segrin, C. (2013). The intergenerational transmission of social skills and psychosocial problems among parents and their young adult children. *Journal of Family Communication, 13*, 77–91. doi: 10.1080/15267431.2013.768247

Cacioppo, J. T., Ernst, J. M., Burleson, M. H., McClintock, M. K., Malarkey, W. B., Hawkley, L. C., Bernston, G. G. (2000). Lonely traits and concomitant physiological processes: The MacArthur social neuroscience studies. *International Journal of Psychophysiology, 35*, 143–154.

Cacioppo, J. T., Fowler, J. H., & Christakis, N. A. (2009). Alone in the crowd: The structure and spread of loneliness in a large social network. *Journal of Personality and Social Psychology, 97*, 977–991. doi: 10.1037/a0016076

Cacioppo, J. T., Hawkley, L. C., & Thisted, R. A. (2010). Perceived social isolation makes me sad: 5-year cross-lagged analyses of loneliness and depressive symptomatology in the Chicago Health Aging, and Social Relations Study. *Psychology and Aging, 25*, 453–463. doi: 10.1037/a0017216

Coyne, J. C. (1976a). Toward an interactional description of depression. *Psychiatry, 39*, 28–40.

Coyne, J. C. (1976b). Depression and the response of others. *Journal of Abnormal Psychology, 85*, 186–193. doi: 10.1037/0021-843X.85.2.186

DeVellis, R. F., Lewis, M. A., & Sterba, K. R. (2003). Interpersonal emotional processes in adjustment to chronic illness. In J. Suls & K. A. Wallston (Eds.), *Social psychological foundations of health and illness* (pp. 256–287). Malden, MA: Blackwell Publishing. doi: 10.1002/9780470753552.ch10

Eshbaugh, E. M. (2010). Friend and family support as moderators of the effects of low romantic partner support on loneliness among college women. *Individual Differences Research, 8*, 8–16.

Findlay, L. C., Coplan, R. J., & Bowker, A. (2009). Keeping it all inside: Shyness, internalizing coping strategies and socio-emotional adjustment in middle childhood. *International Journal of Behavioral Development, 33*, 47–54. doi: 10.1177/0165025408098017

Flora, J., & Segrin, C. (2003). Relational well-being and perceptions of relational history in married and dating couples. *Journal of Social and Personal Relationships, 20*, 515–536. doi: 10.1177/02654075030204005

Freud, S. (1966). *Introductory lectures on psychoanalysis*. New York: W. W. Norton & Company. (Original work published in 1917)

Fromm-Reichmann, F. (1960). *Principles of intensive psychotherapy*. Chicago, IL: Phoenix Books.

Givertz, M., Woszidlo, A., Segrin, C., & Knutson, K. (2013). Direct and indirect effects of attachment orientation on relationship quality and loneliness in married couples. *Journal of Social and Personal Relationships, 30*, 1096–1120. doi: 10.1177/0265407513482445 10.1177/0265407513482445

González-Pinto, A., de Azúa, S. R., Ibáñez, B., Otero-Cuesta, S., Castro-Fornieles, J., Graell-Berna, M., Ugarte, A., Parellada, M., Moreno, D., Soutullo, C., Baeza, I., & Arango, C. (2011). Can positive family factors be protective against the development of psychosis? *Psychiatry Research, 186*, 28–33. doi: 10.1016/j.psychres.2010.05.015

Gottman, J. M. (1994). *What predicts divorce?* Hillsdale, NJ: Lawrence Erlbaum.

Hammen, C., Hazel, N. A., Brennan, P. A., & J. Najman. (2012). Intergenerational transmission and continuity of stress and depression: Depressed women and their offspring in 20 years of follow-up. *Psychological Medicine, 42*, 931–942. doi: 10.1017/S0033291711001978

Hatfield, E., Cacioppo, J. T., & Rapson, R. L. (1992). Primitive emotional contagion. In M. S. Clark (Ed.), *Emotion and social behavior* (pp. 151–177). Newbury Park, CA: Sage.

Hatfield, E., Cacioppo, J. T., & Rapson, R. L. (1994). *Emotional contagion*. Paris: Cambridge University Press.

Holt-Lunstad, J., Birmingham, W., & Jones, B. Q. (2008). Is there something unique about marriage? The relative impact of marital status, relationship quality, and network social support on ambulatory blood pressure and mental health. *Annals of Behavioral Medicine, 35*, 239–244. doi: 10.1007/s12160-008-9018-y

Jackson, T. (2006). Protective self-presentation, sources of socialization, and loneliness among Australian adolescents and young adults. *Personality and Individual Differences, 43*, 1552–1562. doi: 10.1016/j.paid.2007.04.012

Jacob, T. (Ed.). (1987). *Family interaction and psychopathology: Theories, methods, and findings*. New York: Plenum. doi: 10.1007/978-1-4899-0840-7

Jones, W. H., & Moore, T. L. (1990). Loneliness and social support. In M. Hojat & R. Crandall (Eds.), *Loneliness: Theory, research, and applications* (pp. 145–156). Newbury Park, CA: Sage.

Kagan, J., & Snidman, N. (1999). Early childhood predictors of adult anxiety disorders. *Biological Psychiatry, 46*, 1536–1541. doi: 10.1016/S0006-3223(99)00137-7

Kessler, R. C., McGonagle, K. A., Shanyang, Z., Nelson, C., Hughes, M., Eshleman, S., Wittchen, H. U., & Kendler, K. S. (1994). Lifetime and 12-month prevalence of DSM-III-R psychiatric disorders in the United States. *Archives of General Psychiatry, 51*, 8–19. doi: 10.1001/archpsyc.1994.03950010008002

Kessler, R. C., Petukhova, M., Sampson, N. A., Zaslavsky, A. M., & Wittchen, H. U. (2012). Twelve-Month and Lifetime Prevalence and Lifetime Morbid Risk of Anxiety and Mood Disorders in the United States. *International Journal of Methods in Psychiatric Research, 21*, 169–184. http://dx.doi.org/10.1002/mpr.1359

Laing, R. D. (1967). *The politics of experience*. London: Penguin Press.

Lee, C. M., & Gotlib, I. H. (1994). Mental illness and the family. In L. L'Abate (Ed.), *Handbook of developmental family psychology and psychopathology* (pp. 243–264). Oxford, England: John Wiley & Sons.

LeMoyne, T., Buchanan, T. (2011). Does "hovering" matter? Helicopter parenting and its effect on well-being. *Sociological Spectrum, 31*, 399–418. doi: 10.1080/02732173.2011.574038

Lidz, T., Cornelison, A., Fleck, S., & Terry, D. (1957). The intrafamilial environment of schizophrenic patients: 2. Marital schism and marital skew. *American Journal of Psychiatry, 114*, 241–248. doi: 10.1176/ajp.114.3.241

Lovejoy, M. C., Graczyk, P. A., O'Hare, E., & Neuman, G. (2000). Maternal depression and parenting behavior: A meta-analytic review. *Clinical Psychology Review, 20*, 561–592. doi: 10.1016/S0272-7358(98)00100-7

Mammen, O. K., Pilkonis, P. A., & Kolko, D. J. (2000). Anger and parent-to-child aggression in mood and anxiety disorders. *Comprehensive Psychiatry, 41*, 461–468. doi: 10.1053/comp.2000.16567

Manstead, A. S. R., & Fischer, A. H. (2001). Social appraisal: The social world as object of and influence on appraisal processes. In K. R.Scherer, A. Shorr, & T. Johnstone (Eds.), *Appraisal processes in emotion: Theory, methods, research* (pp. 221–232). New York, NY: Oxford University Press.

Miller, S. R., & Coll, E. (2007). From social withdrawal to social confidence: Evidence for possible pathways. *Current Psychology, 26*, 86–101. doi: 10.1007/s12144-007-9006-6

Munich, R. L., & Munich, M. A. (2009). Overparenting and the narcissistic pursuit of attachment. *Psychiatric Annals, 39*, 227–235. doi: 10.3928/00485713-20090401-04

Nelson, M. K. (2010). *Parenting out of control: Anxious parenting in uncertain times.* New York: New York University Press.

Peplau, L. A., Russell, D., & Heim, M. (1979). The experience of loneliness. In I. H. Frieze, D. Bar-Tal, & J. S. Caroll (Eds.), *New approaches to social problems* (pp. 53–78). San Francisco, CA: Jossey-Bass.

Poulin, J., Deng, R., Ingersoll, T. S., Witt, H., & Swain, M. (2012). Perceived family and friend support and the psychological well-being of American and Chinese elderly persons. *Journal of Cross-Cultural Gerontology, 27*, 305–317. doi: 10.1007/s10823-012-9177-y

Price, A. R. (1994). Genetic approaches to mental illness. In A. Frazer, P. B. Molinoff, & A. Winokur (Eds.), *Biological bases of brain function and disease* (pp. 281–299). New York, NY: Raven Press.

Ritchie, L. D., & Fitzpatrick, M. A. (1990). Family communication patterns: Measuring intrapersonal perceptions of interpersonal relationships. *Communication Research, 17*, 523–544. doi: 10.1177/009365090017004007

Roese, N. J., & Summerville, A. (2005). What we regret most ... and why. *Personality and Social Psychology Bulletin, 31*, 1273–1285. doi: 10.1177/0146167205274693

Rokach, A. (1989). Antecedents to loneliness: A factorial analysis. *The Journal of Psychology, 123*, 369–384. doi: 10.1080/00223980.1989.10542992

Rokach, A. (2012). Loneliness, support, marriage and the family. *Psychology and Education: An Interdisciplinary Journal, 49*, 19–33.

Rothon, C., Goodwin, L., & Stansfeld, S. (2012). Family social support, community "social capital" and adolescents' mental health and educational outcomes: A longitudinal study in England. *Social Psychiatry and Psychiatric Epidemiology, 47*, 697–709. doi: 10.1007/s00127-011-0391-7

Schachter, S. (1959). *The psychology of affiliation.* Minneapolis, MN: University of Minnesota Press.

Segrin, C. (1996). The relationship between social skills deficits and psychosocial problems: A test of a vulnerability model. *Communication Research, 23*, 425–450. doi: 10.1177/009365096023004005

Segrin, C. (1999). Social skills, stressful life events, and the development of psychosocial problems. *Journal of Social and Clinical Psychology, 18*, 14–34. doi: 10.1521/jscp.1999.18.1.14

Segrin, C. (2001). *Interpersonal processes in psychological problems.* New York: Guilford Press.

Segrin, C. (2003). Age moderates the relationship between social support and psychosocial problems. *Human Communication Research, 29*, 317–342. doi: 10.1111/j.1468-2958.2003.tb00842.x

Segrin, C., & Badger, T. A. (2013). Interdependent psychological distress between Latinas with breast cancer and their supportive partners. *Journal of Latina/o Psychology, 1*, 21–34. doi: 10.1037/a0030345

Segrin, C., & Badger, T. A. (2014). Psychological and physical distress are interdependent in breast cancer survivors and their partners. *Psychology, Health, and Medicine, 19*, 716–723. doi: 10.1080/13548506.2013.871304

Segrin, C., Badger, T. A., Dorros, S. M., Meek, P., & Lopez, A. M. (2007). Interdependent anxiety and psychological distress in women with breast cancer and their partners. *Psycho-Oncology, 16, 634–643.* doi: 10.1002/pon.1111

Segrin, C., Badger, T. A., & Harrington, J. (2012). Interdependent psychological quality of life in dyads adjusting to prostate cancer. *Health Psychology, 31*, 70–79. doi: 10.1037/a0025394

Segrin, C., Badger, T. A., Meek, P., Lopez, A. M., Bonham, E., & Sieger, A. (2005). Dyadic interdependence on affect and quality of life trajectories among women with breast cancer and their partners. *Journal of Social and Personal Relationships, 22*, 673–689. doi: 10.1177/0265407505056443

Segrin, C., Burke, T. J., & Dunivan, M. (2012). Loneliness and poor health within families. *Journal of Social and Personal Relationships, 29*(5), 597–611. doi: 10.1177/0265407512443434

Segrin, C., & Flora, J. (2000). Poor social skills are a vulnerability factor in the development of psychosocial problems. *Human Communication Research, 26*, 489–514. doi: 10.1111/j.1468-2958.2000.tb00766.x

Segrin, C., & Flora, J. (2001). Perceptions of relational histories, marital quality, and loneliness when communication is limited: An examination of married prison inmates. *Journal of Family Communication, 1*, 151–173. doi: 10.1207/S15327698JFC0103_01

Segrin, C., Givertz, M., Swiatkowski, P., & Montgomery, N. (2015). Overparenting is associated with child problems and a critical family environment. *Journal of Child and Family Studies, 24*, 470–479. doi: 10.1007/s10826-013-9858-3

Segrin, C., Nevarez, N., Arroyo, A., & Harwood, J. (2012). Family of origin environment and adolescent bullying predict young adult loneliness. *The Journal of Psychology, 146*, 119–134. doi: 10.1080/00223980.2011.555791

Segrin, C., Woszidlo, A., Givertz, M., Bauer, A., & Murphy, M. T. (2012). The association between overparenting, parent-child communication, and entitlement and adaptive traits in adult children. *Family Relations, 61*, 237–232. doi: 10.1111/j.1741-3729.2011.00689.x

Segrin, C., Woszidlo, A., Givertz, M., & Montgomery, N. (2013). Parent and child traits associated with overparenting. *Journal of Social and Clinical Psychology, 32*, 569–595. doi: 10.1521/jscp.2013.32.6.569

Silberg, J. L., Maes, H., & Eaves, L. J. (2012). Unraveling the effect of genes and environment in the transmission of parental antisocial behavior to children's conduct disturbance, depression and hyperactivity. *Journal of Child Psychology and Psychiatry, 53*, 668–677. doi: 10.1111/j.1469-7610.2011.02494.x

Sullivan, H. S. (1953). *The interpersonal theory of psychiatry.* New York: Norton.

Turner-Cobb, J. M., Steptoe, A., Perry, L., & Axford, J. (1998). Adjustment in patients with rheumatoid arthritis and their children. *Journal of Rheumatology, 25*, 565–571.

Wang, Y., & Dix, T. (2013). Patterns of depressive parenting: Why they occur and their role in early development risk. *Journal of Family Psychology, 27*, 884–895. doi: 10.1037/a0034829

Watzlawick, P., Bavelas, J. B., & Jackson, D. D. (1967). *Pragmatics of human communication.* New York: W. W. Norton & Company Inc.

Weihs, K., Fisher, L., & Baird, M. (2002). Families, health, and behavior. *Family Systems and Health, 20*, 7–46. doi: 10.1037/h0089481

Westen, D. (1990). Psychoanalytic approaches to personality. In L. A. Pervin (Ed.), *Handbook of personality: Theory and research* (pp. 21–65). New York: Guilford Press.

Westman, M., Keinan, G., Roziner, I., & Benyamini, Y. (2008). The crossover of perceived health between spouses. *Journal of Occupational Health Psychology, 13*, 168–180. doi: 10.1037/1076-8998.13.2.168

Williams, D. R., Gonzalez, H. M., Neighbors, H., Nesse, R., Abelson, J. M., Sweetman, J., & Jackson, J. S. (2007). Prevalence and distribution of major depressive disorder in African Americans, Caribbean blacks and non-Hispanic whites: Results from the National Survey of American life. *Archives of General Psychiatry, 64*, 305–315. doi: 10.1001/archpsyc.64.3.305

Wynne, L., Ryckoff, I., Day, J., & Hirsch, S. (1958). Pseudo-mutuality in the family relations of schizophrenics. *Psychiatry, 21*, 205–220.

CHAPTER TWO

The Impact OF Maternal AND Paternal Communication Dominance ON Offspring's Negative Self-Talk, Depression, AND Suicidality

MICHELLE MILLER-DAY
Chapman University

SAM M. DORROS
Chapman University

L. EDWARD DAY
Chapman University

According to the Centers for Disease Control and Prevention (CDCP) (2010), suicide was the 10th leading cause of death in the United States and the 3rd leading cause of death among Americans between the ages of 15 and 24. Among 15- to 24-year-olds, suicide accounts for 20% of all deaths annually and the prevalence of suicidal thoughts, suicide planning, and suicide attempts is significantly higher among emerging adults aged 18–29 years than among adults over 30 years of age (Crosby, Han, Ortega, Parks, & Gfoerer, 2011). Young adults aged 18–24 years have the highest incidence of reported suicide ideation (Crosby, Cheltenham, & Sacks, 1999). The American College Health Association's National College Health Assessment (2011) found that within the past 12 months, 30.3% of students felt so depressed they found it difficult to function, 6.6% seriously considered suicide, 5.2% intentionally cut, burned, bruised, or otherwise injured themselves, and 1.1% attempted suicide. Moreover, nearly a third of those who report past suicide attempts will make subsequent repeated attempts (Kessler, Bergland, Borges, Nock, & Wang, 2005). Beyond loss of life, states spend more than $900 million annually on medical costs associated with suicides and suicide attempts by youths up to 21 years of age (Children's Safety Network, 2000). Suicidal tendencies (referred to here as suicidality) including ideation, suicide-related behaviors, and suicide attempts are a significant public health issue (U.S. Public Health Service, 1999).

In the research area of suicidality, general family functioning has been implicated in a variety of suicide risk factors such as depression (Miller, McDermut, Gordon, Keitner, Ryan, & Norman, 2000), alcohol and substance use disorders (Andrews, Hops, Ary, Tildesley, & Harris, 1993), and poor problem solving (Kazdin, 2010). While we are beginning to understand how general family processes may influence suicide risk (Wagner, Silverman, & Martin, 2003), much of this research focuses on family history of suicide or general family functioning constructs such as cohesion, conflict, or attachment, with a paucity of research examining specific parent-offspring communicative interaction that facilitates this functioning. Parent-child communication is implicated in suicide risk but often in very general terms such as "poor communication" or "unsatisfying communication" (Gould, Fisher, Parides, Flory, & Shaeffer, 1996). More recently, however, specific parent-offspring interaction patterns such as parental psychological control (Barber, 2002; Grolnick, 2003) and dominant-submissive parent-child communication (Miller-Day & Walker-Jackson, 2012) have been correlated with depression (McClellan, Heaton, Forste, & Barber, 2004) and suicide (Diamond, Didner, Waniel, Priel, Asjerov, & Arbel, 2005).

Given the importance of understanding the role of parental communication in offspring suicidality and the methodological gaps in existing work in this area, the purpose of this study is to examine maternal and paternal dominant communication as a predictor of offspring's suicidality in an emerging adult sample. To fully develop a model for testing, we first review the research literatures on suicidality and family interaction, communication dominance, negative intrapersonal communication, depression, and suicidality.

LITERATURE REVIEW

Suicidality and Family Interaction

Suicidality has been described on a continuum that begins with ideation (consideration of suicide) followed by planning and preparing for suicide, and then finally threatening, attempting, and completing suicide (Kachur, Potter, Powell, & Rosenberg, 1995). A history of attempts and serious ideation remain the best predictors of future attempts and completed suicide (Lewinsohn, Rhode, &

Seeley, 1996). On college campuses, those who typically seek help for suicidality and suicide-related risk factors are women (Lucas & Berkel, 2005; Stone, Vespia, & Kanz, 2000). Women have a higher incidence of depression than do men, with depression being a significant predictor of suicide; up to 60% of individuals who commit suicide have a depressive disorder at the time of death (Barbe, Bridge, Birmailer, Kolko, & Brent, 2004). For both males and females, rates of depression, suicidal ideation, and suicide attempts rise during adolescence and are especially high during young adulthood (Lewinsohn, Rohde, & Seeley, 1996).

Some research indicates that supportive family relationships may function as deterrents to suicide (Wagner, Silverman, & Martin, 2003); however, little research has been conducted on the interpersonal dynamics of college students and their parents as the student gains increased autonomy and differentiation from parental figures. Clinical research by Richards (1999) reported that intrafamily dynamics significantly predicted suicidality. Across all therapists' reports in this study, over half (52.9%) of the patients reported perceptions that their parents were indirectly rejecting and that their intrafamilial communication was dysfunctional. Other research on family factors and suicide outcomes lends additional support to the importance of parent-offspring communication and suicide risk (Firestone, 1997; Firestone & Macey, 1997; Gould et al., 1996). The findings from these studies strongly suggest that interpersonal interactions with significant primary figures, especially parents, that are intrusive and/or rejecting are likely to be internalized and can increase the risk of suicide in later life. This research points out that covert parental control strategies for gaining offspring conformity may result in self-attacks and suicidal ideation (Firestone & Firestone, 1998; Firestone & Macey, 1997). Also compelling are studies by Kim et al. (2005) and Lieb et al. (2005), which both found that interpersonal interactions with parents predicted suicide over and above mental health diagnoses such as depression or bipolar disorder. Despite an increased interest in family and interpersonal foundations of suicide, there has been little research attention paid to parental communication and suicide until recently.

Indirect and insidious parent-offspring interpersonal interactions (e.g., put-downs, coercion, rejection, hostility, dismissiveness) disrupt the emotional competence of offspring and affect offspring's socio-emotional adjustment across the lifespan, not just in childhood (Barber, 2002; Nussbaum, Pecchioni, Baringer, & Kundrat, 2002). Family processes, especially interactions with parents, remain consequential for emerging adult offspring as they move toward greater autonomy and control of their own lives, differentiating themselves from parents (Lawson & Brossart, 2004; West et al., 1999). Insidious family interaction such as dominant communication does not abruptly stop upon high school graduation and may continue to intrude on the offspring's psychological autonomy into adulthood, encroaching on the young adult's perception of self and self-talk, while increasing the risk for depression and suicide. Yet despite the importance of parent-offspring interaction in the lives of sons and daughters, there is little research available examining parental communication dominance among emerging adults.

Deleterious Effects of Communication Dominance

Dominant parent-offspring communication is an intrusive, coercive, and manipulating form of parental communication in which parents appear to maintain their own self at the expense and violation of the child's self by requiring compliance, discouraging the child to think for him or herself, providing sanctions for disagreement, inhibiting offspring's verbal and nonverbal expression, and employing guilt induction (Miller-Day, 2004). Dominant parental communicative interaction increases the risk of problems such as depression and suicide (Barber, 1996, 2002; Barber, Olsen, & Shagle, 1994) with different models for paternal and maternal dominant communication (Miller-Day, 2004; Miller-Day & Walker-Jackson, 2012). A study by Barber and Harmon (2002) revealed that across nine different cultures, parental dominance was related to depression. Moreover, Diamond et al. (2005) found a positive association between parental dominance and suicide ideation of offspring. Specifically, these studies have addressed two separate dimensions of communication dominance—*parental psychological control* and *necessary convergence communication* (NCC). Barber and colleagues defined parental psychological control as a "psychologically oriented, intrusive, constraining, and manipulating form of parental control in which parents appear to maintain their own self at the expense and violation of the child's self" (Barber, Bean, & Erickson, 2002, p. 16). This definition describes a process whereby (1) a parent controls offspring psychologically through the use of dominance, controlling their thoughts and feelings rather than behavior; (2) a parent encourages emotional and psychological dependence, intruding on the offspring's sense of differentiation and identity, restricting the offspring to the psychological world of the parent; (3) efforts are made by a parent to constrain individuation and independence of offspring and inhibit offspring's verbal and nonverbal expression, affecting psychological distance; and (4) a parent manipulates the emotional balance between self and offspring by withdrawing love and approval, using guilt induction, and instilling anxiety in children (Barber, 2002).

According to this research, parental psychological control encourages emotional fusion and inhibits individuation (Barber, 2002; Barber, Olsen, & Shagle, 1994.) This interpersonal communication process of psychological control is not clearly explicated in the research literature. However, Miller and colleagues (Miller-Day, 1994, 2004;) Miller-Day & Walker-Jackson, 2012) report a convergence communication pattern that links psychological control to communication practice. This convergence communication pattern emerged through work with adult women with a history of one or more suicide attempts and led to the development of the Necessary Convergence Communication Theory (NCCT, Miller-Day, 2004). This research suggests that when a parent engages in chronic dominant communication with adult offspring, offspring learn to be submissive, and meanings can be easily coerced (e.g., "You don't think for yourself, you are told what to think"). Within the NCCT, *necessary* infers that convergence is perceived as essential to achieving a certain result, and *convergence* indicates a tendency toward one point (Miller-Day, 2004). Thus, to obtain parental approval and avoid the withdrawal of affection, offspring will overaccommodate the parent's thoughts, attitudes, and feelings and converge with the parent's assigned meanings at the expense of his/her own. Convergence communication has been linked to eating disorders (Miller-Day & Fisher, 2008; Miller-Day & Marks, 2006), and suicidality (Miller, 1995; Miller-Day & Walker-Jackson, 2012). According to the research, this overaccommodation blurs individual psychological boundaries, encourages emotional fusion, and offspring incorporate negative messages into their own self-talk and personal identity and may function differently with mothers and fathers (Miller & Day, 2002; Miller & Lee, 2001; Miller-Day & Walker-Jackson, 2012). Yet what this line of research does not fully explicate is the process by which parental communication dominance with offspring impacts suicidality. Early work on self-destructive intrapersonal communication resulting from parental dominance, however, provides a direction for our inquiry.

Intrapersonal Communication: Negative Self-Talk and Self-Destructive Thoughts

Toward the end of the 1990s, what was first identified in the clinical research of Firestone and Firestone (1996, 1998) and Richards (1999) resurfaced in the parenting and communication literature. This research investigated parent-offspring communicative interaction that is psychologically controlling and leads to disturbances in offspring's development and found that suicide may be a result of self-rejecting attitudes that develop during interpersonal interactions with parents (Firestone, 2014). These interactions may include put-downs, devaluations, and "conditions of worth" (Rogers, 1961) that are not one-time events but are cumulative developmental traumas (Renn, 2012). If young adults and adults remain undifferentiated from family systems with these interactions, they tend to incorporate into themselves the critical and hostile attitudes directed toward them, leading to thoughts of, planning for, and carrying out suicide (Firestone, Firestone, & Catlett, 2012). Similarly, Orbach, Mikulincer, Stein, and Cohen (1998) discovered that suicidal patients were less differentiated from parents and had more negative self-representations than nonsuicidal controls.

Firestone and colleagues' (e.g., 2012, 2014) body of research suggests that self-rejecting attitudes manifest in negative self-talk, and self-destructive thoughts contribute to suicide risk. Findings from this research demonstrate a strong connection between parental introjects or "voices" and self-destructive behavior. Firestone and colleagues characterize the "voice" as a systematized, integrated pattern of negative self-talk and attitudes, antithetical to the self and hostile toward others; that is, the basis of an individual's maladaptive behavior. "Voices" of self-attack vary along a continuum of intensity from mild self-reproach to strong self-accusations and suicidal ideation (Firestone, 2014; Firestone & Firestone, 1996, 1998; Firestone, Firestone, & Aurelius, 2012). Similarly, self-destructive behavior exists on a continuum ranging from self-denial to self-criticism to self-defeating behaviors (i.e., behavior contrary to one's goals, accident-proneness, substance abuse) and eventually to direct actions that cause bodily harm. Firestone and colleagues argue that clinical evidence supporting the relationship between self-destructive thoughts (internal voices) and self-destructive living would lead to an accurate prediction of an individual's suicide potential. What remain unclear are the associations among dominant parental communication, negative self-talk, and their associations and effects on emerging adults who are developmentally differentiating from parents and who are prone to suicidality and depression.

The Significance of Depression

Depression is a pathological and pervasive state of mood and is consistently the most prevalent disorder among adolescent suicide victims (Gould et al., 2003). Globally, major depression is projected to become the world's second leading cause of disability by 2020 (Murray & Lopez, 1996), is currently one of the leading causes of disability worldwide, and is a consistent predictor of suicide, which is the second leading cause of death in 15- to 20-year-olds (World Health Organization, 2014). A high proportion of adolescents with suicidal ideation or who have engaged in suicide acts also meet the criteria for depression (Lewinsohn, et al., 1996). Eighty-five percent of clinically depressed adolescents will also have suicide ideation (Barbe et al., 2004), and 32% will make a suicide attempt sometime during their adolescence or young adulthood (Kovacs, Goldston, & Gatsonis, 1993). Kessler and colleagues' (1999, 2005) studies on national trends in suicide ideation and attempts revealed that depression is a better predictor of suicide than other mental or substance use disorders. But rarely are family communication variables factored into these investigations of depression and suicidality. Therefore, given findings from past research and methodological gaps, we created a conceptual model of the communication factors that may predict emerging adult depression and suicidality.

The Conceptual Model

Because research has revealed that dominant parental communication is associated with negative self-talk (mild self-reproach to suicidal ideation) (Firestone, 2014; Firestone & Firestone, 1998; Firestone, Firestone, & Catlett, 2012) and suicidality (Miller-Day & Walker-Jackson, 2012), we posit that the influence of mother's and father's dominant communication on suicidality would be both direct and indirect through offspring's negative self-talk. In addition to understanding how dominant parental communication affects sons' and daughters' negative self-talk and suicidality, it is important to consider the role of depression in each parental model. Although we know that there is a strong relationship between depression and suicidality, the research literature is unclear about the effect of dominant parental communication on depression and if the impact of dominant parental communication on suicidality is indirect through depression. Considering that depression is one of the best predictors of suicide and that dominant parental communication may predict depression (McClellan et al., 2004), we posit that dominant parental communication effects suicidality through depression. These relationships are portrayed in Figure 1. The five hypotheses in this conceptual model are:

H1: Dominant parental communication increases offspring's negative self-talk.

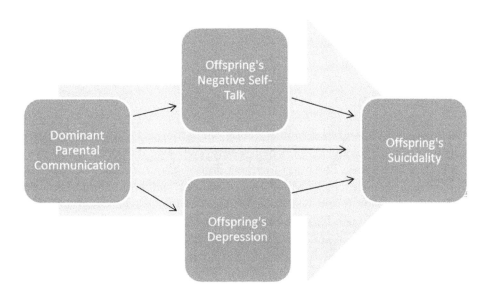

Fig 1. Effect of Dominant Parental Communication on Negative Self-talk, Depression, and Suicidality.

H2:   Dominant parental communication increases offspring's suicidality.
H3:   Dominant parental communication increases offspring's depression.
H4:   Offspring's negative self-talk increases offspring's suicidality.
H5:   Offspring's depression increases offspring's suicidality.

Two models were tested—one for maternal communication and one for paternal communication.

METHODS

Sample

The present sample included a total of 252 participants ranging in age from 18–23 (M = 20.06, SD = 1.26). The sex of participants was relatively equal, with a breakdown of 49.6% male and 50.4% female participants. We administered a self-report, web-based survey to university students currently enrolled at a mid-Atlantic university in a required general education public speaking course. These participants were part of a university research subject pool, and they received course credit for their participation. Self-report is an efficient approach given the nature of the study variables. As Rohner (1986) pointed out, perceptions of parental love and control are beliefs held by the offspring, not merely a set of actions by the parent. Self-reports are a valid way to measure interpersonal interaction variables such as parental dominance "since feeling dominated, controlled, devalued, manipulated, and criticized is very much a subjective experience" (Barber, 1996, p. 3303).

Measures

Communication Dominance. Communication dominance was conceived as a latent construct with three dimensions. The first was psychological control as defined by Barber and colleagues. The other two were dimensions of necessary convergence communication as defined by Miller-Day (motivation and disequilibrium). For the first dimension, the Psychological Control Scale-Youth Self-Report [PCS-YSR] (Barber, 1996) was used. This is a seven-item scale designed to measure perceptions of psychological control and was administered separately to assess maternal psychological control and paternal psychological control. Sample items included "my mother is always trying to change how I feel or think about things" and "would like to be able to tell me how to feel or think about things all of the time." Each item is rated using a five-point Likert-type scale ranging from 1 (*"Not at all like her/him"*) to 5 (*"Very much like her/him"*). This instrument had been validated and exhibited reliabilities ranging from .72-.85 among a samples of adolescents (Barber, 2002); however, to our knowledge this instrument had not been previously validated among a college-student population. In our sample, internal consistency was lower than that reported by Barber (2002). Cronbach's alpha for mothers' psychological control was .69, and fathers' psychological control was .59. Removing items did not significantly improve reliability. Means (and standard deviations) for mothers' and fathers' psychological control were 1.39 (0.35) and 1.29 (0.28), respectively.

For the other two dimensions, an adapted version of the Necessary Convergence Communication Scale (NCCS) (Miller-Day & Walker-Jackson, 2012) was used in this study to measure dominance. This is a 16-item instrument designed to measure two dimensions of convergent communicative interaction—motivation and disequilibrium. The NCCS was adapted to assess both mothers and fathers separately. Each item was designed to assess how much the statement characterizes communicative interactions with the relational partner and was rated using a five-point Likert-type scale ranging from 1 ("Not at all") to 5 ("Very much"). Sample items for motivation included "When my father and I disagree, he tends to be coercive," "My mother's dominance requires my submission," and "My mother insists that I agree with her," and a sample item for disequilibrium was "Only my mother offers opinions in our conversations." The NCCS was normed on university students and demonstrated a reliability of .91. Both scales were internally consistent for both mother's and father's motivation (α = .83 and α = .86, respectively). The mean (standard deviation) for mother's motivation was 1.70 (0.63), and for father's motivation, the mean (standard deviation) was 1.78 (0.69). The disequilibrium scale was also internally consistent for both mother's and father's disequilibrium (α = .88 and α = .86, respectively). The means (standard deviations) for mother's disequilibrium was 2.12 (.88) and for father's disequilibrium 2.22 (.87), respectively.

Self-destructive thoughts. The Firestone Assessment of Self-Destructive Thoughts (FAST) (Firestone & Firestone, 1996) was developed based on 20 years of research into the self-destructive thoughts related to suicide risk and shows promise as a reliable instrument to assess suicide risk. It is a self-report questionnaire consisting of 84 items used to assess a continuum of voice attacks that are correlated with suicidality and depression.

As indicated earlier, voice attacks are considered a systematized, integrated pattern of negative self-talk and attitudes, antithetical to the self and hostile toward others, that vary along a continuum of intensity from mild self-reproach to strong self-accusations and suicidal ideation (Firestone & Firestone, 1996, 1998). For this analysis, 19 of the 84 items were eliminated because they were confounded with suicidality. These items involved injunctions to plan suicide (e.g., "When are you going to kill yourself? You have to find a good time.") or injunctions to carry out suicide plans (e.g., "Just kill yourself! It's the only way out").

Each of the remaining items was designed to assess the current frequency of a self-destructive thought and was rated using a five-point Likert-type scale ranging from 0 ("Never") to 4 ("Most of the Time") with sample items including, "You can't do anything right, you're disgusting" and "You idiot! You don't deserve anything." The FAST has been administered to adult patients in psychiatric hospital settings and a variety of outpatient treatment settings, as well as nonclinical samples of college students (Firestone & Firestone, 1996). Cronbach's alpha for the remaining 65 items was .94, with a mean (standard deviation) of 1.64 (.46).

Depression. The Beck Depression Inventory-II (BDI-II; Beck, Steer, & Brown, 1996) is a 21-item self-report scale of depressive symptoms (including sad affect, apathy, disappointment/guilt, and physical symptoms) as listed in the American Psychiatric Association's *Diagnostic and Statistical Manual of Mental Disorders* Fourth Edition (DSM-IV; 1994). A total score is computed by summing the scores on the 21 symptoms. The BDI has been used for 35 years to identify and assess depressive symptoms and has been reported to be highly reliable regardless of the population. It has a high alpha coefficient (.80), its construct validity has been established, and it is able to differentiate depressed from nondepressed patients. The BDI-II has high alpha coefficients for outpatients (.92) and for college students (.93) (Beck, Steer, & Brown, 1996).

For this study, 2 of the 21 items were deleted. One ("Thought of killing myself") was eliminated because of a confound with suicidality. The other ("Loss of interest in sex") was eliminated because analysis of results of a pilot test showed that the item did not correlate with the other items in a college student population. This scale computed from the 19 remaining items for this study was internally consistent (α = .84), with a mean (standard deviation) of 1.38 (0.33).

Suicidality. Suicidality was measured using the Adult Suicidal Ideation Questionnaire (ASIQ; Reynolds, 1991b). The ASIQ is a 25-item self-report measure of suicide ideation in adults. Respondents rate the frequency of suicidal thoughts during the past month using a seven-point scale for each item. The scale ranges from 0 ("*never had the thought*") to 6 ("*almost every day*"). Item content ranges from general wishes that one were dead or never born to distinctive risk factors such as thoughts of how and when to kill oneself. The instrument is consistent with the O'Carroll et al. (1996) definition of suicide-related thoughts and behaviors.

The ASIQ has been administered to undergraduate college students (Reynolds, 1991a), adults seeking outpatient psychiatric treatment, and adults in the community (Reynolds, 1991b). The ASIQ taps a single dimension of suicide ideation. The ASIQ has high internal consistency with Cronbach alpha coefficients ranging from .96 to .98 in clinical and nonclinical samples (Reynolds, 1991a, 1991b). The ASIQ also has high test-retest reliability in psychiatric outpatients ($r = .95$; Reynolds, 1991b) over a one-month period and in undergraduate college students ($r = .86$; Reynolds, 1991a) over a one-week period. In this sample, the scale was internally consistent ($\alpha = .97$), with a mean (standard deviation) of 1.23 (0.48).

Research Ethics

All study procedures were approved by the institutional review board (IRB) of the respondents' institution. All students in the randomly assigned sections of the university course were provided equal access to completing the survey and were provided with an alternative speech analysis assignment if they elected to not participate in the study. Each participant was provided with information on university and community counseling resources in both the consent form and on the final page after completing the survey. Since participants received course credit for their participation, the survey results were not anonymous. Therefore, in addition to providing counseling resources to participants, study personnel identified all participants who scored above the mean on either depression, suicidality, or negative self-talk and emailed them directly to be assured that they were aware of counseling services available to them. The lead author personally called five students who scored in the top quartile on one or more of these measures to encourage the students to seek assistance. All five were already receiving counseling or treatment.

RESULTS

Procedures and Statistical Analysis

Missing data were checked before the data analyses. A listwise deletion was performed for participants who were missing more than 10 data points, which resulted in 15 cases being deleted from the data set. Given that the proportion of cases with missing data was small (i.e. approximately 5%), listwise deletion may be considered an acceptable form of handling missing data (Roth, 1994). The listwise deletion resulted in a total of $N = 252$ for each path analysis (mothers and fathers separately).

Correlations among all measures are shown in Table 1. Any additional remaining missing single-item variables were replaced with the mean of the scale (i.e. mean substitution), which can shrink the variance of the variables. Although not necessarily appealing, it was required to do so in order to perform analyses using AMOS statistical software. Path model analyses were conducted using the AMOS 22 program. Two separate path model analyses were conducted testing the theoretical model presented in Figure 1, one for the effect of mother's dominant communication and the other for father's dominant communication on negative self-talk, depression, and suicidality.

Table 1. Correlation Matrix of Maternal and Paternal Communication Dominance and Offspring's Depression, Negative Self-Talk, and Suicidality.

Measure	1	2	3	4	5	6	7	8	9
1. Depression	–								
2. Negative Self-Talk	.52**	–							
3. Suicidality	.39**	.69**	–						
4. Mother's Disequilibrium	.16*	.21**	.11	–					
5. Mother's Motivation	.20**	.30**	.11	.37**	–				
6. Mother's Psychological Control	.35**	.32**	.19**	.35**	.50**	–			
7. Father's Disequilibrium	.19**	.20**	.12	.60**	.11	.21**	–		
8. Father's Motivation	.21**	.31**	.15*	.11	.52**	.16*	.23**	–	
9. Father's Psychological Control	.16*	.29**	.19**	.04	.11	.30**	.10	.46**	–

Note: *$p < .05$, **$p < .01$.

Overall Model Fit for Mother's Dominant Communication

Following the original hypothesized model (see Figure 1), five paths were examined for goodness of fit, including: mother's dominance to negative self-talk (H1), dominance to suicidality (H2), dominance to depression (H3), negative self-talk to suicidality (H4), and depression to suicidality (H5). Three paths were significant, from mother's dominance to negative self-talk (H1), dominance to depression (H3), and negative self-talk to suicidality (H4). Two paths, dominance to suicidality (H2) and depression to suicidality (H5), were not statistically significant, so we deleted those paths and examined the goodness of fit of the revised model. Modification indices suggested an additional pathway from depression to negative self-talk, which we included in the final model (see Figure 2). The final model fit the data very well (x^2 (8, N = 252) 12.86, p = .12; RMSEA = .05 ([CI] = .00-.10); CFI = .99).

Overall Model Fit for Father's Dominant Communication

When the original model was tested for fathers, the same three paths were significant: from father's dominance to negative self-talk (H1), dominance to depression (H3), and negative self-talk to suicidality (H4). Two paths, dominance to suicidality (H2) and depression to suicidality (H5), were not statistically significant, so we deleted those paths and examined the goodness of fit of the revised model (see Figure 3). The final model fit the data very well (x^2 (8, N = 252) = 10.50, p = .23; RMSEA = .04 [CI] = .00-.09); CFI = .99). No other paths were suggested by the modification indices.

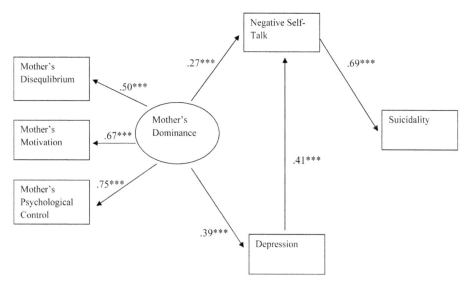

Fig 2. Final Model of Mother's Dominant Communication on Negative Self-talk, Depression, and Suicidality.
****p < .001.

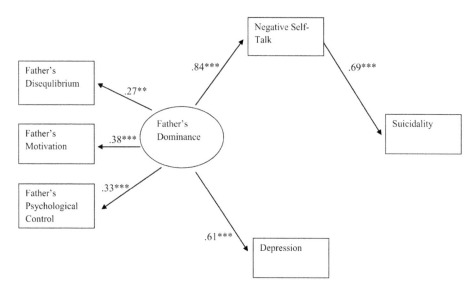

Fig 3. Final Model of Father's Dominant Communication on Negative Self-talk, Depression, and Suicidality.
***p < .001, **p < .01.

DISCUSSION

The purpose of this investigation was to assess if maternal and paternal dominant communication predicted offspring's negative self-talk, depression, and suicidality in an emerging adult sample. The results supported a number of our hypothesized relationships and revealed one surprising finding. In the model testing maternal communication dominance, mother's dominance predicted negative self-talk (H1), dominance predicted depression (H3), and negative self-talk predicted suicidality (H4). Dominant communication did not have a direct effect on suicidality as predicted (H2). The effect of dominant communication on suicidality was indirect through negative self-talk. Most surprisingly, in this model, depression did not directly affect suicidality (H5). This is surprising given that depression is one of the most consistent predictors of suicidality (WHO, 2014). Results were similar in the model testing paternal communication dominance, with father's dominance predicting negative self-talk (H1), dominance predicting depression (H3), and negative self-talk predicting suicidality (H4). Again, as in the paternal model, the effect of dominance was indirect through negative self-talk rather than being a direct effect, and depression did not predict suicidality (H5).

The Surprise: Depression only linked to Suicidality through Intrapersonal Communication

As noted above, the most striking and counterintuitive finding is that a direct causal link between depression and suicidality does not fit these data for either model. Although research consistently finds that depression is one of the best predictors of suicidality (Harrington, 1993; Lewinsohn et al., 1996; WHO, 2014), there was no causal link between depression and suicidality in this study. For the father's model, there was also no indirect path. This, of course, does not mean that the two constructs are unrelated. It does suggest, however, that when one examines communication patterns as an exogenous construct, depression and suicidality are likely both outcomes of a maladaptive communication style rather than directly causally linked. They are symptoms of the same maladaptive pattern. This is a particularly important finding, because depression is one of the single best predictors of suicidality in the psychology literature. This finding indicates that while depression may be a significant risk factor for suicidality when not considering the impact of communication, once negative self-talk is added to the model, this dissipates the effect of depression on suicidality.

Salience of Negative Self-Talk

Negative self-talk had the only direct link to suicidality in both models. Dominant communication patterns from both mothers and fathers increased the likelihood of negative self-talk. Dominant communication patterns from mothers also affects negative self-talk indirectly through depression. Both models lead to the general conclusion that the key to understanding the immediate precursors of suicide is understanding how at-risk individuals negatively define themselves through intrapersonal communication and how parental communication shapes those intrapersonal messages; that is, a key factor contributing to that negative intrapersonal communication is interaction style with parents. Firestone (2010) pointed out that there is an intergenerational transmission of self-critical and self-destructive "voices" from dominating parents to the minds of offspring who internalize self-critical voices. While cognitive-behavioral therapy is often employed with depressed or suicidal patients to modify a patient's thinking to bring about cognitive and behavioral change (Beck, 2011), these traditional approaches do not always help individuals try to identify the destructive voices in their heads that interfere with their personal growth and struggle toward autonomy from parental beliefs (Firestone et al., 2012).

Dominant Parental Communication as a Risk Factor

These results add to previous research that indicates dominant parent-offspring communication increases the risk of problems such as depression and suicide (Barber, 1996; Barber, 2002; Barber, Olsen, & Shagle, 1994) with different models for paternal and maternal dominant communication (Miller-Day, 2004; Miller-Day & Walker-Jackson, 2012). While the psychological control literature suggests this pattern of interaction is especially deleterious in childhood, the results from this study suggest that when parental communication dominance continues into early adulthood, the impact can be just as problematic. Dominant parent-offspring communication tends to dominate offspring verbally and nonverbally, providing sanctions for disagreement, and inhibits offspring's verbal and nonverbal expression, and, as Miller-Day (2004) points out, this may result in the "hijacking of meaning" where offspring do not think for themselves but internalize and embrace parental messages as their own. Emerging adulthood (ages 19–29) (Arnett, 2000) is a time of differentiating and developing a unique sense of self, not just reflecting our parents' values, attitudes, beliefs, and voices. As this study suggests, dominant parental communication has implications for emerging adults' mental health and that the effect of maternal and paternal dominance may differ. While dominant parental communication significantly influenced both negative self-talk (intrapersonal communication) and depression for sons and daughters, the effect was much stronger for father's dominant communication.

Implications

Among the implications of these findings are that suicidality could be targeted with primary prevention programs that focus on parenting communication skills. Addressing dysfunctional parent-child interaction patterns by promoting prosocial interactions could reduce the precursors of suicide. Also, directly addressing the intrapersonal communication of offspring with dominant parental communication using "voice therapy" may be useful. Voice therapy (Firestone, 2010) is a "self under siege" therapy designed to help offspring differentiate themselves from destructive parental voices. In this therapy, differentiation is becoming an independent person who functions primarily in the adult mode and who transcends destructive familial influences, and the more differentiated the self, the more a person can be an individual while still retaining emotional contact with the family group (Firestone, 2010; Firestone et al., 2012; Kerr & Bowen, 1988). As described in Firestone et al. (2012), voice therapy employs a dialogue format that allows the person to identify and state the inner voice out loud and direct the statements to him or herself. This therapeutic approach employs innovative methods to directly address internal dialogue that is critical, restrictive, and sometime self-destructive by identifying their source, challenging them, exploring the voices, and seeking to gain a new perspective. Voice therapy is intended to split the "real" self from the "anti-self" that consists of negative parental attitudes incorporated into identity and to emancipate offspring from these messages (Firestone et al., 2012). University programs might focus on voice therapy strategies with students to manage negative self-talk in ways to mitigate the risks of parental communication dominance.

This study also lends additional support for necessary convergence communication theory (Miller-Day, 1995; Miller-Day & Walker-Jackson, 2012), supporting the prediction that offspring of parents using dominant communication may over-accommodate parents' thoughts, attitudes, and feelings at the expense of their own. By becoming emotionally and psychologically dependent on the dominant parent, the internalization of parental critical voices may lead to the negative self-talk and self-destructive thoughts that contribute to suicide risk.

Future Research

The findings of this study suggest that negative self-talk may have more proximal direct effects on suicide than depression and may even mediate the effects of depression. This has significant implications for mental health research and clinical applications. Yet while this study is promising for increasing understanding of communication-related risk factors to depression and suicidality, communication researchers have the opportunity to further develop more nuanced measures of dominant parental communication. It falls to the field of family communication to conceptualize and measure communication beyond "poor or good" communication. The measures used in this study are a start, but further refinement is needed. For example, perhaps different measures are needed that are sensitive to different stages of the offspring's development. It is unclear if parental communication dominance should be measured similarly at early adolescence and early adulthood.

Additionally, while dominant parental communication significantly influenced negative self-talk and depression of offspring in this sample, the effect was much stronger for father's dominant communication. It is unclear why this may be, nor do we know if the effect is similar for sons and daughters. Further research is warranted to fully understand these effects. Moreover, this study utilized emerging adult self-report of both parent and offspring behaviors. Although we believe that offspring reports are the most valid source for these constructs, it is possible that there may be same-source bias introduced into these data. Further research in this area may obtain parent reports of communication in addition to offspring reports.

Conclusion

Investigating parental communication dominance and offspring's intrapersonal communication has a lot to offer in understanding the dark side of family communication. Parental communication dominance and negative self-talk as risk factors for suicidality have rarely been studied, and these constructs are centrally related to the field of communication. This study reveals that these constructs are consequential for understanding both depression and suicidality in an emerging adult population, and the differential importance of mothers and fathers in predicting both depression and negative self-talk is noteworthy.

In all, the challenge for some emerging adults may be to process parental dominant messages without internalizing those messages into their own self-talk. Voice therapy outside or within the context of university settings may be a useful method to directly address this critical self-talk, challenge it, and come to a new understanding of the intrapersonal communication. Parents may or may not be aware of the effect of dominant communication or, as Miller-Day (2004) found, they may be psychologically controlling "out of love" and concern for offspring. Dominant parental communication may function as a risk factor and, if identified, might be addressed through parenting interventions such as parent education programs through communities or schools. Communication is consequential, and perhaps communication scholars might collaborate with clinicians and prevention experts to develop programs for these families.

REFERENCES

American College Health Association. (2011). *American College Health Association. National College Health Assessment II. Reference group executive summary.* Hanover, MD: American College Health Association.

American Psychiatric Association. (2000). *Diagnostic and statistical manual of mental disorders DSM-IV-TR Fourth Edition* (Text Revision) Author: American Psychiatric Association.

Andrews, J. A., Hops, H., Ary, D. W., Tildesley, E., & Harris, J. (1993). Parental influence in early adolescent substance use: Specific and nonspecific effects. *Journal of Early Adolescence, 13*, 285–310. doi: 10.1177/0272431693013003004

Arnett, J. J. (2000). Emerging adulthood: A theory of development from the late teens through the twenties. *American Psychologist, 55*, 469–480. doi: 10.1037//0003-066X.55.5.469

Barbe, R. P., Bridge, J., Birmailer, B., Kolko, D., & Brent, D. A. (2004). Suicidality and its relationship to treatment outcomes in depressed adolescents. *Suicide & Life -Threatening Behavior, 34*, 44–55. doi: 10.1521/suli.34.1.44.27768

Barber, B. (1996). Parental psychological control: Revisiting a neglected construct. *Child Development, 67*, 3296–3319. doi: 10.1111/j.1467-8624.1996.tb01915.x

Barber, B. (2002). *Intrusive parenting: How psychological control affects children and adolescents.* Washington, DC: American Psychological Association. doi: 10.1037/10422-000

Barber, B., Bean, R. L., & Erickson, L. D. (2002). Expanding the study of psychological control. In B. Barber (Ed.), *Intrusive parenting: How psychological control affects children and adolescents* (pp. 263–289). Washington, DC: American Psychological Association. doi: 10.1037/10422-009

Barber, B. K., & Harmon, E. L. (2002). Violating the self: Parental psychological control of children and adolescents (pp. 15–52). In B. Barber (Ed.), *Intrusive parenting: How psychological control affects children and adolescents.* Washington, DC, US: American Psychological Association. doi: 10.1037/10422-002

Barber, B., Olsen, J. A., & Shagle, S. (1994). Associations between parental psychological control and behavioral control and youth internalized and externalized behaviors. *Child Development, 65*, 1120–1136. doi: 10.1111/j.1467-8624.1994.tb00807.x

Beck, J. S. (2011). *Cognitive behavior therapy: Basics and beyond.* Guilford Press.

Beck, J., Steer, R. A., & Brown, G. K. (1996). *Beck Depression Inventory Manual* (2nd ed.). San Antonio, TX: Psychological Corporation.

Centers for Disease Control and Prevention, National Center for Injury Prevention and Control. (2010). *Web-based Injury Statistics Query and Reporting System (WISQARS)* [online]. [cited 2012 Oct. 19]. Available from www.cdc.gov/injury/wisqars/index.html.

Centers for Disease Control and Prevention, National Center for Injury Prevention and Control. (2010). *Injury Prevention & Control: Data & Statistics (WISQARS).* (2014, July 7). Retrieved from http://www.cdc.gov/injury/wisqars/index.html

Children's Safety Network National Injury and Violence Prevention Resource Center, Education Development Center. (2000). *Costs of Completed and Medically Treated Youth Suicide Acts by State, 1996.* See http://www.nga.org/files/live/sites/NGA/files/pdf/0504SUICIDEPREVENTION.pdf

Crosby, A., Cheltenham, M., & Sacks, J. (1999). Incidence of suicidal ideation and behavior in the United States, 1994. *Suicide and Life-Threatening Behavior, 29*, 131–140. doi: 10.1111/j.1943-278X.1999.tb01051.x

Crosby A. E., Han B., Ortega L. A. G., Parks S. E., & Gfoerer, J. (2011). *Suicidal thoughts and behaviors among adults New York: Guilford Press. aged ≥18 years—United States, 2008–2009.* MMWR

Surveillance Summaries: 60 (no. SS-13). Atlanta: Division of Violence Prevention, National Center for Injury Prevention and Control, Centers for Disease Control and Prevention.

Diamond, G. M., Didner, H., Waniel, A., Priel, B., Asherov, J., & Arbel, S. (2005). Perceived parental care and control among Israeli female adolescents presenting to emergency rooms after self-poisoning. *Adolescence, 40*, 257–72.

Firestone, R. W. (1997). *Suicide and the inner voice: Risk assessment, treatment, and case management.* Thousand Oaks, CA: Sage.

Firestone, R. W. (2010). Voice therapy. In H. G. Rosenthal (Ed.), *Favorite counseling and therapy techniques* (2nd ed., pp. 121–124). New York: Routledge/Taylor & Francis Group.

Firestone, R. W. (2014). The ultimate resistance. *Journal of Humanistic Psychology, 55* (1), 77–101. doi: 10.1177/0022167814527166

Firestone, R. W., & Firestone, L. (1996). *Firestone assessment of self-destructive thoughts manual.* San Antonio, TX: Psychological Corporation.

Firestone, R. W., & Firestone, L. (1998). Voices in suicide: The relationship between self-destructive thought processes, maladaptive behavior, and self-destructive manifestations. *Death Studies, 22,* 411–443. doi: 10.1080/074811898201443

Firestone, R. W., & Firestone, L. (2012). Separation theory and voice therapy methodology. In P. R. Shaver and M. Mikulincer (Eds.), *Meaning, mortality, and choice: The social psychology of existential concerns* (pp. 353–377). Washington, DC, US: American Psychological Association.

Firestone, R., Firestone, L., & Catlett, J. (2012). *The self under siege: A therapeutic model for differentiation.* New York, NY: Routledge.

Firestone, R. W., & Macey, D. (1997). *Suicide and the inner voice: Risk assessment, treatment, and case management.* Thousand Oaks, CA: Sage Publications.

Gould, M. S., Fisher, P., Parides, M., Flory, M., & Shaffer, D. (1996). Psychosocial risk factors of child and adolescent completed suicide. *Archives of General Psychiatry, 53*, 1155–1162. doi: 10.1001/archpsyc.1996.01830120095016

Gould, M. S., Greenberg, T., Velting, D. M., & Shaffer, D. (2003). Youth suicide risk and preventive interventions: A review of the past 10 years. *Journal of the American Academy of Child and Adolescent Psychiatry, 42*, 386–405. doi: 10.1097/01.CHI.0000046821.95464.CF

Grolick, W. (2003). *The psychology of parental control: How well-meant parenting backfires.* Mahwah, NJ: Lawrence Erlbaum Associates.

Harrington, R. (1993). *Depressive disorder in childhood and adolescence.* Chichester, UK: John Wiley & Sons.

Kachur, S., Potter, L., Powell, K., & Rosenberg, M. (1995). Suicide: Epidemiology, prevention, treatment. *Adolescent Medicine: State of the Art Reviews, 6*, 171–182.

Kazdin, A. E. (2010). Problem-solving skills training and parent management training for oppositional defiant disorder and conduct disorder. In J. R. Weisz and A. E. Kazdin (Eds.), *Evidence-based psychotherapies for children and adolescents* (pp. 211–226). New York: Guilford Press.

Kerr, M., & Bowen, M. (1988). *Family evaluation: An approach based on Bowen theory.* New York: Norton.

Kessler, R. C., Bergland, P., Borges, G., Nock, M., & Wang, P. S. (2005). Trends in suicide ideation, plans, gestures, and attempts in the United States, 1990–1992 and 2001–2003. *Journal of the American Medical Association, 293*, 2487–2495. doi: 10.1001/jama.293.20.2487

Kessler, R. C., Borges, G., Walters, E. E. (1999). Prevalence of risk factors for lifetime suicide attempts in the National Comorbidity Survey. *Archives of General Psychiatry, 56*, 617–626. doi: 10.1001/archpsyc.56.7.617

Kim, C. D., Seguin, M., Therrian, N., Riopel, G., Chawky, N., Lesage, A. D., & Turecki, G. (2005). Family aggregation of suicidal behavior: A family study of suicide completers from the general population. *The American Journal of Psychiatry*, *162*, 1017–1019. doi: 10.1176/appi.ajp.162.5.1017

Kovacs, M., Goldston, D., & Gatsonis, C. (1993). Suicidal behaviors and childhood depressive onset disorders: A longitudinal investigation. *Journal of the American Academy of Child and Adolescent Psychiatry*, *32*, 8–20. doi: 10.1097/00004583-199301000-00003

Lawson, D. F., & Brossart, D. M. (2004). The developmental course of personal authority in the family system. *Family Process*, *43*, 391–410. doi: 10.1111/j.1545-5300.2004.00029.x

Lewinsohn, P. M., Rohde, P., & Seeley, J. R. (1996). Adolescent suicidal ideation and attempts: Prevalence, risk factors and clinical implications. *Clinical Psychology: Science and Practice*, *3*(1), 25–46. doi: 10.1111/j.1468-2850.1996.tb00056.x

Lieb, R., Bronisch, T., Hofler, M., Scheirer, A., & Wittchen, H. U. (2005). Maternal suicidality and risk of suicidality in offspring: Findings from a community study. *The American Journal of Psychiatry*, *162*, 1665–1671. doi: 10.1176/appi.ajp.162.9.1665

Lucas, M. S., & Berkel, L. A. (2005). Counseling needs of students who seek help at a university counseling center: A closer look at gender and multicultural issues. *Journal of College Student Development*, *46*, 251–266. doi: 10.1353/csd.2005.0029

McClellan, C., Heaton, T., Forste, R., & Barber, B. (2004). Familial impacts on adolescent aggression and depression in Colombia. *Marriage and Family Review*, *36*, 91–118. doi: 10.1300/J002v36n01_05

Miller, M. (1995). An intergenerational case study of suicidal tradition and mother-daughter communication. *Journal of Applied Communication Research*, *23*, 247–270. doi: 10.1080/00909889509365430

Miller, M., & Day, L. E. (2002). Family communication, maternal and paternal expectations, and college students' suicidality. *Journal of Family Communication*, *2*, 167–184. doi: 10.1207/S15327698JFC0204_01

Miller, M., & Lee, J. (2001). Communicating disappointment: The viewpoint of sons and daughters. *Journal of Family Communication*, *1*, 111–131. doi: 10.1207/S15327698JFC0102_02

Miller, I. W., McDermut, W., Gordon, K. C., Keitner, G. I., Ryan, C. E., & Norman, W. (2000). Personality and family functioning in families of depressed patients. *Journal of Abnormal Psychology*, *109*, 539–545. doi: 10.1037/0021-843X.109.3.539

Miller-Day, M. (2004). *Communication among grandmothers, mothers and adult daughters: A qualitative study of maternal relationships*. Mahwah, NJ: Lawrence Erlbaum Associates.

Miller-Day, M., & Fisher, C. (2008). Family communication and disordered eating patterns. *International Journal of Psychology Research*, *3*(3), 1–26.

Miller-Day, M., & Marks, J. L. (2006). Perceptions of parental communication orientation, perfectionism, and disordered eating behaviors of sons and daughters. *Health Communication*, *19*, 153–163. doi: 10.1207/s15327027hc1902_7

Miller-Day, M., & Walker-Jackson, A. (2012). The Convergence Communication Scale (CCS): Development and evaluation of an interpersonal submission assessment. *Journal of Social and Personal Relationships*, *29*, 1036–1057. doi: 10.1177/0265407512443617

Murray, C. J., & Lopez, A. D. (1996). Evidence-based health policy—Lessons from the Global Burden of Disease Study. *Science*, *274*(5288), 740–743.

Nussbaum, J. F., Pecchioni, L. L., Baringer, D. K., & Kundrat, A. L. (2002). Lifespan communication. In W. B. Gudykunst (Ed.), *Communication yearbook 26* (pp. 366–389) Mahwah, NJ: Lawrence Erlbaum Associates.

O'Carroll, P. W., Berman, A. L., Maris, R. W., Moscicki, E. K., Tanney, B. L., & Silverman, M. M. (1996). Beyond the tower of Babel: A nomenclature for suicidology. *Suicide & Life-Threatening Behavior, 26*, 227–252. doi: 10.1111/j.1943-278X.1996.tb00609.x

Orbach, I., Mikulincer, M., Stein, D., & Cohen, O. (1998). Self representation of suicidal adolescents. *Journal of Abnormal Psychology, 107*, 435–439. doi: 10.1037/0021-843X.107.3.435

Renn, P. (2012). *The silent past and the invisible present: Memory, trauma, and representation in psychotherapy.* New York, NY: Routledge.

Reynolds, W. M. (1991a). Psychometric characteristics of the Adult Suicidal Ideation Questionnaire in college students. *Journal of Personality Assessment, 56*, 289–307. doi: 10.1207/s15327752jpa5602_9

Reynolds, W. M. (1991b). *Adult Suicide Ideation Questionnaire: Professional manual.* Odessa, FL: Psychological Assessment Resources.

Richards, B. M. (1999). Suicide and internalised relationships: A study from the perspective of psychotherapists working with suicidal patients. *British Journal of Guidance & Counselling, 27*, 85–99. doi: 10.1080/03069889908259717

Rogers, C. R. (1961). *On becoming a person: A therapist's view of psychotherapy.* Boston, MA: Houghton Mifflin.

Rohner, R. P. (1986). *The warmth dimension: Foundations of parental acceptance-rejection theory.* Beverly Hills, CA: Sage.

Roth, P. L. (1994). Missing data: A conceptual review for applied psychologists. *Personnel Psychology, 47*, 537–560. doi: 10.1111/j.1744-6570.1994.tb01736.x

Stone, V. L., Vespia, K. M., & Kanz, J. E. (2000). How good is mental health care on college campuses? *Journal of Counseling Psychology, 7*, 498–510. doi: 10.1037/0022-0167.47.4.498

U.S. Public Health Service. (1999). *The Surgeon General's call to action to prevent suicide.* Washington, DC: Dept. of Health and Human Services.

Wagner, B. M., Silverman, M. A., & Martin, C. E. (2003). Family factors in youth suicidal behaviors. *The American Behavioral Scientist, 46*, 1171–1191. doi: 10.1177/0002764202250661

West, M. L., Sprang, S. W., Rose, S. M., & Adam, K. S. (1999). Relationship of attachment-felt security and history of suicidal behavior in clinical adolescents. *Journal of Canadian Psychiatry, 44*, 578–582.

World Health Organization. (2014). *Preventing suicide: A global imperative.* Geneva, Switzerland: World Health Organization.

CHAPTER THREE

Parental AND Sibling Behaviors THAT Encourage Daughters' Continued Eating Disorders

An Inconsistent Nurturing as Control Perspective

ASHLEY P. DUGGAN
Communication Department, Boston College

BRIELLE KILMARTIN
Student, New York Law School

Therapeutic interventions for eating disorders often involve multiple family members in treatment (Loeb & Le Grange, 2009). However, relationships and control dynamics within families may actually impede treatment and instead exacerbate disordered eating. Eating disorders are most commonly diagnosed during adolescence (American Psychiatric Association; APA, 2013), which is an already stressful time in human development that can be further complicated by inconsistent or volatile family dynamics. Research provides evidence that families with eating-disordered children overall are more conflicted (Vandereycken, 2002), dysfunctional, and chaotic, with less support and involvement (Benninghoven, Schneider, Strack, Reich, & Cierpka, 2003; Vandereycken, 2002) than families without anyone with an eating disorder. Families of individuals with eating disorders also indicate low family cohesion, poor communication, limited emotional expressiveness, and minimal overall family satisfaction (Benninghoven et al., 2003). Eating-disordered individuals may have problems identifying and expressing their emotions (Nilsson et al., 2007) and instead rely on food as an external source of emotion regulation. Eating-disordered behaviors can serve an expression of needs and can indicate experiencing problems beyond eating (Norbo et al., 2006; Ringer & Crittenden, 2007). Eating-disordered individuals often have perfectionist tendencies, and families including an eating-disordered individual tend to face other manifestations of control across multiple members of the family (Miller-Day & Marks, 2006; Norbo et al., 2006). Eating-disordered behaviors may indirectly indicate family problems (Ringer & Crittenden, 2007), and eating-disordered individuals may lack the ability to express themselves in more adaptive ways (Norbo et al., 2006). Thus, family interaction patterns about eating disorders provide a rich context for examining the dark side of family communication.

Family dynamics may play a role in the development and progression of eating disorders, particularly in female adolescents. The current research suggests that mothers, fathers, and siblings of eating-disordered daughters can exacerbate disordered eating through their attempts to "help" the daughter curtail disordered eating behaviors. This research extends previous applications of Inconsistent Nurturing as Control (INC) theory (Le Poire, 1995; Duggan & Le Poire Molineux, 2013) to the domain of eating disorders and is the first to examine the interplay between parental and sibling behavior of eating-disordered daughters. Daughters with eating disorders were interviewed about family members' strategies to curtail disordered eating. We suggest that parents and siblings of eating-disordered daughters have competing goals of nurturing the disorder and controlling the disordered eating. INC poses that paradoxical injunctions ultimately impact expressions of control in relationships where a compulsive behavior (the eating disorder) interferes with everyday functioning. Qualitative evidence shows the interplay between parent and sibling strategies that may ultimately encourage disordered eating. Based on INC theory, we assert that family members unintentionally and subtly encourage compulsive behavior through their well-intentioned efforts to help.

OCCURRENCE AND CONTEXT OF EATING DISORDERS

The two primary eating disorders are anorexia nervosa and bulimia nervosa (DSM-V; American Psychiatric Association, 2013). Eating disorders generally occur during adolescence and early adulthood, often endure throughout life, and can have a devastating impact on individuals and families. Women represent a vast majority of all eating-disordered individuals, and eating disorders have a higher mortality risk than other mental health disorders (Fairburn & Harrison, 2003). Anorexia and bulimia usually comprise a characteristic attitude in which self-worth is judged largely in terms of body shape and weight (Fairburn & Harrison, 2003). Individuals with anorexia nervosa refuse to maintain normal weight (body weight less than 85% of expected); they have intense fear of gaining weight; and they deny the seriousness of their low body weight (APA, 2013). Treatment is notoriously difficult for anorexia patients who resist change; people seek help only with persistent urging of close friends and family.

Bulimia involves attempted purging through overexercise, self-induced vomiting, or taking laxatives or diuretics (APA, 2013). Bulimic individuals' body weight may be within normal range because of repeated overeating episodes. Bulimic episodes or "binges" involve the consumption of unusually large amounts of food and perceived loss of control (APA, 2013). Researchers discuss the importance of addressing both cultural and social factors, like intense pressure placed on women and girls to be thin, as well as on behavioral, health, and medical factors (Fairburn & Harrison, 2003).

Eating disorder prevalence estimates vary, perhaps because many who suffer from these disorders are reluctant to reveal their condition. Lifetime prevalence estimates from population-based studies are relatively low (0.5%–1.0% for anorexia nervosa and 0.5%–3.0% for bulimia), but community studies with dimensional measures yield far higher estimates of the prevalence of disordered eating (14%–22%) than reports that apply strict DSM diagnostic criteria (Swanson et al., 2011). Individuals with anorexia frequently deny any illness and are often seen for treatment only because people close to them express concern that their lives may be in imminent danger (Polivy & Herman, 2002). Bulimia is usually more difficult to detect through appearance, but bulimic patients may seek treatment because they find the binge-purge cycle disturbing (Polivy & Herman, 2002). Eating disorders often co-occur with other psychiatric disorders and disturbances, including depression, anxiety, obsessiveness, substance abuse disorders, marked impairments in social functioning, and suicide (Swanson et al., 2011).

Issues of family interaction and environment may contribute to the development and progression of eating disorders. Family environments highly concerned with eating patterns and weight also are associated with eating disorders (Arroyo & Segrin, 2013; Kluck, 2010). Research provides evidence that the role of family interaction patterns on young adult females' disordered eating attitudes are mediated by both social competence and psychological distress (Arroyo & Segrin, 2013). Families can enact a variety of pathogenic interaction patterns associated with disordered eating, including family expressed emotion, stressful mealtime or food-related communication, disturbed affective communication, and poor problem solving (Segrin & Flora, 2011). Parents of children with eating disorders can experience extreme emotional burden, stress, and anxiety connected to the intensity and duration of the recovery process (Patel et al., 2014). Healthy coping behaviors may increase family members' ability to participate more effectively in recovery (Patel et al., 2014), but family dynamics are often more complicated than coping strategies can address.

COMPETING FAMILY COMMUNICATION GOALS: INCONSISTENT NURTURING AS CONTROL

Family members seek to nurture, encourage, show warmth, and support each other, but family members also use harsher behaviors to control or minimize potential risk or harm to the family. When a family member engages in behaviors that interfere with daily functioning, parents and siblings seek to nurture the individual but also to control the risky or harmful behavior. Inconsistent Nurturing as Control (INC) theory is based on the assumption that functional family members (parents and siblings) of someone with a compulsive behavior have competing goals of nurturing and controlling (see Le Poire, 1995; Duggan & Le Poire Molineux, 2013). Originally written to explain relationships between substance-abusive individuals and their nonaddicted relational partners (Le Poire, 1995), subsequent theoretical and applied research provides evidence that daughters with eating disorders face similar patterns with mothers' inconsistent attempts to control disordered eating (Duggan, Le Poire, Prescott, & Baham, 2009; Prescott & Le Poire, 2002) as well as depression (Duggan & Le Poire, 2006; Duggan, Le Poire, & Addis, 2006) and spousal violence (Duggan, Le Poire, Prescott, & Baham, 2009).

INC poses paradoxical injunctions in relationships with afflicted partners (e.g., drug abusers, physically abusive individuals, depressed individuals, eating-disordered individuals), paradoxes that ultimately impact expressions of control by functional family members (family members without a problem that interferes with daily functioning) (Le Poire, 1995). INC suggests that family members' nurturing is highly rewarding during times of crisis such that ending the compulsive behavior is not the ultimate goal (Le Poire, 1995). The contradictory nature of family relationships means that functional family members exhibit nurturing relationship maintenance behaviors while they attempt to extinguish the undesirable behavior (e.g., Duggan & Le Poire, 2006; Duggan & Le Poire Molineux, 2013; Prescott & Le Poire, 2002). Assumptions lead to the paradoxical conclusion that if family members actually control the undesirable behavior, they also lose their ability to utilize their nurturing resources in response to undesirable behavior. Thus, family members may ultimately be driven by fear that successfully treating the eating disorder will decrease the daughter's dependency on them. Competing goals lead to inconsistent reinforcement and punishment in influence attempts. INC theory predicts that partners and family members will reinforce the compulsive behavior in the pre-label stage (when they might recognize concerns about behavior), use their best attempts at punishing in the post-label stage (following an event that flags concerns), and revert to a mix of reinforcement and punishment in the post-frustration stage (when they realize nurturing behaviors are not working) (Duggan & Le Poire Molineux, 2013).

In contradistinction to curtailing disordered eating, inconsistent influence may actually increase compulsive behavior (Duggan & Le Poire Molineux, 2013; Le Poire, 1995). Even more problematic, family members may *intermittently* reinforce compulsive behaviors by shifting strategies across labeling stages or by family members using inconsistent strategies. When family members become resentful of the amount of nurturing, they may instead reinforce disordered eating. This intermittent reinforcement may ultimately strengthen disordered eating. Family members' subsequent lack of nurturing is likely an attempt to *punish* or extinguish the disordered eating. Unfortunately, INC theory argues that similar to intermittent reinforcement, the punishment also *increases* the disordered eating (Duggan & Le Poire Molineux, 2013). As demonstrated through evidence for learning theory, intermittent reinforcement or punishment has stronger effects on behavior than continuous reinforcement or continuous punishment. Family members may ultimately strengthen disordered eating through both intermittent reinforcement and intermittent punishment.

This inconsistency is documented over the life span of the relationship, with evidence primarily in substance abuse and depression contexts. Partners of substance-abusive individuals reinforced the substance-abusive behavior (e.g., offering a drink after work) in the pre-labeling phase, before they realized the substance abuse interfered with daily functioning; partners punished substance abuse (e.g., calling the police, threatening to leave) in the post-label phase (e.g., after a drunken car accident), after they realized the depth of interference of drinking on everyday functioning. Partners at some point became frustrated that their control attempts were ineffective and reverted to a mix of reinforcing and punishing strategies (Le Poire, Hallett, & Erlandson, 2000). In addition, partners' consistency in punishing substance abuse and reinforcing alternative behavior (e.g., encouraging attendance at AA meetings) predicted lower relapse and lower depression (Le Poire et al., 2000). Subsequent research examined nonverbal and verbal communication in videotaped conversations and found that consistent verbal punishment (e.g., threats, nagging) predicted lower relapse rates, while verbal reinforcement (e.g., telling the partner he or she is more fun drunk) predicted higher rates of relapse. Nonverbal communication, including vocal qualities associated with punishment (i.e., harsh tone, sharpness in pitch) and vocalic reinforcement (i.e., melodic softness), also predicted relapse and persuasive effectiveness (Duggan, Dailey, & Le Poire, 2008).

Similar patterns of reinforcement and punishment are documented in couples' strategies to curtail depression, where partners contributed to the depression before labeling it problematic, encouraged positive emotional outlets after labeling depression problematic, but over time reverted to reinforcement mixed with punishment (Duggan & Le Poire, 2006). Four contexts of interpersonal influence shed light on power dynamics of helping-type relationships between substance-abusive individuals and romantic partners, relationships between eating-disordered daughters and their mothers, relationships between physically abused women and their violent partners, and relationships between depressed individuals and their romantic partners (Duggan, Le Poire, Prescott, & Baham, 2009). Romantic partners put their own needs aside in order to nurture through crisis, but they also became resentful that their own needs were not being met and used a combination of sometimes nurturing and sometimes reverting to harshness and punishment. In addition, strategies to curtail the compulsive behavior were qualitatively similar across substance-abusive and depressive contexts, with evidence for partners' relational roles enmeshed in the combination of nurturing and controlling (Duggan, Le Poire, & Addis, 2006). Results suggest the combination of behaviors resembles intermittent reinforcement and punishment and should actually strengthen the compulsive behavior.

INCONSISTENT STRATEGIES AMONG FAMILY MEMBERS

The ongoing interdependence and long-term commitment of family members poses rich implications for the interconnection of intentional and unintentional messages among parents and siblings of eating-disordered daughters, and the current study provides an initial test of changes in strategies across family members. Eating disorder relapse is common, and the trajectory of an eating disorder can span a lifetime. Parental involvement in eating disorder treatment can improve outcomes (Bulik, et al., 2007), but parents also may become resentful of neglecting their own well-being during years of treatment. Eating-disordered individuals resist treatment, and caregiving can involve prolonged, challenging processes (Loeb & Le Grange, 2009).). Furthermore, family members may blame eating-disordered individuals for the compulsive behavior, and individuals outside the family may similarly attribute the eating disorder to dysfunctional family dynamics. Parents report negative effects of eating disorders on the family, stress in dealing with difficult eating behaviors, stress over dependency of the eating-disordered child, and social stigma and shame (Treasure et al., 2001). Family members navigate difficult treatment processes, such as refeeding after meals and careful monitoring to discourage purging. Parents' development and maintenance of adaptive coping and self-care may be an important foundation for their ability to provide needed ongoing support for the eating-disordered child, but parents may be confined by stigma or by the eating-disordered child not wanting people to know about the condition (Patel et al., 2014).

Mothers. Paradoxical injunctions within the mother-daughter relationship may pose particular difficulties for mothers to effectively help their daughters diminish eating-disordered behavior (Prescott & LePoire, 2002). INC research provides evidence that mothers reinforce the disordered eating behaviors before labeling the eating disorder, then punish the disordered eating behaviors, but over time revert to a mixture of reinforcing and punishing strategies (Prescott & Le Poire, 2002). Broader psychoanalytic and clinical attention has focused on problematic aspects of the mother-daughter relationship as connected to the eating disorder. Mothers of eating-disordered daughters may feel intense emotions such as confusion, guilt, helplessness, anger, self-doubt, and hope during treatment. Mothers may also experience challenges of time and energy for the daughter's treatment that comes at the expense of their own priorities and of other family members.

Fathers. Fathers may be involved in conflict about the eating disorder. Research on adolescent daughters tends to see their fathers as more judgmental than mothers, less willing to listen, and more likely to impose their authority rather than to try to understand (Noller & Fitzpatrick, 1993). Skilled conflict resolution and open communication between fathers and their daughters may offset eating-disordered. Fathers and daughters resorting to resolving conflict in ways that do not offer long-term resolution for both father and daughter can lead to increased eating disordered behaviors (Botta & Dumlao, 2002). One parent may encourage communication more than the other and handle conflicts differently, and fathers may be caught in conflicts with daughters (Miller-Day & Marks, 2006). In addition, research indicates that father-child conformity communication patterns that stress a climate of homogeneity of attitudes, values, and beliefs, and paternally prescribed perfectionism predicted maladaptive eating when controlling for individual factors such as offspring perfectionism and perceived loss of personal control (Miller-Day & Marks, 2006). Parents may create a climate that enforces similar attitudes, values, and beliefs among family members; these assumptions of similarity may translate into closed and restricted family communication that reinforces parental power and control (Miller-Day & Marks, 2006). Reinforcing parental attitudes may translate into manifestations in father-daughter communication that focus on control.

Siblings. Sibling relationships also face difficulties about eating disorders. Healthy siblings living in the shadow of illness experience difficulties that can have emotional, structural, familial, and social ramifications (Corrigan & Miller, 2004). Siblings may compete for parental attention, and parental attention when one child is diagnosed with an eating disorder is often characterized by ambivalence, frustration, conflict, and frequent transitions between love-hate relationships (Blessing, 2007). Siblings may assume extra responsibility to care for the sister with an eating disorder, which could lead to a sense of frustration, anger, jealousy, hatred, and fear of losing the sister (Latzer, Katz, & Berger, 2013). Ambivalent feelings can create a sense of guilt and fear and reinforce the vicious cycle of closeness-distance, love, and hate (Latzer, Katz, & Berger, 2013). Siblings may feel family dynamics depend on the sick sister, who makes little effort to eat and is deliberately making life difficult for the family (Latzer, Katz, & Berger, 2013). Siblings may feel intense anger at times and empathy and compassion at other times.

Ongoing inconsistency among family members in their attempts to curtail disordered eating would translate into unintentional messages among parents and siblings of eating-disordered daughters, likely reinforcing the disordered eating over time. This study provides an initial test of changes in strategies across family members to examine reinforcement and punishment of the disordered eating among family members and to examine how the interplay among family members changes over the course of labeling the disordered eating problematic. The following research question guides the analysis:

RQ: According to eating-disordered daughters, what strategies were used by mothers, fathers, and siblings during the different labeling stages (pre-label, post-label, and post-frustration), and how did the strategies vary across stages and among family members?

METHOD

Eating-disordered women were recruited through the department research participation pool and through flyers in the campus counseling center and health promotion office. Participants (15 women) were current students at a university in the Northeast who had received formal treatment for an eating disorder. Before scheduling interviews, participants confirmed over the phone that they were told they had an eating disorder. Following consent, hour-long interviews with daughters were conducted in two stages about their perceptions of what each family member did to help curtail disordered eating. First, the researcher introduced the study and asked about the timeframe of the eating disorder diagnosis, prompting participants to remember the event in which the eating disorder became apparent and was diagnosed. All of the women easily identified the time period and event surrounding diagnosing the eating disorder.

The second stage of the interview addressed the daughter's recollections of strategies each family member used to help curtail her disordered eating. Questions were organized by labeling stages consistent with INC theory (pre-label, post-label, and post-frustration) and addressed strategies of the parent who labeled the eating disorder (the mom, in every interview), and then the other parent (the dad), and then the sibling(s). Thus, the interviewer asked what the mom did immediately following labeling the eating disorder problematic (post-label period), how long she tried that strategy, what she did after that (for how long), etc., until the daughter had no new strategies to report. The interviewer then asked about what the dad did after labeling the eating disorder problematic, and then what sibling(s) did. Next, the interviewer asked whether there was a time when control attempts were not working (post-frustration stage). Specific strategies were again prompted in order and about one family member at a time. The last part of the interview related to the time period between when the mom initially commented about potential concerns with the daughter's eating and when the eating disorder was officially diagnosed. Interviewers prompted strategies until the interviews reached saturation.

A total of twenty-six pages (double-spaced) of strategies were reported, with each participant easily recounting perceptions of strategies used by each family member. Each strategy (N = 102 total strategies) was initially entered into a data spread sheet in the order provided by the participants with the family member who used the strategy recorded on the back of the card. The two authors read through the entire data set each independently and then together, identifying themes and mani-fest and latent content areas that emerged from the reported strategies (Graneheim & Lundman, 2004). Manifest content included strategies directly addressing the disordered eating (i.e., carefully monitoring what the daughter ate). Latent content included context of strategies that the eating-disordered daughters interpreted as connected to the eating disorder but could have other meaning in a different con-text (i.e., telling the daughter her toilet was dirty again, implying finding evidence of throwing up in the toilet). Emerging themes and occurrences of communication were quantified/counted with the reported strategy as the unit of analysis and then sorted qualitatively and independently by the second author. This process allows for combining the deductive, post-positivistic approach, in which INC theory is tested, with an iterative process of systematically and inductively identifying themes and creating categories within the reflections (Graneheim & Lundman, 2004). To guard against arbitrary decision making, coders reanalyzed discrepancies in data (8 of the 102 total strategies) together after developing categories to minimize force-fit-ting data. Consistent with earlier qualitative INC analyses (Duggan, Le Poire, & Addis, 2006; Prescott & Le Poire, 2002), strategies were then sorted into groups of similar responses, and frequencies per family member were recorded, allowing for analysis of consistency/inconsistency in strategies that reinforced or punished eating-disordered behavior across family members.

RESULTS

My mom left for work that morning, but then came home because she forgot something. She walked in on me puking in the bathroom. For several weeks after that she really worked with me to buy the healthy foods I wanted to eat. Salads for every lunch and dinner, few carbs, letting cucumbers and oranges be the substance of the toppings, and not giving me a hard time for vinegar only as the salad dressing. My dad told me I looked good, and my little sister seemed to know that something was up, but she didn't push too hard. A couple months later I had lost ten more pounds, and my sister followed me to the bathroom after every meal. I think she stood outside the door just to see if I was puking. I would turn on the water to try to keep them from hearing me. When my mom took me shopping she said it was "absurd" that I needed a size zero, and she was tired of how the whole family's eating was dependent upon my selfishness and how I needed to control everyone else. We had a long talk about how she had suspected for almost a year that I was making myself throw up. My dad came into my room that night and said he was tired of me playing hard ball with my mom, and that he demanded that I cut out the drama. My mom took the lock off the bathroom door. They sent me to rehab, but we never really talked about it after I came home. When I left for college it was unspoken that they all worried things would go downhill with me.

This story is compiled from our interviews and shows how daughters recognize points of labeling the eating disorder and how daughters make sense of the interplay between family members' attempts to curtail the daughter's disordered eating. Interviews with eating-disordered daughters document their perceptions of family members' strategies to curtail disordered eating. In addition, interviews provided insight into daughters' perceptions of family members' strategies to better understand family dynamics with regard to punishment and reinforcement. Overall, the interviews provided examples of strategies each family member used within each labeling period, which allows for better understanding changes across time periods for each family member as well as the interplay among the types of family members' strategies. Results show change across mothers, fathers, and siblings. See Table 1 for a thematic description of strategies reported for each family member during each time period. Summaries of strategies are included below, with interpretations of interconnections among family members addressed in the discussion section.

This is the first study to examine inconsistent strategy use across multiple family members, and qualitative analysis of strategies provides evidence of simultaneous reinforcement and punishment among the interconnection of family members at each stage of labeling. This study identifies simultaneous reinforcement and punishment. Family members may be using a combination of reinforcement and punishment in their attempts to stop the eating-disorder behavior, which would support the INC theory's contention that family members use intermittent reinforcement and intermittent punishment. Thus, the current study provides evidence that supports INC predictions (Duggan & Le Poire Molineux, 2013; Le Poire, 1995) that family members change their strategy over time such that an overall pattern of inconsistent reinforcement and punishment results.

MOTHERS

Eating-disordered daughters reported that their mothers used nonconfrontational subtleties and questions before the disordered eating was labeled problematic; mothers used intentional support and strategically encouraged healthy eating after labeling the disordered eating problematic; and mothers used emotional

Table 1. Thematic Analysis of Strategies of Family Members within Labeling Stages.

	Mom	Dad	Siblings
Pre-label	Non Confrontational Subtleties and Questions	Never Noticed	Active Confront and Control WHEN They Notice
Examples	Made little suggestions to eat one thing over another	Seemed to never notice	Hugged and asked where I disappeared
	Asked why I kept exercising and encouraged me to do a bit less	Thought losing weight was a good thing	Come see what I was ordering to be sure it was enough
	Cooked healthier food for me to eat at home	Double checked I did not want more food before cleaning up kitchen	Told me I was so skinny (perceived as jealous)
	Told me to value health over being skinny	No expressed suspicion	Constant suspicious glances and inquisitions about bathroom activity
	Discouraged me from reading diet books	Never said anything	Too young to notice
	Asked why my toilet was a mess	Heard concerns from tennis coach and told my mom	Did not realize what was going on
Post-label	Intentional Support/ Strategically Encouraged Healthy Eating	Alongside Mom But Shift Intensity	Threaten to Take More Extreme Action
Examples	Helped me make changes to my diet (fewer carbs, healthy calories, all food groups included)	Said it was not his place to intervene	Said she would tell mom and dad if I hid anything about food
	Set up appointment with nutritionist and therapist	Expressed concern but only alongside mom	Hypersensitive to what I was eating at meals
	Said she knew I was making myself throw up in the bathroom	He obviously knew but never said anything about it	Cried a lot when she saw me
	Told me she was worried about me	Was present for dialogue but never independently involved	Constantly saying I need to eat more

Post-label	Intentional Support/ Strategically Encouraged Healthy Eating	Alongside Mom But Shift Intensity	Threaten to Take More Extreme Action
	Allowed only healthy food into the house	Still unaware there ever was a problem	Threatened to encourage mom to take more extreme action
	Affirmed I was beautiful every day	Told me I was stupid to be so selfish	Discouraged junk food eating
	Focused on my academic accomplishments to make me feel good. Said she was proud of me no matter what.	Told me to suck it up and get over it	Told my parents I was working out too much
Post-frustration	Emotional confrontation/Intervention mixed with support	Stronger Shifts in Emotional Intensity (Increase OR Decrease)	Emotional Reactions and Expressions of Own Frustration
Examples	Told me I did not care about my well-being	Yelled at me, told me to suck it up and be normal	Told me how stupid it was to never eat
	After dinner refused to let me go to my room by myself	Rewarded behavior; Offered me $$$ to lose weight	Always crying
	Took lock off bathroom door	Got mad to back up mom	Started lashing out at school
	Refused to follow nutritionist diet plan and instead asked for other resources	Lack of investment in the issue	Sarcastic—said things like "we all know you won't eat anyway"
	Showed me pictures of people who had serious eating disorders (hair falling out, going blind, bad teeth, stomach problems)	Kept following mom's lead, but when she got mad he did too	Angry demeanor all the time
	Often aggressive and angry	Felt it wasn't his place to chime in	Did not realize what was going on
	Put a lot of food on my plate at dinner every night	Called me dramatic for saying I can't go to dinner for fear of purging	Threatened to tell parents when suspected behavior still occurred

confrontation and intervention mixed with support once they became frustrated in their attempts to curtail the disordered eating were not working (See Table 1). Daughters reported their mothers' strategies during the **pre-label period** encouraged healthy eating, but also with subtleties and questions about particular aspects of the daughters' eating. Examples include making suggestions to eat one thing over another, cooking healthier meals for the daughter, discouraging reading diet books, and asking why the toilet was a mess (suggesting she noticed purging). Interviews suggested that mothers were usually involved in the event that led to labeling the eating disordered, including seeing the daughter purging or seeing the daughter losing excess weight during a short time period.

Daughters' reports of their mothers' strategies during the **post-label period** provided direct support to curtail disordered eating. Examples include setting up an appointment with nutritionist and therapist, allowing only healthy food into the house, and helping the daughter make changes to her diet that were healthy calories but in which all food groups were included. Mothers' strategies during the **post-frustration period** were characterized by emotional confrontation and intervention mixed with support. Examples include refusing to let the daughter go to her room by herself after dinner, taking the lock off the bathroom door, showing aggression and anger, and showing pictures of side effects of serious eating disorders.

Fathers

Eating-disordered daughters' reports of their fathers' strategies suggested that fathers seemed not to notice potential disordered eating behaviors ahead of labeling; fathers expressed concerns alongside the mother but with distinctions in intensity from the mother after labeling the disordered eating problematic; and fathers used stronger shifts in emotional intensity once they became aware that attempts to curtail disordered eating were not working (see Table 1). Daughters report of their fathers' strategies during the **pre-label period** were thematically conceptualized as never noticing, as not expressing concern, as never saying anything to indicate losing weight was problematic.

Daughters' reports of their fathers' strategies during the **post-label period** suggested that fathers provided support for the mother in her intervention. Daughters' reports of fathers' post-label strategies indicated emotional shifts from the mother, where daughters indicated their fathers used either lower intensity than mothers by saying it was not their place to intervene and expressed concern only alongside the mother, or higher intensity than mothers by telling the daughter she was stupid to be so selfish and to suck it up and get over it. Daughters' reports of fathers' strategies during the **post-frustration** period indicate stronger shifts in emotional intensity from their previous strategies and further distinctions from the tone of mothers' strategies used during this time period. Examples of fathers increasing emotional intensity in post-frustration strategies include getting mad when mom was angry to back up the mom, yelling at the daughter, and calling daughter dramatic. Examples of decreasing emotional intensity include indicating the father felt it was not his place to chime in and lack of investment in the issue.

SIBLINGS

Eating-disordered daughters' reports of their siblings' strategies suggested that siblings actively confronted and tried to control indications of disordered eating before labeling the eating disorder problematic; siblings threatened to take more extreme action after labeling the disordered eating problematic; and siblings used emotional reactions and expressions of their own frustration once they became aware that attempts to curtail disordered eating were not working (see Table 1). Daughters' reports of siblings' strategies during the **pre-label period** indicated active confrontation and attempts to control when they noticed problematic eating, but some siblings were either too young to notice or did not realize eating might be problematic at this point. Examples included checking to see what sister was ordering to be sure she was eating enough, telling her sister she was so skinny (which sister perceived as jealous), and reportedly constant suspicious glances and inquisitions.

Eating-disordered daughters' reports of siblings' strategies during the **post-label period** suggested that siblings threatened to take more extreme action if the sister did not adhere to guidelines about food and indicated (hyper)sensitivity to details about the sister and her eating. Examples of more extreme action include threatening to tell mom and dad if sister hid anything about food and telling parents when sister worked out too much. Examples of acute sensitivity to details of eating disorder included crying a lot when seeing the sister and hypersensitivity to what the sister ate. Daughters' reports of siblings' strategies during the **post-frustration period** were characterized by further emotional reactions and expressions of their own anxiety. Examples include telling sister how stupid it was to never eat, making sarcastic comments ("we all know you won't eat anyway"), crying when tears seemed to be a disproportionate response (described as "always" crying), and starting to lash out at school.

DISCUSSION

Results support predictions from INC theory and provide evidence for inconsistency in family members' strategic attempts to curtail disordered eating as well as inconsistency among family members within each time period. We summarize the major points of the study in terms of INC theory such that we interpret the strategies through the lens of INC theory.

Overall, eating-disordered daughters reported that mothers shifted from nonconfrontational subtleties to intentional support to emotional confrontation. Daughters reported that fathers shifted from not noticing to expressing concern to stronger emotional persuasion. Daughters reported that siblings actively confronted and then shifted to threats of more extreme action and then expressed frustration. Overall, results suggest inconsistency in any one family member's influence attempts over time, as well as inconsistency across family members' interplay of influence attempts. We share implications for dark-side interpretations of influence attempts.

Inconsistency Over Time

Eating-disordered daughters' reports of strategies suggested inconsistency in strategy use over time. Since only daughters were interviewed, the inconsistency may be a product of the daughters' perceptions. Perceptions may translate into continued disordered eating even if other family members may have reported different family dynamics. Daughters' reports suggested that mothers encouraged healthy eating but with subtleties in questions about possible eating concerns before labeling the eating disorder problematic. Mothers provided direct support to curtail disordered eating after labeling it problematic and reverted to emotional confrontation and intervention mixed with support once they concluded the attempts to curtail disordered eating were not working. Similar to previous research about mothers of eating-disordered daughters (Prescott & Le Poire, 2002), strategies reported in this study provide evidence that mothers reinforce the eating disorder before labeling it problematic, punish/curtail the eating disorder after labeling it problematic, but then revert over time to intermixing reinforcement and punishment.

Daughters' perceptions of their fathers' strategies also changed across time. Daughters suggested that their fathers did not notice eating concerns before labeling the eating disorder problematic, provided support for mothers' behaviors after labeling but sometimes with statements of higher intensity than mothers such as telling the daughter not to be so stupid and selfish. Fathers' strategies in the post-frustration period suggest more extreme emotional shifts to more intensity such as yelling at the daughter or to decreased emotional intensity by showing lack of investment and saying it was not their place to address the eating disorder.

Daughters reported that siblings' strategies similarly changed over time. Siblings who were old enough to notice problematic eating actively confronted the eating behaviors before labeling the eating disordered, threatened to take more extreme actions, and indicated much sensitivity to the issue after labeling the eating disordered. During the post-frustration period, siblings expressed their own anxiety through crying, lashing out at school, and direct confrontational comments.

Interplay Across Family Members

Within each time period, the inconsistency among family members suggests simultaneous punishment and reinforcement. The interplay of family members' strategies may simultaneously encourage disordered eating. While one family member may use strategies to curtail disordered eating, another family member may encourage problematic eating. Before labeling the eating behavior problematic, siblings' active confrontation behavior and comments about (the sister) being skinny are in contrast to the fathers not noticing concerns. During this pre-label period, mothers' healthier cooking and nonconfrontational questions are further in contrast to the active confrontation of siblings and to fathers' lack of suspicion.

After labeling the eating disorder problematic, siblings demonstrate high emotional sensitivity, with crying and threats to tell parents about escalated eating problems, again in contrast to mothers' strategic support and active participation in a program to address disordered eating. During this post-label period, fathers left confrontation to the mothers or demonstrated higher emotional reactivity than mothers. Fathers who escalated intervention efforts criticized the daughters' selfishness and exacerbated emotions.

In the post-frustration phase, we see further contradictions in family dynamics. Emotional escalation across family members includes mothers' emotional confrontation, fathers' yelling, and siblings' emotions spilling into school behavior. We see inconsistency across family members in mothers' direct interventions through pictures of irreversible side-effects of eating disorders (hair falling out, blindness, rotted teeth), fathers' bouts of backing off emotional investment, and some siblings who were too young to be included in discussions about why the family's emotional life as connected to food was complicated. In addition, the eating-disordered daughters described their brothers as oblivious, naïve or nonchalant. As interpreted through an INC framework, the inconsistency and volatility in expressed emotions connected to eating are likely to further enmesh family reactivity with eating concerns.

Dark-Side Implications

A dark-side lens suggests that family members use messages overall that likely encourage the progression of a daughter's eating disorder. Thus, this chapter provides evidence of messages deemed harmful that cause temporary and long-term negative effects within the family system (adapted from Olson, Baiocchi-Wagner, Wilson Kratzer, & Symonds, 2012). Similar to other dark contexts, including drug and alcohol abuse, depression, and physical violence, strategy change over time and the inconsistency among family members' strategies within each labeling period suggest that family members face competing goals in their relationship with the eating-disordered daughter such that they unwittingly encourage disordered eating through their attempts to help. Paradoxical injunctions in the relationship are likely explanations for the inconsistency in control attempts. Parents and siblings live in the shadow of the eating disorder, and they likely experience emotional, familial, and social difficulties connected to the disorder (Latzer, Katz, & Berger, 2013). In addition to likely contributing to the eating disorder, other health and relational complications may arise. Healthy sisters already at risk for developing an eating disorder may also display disordered eating behaviors. The eating disorder can become a paradoxical position of power, where family dynamics revolve around the daughter with the eating disorder in an attempt to respond to the ongoing challenges of the eating. Thus, the nurturing behaviors of the family may be rewarding to the daughter with the eating disorder such that ultimate "success" in treating the disorder would compromise the family roles and relationships and threaten homeostasis of the family system. Developing social competence and psychological distress identified as mediators of disordered eating attitudes (Arroyo & Segrin, 2013) may be subsumed by the ongoing stress of caretaking. In addition, a dark lens suggests developing these attributes may be in contradistinction with the emotionality of family systems that serve to dance around the eating disorder. Results are consistent with the idea that dysfunctional family interaction variables are associated with competing goals that cannot be easily resolved. Previous research describes sibling need for social support and for regular time apart from the stressful events and interactions about the eating disorder in order to be helpful in addressing the eating disorder (Withers et al., 2014). Similarly, this study poses a need to better understand how family members recognize and respond to the simultaneous reinforcement and punishment that moves beyond just "including" multiple family members in eating disorder treatment. Instead, involvement in family-based treatment should include recognition of communication dynamics that function differently than intended.

Furthermore, sociocultural theories suggest that societies emphasize a narrow definition of women's physical attractiveness such that discontent becomes normative. Family members may reinforce the narrow definition of a thin ideal. Attempts to cook healthy food may translate into endorsing products or services that promise thinness and a happier life because of it. Family members may make appearance-related social comparisons even when they have detrimental consequences. An unrealistic "body perfect" ideal may be transmitted and reinforced by ongoing familial and social influences. The fine line between healthy and excessive focus on a thin ideal as a source of identity can be easily blurred. Family members may directly and indirectly contribute to the ongoing eating disorder.

Limitations and Future Directions

Limitations of this study also point to directions for future research. Because of the cross-sectional nature of the interviews, we cannot make causal claims. Future research should document over-time data connected to the progression of the eating disorder, as well as related variables such as emotions expressed and family cohesiveness. Further examination of family members' reports is also needed. Finally, we were able to qualitatively examine strategies reported across time periods, but our sample size was too small to develop empirical models. Additional analyses would benefit by subsequent interviews and multimethod research that builds social scientific models from the identified interconnection in strategies. With that said, the current study provides preliminary yet important evidence for how harmful communication can translate into temporary and long-term negative effects within the family system.

REFERENCES

Arroyo, A., & Segrin, C. (2013). Family interactions and disordered eating attitudes: The mediating role of social competence and psychological distress. *Communication Monographs, 80*(4), 399–424.

American Psychiatric Association (APA). (2013). *Diagnostic and statistical manual of mental disorders* (5th ed.). Washington, DC: Author.

Benninghoven, D., Schneider, H., Strack, M., Reich, G., & Cierpka, M. (2003). Family representations in relationship episodes of patients with a diagnosis of bulimia nervosa. *Psychology and Psychotherapy: Theory, Research, and Practice, 76*, 323–336.

Blessing, D. (2007). Hiding in plain site: The sibling connection in eating disorders. *Journal of Child Psychotherapy, 33*, 36–50.

Botta, R. A., & Dumlao, R. (2002). How do conflict and communication patterns between fathers and daughters contribute to or offset eating disorders? *Health Communication, 14*, 199–219.

Bulik, C. M., Berkman, N., Brownley, K., Sedway, J., & Lohr, K. (2007). Anorexia nervosa treatment: A systematic review of randomized controlled trials. *International Journal of Eating Disorders, 40*, 310–320.

Corrigan, P. W., & Miller, F. E. (2004). Shame, blame, and contamination: A review of the impact of mental illness stigma on family members. *Journal of Mental Health, 13*, 537–548.

Duggan, A. P., Dailey, R., & Le Poire, B. A. (2008). Reinforcement and punishment of substance abuse during ongoing interactions: A conversational test of Inconsistent Nurturing as Control Theory. *Journal of Health Communication, 13*(5), 417–433.

Duggan, A. P., & Le Poire, B. A. (2006). One down; two involved: An application and extension of Inconsistent Nurturing as Control theory to couples including one depressed individual. *Communication Monographs, 73*, 379–405.

Duggan, A. P., Le Poire, B. A., & Addis, K. (2006). A qualitative analysis of communicative strategies used by partners of substance abusers and depressed individuals during recovery: Implications for Inconsistent Nurturing as Control Theory. In R. M. Dailey, & B. A. Le Poire (Eds.) *Applied interpersonal communication matters: Family, health, and community relations* (pp. 150–174). New York: Peter Lang.

Duggan, A. P., Le Poire, B. A, Prescott, M., & Baham, C. S. (2009). Understanding the helper: The role of codependency in health care and health care outcomes. D. E. Brashers & D. Goldsmith (Eds.), *Communicating to manage health and illness* (pp. 271–300). New York: Routledge.

Duggan, A. P., & Le Poire Molineux, B. A. (2013). The reciprocal influence of drugs and alcohol abuse on family members' communication. In A. Vangelisti (Ed.), *The Routledge Handbook of Family Communication* (pp. 463–478). New York: Routledge.

Fairburn, C. G., & Harrison, P. J. (2003). Eating disorders. *Lancet, 361*, 407–416.

Graneheim, U. H., & Lundman, B. (2004). Qualitative content analysis in nursing research: Concepts, procedures, and measures to achieve trustworthiness. *Nurse Education Today, 24*, 105–112.

Kluck, A. S. (2010). Family influence on disordered eating: The role of body image dissatisfaction. *Body Image, 7*, 8–14.

Latzer, Y., Katz, R., & Berger, K. (2013). Psychological distress among sisters of young females with eating disorders: The role of negative sibling relationships and sense of coherence. *Journal of Family Issues*, Online ahead of print publication, 1–21.

Le Poire, B. A. (1995). Inconsistent nurturing as control theory: Implications for communication-based research and treatment programs. *Journal of Applied Communication Research, 23*, 1–15.

Le Poire, B. A., Hallett, J. S., & Erlandson, K. T. (2000). An initial test of inconsistent nurturing as control theory: How partners of drug abusers assist their partners' sobriety. *Human Communication Research, 26*, 432–457.

Loeb, K., & Le Grange, D. (2009). Family based treatment for adolescent eating disorders: Current status, new applications and future directions. *International Journal of Adolescent Health, 2*, 243–254.

Miller-Day, M., & Marks, J. (2006). Perceptions of parental communication orientation, perfectionism, and disordered eating behaviors of sons and daughters, *Health Communication, 19*(2), 153–163.

Nilsson, K., Abrahamsson, E., Torbiornsson, A., & Hagglof, B. (2007). Causes of adolescent onset anorexia nervosa: Patient perspectives. *Eating Disorders: The Journal of Treatment & Prevention, 15*(2), 125–133.

Noller, P., & Fitzpatrick, M. A. (1993). *Communication in family relationships*. Englewood Cliffs, NJ: Prentice Hall.

Norbo, R., Espeset, E., Gulliksen, K., Skarderud, F., & Holte, A. (2006). The meaning of self-starvation: Qualitative study of patients' perception of anorexia nervosa. *International Journal of Eating Disorders, 39*(7), 556–564.

Olson, L. N., Baiocchi-Wagner, E., Wilson Kratzer, J., & Symonds, S. (2012). *The dark side of family communication*. Cambridge, UK: Polity Press.

Patel, S., Shafer, A., Brown, J., Bulik, C., & Zucker, N. (2014). Parents of children with eating disorders: Developing theory-based health communication messages to promote caregiver well-being. *Journal of Health Communication, 19*, 593–608.

Polivy, J., & Herman, C. P. (2002). Causes of eating disorders. *Annual Review of Psychology, 53*, 187–213.

Prescott, M. E., & Le Poire, B. A. (2002). Eating disorders and the mother-daughter communication: A test of Inconsistent Nurturing as Control theory. *Journal of Family Communication, 2*, 59–78.

Ringer, F., & Crittenden, P. (2007). Eating disorders and attachment: The effects of hidden family processes on eating disorders. *European Eating Disorders Review, 15*(2), 119–130.

Segrin, C., & Flora, J. (2011). *Family communication* (2nd ed.). New York, NY: Routledge.

Swanson, S. A., Crow, S. J., Le Grange, D., Swendsen, J., & Merikangas, K. R. (2011). Prevalence and correlates of eating disorders in adolescents: Results from the national comorbidity survey replication adolescent supplement. *Archives of General Psychiatry, 68*(7), 714–723.

Treasure, J., Murphy, T., Szmukler, T., Todd, G., Gavan, K., & Joyce, J. (2001). The experience of care-giving for severe mental illness: A comparison between anorexia nervosa and psychosis. *Social Psychiatry and Psychiatric Epidemiology, 36*, 343–347.

Vandereycken, W. (2002). Families of patients with eating disorders. In C. Fairburn & K. Brownell (Eds.), *Eating disorders and obesity: A comprehensive handbook* (2nd ed., pp. 215–220). New York: Guilford Press.

Withers, A., Mullan, B., Madden, S., Kohn, M., Clarke, S., Thornton, C., … Touyz, S. (2014). Anorexia nervosa in the family: A sibling's perspective. *Advances in Eating Disorder: Theory, Research, and Practice, 2*(1), 53–64.

CHAPTER FOUR

The ADHD-Diagnosed Child

Does Family Communication Environment Contribute to the Decision to Medicate?[1]

DANNA M. GIBSON
Columbus State University

LYNNE M. WEBB
Florida International University

LAVEDA I. JOSEPH
Columbus State University

Children can behave in unexpected ways. When such behaviors are associated with an ambiguous disorder, such as attention deficit/hyperactivity disorder (ADHD), parents may seek diagnosis and treatment, including the administration of powerful medications. Given the potential long-term, negative impact of medications such as Ritalin, parents face difficult treatment decisions. In an attempt to understand what conditions accompany parental willingness to medicate ADHD children, we surveyed and interviewed a stratified random sample of 48 mothers of 1st, 2nd, and 3rd grade children in rural Tennessee. Half the mothers had children clinically-diagnosed with ADHD and half did not. We queried simply whether the ADHD diagnosis was associated with willingness to medicate or, alternatively, whether certain patterns of communication within the family were more strongly associated with willingness to medicate. Could certain family communication patterns accompany the tendency to seek medication?

ADHD ETIOLOGY, DIAGNOSIS, AND TREATMENT

To date, childhood ADHD remains an ambiguous disorder with no single definitive test and no agreed upon etiology (APA, 2013; Breggin, 2011; Sadek, 2013). Because ADHD is a medical diagnosis, lay people might assume its etiology is physiological. In contrast, scholars believe that many factors might contribute to its development and diagnosis (APA, 2013; Anderson, Barabasz, Barabasz, & Warner, 2000; Breggin, 2007, 2008; Doggett, 2004; Iudici, Faccio, Belloni, & Costa, 2014; Hoagwood, Kelleher, Feil, & Conner, 2000), including the following:

- physical environment (e.g., exposure to toxic metals and diet);
- biology (e.g., genetic pre-disposition, heredity, medical problems, brain damage resulting from head trauma, and bacterial or viral infections);
- neurology (e.g., depressed activity of frontal lobes, brain's inability to stop receiving messages, and slow brain wave activity);
- culture (e.g., differences in frequency of diagnoses and preference of treatment types among different populations);
- social considerations (e.g., personal, parental, or societal reasons for preferring an ADHD diagnosis and particular treatment types); and
- family environment (e.g., parental standard for acceptable behavior and the orderliness/chaos within the household).

In the absence of a medical test for ADHD, diagnosis remains subjective in terms of the behavioral symptoms that constitute evidence of ADHD as well as who must observe the behaviors and under what conditions (Anderson et al., 2000; Baughman, 2006; Doggett, 2004). In addition to the subjective diagnosis, multiple treatment methods exist to address ADHD symptoms, including medication, behavior modification, neurological therapy, and change of environment or diet; treatments can be used individually and in combinations such that each treatment method can incorporate medication (Anderson, et al., 2000; Baughman, 2006; Breggin, 2000; Diller, 1998; Diller & Goldstein, 2006; Doggett, 2004). Currently, there is no established procedure for determining, before medication is prescribed, which drugs, if any, will be useful for a given child's symptomology (Breggin, 2013).

Despite the potential of dangerous side effects associated with prescribed medications (depression, sleeplessness, nervousness, loss of appetite, abdominal pain, weight loss, abnormal heartbeat, blood pressure changes, chest pains, dizziness, fever, headaches, hives, jerking, joint pain, Tourette's Syndrome, seizures and drug tolerance; see Breggin, 2000; Diller, 1996), powerful amphetamine-like stimulant drugs, such as Ritalin, remain the treatment of choice in over 40% of ADHD cases (Breggin, 2008). Moreover, ADHD medication information typically fails to include the warning that 50% to 65% of the medicated children will remain medicated throughout adulthood (Breggin, 2013). As children on Ritalin mature, their diagnoses and medication treatment often change; nonetheless, they typically remain on medication across the lifespan (Breggin, 1994, 2008, 2011; Diller, 1998; Diller & Goldstein, 2006).

Currently, stimulant medication is prescribed yearly to more than 6.4 million U.S. children (Visser et al., 2014). As the prescription numbers rise, so too have the drug options for treating ADHD, which now include Ritalin, Amphetamine (Adderall), Dextroamphetaine (Dexedrine), Atomoxetine (Strattera), and Lisdexametamine Dimesylate (Vyvanse) (National Institute of Mental Health, 2008).

Research suggests that approximately 11 percent of U.S. children actually suffer from ADHD, yet as many as 50% of the children in certain grades in some school districts are on ADHD medication (Breggin, 2008, 2011). During the past decade, the number of times U.S. children saw physicians for suspected ADHD and were *not* prescribed drugs decreased 45% (Hoagwood et al., 2000); thus, U.S. physicians are increasingly prescribing medication to children suspected of having ADHD. Such statistics may have encouraged the United Nations' International Narcotics Control Board to issue a warning to the U.S. against the over-diagnosis of ADHD. Furman (2005) argued that the increase in ADHD diagnoses is due to less parental tolerance of associated childhood behaviors. Similarly, Panksepp (2004) noted that with the exception of rare medical problems (i.e., hyperthyroidism and explicit brain injuries), the majority of normal, highly playful children who have difficulties adjusting to certain institutional expectations are erroneously diagnosed with ADHD. Thus, there appears to be an increased willingness to pursue medical treatment and to treat ADHD with such stimulants as Ritalin among parents, doctors, and teachers.

A COMMUNICATIVE PERSPECTIVE ON ADHD

Given the lack of agreement on ADHD etiology and concerns about the long-term effects of medication on children, many scholars search for an environmental cause of children's ADHD-like behaviors. Recent speculation has turned to the family and home environment, especially family communication, as a catalyst for the ADHD diagnosis and medication (Breggin, 2013; Cohen, Dillon, Gladwin, & De La Rosa, 2013; McLaughlin & Harrison, 2006). Some families may exhibit greater tolerance for unusual behaviors and for active children; others may exhibit less tolerance. Some families may enact a lifestyle so chaotic that children may identify hyperactivity as the only pattern of behavior that garners adult attention. Alternatively, in families that believe that children should be seen but not heard, adults might label even modest activity by children as ADHD. Could certain beliefs about or patterns of family communication facilitate children to behave in ways that become labelled ADHD? Such a chain of events could allow parents to turn to medication as a means of controlling what is perceived as an out-of-control child whose behavior negatively impacts the parents and/or the family.

Our study seeks to understand the family communication dynamics that might surround the decision to medicate an ADHD-diagnosed or misdiagnosed child. To better understand parental willingness to medicate, we examined mothers' perceptions of the communication within their families of creation. We elected to examine family communication environment, with the use of a widely employed assessment of internal family communication dynamics.

FAMILY COMMUNICATION ENVIRONMENT

The family social environment can serve as the primary socialization agent for children (Webb, Ledbetter, & Norwood, 2014). Rules for interaction are established in the family and reinforced by parents and siblings, ultimately creating normative family communication behavior. Parents typically serve as children's first communicative role models; thus, the interactions with parents can have great impact on a child's communicative development (Koesten, 2004; Koesten & Anderson, 2004). However, not all families socialize children to communicate in the same ways. Fitzpatrick and Koerner (1997) concluded, "Family communication environments differentially foster the development of various functional communication skills" (p. 1).

Koerner and Fitzpatrick's (2002) theory of family communication schema explains both the differences and similarities in families' communication patterns. The theory posits that family communication behaviors are governed by cognitive schemas or orientations to family communication and that the schemas can vary from family to family. "These schemata emerge from working models of how parents and children interact; and, ultimately, they shape how family members perceive their social environment and communicate within and outside the family" (Schrodt & Carr, 2012, p. 55). Thus, Koerner and Fitzpatrick's (2002) family communication schema and its accompanying family communication environments or patterns can influence children's communication behaviors in the family and outside the family into the children's adulthood, long after they leave their family of origin (Koerner & Fitzpatrick, 1997).

McLeod and Chaffee (1972) developed, and Ritchie and Fitzpatrick (1990) later refined, the concept of Family Communication Patterns also known as Family Communication Environments (FCE; Fitzpatrick & Ritchie, 1994). FCE has become among the most studied notions in family communication scholarship; the most recent meta-analysis on FCE documents its efficacy in explaining outcomes, particularly in children (Schrodt, Witt, & Messersmith, 2008).

FCE describes two dimensions of family communication: conformity-orientation and conversation-orientation. Conversation-orientation refers to the dialectic between a family's tendency to encourage discussion versus the tendency to encourage members to remain silent and to speak only when necessary. Conversation-orientation correlated positively with adolescent adjustment (Rueter & Koerner, 2008), the development of interpersonal skills (Babin & Palazzolo, 2012; Koesten & Anderson, 2004), emotional connections and self-esteem (Schrodt, Ledbetter, & Ohrt, 2007), daughters' relational closeness with fathers (Scott, Webb, & Amason, 2012), as well as positive relational endeavors including friendship closeness (Ledbetter, 2009) and maintenance behaviors (Ledbetter & Beck, 2014). In sum, conversation-orientation may play a pivotal role in interpersonal interactions inside and outside the family.

The second dimension, conformity-orientation, refers to the dialectic between a family's tendency to stress harmony, children's obedience to parents, and high levels of agreement between parents and children on attitudes, beliefs, and values versus the tendency to respect and encourage the development of individual thought among family members that typically result in the acceptable expression of diverse viewpoints. High conformity families focus on harmonious relationships and uniformity of opinion, allowing little room for individuality (Fitzpatrick & Ritchie 1994). High conformity socialization can result in lower self-esteem, higher stress, and more common instances of communication apprehension and depression (Schrodt et al., 2007) as well as low levels of relational maintenance (Ledbetter, 2009).

Researchers have linked FCE to a variety of communicative outcomes including perspective taking (Koerner & Cvancara, 2002); behavioral outcomes, such as interpersonal competence (Koesten & Anderson, 2004; Koesten, 2004); as well as psychosocial outcomes, such as family adjustment among adopted children (Rueter & Koerner, 2008).[2]

FCE is a parent-driven construct. Indeed, it could be argued that any parental communication behavior is simply a part of FCE–a way for parents to reinforce, enforce, and maintain the FCE they desire for their children, and to socialize parental notions of appropriate communication behaviors embodied in the FCE they advocate. Of course, all family members use communication with other family members (Saphir & McChaffee, 2002) to teach FCE and the specific communication behaviors associated with the parental advocated FCE. Given that communication is omnipresent in the process (the agent, means, and outcome), it seems reasonable to assert the possibility that FCE might influence how parents label their children's talkativeness.

FCE AND ADHD

Research suggests that children's behaviors outside the family can reflect communication in the family environment. For example, a child growing up in a family that values authority over conversation is more likely to exhibit an abrasive, aggressive, and dominating style with peers and be less popular than children from homes that privilege open expression of ideas through conversation (Koerner & Fitzpatrick, 1997; Koesten, 2004; Koesten & Anderson, 2004). When abrasive, aggressive, and dominating antisocial behaviors are associated with a child, they can become part of the symptomology for a childhood malady recognized as ADHD. Children with ADHD are characterized by excessive activity and an inability to self-regulate focused attention (APA, 2013; Anderson et al., 2000; Sadek, 2013). However, those same characteristics can be used to describe children from certain FCE. While ADHD is widely researched, the link between ADHD and FCE has received no attention to date.

Given its ambiguous etiology, leading literature, such as the Diagnostic and Statistical Handbook of Mental Disorders (APA, 2013) warns against assigning an ADHD diagnosis to children from certain chaotic family environments, as they may display hyperactivity and inattention as learned behaviors (Breggin, 1994, 2008; Diller, 1996, 2011; Sadek, 2013). In light of the possible effects of the family environment, some experts argue that an ADHD diagnosis should be reserved for children reared in a stable social environment (Breggin, 1994; Diller, 1998; Sadek, 2013).

DARK SIDE OF FAMILY COMMUNICATION

We do not question the existence of ADHD; however, we place family communication at the heart of its etiology, an issue that extant literature only alludes to in hints and suggestions: What role, if any, could FCE play in producing ADHD-diagnosed children? What purposes could medication serve within these environments, given that some parents view ADHD medication as an "easy and effective way to obtain child compliance" (Eberstadt, 1999, p. 14; Diller, 2011; Iudici et al., 2014). By making a child more agreeable and less argumentative, the drug might accomplish what the parents could not without the medication. If a child is medicated, the parents may feel relieved of pressure (either communicated or perceived) from educators, friends, and family to "control" the child's unruly behavior. Additionally, some parents may view medication as an effective way to help children conform to expectations, thereby absolving the parents of responsibility and blame when children fail to conform to expectations both inside and outside the home (Breggin, 2011; Diller, 2011; Iuduci et al., 2014).

When focusing attention on an ADHD-diagnosed child receiving medication, attention is focused away from parental behaviors, family concerns, and the potential need to examine or change behaviors within the family. Breggin notes that ADHD "is almost always either Teacher Attention Disorder (TAD) or Parent Attention Disorder (PAD). These children need the adults in their lives to give them improved attention" (2011, para. 2). He warns that the diagnosis and medication treatment provide an excuse for some parents to avoid the issue of family dynamics.

PURPOSE AND RESEARCH QUESTIONS

Unlike other approaches to ADHD etiology (e.g., environmental, biological, neurological, cultural, and social), this chapter directly addresses family communication. No previous research has tested for a direct link between family communication and the ADHD phenomenon (diagnosis and willingness to medicate) in children. The purpose of our study was to explore the potential relationship between FCE and mothers' willingness to pursue a medication treatment for an ADHD-diagnosed child. To this end, we posed four research questions:

RQ1. Do mothers with (versus without) ADHD-diagnosed children differ in their willingness to medicate ADHD-diagnosed children?

RQ2. Do mothers with (versus without) ADHD-diagnosed children differ in their FCE?

RQ3. Do mothers from the four FCE types differ in their willingness to medicate?

RQ4. Is conformity- or conversation-orientation directly associated with mothers' willingness to medicate an ADHD-diagnosed child?

METHOD

Sample

Focus on mothers. Mothers' communication continues to attract the attention of communication researchers as a meaningful object of study (e.g., Colander & Rittenour, 2015). Most relevant to our study, mothers spend over twice as much time with their children as fathers (Caumont & Wang, 2014) and thus are in a position to monitor children's behavior, including behaviors associated with the ADHD diagnosis, as well as interact with their children's teachers and coaches who may point out behavioral abnormalities, if they exist. Thus, our study continues the line of research examining mothers' communication patterns. However, given the purpose of our study, we limited our sample to mothers of 1st, 2nd, and 3rd grade students ($N = 60$) enrolled in a rural, county school system in rural Tennessee.

Recruitment of mothers. A university Institutional Review Board and a county Board of Education approved the research before data collection began. We selected participants, hereafter called mothers, from responses to a "Willingness to Participate" letter sent home with each 1st, 2nd, and 3rd grade child in the school district. We sent 650 letters; 300 mothers indicated their willingness to participate in the study by signing and returning the letters (a return rate of 46.2%). During an initial telephone call, we notified mothers that we received their letters and asked them if their child had any clinically diagnosed learning problems, behavior disorders, or combination of both (e.g., ADHD). Based on the mothers' reports, we categorized children as either non-ADHD-diagnosed or ADHD-diagnosed. All children in the latter group had been clinically diagnosed, at least according to the reports of their mothers.

The potential research participant list contained 88 mothers of an ADHD child and 212 mothers of non-ADHD-diagnosed children. Given that we administered the written instruments in a one-on-one format, and given the difficulties of scheduling one-on-one meetings with busy (often single) mothers, we could not conduct administrations with each volunteer mother. Therefore, to keep the project a manageable size, we randomly selected 60 mothers (30 ADHD and 30 non-ADHD) to participate in the study. We notified mothers of their selection and scheduled mutually agreeable dates and times for the 90-minute, data-collection sessions.

Narrowing of the sample. A series of *t*-tests compared the scores from the mothers of male versus female target children across the variables of interest. The *t*-test provides a robust comparison between two groups in situations where the sizes of the groups are uneven and relatively small (Winter, 2013) as well as when scores on the dependent variables are not normally distributed (Kariya, Sinha, & Giri, 1986). The analyses yielded no significant differences. Therefore, we combined data from mothers of sons and daughters for subsequent analyses.

Next, we conducted *t*-tests to assess potential differences between the scores of Caucasian versus non-Caucasian mothers (N = 48 and 12, respectively). One of the three analyses yielded significant results ($t_{(58)willingness\ to\ medicate}$ = −2.14, p = .04; $M_{Caucasians}$ = 3.23; SD = 1.35; $M_{nonCaucasians}$ = 4.19; SD = 1.59) and another result demonstrated a trend toward significance ($t_{(58)conversation-\ orientation}$ = 1.93, p = .06; $M_{Caucasians}$ = 59.67; SD = 13.14; $M_{nonCaucasians}$ = 51.25; SD = 14.96). A conservative interpretation of these findings would be that the Caucasian versus non-Caucasian mothers' scores potentially differ across the variables of interest. Therefore, we elected to not combine the ethnic subsamples for subsequent analyses. Due to the relatively small number of ethnic minorities participating in the study (N = 12), we included data from only Caucasian mothers (N = 48) in the subsequent analyses. Thus, 48 Caucasian mothers served as the research sample for the study.

Description of the sample. Mothers' mean age was 34.85 years (SD = 4.55, range = 26–43). Mothers reported completing, on average, 11.77 years of education (SD = 0.63) and giving birth to their first child at the age of 24.23 (SD = 4.25, range = 16–36). Mothers' self-reported employment statuses were as follows:

(a) 71% employed outside of the home (n = 34); (b) 21% full-time homemakers (n = 10); and (c) 8% employed part-time outside of the home (n = 4). Mothers' reported marital statuses as follows: (a) 56.25% married; (b) 27.08% divorced; (c) 12.50% widowed or separated from their spouse; and (d) 4.17% never married. Although 54% (n = 26) of the research sample did not report an ADHD-diagnosed child in the home, 40% (n = 19) reported one ADHD-diagnosed child and 6% (n = 3) reported having two ADHD-diagnosed children. Finally, the 22 mothers with at least one ADHD-diagnosed child self-reported the children's treatment as: (a) 68.18% stimulant medication; (b) 22.72% counseling; (c) 4.55% behavior modification; and (d) 4.55% a combination of medication and counseling. This sample's self-reported treatments are consistent with other U.S. samples. For example, Hoagwood et al. (2000) reported that ADHD treatment with stimulant prescriptions increased to 75.4%, and counseling treatment dropped just below 25%.

Instruments

Each mother completed written, counter-balanced questionnaires. All data were collected in the mothers' homes. Although we employed extant written instruments, we conducted a factor analysis of the items using principal components varimax rotation with Kaiser Normalization to assess the validity of the instruments with our sample.[3] The factor analysis across every item of all instruments yielded the anticipated factors with acceptable Cronbach's alphas ranging from .87 to .96.

Demographic variables. The mothers completed a 29-item questionnaire that requested information used to describe the sample (e.g., age, ethnicity, marital status). Mothers who reported being the parent of an ADHD-diagnosed child received a version of the questionnaire that asked about their preferred treatment options: (a) medicine treatment, (b) behavior modification, (c) counseling treatment, and/or (d) other.

Family Communication Environment. Ritchie and Fitzpatrick's (1990) Revised Family Communication Pattern (RFCP) instrument assessed the mothers' perceived FCE. Designed to measure perceptions of family conversation (questions 1–15) and conformity (questions 16–26) orientations, the RFCP allows responses of 1 to 5 to the 26 items, where 1 indicates "always" true of the family and 5 indicates "never" true of the family. Typical items include the following: "In our family, we often talk about our future" and "In my family, I feel it is important for my children to obey me without question." The Cronbach alphas for conversation-orientation (a = .96) and for conformity-orientation (a = .87) compared favorably to those reported by Ritchie and Fitzpatrick (1990).

Following the standard scoring procedure for the RFCP, we categorized the scores into four types, via a median split along the two underlying dimensions of conversation- and conformity- orientations, employing the medians of our research sample as the mid-points for the categories: laissez-faire (low in both conversation and conformity), protective (low in conversation and high in conformity), consensual (high in both conversation and conformity), and pluralistic (high in conversation and low in conformity). Our 48 mothers were distributed across the four categories as follows: laissez-faire (n = 9), protective (n = 10), consensual (n = 12), and pluralistic (n = 17).

Willingness to Medicate. The ADHD Knowledge and Opinion Scale (AKOS-R; Bennett, Power, Rostain, & Carr, 1996) measured mothers' willingness to medicate their ADHD-diagnosed child, hereafter called "willingness to medicate." Response scales for the individual items on the AKOS-R instrument ranged from 1 to 6, where 1 indicates *strongly disagree* and 6 indicates *strongly agree*. To allow for direct comparisons between groups as well as to follow the procedure employed by Bennett et al. (1996), mothers of non-ADHD-diagnosed children were requested to respond to the questions as if their child was diagnosed with ADHD. In our sample, the Cronbach alpha for the instrument was .95.

Procedures

Administration of Questionnaires and Interviews. Following selection, each mother signed a consent form. We informed the mothers that their participation in the study was voluntary and guaranteed confidentiality within the limits of the law. We conducted the data-collection sessions in the mothers' homes. To avoid possible distraction or confidentiality concerns, an assistant removed children from the interview room either to play outside or to view an age-appropriate movie in another room of the home.

On arriving at the interviewee's home, the first author allowed a few minutes for introductions and to explain the study to the mother. The research was characterized as a study of challenges families face with elementary school-age children and how mothers communicate about those challenges. Then, explanations and instructions were provided for each instrument and mothers were encouraged to ask questions whenever clarification was needed. Following data collection, each mother received $5.00 compensation for her participation.

Pretest. Before data collection, we pretested the instruments, interview protocol, and procedures with ten mothers randomly selected from the subject pool (i.e., five mothers of ADHD children and five mothers of non-ADHD children). Based on pretest feedback as well as our experiences during the pretest, we made minor spelling and grammatical changes to the written questionnaires. However, we made no changes to the administrative protocol.

RESULTS

Differences between mothers with versus without ADHD-diagnosed children. A series of *t*-tests compared the scores of mothers with ADHD-diagnosed versus non-ADHD-diagnosed children across the variables of interest. The analyses yielded no significant results. These results answer RQ1 and 2 in the negative. Mothers with (versus without) ADHD-diagnosed children did not differ in their willingness to medicate their ADHD-diagnosed children, their conversation-orientations, nor their conformity-orientations.

Differences in willingness to medicate an ADHD-diagnosed child by FCE types. A univariate analysis of variance revealed that mothers from the four FCE subsamples differed significantly in their willingness-to-medicate scores ($F_{(3,30)}$ = 13.21, $p < .01$,), thus answering RQ3 in the affirmative. Parents from some FCE types reported significantly higher willingness to medicate scores than those from other FCE types. Post hoc Bonferroni multiple comparisons revealed a pattern of significant differences between Laissez-faire and Protective mothers versus Consensual and Pluralistic mothers. As a means of summarizing our results and profiling the FCE types, we constructed the table below to depict the results for each

		Conformity	
		High:	Low:

Conversation	High	Consensual
		• Willingness to Medicate Score:
		  ◦ $M = 2.24$
		  ◦ $SD = 0.88$
		• $N = 12$
			Pluralistic
			• Willingness to Medicate Score:
			  ◦ $M = 2.54$
			  ◦ $SD = 0.59$
			• $N = 17$

	Low	Protective
		• Willingness to Medicate Score:
		  ◦ $M = 4.55$
		  ◦ $SD = 1.25$
		• $N = 10$
			Laissez-faire
			• Willingness to Medicate Score:
			  ◦ $M = 4.39$
			  ◦ $SD = 1.02$
			• $N = 9$

Note: Overall willingness-to-medicate scores were $M = 3.23$, $SD = 3.23$.

FCE type. Please note that one-way analysis of variance is tolerant of small and uneven group sizes (Kastenbaum, Hoel, & Bowman, 1970) when the dependent variable approximates a normal distribution, as was the case with willingness to medicate.

Associations between conformity-orientation, conversation-orientation, and willingness-to-medicate scores. We examined the frequency distributions of our three variables (i.e., conformity-orientation, conversation-orientation, and willingness-to-medicate scores); only one distribution was normally distributed (i.e., willingness-to-medicate scores). Therefore, we calculated a series of non-parametric Spearman's rho statistics to assess the potential associations the three variables of interest. "The efficiency of the Spearman rank correlation when compared to the most powerful parametric correlation, the Pearson r, is about 91 percent" (Siegel, 1956, p. 213). Two of the correlations were nonsignificant. However, the analysis revealed one significant negative correlation ($rho = -72$, $p = .00$, $r^2 = .51$) between conversation-orientation and willingness to medicate. The lower the conversation among orientation, the more willing to medicate. These mixed results provided a clear answer to RQ4: The analyses documented a significant negative association between conversation-orientation and willingness to medicate. The analyses relevant to both RQ3 and 4 revealed consistent results: Willingness-to-medicate was negatively associated with conversation-orientation and the two FCE types with low conversation-orientation (Protective and Lais-sez-faire families) displayed the highest willingness-to-medicate scores. The more families promoted conversation, the less likely they were to mediate their ADHD-diagnosed children.

DISCUSSION

A Communicative Explanation for Willingness to Medicate

Overall, the results of this study provide support for a communication-based understanding of ADHD diagnosis and treatment. It seems rational to assume that mothers' willingness to medicate would be differentiated by the diagnosis of ADHD (rather FCE). That was not the case in our sample. Instead, mothers' willingness to medicate their ADHD-diagnosed child was significantly and neg-atively correlated with their family conversation-orientation. In this sample, the more mothers valued conversation and open discussion in the family, the less likely they reported being willing to medicate. Conversely, the less the mothers privi-leged family conversation, the more willing they were to medicate their ADHD children, perhaps medicating the children into silence.

The results of the one-way analysis of variance provided further support that conversation-orientation may be the critical variable at play in willingness to medicate. The Laissez-faire and Protective mothers posted significantly higher willingness-to medicate scores than the Consensual and Pluralistic mothers. Recall that the major difference between the Laissez-faire and Protective versus the Consensual and Pluralistic family types is that the former two types are low in conversation-orientation, whereas the latter two are high in conversation-orientation. Support for these results can be found in additional family communication research that also documents the significant impact of conversation-orientation on the thoughts and behaviors of family members (Fitzpatrick et al., 1996; Koesten & Anderson, 2004; Ledbetter, 2009; Ledbetter & Beck, 2014; Rueter & Koerner, 2008; Schrodt et al., 2007; Scott et al., 2012).

For example, previous research documents that when families encounter challenging situations (e.g., exposure to violence, conflict, or deployment), members from high-conversation-oriented families did not display some of the more negative results of living in a troubled family (Babin & Palazzolo, 2012; Sillers, Holman, Richards, Jacobs, Koerner, & Reynolds-Dyk, 2014; Wilson, Chernichky, Wilkum, & Owlett, 2014). In such cases, the higher conversation-orientation may allow family members to talk through and appropriately address their problems. Conversely, mothers from low-conversation-oriented families may refrain from engaging in talk necessary to problem solving.

Members of low-conversation-oriented families are more likely to possess fewer social interaction skills and to withdraw from conversation (Koerner & Fitzpatrick, 1997, 2002, 2004; Koesten & Anderson, 2004). Given these tendencies, it is reasonable to believe that low-conversation mothers might shy away from the more conversation-oriented ADHD treatment programs (e.g., counseling or behavior modification). Thus, mothers from low-conversation families may co-construct their children's ADHD diagnosis with their pediatrician by communicating less tolerance for their children's talkativeness, showing more willingness to recognize that behavior as a disorder, and desiring a quick and effective treatment of the ambiguous disorder via medication.

Note that conformity-orientation was unrelated to willingness to medicate across multiple analyses. Indeed, all parents might desire their children to conform to a reasonable extent to family and household norms. But what are the family norms for conversation? Conversational norms seem to differentiate mothers who are willing to medicate from mothers who are not.

Our results lend credence to the notion that certain FCEs may create affordances that encourage medicating ADHD-diagnosed children. Indeed, the consistencies of the findings lend credence to a notion of a communicative etiology to the tendency to medicate the ADHD-diagnosed child. We report correlations here and do not document causation or predict behavior. Nonetheless, our findings provide a warrant for a line of research testing for causal relationships. Such findings would provide further support for Koerner and Fitzpatrick's (2002) theory of family communication schema and their claim that FCE can influence behaviors inside and outside the family.

Limitations

Conclusions drawn from this study must be tempered with an understanding of the study's limitations. Our study's sample, although randomly drawn from among volunteers, contained multiple characteristics that limit the generalizability of the findings. Our relatively small sample contained only Caucasian mothers living in a rural area in one Southern state in the United States. Furthermore, we employed self-report methods and such methods can be negatively influenced by social desirability and recall issues. We also allowed mothers with no ADHD-diagnosed child to participate in the sample and in some assessments to report projected behavior *if* her child was diagnosed with ADHD. Here we asked mothers to engage in hypothetical thinking; when faced with an actual diagnosis, mothers may behave quite differently than they here reported that they would.

Conclusions

Our study provides evidence that a communication perspective on ADHD can be useful in providing insight into mothers' willingness to medicate their ADHD-diagnosed children. Despite our study's limitations, it contributes to knowledge about the dark side of family communication. The study provides the first evidence that specific FCEs (i.e., Laisse-Faire, Protective) are associated with willingness to medicate ADHD-diagnosed children. Second, the study identifies conversation-orientation as strongly associated with mothers' willingness to medicate their ADHD-diagnosed children. Third, these findings may point to the need for psychological assessment of an entire family, when parents request an ADHD evaluation for a child. Given that lower conversation-orientation scores would be associated with lower adolescent adjustment (Rueter & Koerner, 2008), less developed interpersonal skills (Babin & Palazzolo, 2012; Koesten & Anderson, 2004), fewer emotional connections and lower self-esteem (Schrodt, Ledbetter, & Ohrt, 2007), as well as fewer relational endeavors including friendship closeness (Ledbetter, 2009) and maintenance behaviors (Ledbetter & Beck, 2014), these parents may lack communication skills and/or experience psychological problems. Fourth, the study suggests fruitful directions for further communication-based research on ADHD.

REFERENCES

American Psychiatric Association (2013). *DSM-5: Diagnostic and statistical manual of mental disorders* (5th ed.). Washington, DC: American Psychiatric Publishing.

Anderson, K., Barabasz, M., Barabasz, A., & Warner, D. (2000). Efficacy of Barabasz's instant alert hypnosis in the treatment of ADHD with neurotherapy. *Child Study Journal, 30*(1), 51–63. Retrieved from http://eric.ed.gov/?id=EJ620290

Babin, E. A., & Palazzolo, K. E. (2012). The relationships between parent communication patterns and sons' and daughters' intimate partner violence involvement: Perspectives from parents and adult children. *Journal of Family Communication, 12,* 4–21. doi: 10.1080/15267431.2011.607740

Baughman, F. A. (2006). *The ADHD fraud: How psychiatry makes "patients" of normal children.* Victoria, BC: Trafford.

Bennett, D., Power, T., Rostain, A., & Carr, D. (1996). Parent acceptability and feasibility of ADHD interventions: Assessment, correlates, and predictive validity. *Journal of Pediatric Psychology, 21*(5), 643–657. doi: 10.1093/jpepsy/21.5.643

Breggin, P. (1994). *Toxic psychiatry.* New York: St. Martin's Press.

Breggin, P. (2000). Confirming the hazards of stimulant drug treatment. *Ethical human sciences and services, 2*(3), 2003–2005. Retrieved from http://breggin.com/index.php?option=com_doc-man&task=cat_view&gid=53&dir=DESC&order=date&Itemid=37&limit=10&limitstart=20

Breggin, P. (2007). *Talking back to Ritalin.* New York: St. Martin's Press.

Breggin, P. (2008). *Medication madness. The role of psychiatric drugs in cases of violence, suicide, and crime.* New York: St. Martin's Press.

Breggin, P. (2011, October 13). A misdiagnosis, anywhere. *The New York Times.* Retrieved from http://www.nytimes.com/roomfordebate/2011/10/12/are-americans-more-prone-to-adhd/adhd-is-a-misdiagnosis

Breggin, P. (2013). *Psychiatric drug withdrawal: A guide for prescribers, therapists, patients and their families.* New York: Springer.

Caumont, A., & Wang, W. (2014, May 9). 5 questions (and answers) about American moms today. Pew Research Report. Retrieved from http://www.pewresearch.org/fact-tank/2014/05/09/5-questions-and-answers-about-american-moms-today/

Cohen, D., Dillon, F. R., Gladwin, H., & De La Rosa, M. (2013). American parents' willingness to prescribe psychoactive drugs to children: A test of cultural mediators. *Social Psychiatry and Psychiatric Epidemiology, 48*(12), 1873–1887. doi: 10.1007/s00127-013-0710-2

Colander, C. W., & Rittenour, C. E. (2015). "Feminism begins at home": The influence of mother gender socialization on daughter career and motherhood aspirations as channeled through feminist identification. *Communication Quarterly, 63,* 81–98. doi: 10.1080/01463373.2014.965839

Diller, L. (1996). The run on Ritalin: Attention Deficit Disorder and stimulant treatment in the 1990s. *Hastings Center Report, 26*(2), 12–18. doi: 10.2307/3528571

Diller, L. (1998). *Running on Ritalin: A physician reflects on children, society, and performance in a pill.* New York: Doubleday.

Diller, L. (2011). *Remembering Ritalin: A doctor's and Generation Rx reflection on life and psychiatric drugs.* New York: Penguin Group.

Diller, L. & Goldstein, S. (2006). Science, ethics, and the psychosocial treatment of ADHD. *Journal of Attention Disorders, 9,* 571–574. doi: 10.1177/1087054705286052

Doggett, A. M. (2004, March). ADHD and drug therapy: Is it still a valid treatment? *Child Health Care, 8,* 1, 60–81. doi: 10.1177/1367493504041856J

Eberstadt, M. (1999, April-May). Why Ritalin rules. *Policy Review, 1*–14.

Fitzpatrick, M. A., & Badzinski, D. (1994). All in the family: Interpersonal communication in kin relationships. In M. Knapp & G. Miller (Eds.), *Handbook of Interpersonal Communication.* (2nd ed.) (pp. 726–771). Thousand Oaks, CA: Sage.

Fitzpatrick, M. A., & Ritchie, L. D. (1994). Communication schemata within the family. *Human Communication Research, 20,* 275–301. doi: 10.1111/j.1468-2958.1994.tb00324.x

Furman, L. (2005). What is attention-deficit hyperactivity disorder (ADHD)? *Journal of Child Neurology, 20,* 994–1002. doi: 10.1177/08830738050200121301

Hoagwood, K., Kelleher, K. J., Feil, M., & Conner, D. M. (2000). Treatment services for children with ADHD: A national perspective. *Journal of the American Academy of Child and Adolescent Psychiatry, 39*(2), 198–218. doi: 10.1097/00004583-200002000-00020

Horan, S. M., Houser, M. L., & Cowan, R. L. (2007). Are children communicated with equally? An investigation of parent-child sex composition and gender role communication differences. *Communication Research Reports, 24,* 361–372. doi: 10.1080/08824090701624262

Iudici, A., Faccio, E., Belloni, E. & Costa, N. (2014, March). The use of the ADHD diagnostic label: What implications exist for children and their families? *Procedia—Social and Behavioral Sciences, 122,* 506–509. doi: 10.1016/j.sbspro.2014.01.1383

Kariya, T., Sinha, B. K., & Giri, N. C. (1986). Robustness of *t*-test. (Research Report ADA176972). Retrieved from Pittsburgh University Pennsylvania Center for Multivariate Analysis website: http://www.dtic.mil/docs/citations/ADA176972

Kastenbaum, M. A., Hoel, D. G., & Bowman, K. O. (1970). Sample size requirements: One-way analysis of variance. *Biometrika, 57*(3), 421–430. doi: 10.1093/biomet/57.2.421

Koerner, A., & Cvancara, K. E. (2002). The influence of conformity orientation on communication patterns in family conversations. *Journal of Family Communication, 2*(3), 133–152. doi: 10.1207/S15327698JFC0203_2

Koerner, A., & Fitzpatrick, M. A. (1997). Family type and conflict: The impact of conversation orientation and conformity orientation on conflict in the family. *Communication Studies, 48,* 59–75. doi: 10.1080/10510979709368491

Koerner, A. F., & Fitzpatrick, M. A. (2002). Toward a theory of family communication. *Communication Theory, 12,* 70–91. doi: 10.1111/j.1468-2885.2002.tb00260.x

Koesten, J. (2004). Family communication, patterns, sex of subject, and communication competence. *Communication Monographs, 71,* 226–244. doi: 10.1080/0363775052000343417

Koesten, J. & Anderson, K. (2004). Exploring the influence of family communication patterns, cognitive complexity, and interpersonal competence on adolescent risk behaviors. *Journal of Family Communication, 4,* 99–121. doi: 10.1207/s15327698jfc0402_2

Ledbetter, A. M. (2009). Family communication patterns and relational maintenance behavior: Direct and mediated associations with friendship closeness. *Human Communication Research, 35,* 130–147. doi: 10.1111/j.1468-2958.2008.01341.x

Ledbetter, A. M. (2010). Family communication patterns and communication competence as predictors of online communication attitude: Evaluating a dual pathways model. *Journal of Family Communication, 10,* 99–115. doi: 10.1080/15267431003595462

Ledbetter, A. M., & Beck, S. J. (2014). A theoretical comparison of relationship maintenance and closeness as mediators of family communication patterns in parent-child relationships. *Journal of Family Communication, 14,* 230–252. doi: 10.1080/15267431.2014.908196

McLaughlin, D. P., & Harrison, C. A. (2006). Parenting practices of mothers of children with ADHD: The role of maternal and child factors. *Child & Adolescent Mental Health, 11,* 82–88. doi: 10.1111/j.1475-3588.2005.00382.x

McLeod, J. M, & Chaffee, S. H. (1972). The construction of social reality. In T. Tedeschi (Ed.), *The social influence processes* (pp. 50–99). Chicago: Aldine-Atherton.

National Institute of Mental Health (U.S.). (2008). *Mental health medications* (Rev. 2008.). [Rockville, Md.]: National Institute of Mental Health, U.S. Dept. of Health and Human Services, National Institutes of Health. Retrieved from http://search.library.wisc.edu/catalog/ocn613111665

Panksepp, J. (2004). *Textbook of biological psychiatry*. Hoboken, NJ: Wiley-Liss, Inc.

Ritchie, L. D., & Fitzpatrick, M. A. (1990). Family communication patterns: Measuring intrapersonal perceptions of interpersonal relationships. *Communication Research, 17,* 523–544. doi: 10.1177/009365090017004007

Rueter, M. A., & Koerner, A. F. (2008). The effect of family communication patterns on adopted adolescent adjustment. *Journal of Marriage and Family, 70,* 715–727. doi: 10.1111/j.1741-3737.2008.00516.x

Sadek, J. (2013). *A clinician's guide to ADHD*. New York: Springer.

Saphir, M. N., & Chaffee, S. H. (2002). Adolescents' contributions to family communication patterns. *Human Communication Research, 28,* 86–108. doi: 10.1111/j.1468-2958.2002.tb00799.x

Schrodt, P., & Carr, K. (2012). Trait verbal aggressiveness as a function of family communication patterns. *Communication Research Reports, 29,* 54–63. doi: 10.1080/08824096.2011.639914

Schrodt, P., Ledbetter, A. M., & Ohrt, J. K. (2007). Parental confirmation and affection as mediators of family communication patterns and children's mental well-being. *Journal of Family Communication, 7,* 23–46. doi: 10.1080/15267430709336667

Schrodt, P., Witt, P. L., & Messersmith, A. S. (2008). A meta-analytical review of family communication patterns and their associations with information processing, behavioral, and psychosocial outcomes. *Communication Monographs, 75,* 248–269. doi: 10.1080/03637750802256318

Scott, T. M., Webb, L. M., & Amason, P. (2012). Professionally accomplished women's perceptions of father-daughter communication: An exploratory study. *Iowa Journal of Communication, 44*(1), 64–92. Retrieved from http://webcache.googleusercontent.com/search?q=cache:_Zz0ht-WP2rYJ:connection.ebscohost.com/c/articles/82603731/professionally-accomplished-womens-perceptions-father-daughter-communication-exploratory-study+&cd=1&hl=en&ct=clnk&gl=us

Siegel, S. (1956). *Nonparametric statistics for the behavioral sciences*. New York: McGraw-Hill.

Sillars, A., Holman, A. J., Richards, A., Jacobs, K. A., Koerner, A., & Reynolds-Dyk, A. (2014). Conversation and conformity orientations as predictors of observed conflict tactics in parent-adolescent discussions. *Journal of Family Communication, 14,* 16–31. doi: 10.1080/15267431.2013.857327

Steinberg, L. D., & Silverberg, S. B. (1986). The vicissitudes of autonomy in early adolescence. *Child Development, 57,* 841–851. Retrieved from http://www.jstor.org/stable/1130361

Visser, S. N., Danielson, M. L., Bitsko, R. H., Holbrook, J. R., Kogan, M. D., Ghandour, R. M., ... Blumberg, S. J. (2014). Trends in the parent-report of health care provider—diagnosed and medicated Attention-Deficit/Hyperactivity Disorder: United States, 2003–2011. *Journal of the American Academy of Child & Adolescent Psychiatry, 53,* 34–46. doi: 10.1016/j.jaac.2013.09.001

Webb, L. M., Ledbetter, A., & Norwood, K. M. (2014). Families and technologically-assisted communication. In L. H. Turner & R. West, Eds., *Sage handbook of family communication* (pp. 354–369). Thousand Oaks, CA: Sage. doi: 10.4135/9781483375366

Wilson, S. R., Chernichky, S. M., Wilkum, K., & Owlett, J. S. (2014). Do family communication patterns buffer children from difficulties associated with a parent's military deployment/

Examining deployed and at-home parents' perspectives. *Journal of Family Communication, 14*, 32–52. doi: 10.1080/15267431.2013.857325

Winter, J. C. F. (2013). Using the Student's *t*-test with extremely small samples sizes. *Practical Assessment, Research, & Evaluation: A Peer Reviewed Electronic Journal, 18*(10). Retrieved from http://pareonline.net/pdf/v18n10.pdf

NOTES

1. This chapter is based on the first author's PhD dissertation. The authors thank Joann Keyton (PhD, 1987, Ohio University) who chaired the defense of the dissertation as well as Dixie R. Crase (PhD, 1967, Ohio State University), Walter G. Kirkpatrick (PhD, 1974, University of Iowa), and D. Gray Mathews (PhD, 1993, Pennsylvania State University) who also served as members of Ms. Gibson's dissertation committee.
2. For a more detailed list of outcomes associated with FCE, please see Schrodt et al. (2008).
3. The findings here reported are drawn from a larger data collection. One of the instruments used in that larger data collection was designed to assess communication in public venues and had not previously been employed to assess communication in a family setting. Given that the instrument was significantly modified in wording and context to address the focus of this study, we opted to employ a rigorous form of factor analysis.

CHAPTER FIVE

Dark Climates AND Media Use IN THE Family

The Associations Among Child Temperament, Maternal Mental Well-Being, and the Frequency of Mothers' Use of Television Viewing to Soothe Their Children

INE BEYENS & STEVEN EGGERMONT
School for Mass Communication Research, University of Leuven, Belgium

Family life can be filled with darkness, ranging from light and mild tints of darkness to very intense shades of darkness (Fitness & Duffield, 2004; Olson, Baiocchi-Wagner, Wilson Kratzer, & Symonds, 2012). Within some families, darkness in the family impacts familial functioning and affects the dyadic interactions in a family (Olson et al., 2012). With respect to parent-child relationships, dark issues can affect processes at the level of parent-child pairs and may result in negative forms of parenting (Lee, Zhou, Eisenberg, & Wang, 2013; Olson et al., 2012). The present chapter will explore the extent to which dark individual traits on behalf of the child and the parent may result in parenting strategies that promote the use of television for children.

Research on young children's television use has increased our understanding of the amount of television that children watch (e.g., Rideout & Hamel, 2006; Vandewater et al., 2005) and the potential effects this exposure may have on children (e.g., Bickham, Wright, & Huston, 2001; Garrison, Liekweg, & Christakis, 2011; Thakkar, Garrison, & Christakis, 2006). Yet this research has rarely taken an interdisciplinary perspective that integrates insights from communication, sociology, psychology, and family studies to investigate the extent to which child and parent characteristics predict the frequency of children's television use (Pinon, Huston, & Wright, 1989).

Nonetheless, such a perspective is needed to understand the motivations behind children's television use, in particular if these are dictated by dark climates in the family.

The present chapter will take an integrative approach to investigate how dark individual traits, on the part of the child as well as on the part of the mother, drive mothers' use of television for their children. In particular, we will focus on the role of television as a potential means for mothers to cope with temperamental problems of their children and their own mental distress. We examine (1) the extent to which children's temperament predicts mothers' use of television to soothe their children, (2) the extent to which mothers' mental well-being predicts their use of television to soothe their children, and (3) the extent to which mothers' mental well-being moderates the relationship between children's temperament and the amount of time that children spend watching television.

CHILDREN'S TELEVISION VIEWING IN THE FAMILY CONTEXT

Media have become an integral part of today's families. Families have access to multiple platforms and likely spend large amounts of their time using media (Common Sense Media, 2013; Nathanson & Fries, 2014; Rideout & Hamel, 2006; Vandewater et al., 2005). For instance, studies have shown that families with young children currently have access to a variety of screen media, from television, videos, and DVDs to mobile devices such as laptops, smartphones, and tablet computers (Common Sense Media, 2013; Wartella, Rideout, Lauricella, & Connell, 2013). Among this range of screen media, television is still the most popular screen medium in the family system and the most frequently consumed by children (Common Sense Media, 2013; Wartella et al., 2013).

It is in this media-immersed family environment that young children start to use television at early ages and often in large amounts (Anderson & Hanson, 2010). For instance, a recent report found that children under eight spend almost two hours a day using screen media, with almost one hour spent watching television (Common Sense Media, 2013). Other studies have reported time spent watching television ranging from an hour and a half a day (Beyens & Eggermont, in press) to almost three hours a day (Nathanson & Fries, 2014).

Television is thus omnipresent in the family system. In many families, the television functions as a constant noise, being on in the background, whether or not the family members are watching (Common Sense Media, 2013; Wartella et al., 2013), or as an electronic babysitter, keeping children occupied when parents need a break (Beyens & Eggermont, 2014; Evans, Jordan, & Horner, 2011; Zimmerman & Christakis, 2007). Also, many families have a television set in the child's bedroom (Common Sense Media, 2013; Nathanson & Fries, 2014;

Wartella et al., 2013). Others have described how television has a functional role within the family system (Jordan, 1992, 2004; Lull, 1990). Routines in the family system evolve around the family's television use, and parents express their authority by controlling television access and content.

While research has increased our understanding of the family routines around children's television viewing (e.g., Jordan, 1992, 2004; Lull, 1990), little is understood about the factors that drive mothers' motivations for children's television viewing (Jordan, 2005; Krosnick, Anand, & Hartl, 2003; Nathanson, 2015). Some studies have described mothers' motivations for children's television viewing, showing that mothers use television for educational or entertainment reasons, as well as for practical reasons (e.g., Evans et al., 2011; Rideout & Hamel, 2006; Vaala, 2014). For instance, mothers use television to get chores done, to establish a routine for their child, or to keep their child safely occupied (Beyens & Eggermont, 2014; Evans et al., 2011; Vaala, 2014).

However, knowledge about the extent to which dark experiences in the family elicit such motivations is scarce. In particular, knowledge is lacking about the extent to which children's temperamental difficulties and maternal mental distress elicit the use of television to soothe children. Nonetheless, understanding the extent to which mothers' motivations regarding children's television use are prompted by dark experiences in the family is important to learn which mothers and children and which dark traits should be targeted in interventions aimed at reducing children's television viewing.

CHILDREN'S TEMPERAMENT AND CHILDREN'S TELEVISION VIEWING

Research has shown that personality traits are driving forces behind a person's media use (Aubrey et al., 2012; Hall, 2005; Kirzinger, Weber, & Johnson, 2012; Langstedt & Atkin, 2013). In this respect, scholars found that personality characteristics such as extraversion and neuroticism predicted individuals' media use and selection of media genres (Aubrey et al., 2012; Hall, 2005; Langstedt & Atkin, 2013; Shim & Paul, 2007). For instance, Langstedt and Atkin (2013) found that while individuals who scored high on neuroticism were more motivated to watch television for companionship, individuals who scored high on extraversion were less motivated to watch television for companionship. Also, individuals with high levels of extraversion spent less time watching television (Langstedt & Atkin, 2013). In a sample of students, Aubrey and colleagues (2012) found that students with high levels of extraversion watched less reality television programs. However, students' level of neuroticism was not associated with reality television exposure.

Researchers studying the uses and gratifications of media have stated that managing emotional states and arousal levels is an important motivation for individuals to use media (Beatty, McCroskey, & Valencic, 2001; Kim & Oliver, 2013; Taylor & Friedman, 2015; Zillman & Bryant, 1994). Therefore, it is not surprising that individuals' temperament has previously been identified as a predictor of the motivations behind people's media use (Sherry, 2001). For instance, research among adults has revealed that temperament predicts adults' motivations to watch television (Sherry, 2001). In particular, Sherry (2001) found that adults' negative mood, behavioral rigidity, and low task orientation predicted their motivation to watch television.

Indications exist that parents' motivations behind young children's television use are influenced by children's temperament as well. Research has indicated that parents develop different parenting strategies to handle their children's temperamental difficulties (Putnam, Sanson, & Rothbart, 2002). Some studies have shown that parents of children with difficult temperaments develop more positive parenting strategies (Belsky & Jaffee, 2006), such as greater involvement with their children (Crockenberg, 1986) or showing more warmth (Rubin, Hastings, Chen, Stewart, & McNichol, 1998). Other studies, however, have demonstrated that children's temperamental problems can elicit negative parenting behaviors (Scaramella & Leve, 2004), such as lower responsiveness (Hemphill & Sanson, 2000), harsh and strict discipline (Katainen, Räikkönen, & Keltikangas-Järvinen, 1997; Kochanska, Friesenborg, Lange, & Martel, 2004), or an authoritarian parenting style (Lee et al., 2013). Children's difficult temperament is thus challenging to parents and often creates problems for managing children efficiently (Belsky, 1984; Sanson, Hemphill, & Smart, 2004).

Although a large body of research has investigated the link between children's temperament and parents' parenting behavior (e.g., Belsky & Jaffee, 2006; Lee et al., 2013), research has not fully addressed the possibility that children's temperament influences parents' decisions around children's television use. It is likely that children's difficult temperament elicits parenting strategies that promote the use of television for children, because studies have shown that parents often rely on television in parenting (Evans et al., 2011; Nathanson & Manohar, 2012). One strategy by which parents may try to cope with difficult child temperament may be to soothe children by letting them watch television. For instance, scholars have suggested that more active or fussier children may encourage parents to use television to entertain their children (Thompson, Adair, & Bentley, 2013). Also, recent studies showed that children with self-regulation problems and children who are more active or fussier watch more television (Radesky, Silverstein, Zuckerman, & Christakis, 2014; Thompson et al., 2013). Likewise, it is possible that children's difficult temperament encourages parents to use television to soothe their children.

CIRCUMSTANCES IN THE FAMILY AND CHILDREN'S TELEVISION VIEWING

Scholars have argued that individual-level factors, such as personality traits, do not affect individuals' media use in a one-dimensional way (Hall, 2005). Rather, the impact of individual-level factors varies according to the social context. Pinon and colleagues (1989) have argued that it is necessary to take into account the social context of children when studying how child characteristics predict children's television use. If one wants to understand why some children watch more television than others, one needs to examine the interaction of individual-level factors with factors in the family environment (Pinon et al., 1989). More specifically, Sherry (2004) stated that the impact of temperament on decisions around media use needs to be examined by looking at interactions with environmental factors.

From family systems and media studies we know that parenting practices, including those relating to children's television viewing, are affected by both parental and child factors (Gingold, Simon, & Schoendorf, 2014; Jordan, 1992, 2004). Through their parenting practices, parents create a reality within the family system that influences how much television their children watch (Jordan, 1992; Taras, Sallis, Nader, & Nelson, 1990). Parents regulate the media environment, set television rules, and may encourage or discourage television viewing for their children. Scholars showed that the quality of the home environment influences parents' decisions regarding children's television viewing and how much time children spend watching television (Certain & Kahn, 2002). A recent study, taking a life logistics perspective that combines insights from family studies and sociology with perspectives from communication and television studies to investigate family life factors associated with children's television time, showed that the circumstances of families' lives predict children's television use (Beyens & Eggermont, in press). In particular, the findings showed that children watch more television if their mothers work longer hours and experience time pressure and mental distress.

MOTHERS' MENTAL WELL-BEING AND CHILDREN'S TELEVISION VIEWING

The chapter by Segrin and Arroyo in this volume summarizes research concerning mental health problems in family contexts and shows that mental health problems are a serious concern for today's families. Mental health problems such as mental distress and depression are highly prevalent among mothers with young children (Beyens & Eggermont, in press; Burdette, Whitaker, Kahn, & Harvey-Berino, 2003; Davé, Petersen, Sherr, & Nazareth, 2010; Giles, Davies, Whitrow, Warin, & Moore, 2011;

Thompson & Christakis, 2007). Prevalence rates of depressive symptoms among mothers with young children found in previous studies range from 21% of the mothers in a study of 0- to 3-year-old children (Thompson & Christakis, 2007) to 30% of the mothers in a study of 3- and 4-year-old children (Burdette et al., 2003) and 31% of the mothers in a study of 2- and 3-year-olds (Giles et al., 2011).

Mental health problems can have important consequences for the family system (Segrin, 2006). In particular, mental health problems largely affect how family members interact with each other within the family system, and, as such, also have an impact on parenting behaviors and parent-child interactions (Brown, McBride, Bost, & Shin, 2011; Segrin, 2006). Scholars have argued that mental distress would also influence parents' decisions regarding children's television viewing (Conners, Tripathi, Clubb, & Bradley, 2007). Recent studies found evidence for an association between mothers' experience of mental distress and higher amounts of television viewing among their children (e.g., Bank et al., 2012; Beyens & Eggermont, in press; Conners et al., 2007; Thompson & Christakis, 2007). Explanations for this association might be that mental distress depletes mothers' energy and motivation to interact with their children or strengthens mothers' belief that children might benefit more from watching television than from engaging in mother-child interactions (Potts & Sanchez, 1994). As such, there is good reason to expect that mothers with mental distress are more often motivated than mothers without mental distress to use television for their children, in particular if their children are fussy and need to calm down.

TELEVISION TO COPE WITH CHILDREN'S DIFFICULT TEMPERAMENT UNDER CONDITIONS OF MATERNAL MENTAL DISTRESS

The effect of temperamental problems on mothers' decisions regarding children's television viewing might vary according to the conditions in the family system. The fact that some studies did (Sherry, 2001; Thompson et al., 2013) and others (Pagani, Fitzpatrick, Barnett, & Dubow, 2010) did not find a relationship between children's temperament and their television use, indicates that the relationship is not simple but dependent on other forces within the family system.

Evidence exists that mothers' mental well-being moderates the impact of children's temperament on mothers' decisions around television viewing. Recently, scholars argued that more research is needed on the role of parents' well-being in the relationship between children's temperament and parents' behavior (Laukkanen, Ojansuu, Tolvanen, Alatupa, & Aunola, 2014). More specifically, scholars have suggested that the relationship between children's temperament and parents' parenting behaviors is moderated by parents' well-being (Mertesacker, Bade,

Haverkock, & Pauli-Pott, 2004; Pauli-Pott, Mertesacker, & Bade, 2000). Studies have indeed found support for a moderating role of mothers' well-being in the relationship between children's difficult temperament and mothers' parenting practices (Mertesacker et al., 2004; Pauli-Pott et al., 2000). For instance, Mertesacker and colleagues (2004) found that children's negative emotionality predicted lower sensitivity only among mothers who had depressive symptoms.

Mothers with poor mental well-being, mental distress, or depression might be in a more difficult position to deal with children's temperamental problems. It is possible that mothers who experience mental distress are more prone to use television to soothe children with difficult temperament, because they may be more unsuccessful in monitoring children's television viewing, as scholars have noted (Bickham et al., 2003; Conners et al., 2007). The extent to which mothers choose television for their children to cope with their children's difficult temperament might thus depend on the mothers' ability to cope with temperamental problems. It is likely that mothers with feelings of mental distress are more likely than their nondistressed counterparts to rely on television to cope with their child's temperamental problems. As such, children with temperamental problems whose mother has mental distress may watch more television than children with temperamental problems whose mother does not have mental distress.

PRESENT STUDY

The current study examines the extent to which characteristics of the individual child and characteristics of the family environment predict mothers' motivations to use television for their children. More specifically, the study focusses on the impact of children's temperament and mothers' well-being on mothers' decisions to use television to soothe their child. In particular, we will test the hypotheses that mothers of children with temperamental problems (H1) and mothers experiencing mental distress (H2) more often use television to soothe their child if their child is fussy and has to calm down. Also, we will investigate the extent to which children with difficult temperaments (H3) and children of mentally distressed mothers (H4) watch more television. Finally, we will test the hypothesis that the impact of children's difficult temperament on the time they spend watching television differs according to the mothers' well-being (H5).

METHOD

In order to investigate potential relations between children's temperament, maternal well-being, and children's television viewing, we conducted a survey of a sample of mothers of children aged 1 to 5 years old (M = 37.00 months old, SD = 17.66; 47.5% boys and 52.5% girls). Participants were recruited from 47 public and private day-care centers and preschools that were randomly selected in different regions in Belgium. Parents received packages including a questionnaire, an informational letter, and a consent form and were invited to complete the questionnaire at home. Participants were guaranteed that participation in the study was voluntary and anonymous and were offered a chance to win a raffle (gift vouchers). Participants provided consent to participate in the study by reading, completing, and signing consent forms and returned their completed questionnaires in sealed envelopes to their day-care center or preschool. The Institutional Review Board of the University of Leuven approved all study procedures.

A total of 944 mothers participated in the study. Mothers who had completed the questionnaire predominantly identified themselves as Caucasian (99.58%), which is representative of the Belgian society (Child and Family, 2012). The majority of mothers had graduate degrees (44.6%) or college graduate degrees (26.7%), one in four held a high school degree (25.8%), 1.9% held an elementary school degree, and 1.0% had no degree. On average, mothers had 1.90 children (SD = 0.79).

Measures

Child Temperament. Mothers completed the Emotionality subscale of the EAS Temperament Survey (Buss & Plomin, 1984) using a five-point Likert scale to assess their children's emotionality, a temperament indicator that is described as "the tendency to become aroused easily and intensely" (Mathiesen & Tambs, 1999). This five-item scale, which includes items such as "My child often fusses and cries" and "My child gets upset easily," has been widely validated and used in previous studies (Mathiesen & Tambs, 1999). Higher scores are indicative of more temperamental difficulties (Cronbach's α = .72, M = 2.75, SD = 0.70).

Mothers' Mental Distress. The Mental Health Inventory (MHI-5; Berwick et al., 1991) was used to measure the extent to which the mother was mentally distressed. On a six-point scale ranging from *(almost) all of the time* (1) to *(almost) none of the time* (6) mothers indicated how much of the time during the past month they "had been a very nervous person" (reverse coded), "felt calm and peaceful," "felt downhearted and blue" (reverse coded), "felt so down in the dumps that nothing could cheer them up" (reverse coded), and "had been a happy person" (Cronbach's α = .85, M = 22.57, SD = 3.65). Lower scores are indicative of poorer mental well-being. A score of 21 has been identified as a cutoff point for having mental distress (Rumpf, Meyer, Hapke, & John, 2001): Mothers scoring 21 or lower were identified as having mental distress; mothers with scores of 22 and higher were identified as not having mental distress. In line with prior research (e.g., Rumpf et al., 2001; Thompson & Christakis, 2007) that has attempted to compare distressed mothers with nondistressed mothers, we dichotomized the sample into mothers having mental distress and mothers without mental distress.

Mothers' Use of Television to Soothe Their Children. Mothers reported how often they use television when their child is fussy (M = 2.02, SD = 0.92) and how often they use television to calm down their child (M = 1.64, SD = 0.88). Response options ranged from *(almost) never (1)* to *very often (5)*.

Children's Time Spent Watching Television. Mothers reported when their child watches television on a typical weekday, a typical Wednesday,[1] and a typical weekend day. Timelines were presented ranging from 6 A.M. until 5 A.M. the next day, each representing the weekday, Wednesday, or weekend day. Each hour on the timeline was divided into four checkboxes of 15 minutes each. Mothers marked a checkbox if their child was watching television during the corresponding 15 minutes. We calculated children's television viewing time by adding up all of the marked checkboxes per timeline. This sum was then divided by four to convert the estimates into hours. We then calculated weekly television viewing time in hours by multiplying the weekday viewing hours by four and adding the result to the number of hours reported for Wednesday and the weekend day times two ([weekday hours × 4] + [Wednesday hours] + [weekend day hours × 2]). Children's mean weekly television viewing averaged 8 hours (M = 8.17, SD = 6.00).

Control Variables. Mothers reported their educational level (1 = *no degree* to 5 = *university degree*), their relationship status (1 = *married or cohabitating* and 2 = *single*), the child's age, the number of children in their family, their attitude toward television (three-item scale, with higher scores reflecting more positive attitudes toward television), and the time they spent watching television (measured with the same procedure as for the children's measure). Based on prior research (Barr, Danziger, Hilliard, Andolina, & Ruskis, 2010; Bickham et al., 2003; Certain & Kahn, 2002), these variables were controlled for in the analyses.

RESULTS

Mothers' Use of Television to Soothe Their Children

In order to investigate whether mothers of children with difficult temperaments and mothers with mental distress would be more often motivated to use television if their child is fussy and if they think that their child has to calm down, we computed χ^2 tests.

First, we found that mothers of children with temperamental problems indicated that soothing a fussy child was more often a reason for letting their child watch television than for mothers whose children did not have temperamental problems (χ^2 (4) = 23.96, p < .001). Almost one in eight mothers of children with difficult temperaments reported that soothing a fussy child was (very) often a reason for them to let their child watch television (12.3%). For mothers who indicated that temperamental problems were *neither typical or atypical* (i.e., the neutral midpoint of the scale) of their child (3.7%) and for mothers who indicated that their child did not experience temperamental problems (2.3%), this was far less a reason. Moreover, we found that mothers of children with temperamental problems indicated that calming down their child was more often a reason for letting their child watch television (χ^2 (4) = 54.33, p < .001). While one in eight mothers who indicated that their child had difficult temperaments used television to this end (13%), only 1.3% of mothers who indicated that difficult temperament was *neither typical or atypical* for their child and 1.7% of mothers whose child did not have difficult temperament used television for this reason.

Second, we found that mothers who experienced mental distress indicated that soothing a fussy child was more often a reason for letting their child watch television than for mothers who did not experience mental distress (χ^2 (2) = 18.46, p < .001). While almost one in ten mothers who experienced mental distress indicated that this was (very) often a reason for her (7.2%), only 2.9% of the mothers who did not experience mental distress indicated that this was a reason for them. Moreover, mothers who experienced mental distress reported that calming down their child was more often a reason for letting their child watch television than for mothers not experiencing mental distress (χ^2 (2) = 28.15, p < .001). While using television to calm down their child was a reason for more than half of the mothers who experienced mental distress (52.9%), this was less of a reason for mothers who did not experience mental distress, with only 35% indicating that this was a reason for them.

Children's Time Spent Watching Television

In order to investigate the extent to which children with difficult temperaments and children of mothers with mental distress watch more television and in order to investigate the interaction effect between children's temperament and mothers' well-being, we conducted hierarchical regression analysis (see Table 1). The mother's education and relationship status, the child's age, and the number of children in their family were entered as control variables in the first step of the equation. In

Table 1. Hierarchical Regression Analysis of the Associations Among Children's Temperament, Mothers' Level of Mental Distress, and Children's Television Viewing Time.

	B	SE	β	t
Step 1				
Mother's education	-.98	.24	-.14***	-4.05
Mother's relationship status	-.99	.96	-.03	-1.03
Child's age	.11	.01	.32***	9.70
Number of children	-.33	.25	-.05	-1.35
Adj. R^2	.18***			
Step 2				
Mother's attitude toward TV	1.32	.35	.12***	3.79
Mother's TV viewing time	.29	.02	.40***	12.00
Incr. R^2/Adj. R^2	.18***/.36***			
Step 3				
Child's temperament	2.29	.91	.27*	2.52
Mother's level of mental distress	-.63	.41	-.05	-1.53
Incr. R^2/Adj. R^2	.00/.36***			
Step 4				
Child's temperament X Mother's level of mental distress	-1.44	.56	-.27**	-2.57
Incr. R^2/Adj. R^2	.01*/.36***			
F	41.87***		df	9

Note: Coefficients are derived from the final regression model (i.e., after all four steps were entered in the regression analysis).

*$p < .05$. **$p < .01$. ***$p < .001$.

the second step, we entered the mother's attitude toward television and the mother's time spent watching television. In the third step, we entered the child's temperament (centered variable) and mother's level of mental distress (dichotomized variable). In the fourth step, we entered the interaction term between the child's temperament and mother's level of mental distress.

First, the regression analysis showed that children's temperament was significantly related to children's time spent watching television, beyond the blocks with control variables. The analyses indicated that children with more temperamental problems watched more television (see Table 1). Second, the regression analysis showed that the mothers' level of mental distress was not significantly related to children's time spent watching television. Hence, we found no evidence that children whose mothers had mental distress watched more television (see Table 1).

However, descriptive analyses showed that children whose mothers had mental distress spent about an hour weekly more watching television (M = 8.82 hours a week; SD = 6.56) than children whose mothers did not experience mental distress (M = 7.73 hours a week; SD = 5.60).

Finally, a significant two-way interaction effect was found—mothers' well-being significantly moderated the relationship between children's temperament and the time they spent watching television (see Table 1). In order to further explore this interaction, we plotted the separate regression lines for children of mothers with mental distress and for children of mothers without mental distress according to the procedure of Aiken and West (1991) and Dawson (2014) (see Figure 1). As shown in Figure 1, and according to our expectations, mothers' mental distress reinforced the relationship between children's temperament and their television viewing, indicating that children with temperamental problems whose mothers had mental distress watched more television than children with temperamental problems whose mothers did not have mental distress. Thus, H5 was supported. The final regression model explained 36.4% of the variance in children's television viewing.

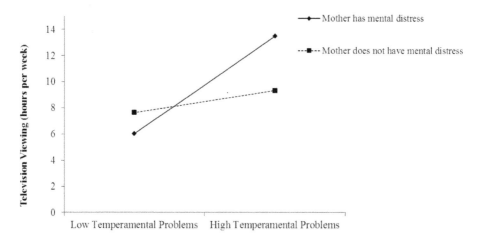

Fig 1. Two-way interaction effect of children's temperamental problems and mothers' level of mental distress on children's television viewing.

DISCUSSION

Dark individual traits have the potential to negatively affect a family (Olson et al., 2012). With respect to parent-child relationships, dark issues at the individual level of the child and the parent may result in negative forms of parenting (Olson et al., 2012). The purpose of the present study was to investigate the extent to which children's temperamental issues and maternal mental health issues affect mothers' decisions around children's television viewing.

Dealing with children's temperamental difficulties can be challenging for parents (Belsky, 1984; Sanson et al., 2004). Children's difficult temperament is clearly a negativity in the family system that, especially under conditions of maternal mental distress, influences parents' parenting practices (Mertesacker et al., 2004; Pauli-Pott et al., 2000). The findings that are presented in the current chapter showed that in a family system that is characterized by temperamental problems on the part of the child, mothers are likely to choose television to soothe their children, especially if these mothers experience high levels of mental distress. As such, our study demonstrates that individual-level issues have an impact on the dyadic interactions in a family (Olson et al., 2012).

Further, the findings emphasized the importance of mothers' mental well-being for their decisions around children's television use. Mothers who experience high levels of mental distress indicated that they are more likely to use television to soothe their children and to calm them down than mothers with lower levels of mental distress. Moreover, their children also watch more television if they have temperamental problems than do children with temperamental problems whose mothers do not experience mental distress (see Figure 1).

Another important finding of the current study is that to understand why some children watch more television than others, the interaction of child factors with maternal factors is important. It is the interplay of children's temperamental problems with mothers' mental distress that increases mothers' likelihood to soothe their children with television and ultimately increases children's actual television viewing time. In this sense, the findings emphasize that screening for maternal mental health problems and children's temperamental difficulties should be incorporated in interventions that aim to reduce children's television viewing.

Implications of Using Television to Soothe Children

While the study that we presented in this chapter demonstrates that mothers see television as an excellent means to calm their child down when the child is upset or fussy, in particular when mothers experience mental distress, nothing is said about whether using television to soothe a child is a positive choice or not, however. It is very likely that children's television viewing negatively affects their emotional, mental, and physical well-being. Television viewing, especially in high amounts, displaces other, more physically active (DuRant, Thompson, Johnson, & Baranowski, 1996), social (Vandewater, Bickham, & Lee, 2006), or cognitively stimulating (Huston, Wright, Marquis, & Green, 1999) activities. Children who watch large amounts of television are likely to have more sleep disorders (Garrison et al., 2011), decreased fitness (Tremblay et al., 2011), and poorer cognitive functioning (Nathanson, Aladé, Sharp, Rasmussen, & Christy, 2014; Nathanson & Fries, 2014), among others. Hence, using television to cope with the negativity of children's temperamental problems might aggravate children's problematic symptoms and result in more negativities in the family system instead of countering the negativities.

However, a distressed mother's use of television for her child could also be a positive coping strategy. It is possible that if a mother is unable to deal with her child, putting the child in front of the television while she calms down could be beneficial. In line with what Thompson and Christakis (2007) have argued, watching television—given that it is high-quality content—could have the potential to offset the negative impact of mothers' feelings of distress.

Further, it is important to note that the meaning of darkness might differ between families: While for some families dark experiences may place a heavy burden on family life and familial functioning, they may be of a more temporary nature for other families (Olson et al., 2012). In this respect, our study showed that some mothers try to cope with children's temperamental problems by using television, but others do not. Also, dark processes in the family can become lighter or darker over time (Olson et al., 2012). However, while it was the aim of our study to investigate the extent to which children's temperamental problems and mothers' mental well-being encourage mothers to use television for their children, the question whether television ultimately soothes children or not remains unanswered and deserves further attention.

It is plausible, for instance, that using television to soothe children does not calm children down but, instead, results in more active and fussier children. As such, it is possible that the relationship between children's temperamental problems and their television viewing is reciprocal and continues in an ongoing chain of reactions. Mothers who use television to soothe their children might in fact keep their children from other more stimulating activities (DuRant et al., 1996; Huston et al., 1999; Vandewater et al., 2006), which may result in continued temperamental difficulties, which might again encourage mothers to use television for their children. Research is needed that examines the extent to which dark experiences such as children's temperamental problems and mothers' mental distress become lighter or darker when mothers use television for their children.

Another implication of mothers' use of television for their children to cope with their children's difficult temperament is that it might create messages for children that television is an appropriate outlet to cope with difficulties. As children learn how to cope with emotions from their parents (Cupach & Olson, 2006), children might perhaps be socialized to think about television as a means for coping with negativities and dark experiences in the family. Further research is needed to investigate the extent to which children who grow up with these dark experiences and whose mothers rely on television to cope with these experiences might be learning to use television themselves as a way to cope with their own stress later in life. Research already showed that older children, whose media use is less controlled by their parents, frequently choose television as a coping strategy when they experience stress (Chen & Kennedy, 2005).

In line with our findings that children's difficult temperament increases the use of television among children and because previous research has shown that children's difficult temperament elicits parenting strategies that are more harsh, more strict, and more authoritarian (Katainen et al., 1997; Kochanska et al., 2004; Lee et al., 2013), it is possible that children's difficult temperament also predicts other parental decisions around children's television, such as parental mediation strategies (Nathanson, 1999, 2001). More research is needed that investigates the impact of children's temperament on parents' decisions and rules around children's television viewing. Also, future studies are needed to examine the extent to which families also use television as a coping strategy for other significant stressors or dark experiences in their family (see for instance Olson et al., 2012).

Potential Ways to Limit the Use of Television to Soothe Children

Mothers' use of television to soothe their children could potentially result in negative media effects on children (e.g., Garrison et al., 2011; Nathanson et al., 2014; Nathanson & Fries, 2014; Tremblay et al., 2011) and might create more negativities in the family instead of alleviating negativities. Yet in a family environment that is more supportive for mothers, mothers might be less inclined to use television to soothe their children. Mothers who receive social support likely have less mental distress (Cutrona & Troutman, 1986). Also, social support has the potential to decrease the impact of mental distress on mothers' parenting practices (Trapolini, Ungerer, & McMahon, 2008). Likewise, social support might decrease the use of television to soothe children. If mothers can turn to their partners, other family members, or friends for emotional help with parenting, or if they can count on someone to watch their child if they need a break, mothers might be less inclined to use television for their children if their children have temperamental problems and if they themselves experience mental distress.

Also mothers' level of parenting self-efficacy could play a role. Some mothers are better than others at soothing their child (Coleman & Karraker, 1997, 2003) and might be less inclined to use television to soothe their child. Mothers who exhibit less efficacy to soothe their child might rely more on television. We recommend that future research investigate the extent to which social support and parents' parenting self-efficacy could limit the use of television to soothe children.

Conclusion

While research has increased our understanding about of amount of television that children watch (e.g., Rideout & Hamel, 2006; Vandewater et al., 2005) and the potential effects that television may have on children (e.g., Bickham et al., 2001; Garrison et al., 2011; Thakkar et al., 2006), this study added to the literature by investigating the role of children's temperament and mothers' well-being in the use of television to soothe children. Of course, this study is not without limitations. The cross-sectional design of our study limits any inferences about the direction of causality. Longitudinal data are needed to more fully investigate the associations among children's temperament, mothers' well-being, and the use of television.

Future research could, for instance, examine our suggestion of a potential mutual relationship between children's temperamental difficulties and the use of television to soothe children. Also, we recommend that research examine how fathers use television with their children. Finally, it is important to underscore that while temperamental difficulties are likely to be associated with problematic behavior among children (e.g., Sanson et al., 2004; Vitaro, Barker, Boivin, Brendgen, & Tremblay, 2006), temperamental problems are not an illness or disease as such (Carey, 1997). Yet this study showed that children's difficult temperament, in particular under conditions of maternal mental distress, encourages mothers to soothe their children with television. More research is needed to investigate the extent to which using television to soothe children with temperamental problems might put these children at increased risk for negative outcomes.

REFERENCES

Aiken, L. S., & West, S. G. (1991). *Multiple regression: Testing and interpreting interactions*. Newbury Park, CA: Sage.

Anderson, D. R., & Hanson, K. G. (2010). From blooming, buzzing confusion to media literacy: The early development of television viewing. *Developmental Review, 30*(2), 239–255. doi: 10.1016/j.dr.2010.03.004

Aubrey, J. S., Olson, L., Fine, M., Hauser, T., Rhea, D., Kaylor, B., & Yang, A. (2012). Investigating personality and viewing-motivation correlates of reality television exposure. *Communication Quarterly, 60*(1), 80–102. doi: 10.1080/01463373.2012.641830

Bank, A. M., Barr, R., Calvert, S. L., Parrott, W. G., McDonough, S. C., & Rosenblum, K. (2012). Maternal depression and family media use: A questionnaire and diary analysis. *Journal of Child and Family Studies, 21*(2), 208–216. doi: 10.1007/s10826-011-9464-1

Barr, R., Danziger, C., Hilliard, M., Andolina, C., & Ruskis, J. (2010). Amount, content and context of infant media exposure: A parental questionnaire and diary analysis. *International Journal of Early Years Education, 18*(2), 107–122. doi: 10.1080/09669760.2010.494431

Beatty, M. J., McCroskey, J. C., & Valencic, K. M. (2001). *The biology of communication: A communibiological perspective*. Cresskill, NJ: Hampton.

Belsky, J. (1984). The determinants of parenting: A process model. *Child Development, 55*(1), 83–96.

Belsky, J., & Jaffee, S. R. (2006). The multiple determinants of parenting. In D. Cicchetti & D. J. Cohen (Eds.), *Developmental psychopathology. Vol. 3. Risk, disorder, and adaptation* (pp. 38–85). Hoboken, NJ: Wiley.

Beyens, I., & Eggermont, S. (2014). Putting young children in front of the television: Antecedents and outcomes of parents' use of television as a babysitter. *Communication Quarterly, 62*(1), 57–74. doi: 10.1080/01463373.2013.860904

Beyens, I., & Eggermont, S. (in press). Understanding children's television exposure from a life logistics perspective: A longitudinal study of the association between mothers' working hours and young children's television time. *Communication Research.* doi: 10.1177/ 0093650215607600

Bickham, D. S., Vandewater, E. A., Huston, A. C., Lee, J. H., Gilman Caplovitz, A., & Wright, J. C. (2003). Predictors of children's electronic media use: An examination of three ethnic groups. *Media Psychology, 5*(2), 107–137. doi: 10.1207/S1532785XMEP0502_1

Bickham, D. S., Wright, J. C., & Huston, A. C. (2001). Attention, comprehension, and the educational influences of television. In D. Singer & J. Singer (Eds.), *Handbook of children and the media* (pp. 101–120). Newbury Park, CA: Sage.

Brown, G. L., McBride, B. A., Bost, K. K., & Shin, N. (2011). Parental involvement, child temperament, and parents' work hours: Differential relations for mothers and fathers. *Journal of Applied Developmental Psychology, 32*(6), 313–322. doi: 10.1016/j.appdev.2011.08.004

Burdette, H. L., Whitaker, R. C., Kahn, R. S., & Harvey-Berino, J. (2003). Association of maternal obesity and depressive symptoms with television-viewing time in low-income preschool children. *Archives of Pediatrics & Adolescent Medicine, 157*(9), 894–899. doi: 10.1001/ archpedi.157.9.894

Buss, A. H., & Plomin, R. (1984). *Temperament: Early developing personality traits.* Hillsdale, NJ: Lawrence Erlbaum Associates, Inc.

Carey, W. B. (1997). Obsessive difficult temperament. *Journal of the American Academy of Child and Adolescent Psychiatry, 36*(6), 722. doi: 10.1097/00004583-199706000-00005

Certain, L. K., & Kahn, R. S. (2002). Prevalence, correlates, and trajectory of television viewing among infants and toddlers. *Pediatrics, 109*(4), 634–642. doi: 10.1542/peds.109.4.634

Chen, J., & Kennedy, C. (2005). Cultural variations in children's coping behaviour, TV viewing time, and family functioning. *International Nursing Review, 52*(3), 186–195.

Child and Family (2012). *The Child in Flanders.* Brussels: Child and Family.

Coleman, P. K., & Karraker, K. H. (1998). Self-efficacy and parenting quality: Findings and future applications. *Developmental Review, 18*(1), 47–85. doi: 10.1006/drev.1997.0448

Coleman, P. K., & Karraker, K. H. (2003). Maternal self-efficacy beliefs, competence in parenting, and toddlers' behavior and developmental status. *Infant Mental Health Journal, 24*(2), 126–148. doi: 10.1002/imhj.10048

Common Sense Media. (2013). *Zero to eight: Children's media use in America 2013.* San Francisco, CA: Common Sense Media.

Conners, N. A., Tripathi, S. P., Clubb, R., & Bradley, R. H. (2007). Maternal characteristics associated with television viewing habits of low-income preschool children. *Journal of Child and Family Studies, 16*(3), 415–425. doi: 10.1007/s10826-006-9095-0

Crockenberg, S. B. (1986). Are temperamental differences in babies associated with predictable differences in care giving? In J. V. Lerner & R. M. Lerner (Eds.), *New directions for child development: Vol. 31. Temperament and social interaction during infancy and childhood* (pp. 53–73). San Francisco, CA: Jossey-Bass.

Cupach, W. R., & Olson, L. N. (2006). Emotion regulation theory: A lens for viewing family conflict and violence. In D. O. Braithwaite & L. A. Baxter (Eds.), *Engaging theories in family communication: Multiple perspectives* (pp. 213–228). Thousand Oaks, CA: Sage.

Cutrona, C. E., & Troutman, B. R. (1986). Social support, infant temperament, and parenting self-efficacy: A mediational model of postpartum depression. *Child Development, 57*(6), 1507–1518. doi: 10.2307/1130428

Davé, S., Petersen, I., Sherr, L., & Nazareth, I. (2010). Incidence of maternal and paternal depression in primary care: A cohort study using a primary care database. *Archives of Pediatrics & Adolescent Medicine, 164*(11), 1038–1044. doi: 10.1001/archpediatrics.2010.184

Dawson, J. F. (2014). Moderation in management research: What, why, when, and how. *Journal of Business and Psychology, 29*(1), 1–19. doi: 10.1007/s10869-013-9308-7

DuRant, R. H., Thompson, W., Johnson, M., & Baranowski, T. (1996). The relationship among television watching, physical activity, and body composition of 5- or 6-year-old children. *Pediatric Exercise Science, 8*(1), 15–26.

Evans, C. A., Jordan, A. B., & Horner, J. (2011). Only two hours?: A qualitative study of the challenges parents perceive in restricting child television time. *Journal of Family Issues, 32*(9), 1223–1244. doi: 10.1177/0192513X11400558

Fitness, J., & Duffield, J. (2004). Emotion and communication in families. In A. L. Vangelisti (Ed.), *Handbook of family communication* (pp. 473–494). Mahwah, NJ: Lawrence Erlbaum.

Garrison, M. M., Liekweg, K., & Christakis, D. A. (2011). Media use and child sleep: The impact of content, timing, and environment. *Pediatrics, 128*(1), 29–35. doi: 10.1542/peds.2010-3304

Giles, L. C., Davies, M. J., Whitrow, M. J., Warin, M. J., & Moore, V. (2011). Maternal depressive symptoms and child care during toddlerhood relate to child behavior at age 5 years. *Pediatrics, 128*(1), e78–84. doi: 10.1542/peds.2010-3119

Gingold, J. A., Simon, A. E., & Schoendorf, K. C. (2014). Excess screen time in US children: Association with family rules and alternative activities. *Clinical Pediatrics, 53*(1), 41–50. doi: 10.1177/0009922813498152

Hall, A. (2005). Audience personality and the selection of media and media genres. *Media Psychology, 7*(4), 377–398. doi: 10.1207/S1532785XMEP0704

Hemphill, S., & Sanson, A. (2000, July). *Relations between toddler and preschooler temperament and parenting style in an Australian sample.* Paper presented at the Sixteenth Biennial Meetings of the International Society for the Study of Behavioral Development, Beijing, China.

Huston, A. C., Wright, J. C., Marquis, J., & Green, S. B. (1999). How young children spend their time: Television and other activities. *Developmental Psychology, 35*(4), 912–925. doi: 10.1037/0012-1649.35.4.912

Jordan, A. B. (1992). Social class, temporal orientation, and mass media use within the family system. *Critical Studies in Mass Communication, 9*(4), 374–386. doi: 10.1080/15295039209366840

Jordan, A. B. (2004). The role of media in children's development: An ecological perspective. *Developmental and Behavioral Pediatrics, 25*(3), 196–206.

Jordan, A. B. (2005). Learning to use books and television: An exploratory study in the ecological perspective. *American Behavioral Scientist, 48*(5), 523–538. doi: 10.1177/0002764204271513

Katainen, S., Räikkönen, K., & Keltikangas-Järvinen, L. (1997). Childhood temperament and mother's child-rearing attitudes: Stability and interaction in a three-year follow-up study. *European Journal of Personality, 11*(4), 249–265. doi: 10.1002/(SICI)1099-0984(199711)11: 4<249:: AID-PER289>3.0.CO;2-Y

Kim, J., & Oliver, M. B. (2013). How do we regulate sadness through entertainment messages? Exploring three predictions. *Journal of Broadcasting & Electronic Media, 57*(3), 374–391. doi: 10.1080/08838151.2013.816708

Kirzinger, A. E., Weber, C., & Johnson, M. (2012). Genetic and environmental influences on media use and communication behaviors. *Human Communication Research, 38*(2), 144–171. doi: 10.1111/j.1468-2958.2011.01424.x

Kochanska, G., Friesenborg, A. E., Lange, L. A., & Martel, M. M. (2004). Parents' personality and infants' temperament as contributors to their emerging relationship. *Journal of Personality and Social Psychology, 86*(5), 744–759. doi: 10.1037/0022-3514.86.5.744

Krosnick, J. A., Anand, S. N., & Hartl, S. P. (2003). Psychosocial predictors of heavy television viewing among preadolescents and adolescents. *Basic and Applied Social Psychology, 25*(2), 87–110. doi: 10.1207/S15324834BASP2502_1

Langstedt, E. R., & Atkin, D. J. (2013). An examination of personality traits and television viewing motives using patterns of interrelation and quadratic analysis. *Atlantic Journal of Communication, 21*(5), 278–293. doi: 10.1080/15456870.2013.842571

Laukkanen, J., Ojansuu, U., Tolvanen, A., Alatupa, S., & Aunola, K. (2014). Child's difficult temperament and mothers' parenting styles. *Journal of Child and Family Studies, 23*(2), 312–323. doi: 10.1007/s10826-013-9747-9

Lee, E. H., Zhou, Q., Eisenberg, N., & Wang, Y. (2013). Bidirectional relations between temperament and parenting styles in Chinese children. *International Journal of Behavioral Development, 37*(1), 57–67. doi: 10.1177/0165025412460795

Lull, J. (1990). *Inside family viewing: Ethnographic research on television audiences.* London: Routledge.

Mathiesen, K. S., & Tambs, K. (1999). The EAS temperament questionnaire—factor structure, age trends, reliability, and stability in a Norwegian sample. *Journal of Child Psychology and Psychiatry, 40*(3), 431–439. doi: 10.1111/1469-7610.00460

Mertesacker, B., Bade, U., Haverkock, A., & Pauli-Pott, U. (2004). Predicting maternal reactivity/sensitivity: The role of infant emotionality, maternal expressiveness/anxiety, and social support. *Infant Mental Health Journal, 25*(1), 47–61. doi: 10.1002/imhj.10085

Nathanson, A. I. (1999). Identifying and explaining the relationship between parental mediation and children's aggression. *Communication Research, 26*(2), 124–143. doi: 10.1177/009365099026002002

Nathanson, A. I. (2001). Mediation of children's television viewing: Working toward conceptual clarity and common understanding. *Communication Yearbook, 25*, 115–152.

Nathanson, A. I. (2015). Media and the family: Reflections and future directions. *Journal of Children and Media, 9*(1), 133–139. doi: 10.1080/17482798.2015.997145

Nathanson, A. I., Aladé, F., Sharp, M. L., Rasmussen, E. E., & Christy, K. (2014). The relation between television exposure and executive function among preschoolers. *Developmental Psychology, 50*(5), 1497–1506. doi: 10.1037/a0035714

Nathanson, A. I., & Fries, P. T. (2014). Television exposure, sleep time, and neuropsychological function among preschoolers. *Media Psychology, 17*(3), 237–261. doi: 10.1080/15213269.2014.915197

Nathanson, A. I., & Manohar, U. (2012). Attachment, working models of parenting, and expectations for using television in childrearing. *Family Relations, 61*(3), 441–454. doi: 10.1111/j.1741-3729.2012.00701.x

Olson, L. N., Baiocchi-Wagner, E., Wilson-Kratzer, J. M., & Symonds, S. (2012). *The dark side of family communication.* Cambridge, UK: Polity Press.

Pagani, L. S., Fitzpatrick, C., Barnett, T. A., & Dubow, E. (2010). Prospective associations between early childhood television exposure and academic, psychosocial, and physical well-being by middle childhood. *Archives of Pediatrics & Adolescent Medicine, 164*(5), 425–431. doi: 10.1001/archpediatrics.2010.50

Pauli-Pott, U., Mertesacker, B., & Bade, U. (2000). Contexts of relations of infant negative emotionality to caregiver's reactivity/sensitivity. *Infant Behavior and Development, 23*(1), 23–39. doi: 10.1016/S0163-6383(00)00029-1

Pinon, M. F., Huston, A. C., & Wright, J. C. (1989). Family ecology and child characteristics that predict young children's educational television viewing. *Child Development, 60*(4), 846–856. doi: 10.2307/1131026

Potts, R., & Sanchez, D. (1994). Television viewing and depression: No news is good news. *Journal of Broadcasting & Electronic Media, 38*(1), 79–90. doi: 10.1080/08838159409364247

Putnam, S. P., Sanson, A. V., & Rothbart, M. K. (2002). Child temperament and parenting. In M. H. Bornstein (Ed.), *Handbook of parenting: Volume I: Children and parenting* (pp. 255–277). Mahwah, NJ: Lawrence Erlbaum.

Radesky, J. S., Silverstein, M., Zuckerman, B., & Christakis, D. A. (2014). Infant self-regulation and early childhood media exposure. *Pediatrics, 133*(5), e1172–e1178. doi: 10.1542/peds.2013-2367

Rideout, V., & Hamel, E. (2006). *The media family: Electronic media in the lives of infants, toddlers, preschoolers and their parents.* Menlo Park, CA: Kaiser Family Foundation.

Rubin, K. H., Hastings, P., Chen, X., Stewart, S., & McNichol, K. (1998). Intrapersonal and maternal correlates of aggression, conflict, and externalizing problems in toddlers. *Child Development, 69*(6), 1614–1629.

Rumpf, H. J., Meyer, C., Hapke, U., & John, U. (2001). Screening for mental health: Validity of the MHI-5 using DSM-IV Axis I psychiatric disorders as gold standard. *Psychiatry Research, 105*(3), 243–253.

Sanson, A., Hemphill, S., & Smart, D. (2004). Connections between temperament and social development: A review. *Social Development, 13*(1), 142–170.

Scaramella, L. V., & Leve, L. D. (2004). Clarifying parent-child reciprocities during early childhood: The early childhood coercion model. *Clinical Child and Family Psychology Review, 7*(2), 89–107. doi: 10.1023/B:CCFP.0000030287.13160.a3

Segrin, C. (2006). Family interactions and well-being: Integrative perspectives. *Journal of Family Communication, 6*(1), 3–21. doi: 10.1207/s15327698jfc0601

Sherry, J. L. (2001). Toward an etiology of media use motivations: The role of temperament in media use. *Communication Monographs, 68*(3), 274–288. doi: 10.1080/03637750128065

Sherry, J. L. (2004). Media effects theory and the nature/nurture debate: A historical overview and directions for future research. *Media Psychology, 6*(1), 83–109. doi: 10.1207/s1532785xmep0601

Shim, J. W., & Paul, B. (2007). Effects of personality types on the use of television genre. *Journal of Broadcasting & Electronic Media, 51*(2), 287–304. doi: 10.1080/08838150701304852

Taras, H. L., Sallis, J. F., Nader, P. R., & Nelson, J. (1990). Children's television-viewing habits and the family environment. *Archives of Pediatrics & Adolescent Medicine, 144*(3), 357–359. doi: 10.1001/archpedi.1990.02150270107036

Taylor, C. L., & Friedman, R. S. (2015). Sad mood and music choice: Does the self-relevance of the mood-eliciting stimulus moderate song preference? *Media Psychology, 18*(1), 24–50. doi: 10.1080/15213269.2013.826589

Thakkar, R. R., Garrison, M. M., & Christakis, D. A. (2006). A systematic review for the effects of television viewing by infants and preschoolers. *Pediatrics, 118*(5), 2025–2031. doi: 10.1542/peds.2006-1307

Thompson, A. L., Adair, L. S., & Bentley, M. E. (2013). Maternal characteristics and perception of temperament associated with infant TV exposure. *Pediatrics*, *131*(2), e390–e397. doi: 10.1542/peds.2012-1224

Thompson, D. A., & Christakis, D. A. (2007). The association of maternal mental distress with television viewing in children under 3 years old. *Ambulatory Pediatrics*, *7*(1), 32–37. doi: 10.1016/j.ambp.2006.09.007

Trapolini, T., Ungerer, J. A., & McMahon, C. A. (2008). Maternal depression: Relations with maternal caregiving representations and emotional availability during the preschool years. *Attachment & Human Development*, *10*(1), 73–90. doi: 10.1080/14616730801900712

Tremblay, M. S., Leblanc, A. G., Kho, M. E., Saunders, T. J., Larouche, R., Colley, R. C., … Connor Gorber, S. (2011). Systematic review of sedentary behaviour and health indicators in school-aged children and youth. *The International Journal of Behavioral Nutrition and Physical Activity*, *8*(1), 98. doi: 10.1186/1479-5868-8-98

Vaala, S. E. (2014). The nature and predictive value of mothers' beliefs regarding infants' and toddlers' TV/video viewing: Applying the integrative model of behavioral prediction. *Media Psychology*, *17*(3), 282–310. doi: 10.1080/15213269.2013.872995

Vandewater, E. A., Bickham, D. S., & Lee, J. H. (2006). Time well spent? Relating television use to children's free-time activities. *Pediatrics*, *117*(2), e181–e191. doi: 10.1542/peds.2005-0812

Vandewater, E. A., Bickham, D. S., Lee, J. H., Cummings, H. M., Wartella, E. A., & Rideout, V. J. (2005). When the television is always on: Heavy television exposure and young children's development. *American Behavioral Scientist*, *48*(5), 562–577. doi: 10.1177/0002764204271496

Vitaro, F., Barker, E. D., Boivin, M., Brendgen, M., & Tremblay, R. E. (2006). Do early difficult temperament and harsh parenting differentially predict reactive and proactive aggression? *Journal of Abnormal Child Psychology*, *34*(5), 685–695. doi: 10.1007/s10802-006-9055-6

Wartella, E., Rideout, V., Lauricella, A. R., & Connell, S. L. (2013). *Parenting in the age of digital technology: A national survey*. Evanston, IL: Northwestern University.

Zillman, D., & Bryant, J. (1994). Entertainment as media effect. In J. Bryant & D. Zillman (Eds.), *Media effects: Advances in theory and research*. Mahwah, NJ: Lawrence Erlbaum Associates, Inc.

Zimmerman, F. J., & Christakis, D. A. (2007). Associations between content types of early media exposure and subsequent attentional problems. *Pediatrics*, *120*(5), 986–992. doi: 10.1542/peds.2006-3322

NOTE

1. Wednesday was singled out because children do not attend preschool on Wednesday afternoons in Belgium, which typically creates extra opportunities to watch television.

PART TWO

Family Interactions AND Processes

CHAPTER SIX

Marital Hostility AND Parent-Youth Hostility During Early Adolescence

CHERYL BUEHLER, BRIDGET B. WEYMOUTH, & NAN ZHOU

Human Development and Family Studies, University of North Carolina Greensboro

The dark side of family communication was investigated by examining the association between marital hostility and parent-youth hostility during early adolescence. Disagreements among family members are inevitable within family systems (Canary, Cupach, & Serpe, 2001), and we conceptualize these differences and incompatibilities as part of typical family functioning. Theoretically, disagreement can result in relationship growth or it can be a risk factor for relationship problems, depending upon the strategies used to manage the differences (Buehler et al., 1998; Koerner & Fitzpatrick, 2002). Expressed hostility is one of the employed strategies in which relationship risk can manifest in families (Buehler, Benson, & Gerard, 2006). We define expressed hostility as specific, overt behavior and expressed communication between family members that includes angry comments, insults, contempt, yelling, swearing, name-calling, and/or physical aggression (Buehler, 2006; Buehler, Krishnakumar, Anthony, Tittsworth, & Stone, 1994).

Early adolescence is an important time to examine the interrelationships between marital and parent-child functioning (Van Doorn, Branje, & Meeus, 2007). Adolescence has been characterized as a transformational period in which conflict between parents and children can serve adaptive relationship functions, as well as a time of increased risk if these conflicts are managed with hostility or arise against a backdrop of broader family problems (Steinberg, 1990). Interconnections with marital hostility are important during this developmental period because the spillover of negative affect and behavior into parent-child relationships may create demands on youth and parents that tax psychological resources needed for developmental tasks (Lindahl, Bregman, & Malik, 2012). Moreover, marital hostility might provide negative templates for intimate relationship functioning during a period in which youth are developing intimate relationship skills and capacities (Buehler, Lange, & Franck, 2007; Linder & Collins, 2005). The current study examined the associations between observed hostile behavior in two central dyads in families—the marital dyad and the parent-youth dyad—during this important developmental period of early adolescence. Four waves of data when youth were in sixth through ninth grades were analyzed from a community-based sample of 416 two-parent families in which the child was a product of the parental union by birth or adoption.

THEORETICAL AND EMPIRICAL BACKGROUND

This study was framed using family systems theory. Three central propositions from the framework were utilized (Cox & Paley, 1997). First, individuals and subsystems (e.g., dyads) are interdependent, and this interdependence is characterized by mutual, though not necessarily equal, influence (Whitchurch & Constantine, 1993). Second, dyads have boundaries, and the nature of influence across dyads depends, in part, on the relative openness of the boundaries (Fosco & Grych, 2010). These influences across dyads can occur at any given point in time and/or across time. Implications of these two propositions for the current study are that there may be a stronger relationship between marital hostility and parent-youth hostility over time in families that have relatively more open boundaries across these two subsystems when compared to families that have somewhat less open boundaries across these two dyads (see a similar suggestion regarding interdependence in Segrin & Arroyo, this volume).

The specific nature of influence, however, might be different when thinking about how parents and youth each contribute to these patterns of mutual influence and overly permeable boundaries. With regard to parents' behavior, marital hostility is thought to affect parent-youth hostility via a negative spillover process (Cox, Paley, & Harter, 2001). Spillover is conceptualized as the transfer of mood, affect, or behavior across family subsystems (Erel & Burman, 1995). We focus specifically on the transfer of negative behaviors across the boundaries of the marital and parent-youth subsystems. Negative affect may come into play by hampering parents' abilities to engage in effective partnering or parenting behaviors (Canary & Messman, 2000). Most of the negative spillover literature has focused, in particular, on the spillover of marital hostility into negative parenting practices or parent-youth conflict/hostility (Canary & Canary, 2013).

With regards to youths' behavior in these dyadic contexts, marital hostility is posited to affect their relationships with parents, in part, through modeling

(Margolin, Christensen, & John, 1996). Youth are observers of the marital relationship. As such, the marital relationship may serve as a template and example for emotional expression and problem solving between relationship partners (Linder & Collins, 2005; Minuchin, 1985). Youth also may act out or behave aggressively to side track parents from their own negative marital interactions (Fosco & Grych, 2008; Schermerhorn, Cummings, DeCarlo, & Davies, 2007).

A third theoretical proposition utilized is that subsystems within families are organized hierarchically (Minuchin, 1985). Systems theory suggests that subsystems and individuals with less power are more susceptible to the influences of more powerful subsystems and individuals. The marital subsystem is theorized to have more power than other subsystems, and this power differential supports healthy family functioning (Bowen, 1978; Minuchin, 1985; Whitchurch & Constantine, 1993). As such, adolescents are more likely to be affected by marital hostility than is marital functioning by parent-youth hostility (Van Doorn et al., 2007).

Although much of the work on the interconnections between marital and parent-child subsystems has focused on the directional spillover effect from the marital relationship to the parent-child relationship, the idea of mutual influence suggests that parent-child hostility also might shape marital hostility over time (Margolin et al., 1996). Potential mechanisms for these linkages may include parental cognitions such as parental efficacy (Moore & Buehler, 2011), youth-initiated triangulation (Fosco & Grych, 2010), differences in the types of cognitive biases demonstrated by parents and youth (Noller, Feeney, Sheehan, & Peterson, 2000; Sillars, Smith, & Koerner, 2010), coparenting difficulties (Margolin, Gordis, & John, 2001), and youth adjustment difficulties to family stressors (Davies & Lindsay, 2004; Schermerhorn, Chow, & Cummings, 2010; Schermerhorn, Cummings, DeCarlo, & Davies, 2007). Although systems theory suggests this potential bidirectionality between marital and parent-youth subsystems, it also suggests that pathways from marital functioning to parent-youth functioning are stronger than those pathways from parent-youth functioning because of the power embedded in the marital subsystem and the hierarchical structuring of these two subsystems in families.

In addition to theory, evidence from cross-sectional studies supports the hypothesis that marital hostility and parent-youth hostility are interdependent. Based on 31 effects, Krishnakumar and Buehler (2000) found a moderately strong, concurrent association between marital hostility and parenting quality (mean effect size = -.32, $p < .05$). In support of our focus on early adolescence, the association was stronger for older children than for younger children. Cross-sectional studies published since the 2000 meta-analysis also have found a positive association between marital conflict and parent-adolescent conflict in a national sample of families (Buehler & Gerard, 2002) and when using observational data (Low & Stocker, 2005).

Short- and long-term longitudinal research also supports the hypothesis of a positive association between marital and parent-youth hostility. In their meta-analysis, Krishnakumar and Buehler (2000) found a significant association between marital conflict and parenting quality over time (mean effect size = .18, $p < .05$). More recently, Chung, Flook, and Fuligni (2009) used daily diary methods and found that marital hostility was associated with both mother-youth ($r = .30$) and father-youth hostility ($r = .25$). Gerard, Krishnakumar, and Buehler (2005) used data from the National Survey on Families and Households (NSFH) and found that marital conflict was associated with parent-adolescent conflict five years later ($\beta = .16$, $p < .05$). Using questionnaire data, Van Doorn et al. (2007) studied Belgian families during early adolescence and found that marital hostility predicted parent-adolescent hostility over two years but that parent-adolescent hostility did not predict subsequent marital hostility. The current study extends these findings by examining the interconnections across four annual waves of data, by using observational assessments of hostility, and by distinguishing between mother- and father-youth relationships.

Moderating Factors: The Role of Individual Family Member Characteristics

Meta-analyses suggest that variability exists in the association between marital hostility and parent-youth hostility (Krishnakumar & Buehler, 2000). As described below, therefore, we examined the moderating effect of four factors that might explain some of this variability: youth gender, youths' appraisals of threat associated with witnessing marital conflict, mothers' depressive symptoms, and fathers' depressive symptoms. This selection of factors was based, in part, on our belief that it is important to consider possible moderating influences from individual family members in the dyads when trying to understand the association between two dyadic family subsystems and by models of communication which suggest that the study of relational processes is strengthened by considering individual factors (Caughlin & Vangelisti, 2006; Cupach, 2000).

Youth gender. Varying perspectives informed our considerations of potential youth gender moderating effects. Davies and Lindsay (2004) suggest that marital conflict may be associated differently with various youth outcomes for sons and daughters and that these gendered patterns differ for younger and older children. They cite literature that suggests that the deleterious effects of marital conflict are stronger for sons than daughters when children are young but are stronger for daughters than sons during early adolescence. Davies and Lindsay found support for daughters' differential susceptibility to the stressful aspects of witnessing marital conflict and found that these effects were stronger when youth held gendered beliefs regarding the importance of valued closeness and concern for others in relationships (which they termed communion beliefs). Tendencies toward communion exacerbated the negative effects of witnessing marital conflict on youth internalizing problems. Cross-sectional research also has found that the association between marital conflict/hostility and parent-adolescent conflict/hostility is stronger for daughters than for sons (Buehler & Gerard, 2002; Krishnakumar & Buehler, 2000).

Other scholars have suggested that associations between marital functioning and youth's relational behavior may be stronger for sons than for daughters. For example, some literature on exposure to marital conflict and youths' romantic relationships during adolescence suggests that, when witnessing marital conflict, boys are more likely than girls to learn and internalize beliefs that aggression is acceptable behavior in intimate relationships (Kinsfogel & Grych, 2004; Simon & Furman, 2010). Extending this theorizing to the parent-youth relationship, boys may come to believe that aggression is appropriate in close relationships by witnessing their fathers' aggressive behavior with their partners. Given these two potential contradictory gender perspectives, we did not forecast the direction of youth gender moderating effects.

Youth appraisal of threat. The cognitive-contextual theory of marital conflict suggests that children assess threat associated with witnessing marital conflict as part of their initial response to this familial stressor (Grych & Fincham, 1990). This primary appraisal of threat level serves an adaptive function that guides subsequent coping behaviors. Although adaptive in the short term, over time these threat appraisals may become a stable template or schema that becomes an additional risk factor for less healthy youth adjustment and functioning (Fosco, Deboard, & Grych, 2007; Grych & Cardoza-Fernandes, 2001). Empirical evidence suggests that threat appraisals exacerbate the deleterious association between marital conflict and children's/youths' adjustment and aggression in dating relationships (El-Sheikh & Harger, 2001; Kerig, 1998; Simon & Furman, 2010). We extended this work by testing the hypothesis that youths' appraisals of threat across early adolescence (i.e., schemas) exacerbate the positive association between marital hostility and parent-youth hostility.

Parents' depressive symptoms. Systems theory suggests a family-wide process model of parent and youth functioning (Cummings, Davies, & Campbell, 2000). Canary and Canary (2013) suggest that, in addition to being a constellation of individual experiences, depression is a communication phenomenon. As such, parental depressive symptoms is one of the parental features that is associated with parenting, children's behavior, and marital functioning (Downey & Coyne, 1990; Du Rocher Schudlich, Papp, & Cummings, 2011; Segrin & Arroyo, this volume).

Although there is evidence of bidirectional effects between marital conflict and parents' depressive symptoms, longitudinal research has supported the proposition that lower marital quality predicts increases in depressive symptoms over time (Proulx, Helms, & Buehler, 2007).

Additionally, family stress theory (McCubbin & Patterson, 1983) suggests that parents' depressive symptoms may exacerbate the association between marital hostility and parent-youth hostility. Segrin (2000) also suggests that poor social skills and negative life events may interact to increase adults' depressive symptoms. Expressed hostility in each dyad functions as a stressor in some families, and individual member resources are expected to mitigate deleterious, system-wide reverberations. Parental depression might decrease the behavioral and emotional resources that parents have to manage marital or parent-child conflict, engage in a positive manner with children and spouses, and enact needed boundary maintenance strategies. Although few studies have examined the interaction between parents' depressive symptoms manifested across early adolescence and marital hostility, there is some evidence that co-experiencing these family stressors compromises parent-child interactions and child well-being (Kouros, Merrilees, & Cummings, 2008; Kouros, Papp, Goeke-Morey, & Cummings, 2014; Segrin & Arroyo, this volume). Both mothers' and fathers' depressive symptoms may compromise systemic functioning, and thus potential crossover effects need to be considered (e.g., fathers' depressive symptoms moderating effects of marital hostility on mother-youth hostility; Du Rocher Schudlich et al., 2011; Kane & Garber, 2004; Kouros et al., 2014; Segrin & Fitzpatrick, 1992). Thus, we tested the potential exacerbating effects of parents' depressive symptoms by aggregating symptomatology across the four data waves of early adolescence and by examining the moderating effects of mothers' and fathers' symptoms in both the mother-youth hostility and father-youth hostility models so as to examine personal and crossover moderating effects.

In sum, based on both theoretical and empirical literature, the following research questions were addressed in this study:

RQ1: Does marital hostility spillover into parent-youth hostility? We hypothesized that marital hostility is associated with increases in parent-youth hostility one year later (mother-youth and father-youth hostility).

RQ2: Does parent-youth hostility spillover into marital hostility? We hypothesized that parent-youth hostility is associated with increases in marital hostility one year later (mother-youth and father-youth hostility).

RQ3: Does youth gender moderate these spillover associations? Given inconsistent theoretical and empirical renderings, we did not make a directional hypothesis.

RQ4: Do youths' appraisals of threat associated with marital conflict moderate these spillover associations? We hypothesized that these appraisals would exacerbate the spillover from marital hostility to parent-youth hostility.

RQ5: Does parents' depressive affect moderate these spillover associations? We hypothesized that both mothers' and fathers' depressive symptoms would exacerbate personal and crossover spillover effects.

Each of these research questions was examined in analyses that controlled for stable hostile interactions across time (i.e., the stability coefficients for marital and parent-youth hostility) and for the concurrent associations between marital hostility and parent-youth hostility at each of the four data waves during early adolescence.

METHOD

Sampling Procedures and Characteristics

This longitudinal sample was taken from a cross-sectional study of marital conflict during early adolescence. For this larger study, 2,346 sixth-grade youth from 13 middle schools in a large, geographically diverse county in the southeastern United States completed a survey about family life. Homeroom teachers sent study recruitment materials home with youth. Two follow-up postal mailings also were sent to parents. Parents consented to their child's participation, and youth assented to complete a questionnaire on family life. This sample of youth was representative of the families in the county on race, parents' marital status, and family poverty status.

Two-parent families for this study were recruited from the larger sample of youth using the following criteria: parents were married or long-term cohabitants, and no stepchildren were in or out of the home. Married or long-term cohabitants were examined because the association between marital conflict and parenting is stronger in married than divorced families (Krishnakumar & Buehler, 2000). Stepfamilies were not included because stepfamilies have complex structures that differ from ever-married families, and a careful study would need to include adequate sample sizes of these various structures to conduct group comparisons, which was beyond the scope of the present study.

Of the 1,131 eligible families from the larger study, 416 (37%) agreed to participate. This response rate was similar to that in studies that have included three or four family members and have used intensive data collection protocols (e.g., National Survey of Families and Households—34%). Using information from the initial youth survey for selection analyses, eligible participating families were similar to eligible nonparticipating families on all study variables, suggesting minimal selection bias.

At wave 1 (W1), when youth were in the sixth grade, youth age ranged from 11 to 14 (M = 11.86, SD = .69). There were 211 daughters (51%). In terms of race, 91% of the families were European American and 3% were African American. This 3% is lower than the percentage of married African American couples with their own children younger than 18 in the county (5%) and in the United States (7.8%) (U.S. Census, 2000, Table PCT27 of SF4). The median level of parents' education in this sample was an associate's degree (two years of college). Parents' educational attainment was similar to that of European American adults in the county who were older than 24 (county median category was some college, no degree; U.S. Census, 2000, Table P148A of SF4). The median level of 2001 household income for families in this study was about $70,000, which was higher than the median 1999 income for married-couple families in the county ($64,689 inflation-adjusted 2001 dollars, U.S. Census, 2000, Table PCT40 of SF3).

To further demonstrate the utility of this sample for the present study, the distribution of marital hostility at W1 (sixth grade) was compared to norms and national distributions. The prevalence of physical marital aggression in the present sample (6.7%) was comparable to rates found in the 1985 National Survey of Family Violence (NSFV; 3.4%) and 1994 National Survey of Families and Households (NSFH; 6.4%) (Straus & Gelles, 1986; Sweet & Bumpass, 2005). The rate of verbal aggression in the sample (78.4%) was comparable to that found in the 1985 NSFV (75%).

Data Collection Procedures

For the larger study and after signing assent forms, youth completed a 40-minute questionnaire about family life and personal well-being during school. This was done in the lunchroom in groups of 30 to 45 youth. Seven to eight research assistants and the project director were present to respond to questions. For the longitudinal study, parents and youth were each mailed a questionnaire and asked to complete it independently (sealed envelope). Completed, sealed questionnaires were collected during the home visit. Parents reaffirmed consent for their child's participation, and each family member provided assent each time data were collected.

Family members also participated in several interaction tasks during the home visit. Home visitors were trained research assistants, hired primarily from the community with extensive experience working with teens and families (e.g., former school teachers). Home visitors were trained to use the data collection protocol by the project director. Two home visitors conducted each home visit. Coded data from two observational tasks were used in the present study. The first task was a problem-solving discussion. This task involved the mother, father, and youth and focused on trying to solve issues of contention selected by family members using the Family Issues Checklist (Conger et al., 1993). The home visitors selected eight areas of disagreements from family members' reports, beginning first with issues identified by all three family members. During the 20-minute discussion task, family members were asked to elaborate on a given issue, identify who usually is involved, and suggest possible solutions. Participants were told they need not get through all of the issues. The second task lasted for 20 minutes, included only the wife and husband, and focused on the marital relationship, conflict strategies, and coparenting.

The semistructured interaction was videotaped. Trained coders rated the interaction using the Iowa Family Interaction Rating Scales (IFIRS; Melby & Conger, 2001). After over 250 hours of training, coders passed an extensive written exam (90% correct criterion) and a viewing exam (criterion level 80% match with ratings by experienced Iowa State University coders). Each family member's behavior was coded during each task. Within each family, different trained coders rated the interaction from the two tasks to minimize coder carryover effects. To assess interrater reliability, a second coder rated 20% of the tasks.

As part of the longitudinal design, assessments were conducted one (W2), two (W3), and three (W4) years later. Most youth were in seventh grade at W2 (mean age = 12.84), in eighth grade at W3 (mean age = 13.83), and in ninth grade at W4 (mean age = 14.84). Data collection procedures were identical for each wave. There were 366 participating families at W2, 340 families at W3, and 320 at W4 (77% retention of W1 families). Families were paid $100 for their participation in W1, $120 for W2, $135 for W3, and $150 for W4. Attrition analyses using MANOVA indicated that there were no differences between the retained and attrited families on any of the study variables.

Measurement

Marital hostility. At each wave, marital hostility was measured using eight observer ratings from the IFIRS. The two content ratings were hostility and antisocial behavior. Each content rating was scored for behavior from wife to husband and husband to wife. Expressed hostility and antisocial behavior were rated from the assessed interaction during the family problem-solving task (youth present) and the marital task (youth not present). Different coders rated the interaction from each of these two tasks. In the IFIRS (Melby et al., 1990), hostile behavior was defined as displays of hostile, angry, critical, disapproving, or rejecting behavior from one family member to another. Antisocial behavior was defined as displays of behavior that are insensitive, obnoxious, rude, uncooperative, or unsociable. The response format for the rating scale ranged from 1 (not characteristic) to 9 (mainly characteristic). The marital hostility measure for this study was created by averaging the eight observer ratings for each data wave (αs range .82–.90). The mean intraclass correlation (ICC) across interrater reliability coders was .74.

Parent-youth hostility. At each wave, parent-youth hostility was measured using four observer ratings from the IFIRS. Hostility and antisocial behavior during the problem-solving task were scored for behavior from parent to youth and youth to parent. At each wave, the measure of mother-youth hostility and father-youth hostility was created by averaging the four observer ratings (αs range .80–.90). The average ICC was .76.

Moderating variables. *Youth gender* was dummy coded (0 = daughters, 1 = sons). At each wave, youths' primary appraisals of *perceived threat* associated with interparental conflict was measured using the six-item subscale from the Children's Perceptions of Interparental Conflict scale (Grych, Seid, & Fincham, 1992) and two items from the conflict resolution subscale of the Multidimensional Assessment of Interparental Conflict (Tschann et al., 1999). A sample item was "When my parents argue I'm afraid something bad will happen." Items were standardized and averaged. Youths' perceptions of perceived threat across the four waves were averaged (αs range .85–.90). At each wave of data collection, mothers and fathers completed the 20-item Center for Epidemiological Studies on Depression measure to assess *parental depressive symptoms* (CES-D; Radloff, 1977). Scores were averaged across the four waves to create one score for mothers' depressive symptoms and one score for fathers' depressive symptoms (αs range .85–.92).

Analytic Procedures

Cross-lagged path analytic models (AMOS 22) were used to examine the associations between marital hostility and parent-youth hostility across early adolescence. Separate models were estimated for mother-youth hostility and father-youth hostility. In contrast to other longitudinal analytic designs, cross-lagged models provide unique insight into the relationships between the marital dyad and the parent-youth dyad because they allow estimation of the relationships between variables of interest while simultaneously controlling for the within-construct correlation (i.e., stability estimates), the cross-sectional concurrent associations between variables, and potential reciprocal associations. Cross-lagged models also allow for the estimation of year-to-year developmental fluctuations in the relationship between marital hostility and parent-youth hostility (McArdle, 2009). There was minimal missing data within each wave (less than 3%). Full information maximum likelihood estimation (FIML) was used to address missing values both within and across waves and is preferable to deleting cases (Schafer & Graham, 2002).

The moderating hypotheses were tested using multiple-group analysis in AMOS. Several cut points were used when examining the moderating role of perceived threat and parents' depressive symptoms in order to assess sensitivity: top 33%, top 25%, and the clinical point in the case of depressive symptoms. The multiple-group analysis was conducted in two steps. First, the cross-lagged model was estimated across the two moderating subgroups with all of the statistical parameters constrained to be the same. Beginning with a fully constrained model minimizes the chance of interpreting the differences inaccurately given all of the remaining parameters are constrained to equality across groups. This analysis produced a chi-square estimate of overall fit for the fully constrained model across two groups. Second, a new model was estimated in which six regression paths (i.e., structural paths) were allowed to vary across the moderating subgroups: (a) each path from marital hostility to parent-youth hostility and (b) each path from parent-youth hostility to marital hostility. This second analysis produced a chi-square estimate of overall fit for the "partially freed" model across two groups. These two chi-square estimates were compared using the chi-square difference test with six degrees of freedom because six paths were allowed to vary in the second analysis. A significant difference in chi-squares indicated that one of the focal associations differed across the two subgroups. The specific nature of the difference was identified using the Critical Ratio (C. R.) estimates in AMOS, which distribute as Z scores; C. R.s greater than 1.96 were considered statistically significant ($p < .05$). If a significant difference between groups was found, the regression coefficients were examined across the two groups to determine the direction of the difference.

RESULTS

The descriptive statistics for the study variables are shown in Table 1. The correlations between marital hostility and parent-youth hostility were statistically significant and in the expected directions.

Marital Hostility and Mother-Youth Hostility

Results from the cross-lagged path analysis are shown in Figure 1. The stability coefficients for marital hostility in this model ranged from .48 to .59. These were statistically significant but not particularly strong in terms of stability effect sizes. Thus, marital hostility was relatively stable over time, but there also was a fair amount of unexplained variance across waves. The same pattern characterized mother-youth hostility, with stability coefficients that ranged from .43 to .52. The within-wave associations between marital hostility and parent-youth hostility were positive and significant; associations ranged from .18 (ninth grade) to .31 (seventh grade).

The central hypothesis of this study was that marital hostility "spills over" into the parent-youth relationship during early adolescence through positive associations with parent-youth hostility across time (RQ1 hypothesis). This hypothesis was supported for two of the three tests in the mother model. Controlling for the reverse association from mother-youth hostility to marital hostility, marital

Table 1. Descriptive Statistics and Correlations.

Variables	1	2	3	4	5	6	7	8	9	10	11
1. Marital hostility – 6th grade		.51	.53	.40	.28	.22	.15	.15	-.00	.21	.20
2. Marital hostility – 7th grade	.51	-	.58	.51	.27	.40	.21	.29	-.04	.15	.18
3. Marital hostility – 8th grade	.53	.58	-	.53	.21	.24	.28	.27	.03	.11	.21
4. Marital hostility – 9th grade	.40	.51	.53	-	.20	.27	.23	.29	.03	.13	.19
5. Parent-youth hostility – 6th grade	.35	.24	.25	.27	-	.46	.44	.50	-.03	.13	.08
6. Parent-youth hostility – 7th grade	.26	.40	.32	.32	.42	-	.51	.51	-.06	.19	.18
7. Parent-youth hostility – 8th grade	.30	.34	.43	.33	.48	.54	-	.53	-.03	.12	.09
8. Parent-youth hostility – 9th grade	.25	.33	.29	.37	.50	.54	.53	-	-.03	.10	.13
9. Youth gender	-.00	-.04	.03	.03	-.01	-.05	-.07	-.06	-	.00	.03
10. Youth perceived IPC threat	.21	.15	.11	.13	.21	.10	.19	.19	.00	-	.17
11. Parents' depressive symptoms	.15	.15	.15	.19	.16	.17	.10	.14	.03	.13	-
M	2.67	2.82	2.75	2.58	3.75	3.88	3.72	3.61	.49	-.01	8.03
					3.61	3.69	3.59	3.38			7.45
SD	1.21	1.23	1.17	1.09	1.59	1.68	1.47	1.53	.50	.60	6.79
					1.59	1.66	1.44	1.49			6.41

Note: Mother-youth model variables are in the upper triangle. Father-youth model variables are in the lower triangle. The means and SDs that are specific to the mother model are in the first mean row; the means and SDs that are specific to the father model are in the second row. Perceived threat is a standardized variable. Bolded correlations are significant at $p < .05$.

hostility when youth were in sixth grade was associated with higher mother-youth hostility during seventh grade; marital hostility during eighth grade was associated with higher mother-youth hostility during ninth grade.

The second research question (RQ2) and associated hypothesis was that mother-youth hostility is positively associated with subsequent marital hostility. This was partially supported. Mother-youth hostility during sixth grade was associated with greater marital hostility when youth were in seventh grade.

Moderating effects. We also examined the potential moderating effects of youth gender, youths' primary appraisals of marital conflict in terms of perceived threat, and parents' depressive affect. Addressing the third research question (RQ3) regarding potential youth gender differences, none of the paths in the model displayed in Figure 1 differed across daughters and sons.

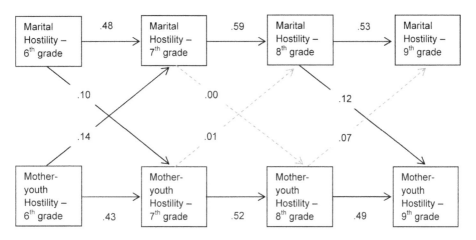

Fig 1. Marital hostility and mother-youth hostility.
Estimates for solid lines were significant at $p < .05$. Estimates for dotted lines were statistically non-significant. The cross-sectional association between marital hostility and mother-youth hostility was .28 at 6th grade, .31 at 7th grade, .22 at 8th grade, and .18 at 9th grade, all $p < .05$.

Focusing next on the fourth research question that addressed the moderating role of perceived threat from marital conflict, we conducted separate analyses using two different cut points to form groups, the top 33% of the sample (versus others) and the top 25% of the sample. Neither of the omnibus tests at 6 df (i.e., whole model test) were statistically significant, suggesting that youths' perceived threat does not moderate the associations between marital hostility and mother-youth hostility over time.

Rather than conducting an omnibus moderating test for the six paths, some multiple-group moderating analyses conduct repeated comparison tests, one association at a time (e.g., Brody et al., 2006; Herman, Lambert, Reinke, & Ialongo, 2008). Although this increases the chance of capitalizing on Type I errors, we also examined the significance of the individual paths given that recent research has utilized this analytic procedure. One of the six individual path comparisons was significant [as evidence by a critical ratio (C. R.) value of greater than 1.96]. The association between marital hostility during sixth grade and mother-youth hostility during seventh grade in the subsample of youth who scored in the top third of perceived threat was significant ($b = .18, p < .05$) but was not significant for the other youth (b = .06, *ns*) (C. R. = 2.18). Thus, there was some evidence that lower levels of perceived threat buffered some of the spillover effects of marital hostility (sixth and seventh grades), but there also was evidence that this protective effect (or vulnerability in terms of higher levels of threat) did not sustain to spillover effects during eighth and ninth grades. Given that this finding may have occurred by chance, this finding should be considered cautiously.

Three separate analyses were conducted to examine the moderating role of mothers' depressive symptoms (part of RQ6): top 33% of mothers (versus others), top 25% of mothers, and the clinical cut point of a score of 16 or higher on the CES-D. Moderating effects were significant for the last analysis. The model in Figure 1 differed for families in which mothers' were in the clinical range of depressive symptom scores ($\Delta\chi^2$ = 19.50, *df* = 6, p = .003). One of six paths differed. Consistent with the finding from youth perceived threat, marital hostility during sixth grade was associated with increased mother-youth hostility during seventh grade in the subsample of families with mothers at the clinical level of depressive symptoms (b = .17, p < .01) but was not significant for the other families (b = .06, *ns*) (C. R. = 2.06).

The last set of moderating analyses for the mother-youth model focused on the potential "crossover" moderating effects of fathers' depressive symptoms (i.e., the second part of RQ5). Two of the three models (not the clinical model) were significant, and the pattern of results was similar across the two analyses. Using the results from the top 33% of families, two of six paths differed across the father symptoms groups. As with mothers' depressive symptoms, marital hostility during sixth grade was associated with increased mother-youth hostility during seventh grade in the subsample of families with fathers in the top third of depressive symptoms (b = .15, p < .01) but was not significant for the other families (b = .05, *ns*) (C. R. = 2.50). In addition, mother-youth hostility during eighth grade was associated with increased marital hostility when youth were in ninth grade in the subsample of families with fathers who were in the top 33% of depressive symptom scores (b = .12, p < .05) but was not significant for the other families (b = .03, *ns*) (C. R. = 2.46).

Marital Hostility and Father-Youth Hostility

Analyses were replicated by focusing on father-youth hostility. Results from the father-youth model are shown in Figure 2. The stability coefficients for marital hostility in this model ranged from .48 to .56. The stability coefficients for father-youth hostility ranged from .31 to .50, suggesting adequate change to model predictors over time. The within-wave associations between marital hostility and parent-youth hostility also were positive and significant; associations ranged from .24 (ninth grade) to .29 (seventh grade).

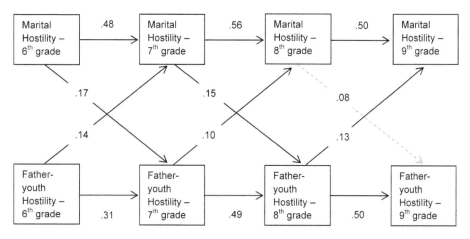

Fig 2. Marital hostility and father-youth hostility.
Estimates for solid lines were significant at $p < .05$. Estimates for dotted lines were statistically non-significant. The cross-sectional association between marital hostility and father-youth hostility was .28 at 6th grade, .29 at 7th grade, .28 at 8th grade, and .24 at 9th grade, all $p < .05$.

The spillover hypothesis from marital hostility to father-youth hostility (RQ1) was supported for two of the three relevant paths in the father model. Controlling for the reverse association from father-youth hostility to marital hostility, marital hostility when youth were in sixth grade was associated with higher father-youth hostility during seventh grade; marital hostility during seventh grade was associated with higher father-youth hostility during eighth grade.

There also was consistent support for the hypothesis associated with the research question regarding the influence of father-youth hostility on marital hostility across time (RQ2). Father-youth hostility during each year of the study (sixth through eighth grade) was associated with greater marital hostility when the youth was in seventh, eighth, and ninth grades, respectively.

Moderating effects. As with the mother-youth model, we also examined the potential moderating effects of youth gender (RQ3), youths' primary appraisals of marital conflict in terms of perceived threat (RQ4), and parents' depressive affect (RQ5). Consistent with the findings regarding mother-youth hostility, the model displayed in Figure 2 that focused on father-youth hostility did not differ across daughters and sons.

Neither of the omnibus tests at 6 *dfs* for youth perceived threat were statistically significant (e.g., $\Delta\chi^2 = 7.79$, $df = 6$, $p = .254$). One of the six individual path comparisons, however, was significant. The association between marital hostility during seventh grade and father-youth hostility during eighth grade was significant for the subsample of youth who scored in the top third of perceived threat (b = .19, p < .001) but was not significant for the other youth (b = .10, ns) (C. R. = 2.34). This significant finding should be considered cautiously because it may have occurred by chance.

Three separate analyses were conducted to examine the moderating role of fathers' depressive symptoms (first part of RQ5): top 33% of fathers (versus others), top 25% of fathers, and the clinical cut point of a score of 16 or higher on the CES-D. Moderating effects were significant for the 25% cutoff ($\Delta\chi^2$ = 17.88, df = 6, p = .007). Two of six paths differed; both involved associations from father-youth hostility to marital hostility. The association between father-youth hostility during ninth grade and increased marital hostility during eighth grade was significant for the subsample of families in which fathers scored in the top 25% of depressive symptoms (b = .16, p < .01) but was not significant for the other families (b = .06, ns) (C. R. = 2.54). This pattern repeated a year later. The association between father-youth hostility during eighth grade and increased marital hostility during ninth grade was significant for the subsample of families in which fathers scored in the top 25% of depressive symptoms (b = .19, p < .01) but was not significant for the other families (b = .10, ns) (C. R. = 2.39).

Finally, the moderating "crossover effects" of maternal depressive symptoms were examined in relation to the father-youth model (Figure 2; second part of RQ5). Mothers' depressive symptoms moderated the model when using the clinical cut point for depression ($\Delta\chi^2$ = 13.12, df = 6, p = .041). Two of six paths differed; the same two paths as for the moderating effects of fathers' depressive symptoms. The association between father-youth hostility during seventh grade and increased marital hostility during eighth grade was significant for the subsample of families in which mothers scored at clinical level of depressive symptoms (b = .17, p < .01) but was not significant for the other families (b = .08, ns) (C. R. = 1.97). The association between father-youth hostility during eighth grade and increased marital hostility during ninth grade was stronger for the group of families in which mothers scored at clinical levels of symptoms (b = .22, p < .01) than for other families (b = .12, p < .05) (C. R. = 2.03), though significant for both groups.

DISCUSSION

This study examined the associations between marital hostility and parent-youth hostility during early adolescence. The findings suggest that: (a) expressed hostility spills over from parent-youth relations to marital relationships, in addition to the more commonly examined form of spillover from marital relationships to the parent-child relationships, (b) parents' depressive mood and behaviors shape these interdependencies, and (c) there were a greater number of statistically significant associations in the father-youth model than in the mother-youth model.

Guided by family systems theory, a system-wide, family process perspective was used to examine the association between marital hostility and parent-youth hostility during early adolescence. The findings from this study supported the proposition that family subsystems are interdependent such that they are characterized by mutual influence (Cox & Paley, 1997). Expressed hostility in the marital dyad was associated with increases in expressed hostility in the parent-adolescent dyad a year later. Contrary to the questionnaire findings reported by Van Doorn et al. (2007), hostile parent-youth interactions also were associated with increased marital hostility a year later. The significant effect sizes in the current study (i.e., .10–.17) were similar to the longitudinal effect size of .16 in the NSFH sample (Gerard et al., 2006).

This pattern of mutual influence suggests that the boundaries between the marital and parent-child subsystems, on average, are fairly permeable during early adolescence. This permeability may be essential to support needed transformations in the parent-youth relationship as children develop, but may present vulnerabilities when the permeability is manifested in the transmission of negative communication behaviors such as expressed hostility (Fosco & Grych, 2010). The vulnerabilities ensconced within these interdependencies are likely complex (Cupach, 2000). Most previous literature has managed this complexity, in part, by focusing on mechanisms that account for the interdependencies between two family members within a dyad (e.g., marital partners, parents and youth). A new generation of research is needed that extends this exploration of mechanisms (i.e., mediators) and conditionalizing factors (i.e., moderators) to a next level of functioning that includes the interconnections between dyads. This study was conducted with this need in mind.

Based on previous conceptual and empirical discourse, we believe that there may be multiple individual and systemic explanations for these interdependencies that should be examined in future research. Expressed hostility between family members may create emotional insecurity (Canary & Canary, 2013; Cummings & Davies, 2010). Cummings and his colleagues have conceptualized emotional insecurity as including emotional reactivity, emotional and behavioral regulatory activity and problems, and internal representations of family life that suggest instability. For youth, emotional insecurity may serve to transmit fears, worries, apprehensions, and rejection sensitivities across the dyads that encompass their social worlds (Cook, Buehler, & Blair, 2012; El-Sheikh & Elmore-Staton, 2004; Lindahl et al., 2012; Schermerhorn et al., 2007). For parents, emotional insecurity may serve to link family subsystems (i.e., dyads) through increased defensiveness, irritability, and anxiety, as well as lower levels of positive interactions with family members (Bowen, 1978; Canary & Canary, 2013; Caughlin, Huston, & Houts, 2000).

In addition to emotional insecurity, negative cognitive appraisals and physiological reactivity may link marital hostility and parent-youth hostility. For youth, negative cognitive appraisals may include self-blame for marital conflict, perceptions of inadequate coping efficacy, and negative perceptions regarding parental over control and intrusion (Buehler, Lange, & Franck, 2007; Canary & Canary, 2013; Fosco & Grych, 2008; Noller et al., 2000). For parents, dysfunctional relationship cognitions may include negative responsibility and blame attributions, globalized self-orientations rather than a relationship focus, and reduced motivation for positive engagement (Caughlin & Vangelisti, 2006; Halford & Sanders, 1990; Sillars, Roberts, Leonard, & Dun, 2000). Research also has begun to implicate physiological dysregulation during conflict interactions as possible linking mechanisms (El-Sheikh & Harger, 2001; Levenson & Gottman, 1985; Lucas-Thompson & Granger, 2014).

We also believe that two important aspects of family functioning may link marital hostility and parent-youth hostility: triangulation and inadequate family warmth and positivity. Triangulation is the process of or the structural characteristic of including children in parental disputes. Triangulation can be characterized as one aspect of boundary ambiguity (Canary & Canary, 2013) and is associated with children's behavior problems, problems with peers, and parent-youth conflict (Buehler, Franck, & Cook, 2009; Buehler & Welsh, 2009; Fosco & Grych, 2008, 2010). We suspect that both triangulating communication processes and triangles that have stabilized structurally may be interconnected with parent-youth hostility. There also is evidence that suggests that inadequate levels of positive communication and interaction may function to exacerbate hostile interactions among family members (Rueter & Conger, 1995). Canary and Canary (2013) discussed this in terms of having adequate relationship maintenance behaviors and suggested that openness, positivity, offering assurances, and sharing activities may help reduce some of the negative interconnections between conflictual communication patterns in families.

The findings from this study did not support Minuchin's (1985) idea that marital functioning is more influential in terms of spillover than functioning in other family subsystems. During early adolescence, parent-youth hostility influenced marital functioning over time as much as marital functioning affected parent-youth interactions. The patterns of mutual influence found in this study, however, do support Minuchin's and Fosco and Grych's (2010) contentions that parents need appropriate boundary maintenance skills, particularly in the context of negative communication behaviors. As such, one of the important implications of these findings is that a key developmental task for parents during early adolescence is to develop or reformulate effective boundary-management strategies.

Given that we found more mutual influence (i.e., negative spillover) in the father-youth model than in the mother-youth model, the developmental task of strengthening boundary maintenance skills may be particularly salient for fathers as children mature and family relationships transform. There is growing evidence that fathers' behavior matters in two-parent families. Some scholars have found that both mothers' and fathers' behaviors matter uniquely in two-parent families (Barber, Stolz, & Olsen, 2005; Buehler, Benson, & Gerard, 2006; Osborne & Fincham, 1996). For example, Buehler et al. found that mothers' (β = .19) and fathers' hostility (β = .30) were each uniquely associated with youth's externalizing problems, including youth's hostile aggression in relationships. Other scholars have found that fathers' behavior was influential in cases where mothers' behavior was not associated with selected outcomes (El-Sheikh & Elmore-Staton, 2004; O'Keefe, 1994; Stocker & Youngblade, 1999). For example, father-youth conflict, but not mother-youth conflict, exacerbated the association between marital conflict and children's externalizing problems. Although most of these studies focused on predicting children's behavior problems and did not examine dyadic functioning in families, there is growing evidence that fathers' negative relationships with family members during early adolescence influence patterns of family functioning. Some scholars have suggested that part of the explanation for these interconnections may center around men's withdrawal behaviors when conflicts are stressful or when family members are emotionally distressed (Caughlin & Malis, 2004; Du Rocher Schudlich et al., 2004).

The interconnections between marital hostility and parent-youth hostility during early adolescence were similar for daughters and sons in this sample of families. Findings in previous studies have found contradictory patterns of youth gender influences, as well as null findings. The two theoretical mechanisms forwarded that suggest possible gendered patterns have focused on tendencies toward communion in relationships (Davies & Lindsay, 2004) and beliefs regarding the legitimacy of aggressive behavior in intimate relationships (Kinsfogel & Grych, 2004; Simon & Furman, 2010). Future research should assess these potential mechanisms directly (rather than use gender as a marker) and conjointly in the same study so that youth gender effects can be better examined.

A system-wide, family process perspective suggests that parents' emotional well-being is important to consider when examining family interactions (Cummings et al., 2000). We found that parents' depressive symptoms exacerbated the negative spillover from the marital relationship to the parent-youth relationship at the beginning of adolescence (sixth to seventh grade). Fathers' depressive symptoms also interacted with parent-youth hostility to increase subsequent marital hostility. Some indicators of depression include lack of energy, disengagement, irritability, and disproportional attention to negative experiences. During this early adolescent adjustment period that includes children starting middle school and entering adolescence, parents dealing with developmental issues associated with midlife, and transformations occurring in family relationships, characteristics associated with depression may exacerbate experienced relationship conflicts (see Canary & Canary's, 2013, section on the marital conflict and depression link for relevant research). These characteristics also suggest a depletion of psychological resources that are needed to address the family-wide transformations and additional stressors that occur during early adolescence. Moreover, depressive symptoms may suggest an additional mechanism that compromises or impairs parents' abilities to manage boundaries well, in addition to enacting other needed social skills (Segrin, 2000). Future research on the "darker side" of interaction patterns across various family subsystems could make significant contributions to the understanding of family communication by examining additional individual and relational factors that may shape interdependencies.

REFERENCES

Barber, B. K., Stolz, H. E., & Olsen, J. A. (2005). Parental support, psychological control, and behavioral control: Assessing relevance across time, culture, and method. *Monographs of the Society for Research in Child Development, 70*(4), 73–103.

Bowen, M. (1978). *Family therapy in clinical practice.* New York: Jason Aaronson.

Brody, G. H., Chen, Y., Murry, V. M., Ge, X., Simons, R. L., Gibbons, F. X., & … Cutrona, C. E. (2006). Perceived discrimination and the adjustment of African American youths: A five-year longitudinal analysis with contextual moderation effects. *Child Development, 77,* 1170–1189. doi: 10.1111/j.1467-8624.2006.00927.x

Buehler, C. (2006). Parents and peers in relation to early adolescent problem behavior. *Journal of Marriage and Family, 68,* 109–124. doi: 10.1111/j.1741-3737.2006.00237.x

Buehler, C., Benson, M. J., & Gerard, J. M. (2006). Interparental hostility and early adolescent problem behavior: The mediating role of specific aspects of parenting. *Journal of Research on Adolescence, 16,* 265–292. doi: 10.1111/j.1532-7795.2006.00132.x

Buehler, C., Franck, K. L., & Cook, E. C. (2009). Adolescents' triangulation in marital conflict and peer relations. *Journal of Research on Adolescence, 19,* 669–689. doi: 10.1111/j.1532-7795.2009.00616.x

Buehler, C., & Gerard, J. (2002). Marital conflict, ineffective parenting, and children's and adolescents' maladjustment. *Journal of Marriage and Family, 64,* 78–92. doi: 10.1111/j.1741-3737.2002.00078.x

Buehler, C., Krishnakumar, A., Anthony, C., Tittsworth, S., Stone, G. (1994). Hostile interparental conflict and youth maladjustment. *Family Relations, 43,* 409–416.

Buehler, C., Krishnakumar, A., Stone, G., Anthony, C., Pemberton, S., Gerard, J., & Barber, B. K. (1998). Interparental conflict styles and youth problem behavior: A two-sample replication study. *Journal of Marriage and the Family, 60,* 119–132.

Buehler, C., Lange, G., & Franck, K. L. (2007). Adolescents' cognitive and emotional responses to marital hostility. *Child Development, 78,* 775–789. doi: 10.1111/j.1467-8624.2007.01032.x

Buehler, C., & Welsh, D. P. (2009). A process model of adolescents' triangulation into parents' marital conflict: The role of emotional reactivity. *Journal of Family Psychology, 23,* 167–180. doi: 10.1037/a0014976

Canary, D. J., Cupach, W. R., & Serpe, R. T. (2001). A competence-based approach to examining interpersonal conflict: Test of a longitudinal model. *Communication Research, 28,* 79–104. doi: 10.1177/009365001028001003

Canary, D. J., & Messman, S. J. (2000). Relationship conflict. In C. Hendrick, & S. S. Hendrick (Eds.), *Close relationships: A sourcebook* (pp. 261–270). Thousand Oaks, CA: Sage Publications, Inc.

Canary, H. E., & Canary, D. J. (2013). *Family conflict: Managing the unexpected.* Malden, MA: Polity.

Caughlin, J. P., Huston, T. L., & Houts, R. M. (2000). How does personality matter in marriage? An examination of trait anxiety, interpersonal negativity, and marital satisfaction. *Journal of Personality and Social Psychology, 78,* 326–336. doi: 10.1037/0022-3514.78.2.326

Caughlin, J. P., & Malis, R. S. (2004). Demand/withdraw communication between parents and adolescents: Connections with self-esteem and substance use. *Journal of Social and Personal Relationships, 21,* 125–148. doi: 10.1177/0265407504039843

Caughlin, J. P., & Vangelisti, A. L. (2006). Conflict in dating and romantic relationships. In J. Oetzel, & S. Ting-Toomey (Eds.), *The Sage handbook of conflict communication* (pp. 129–157). Thousand Oaks, CA: Sage.

Chung, G. H., Flook, L., & Fuligni, A. J. (2009). Daily family conflict and emotional distress among adolescents from Latin American, Asian, and European backgrounds. *Developmental Psychology, 45,* 1406–1415. doi: 10.1037/a0014163

Conger, R. D., Conger, K. J., Elder, G. H., Lorenz, F. O., Simons, R. L., & Whitbeck, L. B. (1993). Family economic stress and adjustment of early adolescent girls. *Developmental Psychology, 29,* 206–219. doi: 10.1037/0012-1649.29.2.206

Cook, E. C., Buehler, C., & Blair, B. L. (2013). Adolescents' emotional reactivity across relationship contexts. *Developmental Psychology, 49,* 341–352. doi: 10.1037/a0028342

Cox, M. J., & Paley, B. (1997). Families as systems. *Annual Review of Psychology, 48,* 243–267. doi: 10.1146/annurev.psych.48.1.243

Cox, M. J., Paley, B., & Harter, K. (2001). Interparental conflict and parent–child relationships. In J. H. Grych, & F. D. Fincham (Eds.), *Interparental conflict and child development: Theory, research, and applications* (pp. 249–272). New York, NY: Cambridge University Press. doi: 10.1017/ CBO9780511527838.011

Cummings, E. M., & Davies, P. T. (2010). *Marital conflict and children: An emotional security perspective.* New York, NY: Guilford Press.

Cummings, E. M., Davies, P. T., & Campbell, S. B. (2000). *Developmental psychopathology and family process.* New York, NY: Guilford Press.

Cupach, W. R. (2000). Advancing understanding of relational conflict. *Journal of Social and Personal Relationships, 17,* 697–703. doi: 10.1177/0265407500174013

Davies, P. T., & Lindsay, L. L. (2004). Interparental conflict and adolescent adjustment: Why does gender moderate early adolescent vulnerability? *Journal of Family Psychology, 18,* 160–170. doi: 10.1037/0893-3200.18.1.160

Downey, G., & Coyne, J. C. (1990). Children of depressed parents: An integrative review. *Psychological Bulletin, 108,* 50–76. doi: 10.1037/0033-2909.108.1.50

Du Rocher Schudlich, T. D., Papp, L. M., & Cummings, E. M. (2011). Relations between spouses' depressive symptoms and marital conflict: A longitudinal investigation of the role of conflict resolution styles. *Journal of Family Psychology, 25,* 531–540. doi: 10.1037/a0024216

El-Sheikh, M., & Elmore-Staton, L. (2004). The link between marital conflict and child adjustment: Parent-child conflict and perceived attachments as mediators, potentiators, and mitigators of risk. *Development and Psychopathology, 16,* 631–648. doi: 10.1017/S0954579404004705

El-Sheikh, M., & Harger, J. (2001). Appraisals of marital conflict and children's adjustment, health, and physiological reactivity. *Developmental Psychology, 37,* 875–885. doi: 10.1037/0012-1649.37.6.875

Erel, O., & Burman, B. (1995). Interrelatedness of marital relations and parent-child relations: A meta-analytic review. *Psychological Bulletin, 118*, 108–132. doi: 10.1037/0033-2909.118.1.108

Fosco, G. M., DeBoard, R. L., & Grych, J. H. (2007). Making sense of family violence: Implications of children's appraisals of interparental aggression for their short- and long-term functioning. *European Psychologist, 12*, 6–16. doi: 10.1027/1016-9040.12.1.6

Fosco, G. M., & Grych, J. H. (2008). Emotional, cognitive, and family systems mediators of children's adjustment to interparental conflict. *Journal of Family Psychology, 22*, 843–854. doi: 10.1037/a0013809

Fosco, G. M., & Grych, J. H. (2010). Adolescent triangulation into parental conflicts: Longitudinal implications for appraisals and adolescent-parent relations. *Journal of Marriage and Family, 72*, 254–266. doi: 10.1111/j.1741-3737.2010.00697.x

Gerard, J. M., Buehler, C., Franck, K., & Anderson, O. (2005). In the eyes of the beholder: Cognitive appraisals as mediators of the association between interparental conflict and youth maladjustment. *Journal of Family Psychology, 19*, 376–384. doi: 10.1037/0893-3200.19.3.376

Gerard, J. M., Krishnakumar, A., & Buehler, C. (2006). Marital conflict, parent-child relations, and youth maladjustment: A longitudinal investigation of spillover effects. *Journal of Family Issues, 27*, 951–975. doi: 10.1177/0192513X05286020

Grych, J. H., & Cardoza-Fernandes, S. (2001). Understanding the impact of interparental conflict on children: The role of social cognitive processes. In J. H. Grych, & F. D. Fincham (Eds.), *Interparental conflict and child development: Theory, research, and applications* (pp. 157–187). New York: Cambridge University Press. doi: 10.1017/CBO9780511527838.008

Grych, J. H., & Fincham, F. D. (1990). Marital conflict and children's adjustment: A cognitive-contextual framework. *Psychological Bulletin, 108*, 267–290. doi: 10.1037/0033-2909.108.2.267

Grych, J. H., Seid, M., & Fincham, F. D. (1992). Assessing marital conflict from the child's perspective: The Children's Perception of Interparental Conflict Scale. *Child Development, 63*, 558–572. doi: 10.1111/j.1467-8624.1992.tb01646.x

Halford, W. K., & Sanders, M. R. (1990). The relationship of cognition and behavior during marital interaction. *Journal of Social and Clinical Psychology, 9*, 489–510. doi: 10.1521/jscp.1990.9.4.489

Herman, K. C., Lambert, S. F., Reinke, W. M., & Ialongo, N. S. (2008). Low academic competence in first grade as a risk factor for depressive cognitions and symptoms in middle school. *Journal of Counseling Psychology, 55*, 400–410. doi: 10.1037/a0012654

Kane, P., & Garber, J. (2004). The relations among depression in fathers, children's psychopathology, and father-child conflict: A meta-analysis. *Clinical Psychology Review, 24*, 339–360. doi: 10.1016/j.cpr.2004.03.004

Kerig, P. K. (1998). Gender and appraisals as mediators of adjustment in children exposed to interparental violence. *Journal of Family Violence, 13*, 345–363. doi: 10.1023/A:1022871102437

Kinsfogel, K. M., & Grych, J. H. (2004). Interparental conflict and adolescent dating relationships: Integrating cognitive, emotional, and peer Influences. *Journal of Family Psychology, 18*, 505–515. doi: 10.1037/0893-3200.18.3.505

Koerner, A. F., & Fitzpatrick, M. A. (2002). Toward a theory of family communication. *Communication Theory, 12*, 70–91. doi: 10.1111/j.1468-2885.2002.tb00260.x

Kouros, C. D., Merrilees, C. E., & Cummings, E. M. (2008). Marital conflict and children's emotional security in the context of parental depression. *Journal of Marriage and Family, 70*, 684–697. doi: 10.1111/j.1741-3737.2008.00514.x

Kouros, C. D., Papp, L. M., Goeke-Morey, M. C., & Cummings, E. M. (2014). Spillover between marital quality and parent-child relationship quality: Parental depressive symptoms as moderators. *Journal of Family Psychology, 28*, 315–325. doi.org/10.1037/a0036804

Krishnakumar, A., & Buehler, C. (2000). Interparental conflict and parenting practices: A meta-analysis. *Family Relations, 49*, 25–44. doi: 10.1111/j.1741-3729.2000.00025.x

Levenson, R. W., & Gottman, J. M. (1985). Physiological and affective predictors of change in relationship satisfaction. *Journal of Personality and Social Psychology, 49*, 85–94. doi: 10.1037/0022-3514.49.1.85

Lindahl, K. M., Bregman, H. R., & Malik, N. M. (2012). Family boundary structures and child adjustment: The indirect role of emotional reactivity. *Journal of Family Psychology, 26*, 839–847. doi: 10.1037/a0030444

Linder, J. R., & Collins, W. A. (2005). Parent and peer predictors of physical aggression and conflict management in romantic relationships in early adulthood. *Journal of Family Psychology, 19*, 252–262. doi: 10.1037/0893-3200.19.2.252

Low, S. M., & Stocker, C. (2005). Family functioning and children's adjustment: Associations among parents' depressed mood, marital hostility, parent-child hostility, and children's adjustment. *Journal of Family Psychology, 19*, 394–403. doi: 10.1037/0893-3200.19.3.394

Lucas-Thompson, R. G., & Granger, D. A. (2014). Parent–child relationship quality moderates the link between marital conflict and adolescents' physiological responses to social evaluative threat. *Journal of Family Psychology, 28*, 538–548. doi: 10.1037/a0037328

Margolin, G., Christensen, A., & John, R. S. (1996). The continuance and spillover of everyday tensions in distressed and nondistressed families. *Journal of Family Psychology, 10*, 304–321. doi: 10.1037/0893-3200.10.3.304

Margolin, G., Gordis, E. B., John, R. S. (2001). Coparenting: A link between marital conflict and parenting in two-parent families. *Journal of Family Psychology, 15*, 3–21. doi: 10.1037//0893-3200.15.1.3

McArdle, J. J. (2009). Latent variable modeling of difference and changes with longitudinal data. *Annual Review of Psychology, 60*, 577–605. doi: 10.1146/annurev.psych.60.110707.163612

McCubbin, H. I, & Patterson, J. M. (1983). Family transitions: Adaption to stress. In H. I. McCubbin, & C. R. Figley (Eds.), *Stress and the family, Vol. 1: Coping with normative transitions* (pp. 5–25). New York, NY: Brunner/Mazel.

Melby, J. N., & Conger, R. D. (2001). The Iowa Family Interaction Rating Scales: Instrument summary. In P. K. Kerig, & K. M. Lindahl (Eds.), *Family observational coding systems: Resources for systematic research* (pp. 33–57). Mahwah, NJ: Erlbaum.

Melby, J. N., Conger, R. D., Rueter, M., Lucy, L., Repinski, D., & Ahrens, K., et al. (1990). The *Iowa Family Interaction Rating Scales* (2nd ed.). Unpublished manuscript, Iowa State University Center for Family Research in Rural Mental Health.

Minuchin, P. (1985). Families and individual development: Provocations from the field of family therapy. *Child Development, 56*, 289–302.

Moore, M. J., & Buehler, C. (2011). Parents' divorce proneness: The influence of adolescent problem behaviors and parental efficacy. *Journal of Social and Personal Relationships, 28*, 634–652. doi: 10.1177/0265407510386991

Noller, P., Feeney, J. A., Sheehan, G., & Peterson, C. (2000). Marital conflict patterns: Links with family conflict and family members' perceptions of one another. *Personal Relationships, 7*, 79–94. doi: 10.1111/j.1475-6811.2000.tb00005.x

O'Keefe, M. (1994). Linking marital violence, mother-child/father-child aggression, and child behavior problems. *Journal of Family Violence, 9*, 63–78. doi: 10.1007/BF01531969

Osborne, L. N., & Fincham, F. D. (1996). Marital conflict, parent–child relationships, and child adjustment: Does gender matter? *Merrill-Palmer Quarterly, 42*, 48–75.

Proulx, C. M., Helms, H., & Buehler, C. (2007). Marital quality and personal well-being: A meta-analysis. *Journal of Marriage and Family, 69*, 576–593. doi: 10.1111/j.1741-3737.2007.00393.x

Radloff, L. S. (1977). The CES-D Scale: A self-report depression scale for research in the general population. *Applied Psychological Measurement, 1*, 385–401.

Rueter, M. A., & Conger, R. D. (1995). Antecedents of parent–adolescent disagreements. *Journal of Marriage and the Family, 57*, 435–448. doi: 10.2307/353697

Schafer, J. L., & Graham, J. W. (2002). Missing data: Our view of the state of the art. *Psychological Methods, 7*, 147–177. doi: 10.1037/1082-989X.7.2.147

Schermerhorn, A. C., Chow, S. M., Cummings, E. M. (2010). Developmental family processes and interparental conflict: Patterns of microlevel influences. *Developmental Psychology, 46*, 869–885. doi: 10.1037/a0019662

Schermerhorn, A. C., Cummings, E. M., DeCarlo, C. A., & Davies, P. T. (2007). Children's influences in the marital relationship. *Journal of Family Psychology, 21*, 259–269. doi: 10.1037/0893-3200.21.2.259

Segrin, C. (2000). Social skills deficits associated with depression. *Clinical Psychology Review, 20*, 379–403. doi: 10.1016/S0272-7358(98)00104-4

Segrin, C., & Arroyo, A. (2015). Mental health problems in family contexts. Olson, L. N. & Fine, M. A. (Eds.) (in production). *The darker side of family communication: The harmful, the morally suspect, and the socially inappropriate.* Peter Lang

Segrin, C., & Fitzpatrick, M. A. (1992). Depression and verbal aggressiveness in different marital couple types. *Communication Studies, 43*, 79–91.

Sillars, A., Roberts, L. J., Leonard, K. E., & Dun, T. (2000). Cognition during marital conflict: The relationship of thought and talk. *Journal of Social and Personal Relationships, 17*, 479–502. doi: 10.1177/0265407500174002

Sillars, A., Smith, T., & Koerner, A. (2010). Misattributions contributing to empathic (in)accuracy during parent-adolescent conflict discussions. *Journal of Social and Personal Relationships, 27*, 727–747. doi: 10.1177/0265407510373261

Simon, V. A., & Furman, W. (2010). Interparental conflict and adolescents' romantic relationship conflict. *Journal of Research on Adolescence, 20*, 188–209. doi: 10.1111/j.1532-7795.2009.00635.x

Steinberg, L. (1990). Autonomy, conflict, and harmony in the family relationship. In S. Feldman, & G. R. Elliott (Eds.), *At the threshold: The developing adolescent* (pp. 255–276). Cambridge, MA: Harvard University Press.

Stocker, C. M., & Youngblade, L. (1999). Marital conflict and parental hostility: Links with children's sibling and peer relationships. *Journal of Family Psychology, 13*, 598–609. doi: 10.1037/0893-3200.13.4.598

Straus, M. A., & Gelles, R. J. (1986). Societal change and change in family violence from 1975 to 1985 as revealed by two national surveys. *Journal of Marriage and the Family, 48*, 465–479.

Sweet, J., & Bumpass, L. (2005). National Survey of Families and Households. http://www.ssc.wisc.edu/nsfh/

Tschann, J. M., Flores, E., Pasch, L. A., & Marin, B. (1999). Assessing interparental conflict: Reports of parents and adolescents in European American and Mexican American families. *Journal of Marriage and the Family, 61*, 269–283. doi: 10.2307/353747

U.S. Census Bureau. (2000). PCT27. Family type by presence of own children under 18 years of age of own children. Families (total), White alone, Black alone. Retrieved September 29, 2004, from http://factfinder.census.gov, Summary File 4.

U.S. Census Bureau (2000). PCT40. Median family income in 1999 (dollars) by family type by presence of own children under 18 years. Retrieved September 3, 2005, from http://factfinder.census.gov, Summary File 3.

Van Doorn, M. D., Branje, S. T., & Meeus, W. J. (2007). Longitudinal transmission of conflict resolution styles from marital relationships to adolescent-parent relationships. *Journal of Family Psychology*, *21*, 426–434. doi: 10.1037/0893-3200.21.3.426

Whitchurch, G. G., & Constantine, L. L. (1993). Systems theory. In P. G. Boss, W. J. Doherty, R. LaRossa, W. R. Schumm, & S. K. Steinmetz (Eds.), *Sourcebook of family theories and methods: A contextual approach* (pp. 325–352). New York: Plenum Press.

CHAPTER SEVEN

Hurt Feelings IN Family Relationships

Social Pain and Social Interaction

ANITA L. VANGELISTI
Department of Communication Studies

"Truth is everybody is going to hurt you: you just gotta find the ones worth suffering for."
—BOB MARLEY

Regardless of how close and caring family members are, they sometimes hurt each other's feelings. They may insult each other without meaning to, blurt out sensitive information, or exchange harsh words during a conflict. They might criticize each other, ignore pleas for attention, or make physical or relational threats. The way family members communicate with each other when they experience, inflict, or observe social pain can have lasting effects on their relationships.

The purpose of the current chapter is to synthesize research relevant to the role of hurtful interactions in family relationships. The chapter begins by describing the various ways that hurt has been conceptualized in the literature. Then research is reviewed covering the characteristics of hurtful events; individuals' cognitive, behavioral, and physiological responses to hurt; and relationship characteristics associated with hurt feelings. Finally, several issues are examined that researchers who study hurt in family relationships might usefully address in the future.

CONCEPTUALIZING HURT

Researchers and clinicians generally agree that hurt arises when a person is emotionally injured by another (Folkes, 1982; L'Abate, 1977). People feel hurt when they perceive that someone else said or did something that made them feel emotional pain. One of the first empirical studies that attempted to distinguish hurt from other emotions was conducted by Shaver, Schwartz, Kirson, and O'Connor (1987). These researchers did a prototype analysis of emotion concepts and found that people perceived that hurt was related to sadness and that it was associated with emotion terms such as anguish and agony. Shaver and his colleagues suggested that the commonality among hurt and these other emotions was that they all involved a degree of suffering.

The early findings of Shaver et al. (1987) paved the way for other researchers to begin to define hurt more precisely and identify the features that distinguish the elicitation of hurt from the elicitation of other emotions. Researchers and theorists have taken a variety of approaches to describing and distinguishing hurt feelings. For instance, Vangelisti and her colleagues (Vangelisti, 1994; Vangelisti & Young, 2000) suggested that hurt is elicited by relationship transgressions and that those transgressions, more specifically, create a sense of vulnerability. By contrast, Leary, Springer, Negel, Ansell, and Evans (1998) argued that the component common to all hurt feelings is relational devaluation or "the perception that another individual does not regard his or her relationship with the person to be as important, close, or valuable as the person desires" (p. 1225). Feeney (2005) adopted aspects of both the Leary et al. and the Vangelisti conceptualizations, arguing that hurt is evoked by relational transgressions that imply negative relationship evaluations.

Feeney (2005) also suggested that hurt feelings are a consequence of threats to individuals' mental models of self and other. As such, when people are hurt, their attachment to significant others is threatened. Feeney's effort to situate hurt as relevant to attachment processes was noted by Shaver, Mikulincer, Lavy, and Cassidy (2009), who suggested the possibility that hurt feelings may be more closely associated with individuals' sense of safety and security than with their mental models of self and other.

The notion that hurt is evoked when people feel unsafe or insecure about their relationships is reflected in much of the literature. For instance, McLaren, Theiss, and their colleagues (McLaren, Solomon, & Priem, 2011; Theiss, Knobloch, Checton, & Magsaman-Conrad, 2009) described hurt feelings in terms of the turbulence or heightened reactivity that partners sometimes experience at certain points in their relationships. These researchers found that the intensity of partners' hurt feelings is linked to their reports of relational turbulence. Lemay, Overall, and Clark (2012) similarly emphasized the possible association between hurt feelings and partners' dependence and vulnerability. They not only found that hurt was linked to dependence and vulnerability but also that individuals who were hurt often made an effort to regain the acceptance of the partner who hurt them.

Although the characteristics of hurt that have been noted by researchers suggest a diversity of theoretical approaches, they also share several features that are relevant to family relationships. First, they underline the idea that a sense of being injured is core to the experience of hurt feelings. When people feel social pain, they perceive they have been wounded by something that someone else said or did. Because family members often interact and maintain their relationships over an extended time period, they have ample opportunity to hurt each other's feelings. Second, the different components of hurt discussed by researchers all involve a sense of vulnerability. Family members often are particularly vulnerable to each other because their relationships are interdependent – the outcomes of each family member typically are influenced by the behavior of other members. Third, hurt feelings are associated with a perceived discrepancy between the current quality of individuals' relationships and the relational quality that individuals desire. In other words, when people are hurt, they perceive their relationship is devalued in some way, and they have a desire to restore or increase its value. People may be especially motivated to restore or increase the value of undervalued family relationships. Because their associations with family members usually are involuntary, individuals may be particularly distressed when they perceive a family relationship as undervalued. They may, as a consequence, be more likely to engage in behaviors geared toward restoring or increasing the value of that relationship.

STUDYING HURT

The features shared by various approaches to studying hurt feelings have provided researchers with a foundation for investigating the ways social pain is evoked and the ways individuals respond to being hurt. Researchers have examined the characteristics of hurtful events; individuals' cognitive, behavioral, and physiological responses to hurt; and relationship characteristics associated with hurt feelings. The findings of these studies have important implications for family members and family relationships.

Characteristics of Hurtful Events

Because the intensity of hurt feelings and outcomes associated with hurt are so varied, one of the first tasks of researchers was to describe the characteristics of hurtful events and note any association between those characteristics and relational outcomes. As such, scholars identified various types of hurtful events and examined the frequency with which those events took place. Both of these characteristics— type and frequency—have been linked to the quality of individuals' relationships.

Type. Several researchers have explored the types of events or behaviors that elicit hurt feelings. Based on the premise that people feel hurt in response to something

that someone else said or did, Vangelisti (1994) initially examined hurtful communication by asking participants to recall and describe interactions when someone
said something that hurt their feelings. She then identified nine speech acts that
evoke hurt, arguing that the form of hurtful messages influences the ways individuals interpret socially painful events. Her data indicated that the most frequently
reported types of hurtful messages were informative statements (e.g., "I never
really liked you."), accusations (e.g., "You're a big fat liar!"), and evaluations (e.g.,
"Well, you really aren't that smart."). She also found that informative statements
tended to be more hurtful than other types of messages. Vangelisti explained this
latter finding by suggesting that informative statements may constrain recipients'
ability to respond to, or challenge, hurtful comments.

Leary and his colleagues (1998) noted, quite correctly, that Vangelisti's
research focused exclusively on situations in which someone said something that
evoked hurt feelings and that it did not account for nonverbal behavior or situations when the absence of a behavior might elicit hurt. To address this limitation, Leary et al. asked their respondents to recall and describe instances when
someone else said or did something that hurt their feelings. The findings of their
study suggested that the majority of hurtful episodes could be described in terms
of four categories including active disassociation, passive disassociation, criticism,
and betrayal. Leary and his associates did not find that the types of hurtful events
differed with regard to the intensity of hurt they elicited, but they did find that
criticism was linked to a lower sense of rejection compared to the other types of
hurtful events.

Feeney (2004) examined hurt feelings in romantic relationships and revised
the typology developed by Leary and his colleagues to fit that context. She classi-
fied the hurtful episodes reported by her participants as active disassociation, passive disassociation, criticism, infidelity, and deception. Feeney found that infidelity
was perceived as more serious than the other types of hurtful events (i.e., as higher
in hurt, powerlessness, perceived intentionality, destructive behavior on the part of
the victim) and that criticism was viewed as relatively less serious. She suggested
that these findings were consistent with Vangelisti's (1994) argument about the
ability of those who are hurt to respond to, or challenge, the individual who hurt
them. The lack of recourse available to individuals who are hurt by infidelity or by
informative statements likely makes those events particularly hurtful.

Frequency. Although the type of hurtful event experienced offers evidence of how
the event might influence individuals' relationships, research and theory suggest
that the frequency with which the event occurs also affects its impact. Hurtful
criticism that is given once or twice by a family member is evaluated differently
than hurtful criticism that is offered over and over again. Further, criticism that is
given in a family where members exchange a preponderance of positive messages

is assessed differently than criticism given in a family where members exchange mostly negative messages.

Because most studies of hurt feelings have asked people to recall and describe single hurtful events, relatively little is known about how variations in the frequency of hurtful behavior affect relationships. The investigations that have focused on frequency have assessed the extent to which individuals perceive hurtful behavior is part of an ongoing pattern. For instance, in one study, Vangelisti and Young (2000) asked participants to describe a hurtful interaction and to report on two variables relevant to frequency. One was the frequency with which they were hurt by the other person (e.g., "He/she often hurts my feelings"); one was the other individual's general tendency to hurt people (e.g., "A lot of people have been hurt by his/her behavior"). Both of the two variables were positively associated with participants' tendency to distance themselves from the individual who hurt them – and this association held up even when perceived intent and relational quality were controlled. The study also revealed an interaction between perceived intent and perceived frequency. When individuals reported that the other person did not hurt them frequently, they responded in line with prior research on intent: Those who saw the hurtful behavior as unintentional did not feel much emotional pain, while those who saw the hurtful behavior as intentional reported much more pain. However, people who said the other individual frequently hurt them responded quite differently. Those who believed the hurtful behavior was intentional reported experiencing very little pain. It may be that as people are hurt repeatedly over time, they come to expect the hurtful behavior and, as a consequence, develop emotional "calluses" that protect them from any pain they might experience.

Another way that researchers have examined the frequency of hurtful interactions has been to investigate interactions that reoccur in close relationships. Hampel and Vangelisti (in progress) have looked at a phenomenon they labelled *serial hurt*. They asked participants to recall and describe their most recent hurtful interaction with a romantic partner and to indicate whether they had had similar interactions with their partner before. Interactions that were reported as one-time events were defined as *discrete* hurt, whereas those described as repeated were defined as *serial* hurt. Analyses revealed that people who said they experienced serial hurt were less satisfied with their relationship than were those who reported on discrete hurt. Further, those describing serial hurt were more likely to say they felt hurt because their partner did not value their relationship and they were worried that the same interaction would reoccur. They also reported feeling more intense pain than did those describing discrete hurt, but this increased pain was due to the topic of the serial interactions being more important to participants. One explanation for this latter finding is that couples engaging in repeated hurtful interactions tend to target particularly important, hurtful topics. Another is that the topics of these interactions become more important to partners over time as partners are hurt repeatedly.

Responses to Hurt

Like the characteristics of hurtful events, the immediate responses that people have to being hurt can influence their subsequent interactions and their relational outcomes. Individuals' reactions to feeling hurt have been examined in terms of three categories: cognitive, behavioral, and physiological responses.

Cognitive. When people feel an aversive emotion such as hurt, they often think about their experience. They evaluate the situation, consider how their feelings were elicited, and try to explain why the other person behaved in the way he or she did.

One of the more important judgments individuals make about their hurt feelings is whether or not the feelings were elicited intentionally or unintentionally. According to Malle and Knobe (1997) judgments of intent are based on individuals' perceptions of whether the behavior in question (a) was volitional (i.e., whether the person chose to engage in the behavior), (b) involved forethought (i.e., whether the person planned the behavior), (c) was foreseeable (i.e., whether the person was aware of the outcomes associated with the behavior), and (d) involved a positively valenced outcome (i.e., whether the person thought the outcome was desirable). In other words, when people judge a hurtful behavior as intentional, they likely perceive that the other person chose to engage in the behavior, planned the behavior, was aware that the behavior would evoke hurt, and saw the evocation of hurt as desirable.

Based on this line of reasoning, Vangelisti and Young (2000) predicted that messages viewed by recipients as intentionally hurtful would be positively associated with the tendency of individuals to distance themselves from the person who hurt them and positively linked to the intensity of people's hurt feelings. The researchers also reasoned that judgments of intent would be negatively associated with two relationship qualities: the degree to which individuals felt satisfied with their relationship with the person who hurt them and the degree to which they felt close to the person who hurt them. These predictions were supported. Messages seen as intentionally hurtful were viewed by participants as creating more distance between recipients and the person who hurt them and as eliciting more intense hurt feelings than were those seen as unintentional. People who felt their hurt feelings were evoked intentionally also were less satisfied with their relationship and felt less close to the person who hurt them than those who perceived they were hurt unintentionally.

While judgments of intent are a telling indicator of relational quality, other cognitive responses offer a more textured view of the relational context associated with hurtful episodes. For instance, individuals who believe their hurt was elicited intentionally may come to different conclusions about the reasons they were hurt.

Those who perceive they were hurt because a relational partner did not care about them probably evaluate the situation differently than do those who perceive they were hurt because they have some sort of personal flaw. The ways people explain their hurt feelings, in short, offer information about the hurtful event and about how individuals feel about themselves and their relationships.

Researchers have explored the reasons people perceive they were hurt by asking them to describe and explain their feelings (e.g., Vangelisti, Young, Carpenter-Theune, & Alexander, 2005). The reasons provided by individuals range from relational denigration (it made them feel like their relationship was not important) to mistaken intent (the other person was not aware that it would hurt) to intrinsic flaw (the interaction focused on a personal defect) to ill-conceived humor (a joke that went bad or was not funny). Studies have indicated that when people perceive that their pain was caused by relational denigration, they report feeling more intense hurt. Similarly, when individuals see an interaction with a romantic partner as high in disaffiliation (characterized by disliking or a lack of appreciation), they are relatively likely to report intense hurt feelings (McLaren et al., 2011). People who say they were hurt because they were humiliated also report more intense pain.

Not surprisingly, some of the reasons associated with particularly intense hurt feelings also are linked to individuals' tendency to distance themselves from the person who hurt them. More specifically, relational denigration and intrinsic flaw both were positively associated with relational distancing. Mistaken intent, by contrast, was negatively linked to distancing (Vangelisti et al., 2005).

Behavioral. In addition to examining individuals' cognitive responses to hurtful events, researchers have explored people's behavioral reactions to being hurt. People describe a wide variety of behavioral responses to hurt including being silent, crying, asking for an explanation, attacking the person who hurt them, apologizing, conceding, being sarcastic, and ignoring the hurtful event.

Vangelisti and Crumley (1998) found that the behavioral responses reported by their participants could be characterized by three factors. The first, labeled active verbal responses, involves efforts by those who were hurt to engage the person who hurt them in interaction (e.g., asking for an explanation, attacking the other person, defending the self). The second factor was called acquiescent responses. It includes conciliatory reactions such as crying, conceding, and apologizing. The third factor, labeled invulnerable responses, is made up of behaviors that might suggest the event in question did not evoke much pain (e.g., laughing, ignoring the event, and being silent). When they examined the links between these three groups of behavioral responses to hurt and other variables, the researchers found a positive association between active verbal responses and relational satisfaction. People who reacted to being hurt by actively engaging their partner in conversation—even if the interaction was somewhat negative—tended to be more satisfied with their relationship. By contrast, individuals who said they responded by being acquiescent tended to report more intense pain. The relatively intense hurt feelings of these individuals may have left them with few resources to engage in interactions with the person who hurt them. Supporting this explanation, Leary and his colleagues (1998) found that crying was associated with the degree of hurt felt by participants. It is important to note, however, that Leary et al.'s data also indicated that saying something critical or nasty and telling the other person about the event both were associated with intense hurt feelings. The idea that intense pain constrains people's active verbal responses, thus, merits further investigation.

One variable that may influence the constraint individuals feel when they respond to hurt is the type of relationship they have with the person who hurt them. Feeney (2005) looked specifically at people's behavioral responses to hurt in the context of couple relationships. She assessed a range of reactions that included expressing anger, crying in front of the other person, crying later, arguing, laughing, and bottling up feelings, among others. Feeney's analysis revealed that partners' behaviors could be described by two factors. One involved responses she deemed constructive for the relationship such as telling the other person, bottling up feelings, ignoring the situation, and asking for an explanation. The other was characterized by responses she characterized as destructive, like saying something critical or nasty, being sarcastic, expressing anger, and getting worked up. Feeney found that destructive responses to hurt were associated with a tendency for partners to report the hurtful event had negative long-term effects on their relationship.

Importantly, people's responses to socially painful communication also depend on gender norms. Women tend to report more intense hurt feelings than men, and women are more likely to note they would confront the source of their social pain than are men (Miller & Roloff, 2005).

Physiological. Some of the most recent work on responses to hurtful events focuses on physiological responses. Given that hurt or social pain is experienced as negative, Priem, McLaren, and Solomon (2008) predicted that it would be associated with a physiological stress response. Priem and her colleagues asked participants to engage in two five-minute conversations with a romantic partner about core traits and values. Partners were coached to be disconfirming and hurtful during the second conversation. The researchers measured participants' hurt feelings as well as changes in their salivary cortisol, a hormone that is released in response to stress. They found that individuals' hurt feelings were positively associated with increases in salivary cortisol.

The conceptualization of hurt as stressful and potentially harmful underlies the bulk of research on physiological responses to hurt. Indeed, a number of scholars have argued that social pain, like physical pain, is a threat to individuals' well-being. Because social and physical pain render people vulnerable, individuals who withdraw from hurtful stimuli are afforded an advantage over those who do not. Indeed, our evolutionary ancestors who learned to evade social pain likely outlived those who failed to do so (MacDonald & Leary, 2005). Based on the centrality of close relationships to survival, Panksepp and his colleagues (Herman & Panksepp, 1978; Panksepp, 1998) argued that the social attachment system in humans coopted the physical pain system to promote well-being. Inasmuch as this is the case, social pain or hurt likely operated as a warning signal for our ancestors, enabling them to avoid the dangers associated with social exclusion.

In line with Panksepp's argument, Eisenberger and Lieberman (2004) developed *pain overlap theory* and proposed that social pain and physical pain share parts of the same underlying processing system. There now is substantial evidence supporting the premises of the theory. For instance, Eisenberger, Lieberman, and Williams (2003) found that the neuroimaging data associated with social and physical pain were quite similar. Their findings indicated that people who were excluded from a virtual ball-tossing game (Cyberball; see Williams, Chung, & Choi, 2000) demonstrated increased activity in the part of the brain that is typically linked to the affective experience of physical pain, the dorsal anterior cingulate cortex (dACC). Further, the amount of activity in the dACC was positively associated with participants' reports of their social distress. Kross, Berman, Mischel, Smith, and Wagner (2011) similarly found that reliving or re-experiencing social pain was linked to increased activity in the regions of the brain that support the affective and sensory experience of physical pain. Research conducted by DeWall and his colleagues (2010) showed that acetaminophen, a commonly used physical pain reliever, reduced people's reports of their hurt feelings or social pain over a three-week period of time. Individuals who took the physical pain reliever once a day for three weeks had less activity in the dACC after they were excluded from a virtual ball-tossing game than did those who took a placebo.

Although the link between hurt feelings and physical pain is relatively clear, research on the way women and men experience pain suggests that it may well be qualified. Studies indicate that women and men may respond in different ways to analgesic drugs (Giles & Walker, 2000) and that women and men experience and react to physical pain in different ways (Fillingrim, 2000). These and other sex differences prompted Vangelisti, Pennebaker, Brody, and Guinn (2014) to investigate the possibility that there are sex differences in the degree to which physical pain relievers reduce hurt feelings. The researchers asked participants to take either ibuprofen, a commonly used physical pain reliever, or a placebo. Then they assessed participants' immediate or acute responses to a socially painful experience (being rejected from a virtual ball-tossing game) as well as their relived or re-experienced reactions to social pain (writing about a hurtful event). They found that women responded as indicated by previous studies and in line with pain overlap theory: Women who took ibuprofen noted that they felt less hurt directly after being excluded from the ball-tossing game and after describing the socially painful experience than did those who took the placebo. Men, however, responded in the opposite fashion: Men who took ibuprofen reported more hurt after being excluded from the game and after describing the socially painful experience than did men who took the placebo.

To further probe their findings, Vangelisti and her colleagues (2014) looked at whether taking the physical pain reliever affected the way women and men expressed their social pain. They examined participants' descriptions of the aforementioned socially painful experience. Because Pennebaker and his colleagues found that people who are prone to social pain use a relatively high proportion of first-person pronouns (Rude, Gortner, & Pennebaker, 2004) and, further, that individuals' emotional involvement in traumatic situations is associated with the frequent use of emotion words (Tausczik & Pennebaker, 2010), the researchers reasoned that the frequency of first-person pronouns and emotion words employed in individuals' descriptions of their painful experiences should be affected by whether or not they took the physical pain reliever. In support of this reasoning, they found that women who took ibuprofen used fewer first-person pronouns and emotion words than women who took the placebo and that men who took ibuprofen used more first-person pronouns and emotion words than did those who took the placebo.

The sex difference evidenced in these findings might be explained in several ways. For instance, it is possible that taking a physical pain reliever provides men with the cognitive resources they need to articulate their social pain. Because men are socialized not to express emotions that involve vulnerability, they may find it more challenging than women to express their hurt feelings. Taking a physical pain reliever may have a disinhibition effect for men, enabling them to express their social pain. This explanation is supported by the finding that men who took ibuprofen described their hurt differently—using more first-person pronouns and marginally more emotion words—than did men who took the placebo.

Another possible explanation is that the neural activity associated with social pain may be linked to the neural activity associated with emotion regulation for men. In line with this explanation, Eisenberger and her colleagues (2009) found that men who had increased levels of interleukin-6 (IL-6, a proinflamatory cytokine produced in response to endotoxin) showed some increase in social pain-related neural activity, but also showed increased activity in several regions of the brain involving emotion regulation. By contrast, women who had increased levels of IL-6 showed almost exclusive increases in social pain-related neural activity. If, indeed, this is the case, taking ibuprofen may affect men's ability to regulate their hurt feelings.

Relationship Characteristics Linked to Hurt

Both the characteristics of hurtful events and people's responses to being hurt have been linked to a number of outcomes relevant to family relationships. More specifically, research suggests that relational satisfaction, commitment, and relationship climate are associated with the way hurt operates.

Satisfaction. Given that hurt feelings typically are experienced as aversive, researchers and clinicians have long argued that the frequency with which people are hurt by a relational partner will negatively affect the way they feel about their relationship. In line with this argument, studies indicate that relational satisfaction is negatively associated with the intensity of individuals' social pain and positively associated with people's tendency to distance themselves from a partner who hurt them. Individuals who are dissatisfied with their relationship are more likely to judge their partner's hurtful behavior as intentional (Vangelisti & Young, 2000) and less likely to engage in active verbal responses to their partner's hurtful behavior (Vangelisti & Crumley, 1998) than are those who are happy with their relationships.

Although a common presumption is that hurt feelings influence relational satisfaction, it is important to recognize that the causal direction of this association has not been established. Researchers do not yet know the extent to which people who are dissatisfied experience more hurtful interactions and engage in fewer constructive responses to social pain than do those who are satisfied or whether, instead, individuals' dissatisfaction with their relationship serves as a lens for interpreting hurtful interactions in relatively negative ways. There is theoretical and empirical evidence in the literature to support both causal paths. For instance, longitudinal research shows that the expression of negative affect negatively predicts satisfaction over time (Gottman & Krokoff, 1989; Levenson & Gottman, 1985; Markman, 1979, 1981)—hinting that hurtful behaviors may create dissatisfaction in relationships. By contrast, studies also show that individuals' relational satisfaction colors their judgments of their partner's behavior (e.g., Murray, Holmes, & Griffin, 1996a, 1996b). Thus, it is possible that people who are dissatisfied see their partner as engaging in more socially painful behaviors than do those who are satisfied. Of course, it is likely that both causal paths occur. Researchers need to determine when each path is predominant and when, for example, positive illusions give way to realistic assessments.

Commitment. Another relational quality that is relevant to the study of hurt feelings is commitment. Among other things, commitment signals how much people value or need a relationship. Inasmuch as commitment involves interdependence with a partner and vulnerability to a partner's behavior, people who are more committed to their relationship are more likely to be hurt by their partner.

The possible link between commitment and hurt feelings was initially explored by researchers who contrasted individuals' responses to being hurt in three types of relationships: romantic relationships, family relationships, and nonfamily/

nonromantic relationships (e.g., acquaintances) (Vangelisti & Crumley, 1998). The researchers argued that people's reactions to social pain in these relationships were likely to differ because family relationships typically are characterized by more constraints and more structural commitment than are the other two types of relationships. In fact, the studies' findings indicated that individuals who described hurtful episodes taking place in the context of family relationships reported feeling more social pain than did those who described episodes taking place in the other two types of relationships. Those who said they were hurt by family members, however, did not engage in more relational distancing as a consequence of their hurt feelings. The researchers suggested that individuals who are hurt by family members may experience more pain because family members are particularly skillful in hurting each other—their lengthy relationships provide them with experiences and information they can use to elicit hurt feelings. But because family relationships typically are involuntary and high in structural commitment (Johnson, 1973, 1991), members may not engage in much relational distancing when they are hurt. In other words, the obligatory nature of family relationships and the constraints that characterize most family associations may discourage individuals from distancing themselves from a family member who hurts them.

Other research supports the notion that relational commitment may give partners an ability to hurt each other without having to incur the costs of relational distancing. For instance, Lemay, Overall, and Clark (2014) found that individuals who are highly committed to their relationship are especially likely to feel social pain in response to perceived devaluation from their partner. Lemay et al.'s work also indicates that people's hurt feelings are associated with dependence and with a desire to restore the acceptance of the perpetrator. Although these findings suggest that high commitment puts individuals at increased risk for being frequently or repeatedly hurt by a partner, Lemay and his colleagues found that partners typically did not exploit this vulnerability. Indeed, their findings indicated quite the opposite. Perpetrators tended to feel guilty about their behavior and empathy toward the person they hurt. They also engaged in more constructive relationship behavior after injuring their partner.

Relational climate. The constructive behavior exhibited by perpetrators in the Lemay et al. (2014) study likely emerged in a relationship context that could be characterized as relatively positive. What happens when the relationship context is less than positive? Do partners interpret hurtful behavior differently when the behavior takes place in a relationship that is fraught with social pain? To explore questions such as these, Vangelisti, Maguire, Alexander, and Clark (2007) examined hurtful family environments. They argued that family members' communication behaviors create a relational climate that varies in terms of the degree to which it evokes hurt. The researchers asked participants to describe and rate behaviors indicative of a socially painful family environment. They found that hurtful family environments are characterized by aggression (belittling, dominating, or blaming family members), a lack of affection (failing to express love, affection, and emotional support toward family members), neglect (not paying attention to family members, ignoring family members), and violence (physically harming or abusing family members).

Of course, the finding that family environments differ with regard to social pain is not surprising. Researchers and clinicians have long known that some family members have a propensity to behave in ways that are nurturant and caring and that others tend to behave in ways that are painful and dismissive. What is more interesting is that the relational climate created by family members' behavior can affect the way they interpret and respond to socially painful interactions. The literature on emotion offers two contrasting models that explain how ongoing exposure to hurt may affect the ways people conceptualize and experience hurtful interactions. The first is a sensitization model. The sensitization model suggests that repeated exposure to hurtful stimuli makes individuals more sensitive so that when they are exposed to the stimuli, their hurt feelings are more intense (Zahn-Waxler & Kochanska, 1990). The second model is a habituation model. This model indicates that ongoing exposure to hurtful stimuli results in people becoming accustomed and less sensitive to social pain (DeWall & Baumeister, 2006).

There is empirical evidence supporting both models. In line with the sensitization model, Will, van Lier, Crone, and Güroğlu (2015) found that chronic rejection from peers during childhood is linked to heightened neural responses to social rejection during adolescence. By contrast, and supporting the habituation model, Vangelisti and her colleagues (2007) found that people who noted their family environment was characterized by a lack of affection rated hurtful family interactions as less emotionally painful than did others.

Although the conditions that predict habituation and sensitization still are unclear, research does suggest that individuals who see their family environment as hurtful differ in some theoretically important ways from people who do not (Vangelisti et al., 2007). For instance, those who perceive their family environment as aggressive have relatively high trait anxiety, low self-esteem, and low verbal hostility. They also are more likely to see other family members' hurtful behavior as intentional. Individuals who perceive their family as lacking affection also have low self-esteem, but they tend to be high (rather than low) in verbal hostility.

FUTURE DIRECTIONS

Researchers have made great progress over the past two decades in understanding hurtful events, the elicitation of social pain, and individuals' responses to feeling hurt. However, there still are major gaps in our understanding of ongoing hurt, its precursors, and its consequences. One reason for these gaps is that the elicitation of social pain and the way people interpret hurtful behavior varies based on the emotional and relational contexts in which hurtful events take place. A pointed insult made in the middle of a one-time argument is different than a pointed insult made in response to an overture of affection. Similarly, an accusation made by a coworker in a meeting differs from an accusation made by a loved one at a family gathering. Much of the research conducted to date focuses on specific emotional or relational contexts. As a consequence, it is unclear which findings are particular to those contexts and which are generalizable to others.

Another limitation of extant research is that it likely confounds relatively isolated hurtful events with events that are part of an ongoing pattern. Researchers often ask participants about individual interactions or ask them to engage in a single interaction, but fail to account for the possibility that those interactions may or may not be associated with an ongoing pattern of hurtful behavior. Research and theory suggest that people's responses to socially painful behavior differ based on their prior exposure to similar behavior (Zahn-Waxler & Kochanska, 1990). As such, scholars need to distinguish hurtful interactions that are relatively isolated from those that are part of a pattern.

In a similar vein, the outcomes associated with any given hurtful event are influenced by the behaviors that precede and follow it. Very little of the research that has been conducted to date has looked at hurtful behavior dyadically. The few studies that have examined hurtful interactions from the perspective of both partners have found that perpetrators often feel guilty about their actions and often respond by engaging in constructive relationship behavior (Lemay et al., 2014). Of course, not all perpetrators recognize—or are concerned with—their partner's social pain. And any guilty feelings a perpetrator experiences might quickly be replaced by defensiveness if those feelings are met by an angry, aggressive victim. Explaining how social pain is elicited and how both victims and perpetrators respond to hurt will require studying hurtful episodes dyadically.

Finally, researchers have yet to systematically examine the influence of individuals' social networks on hurt feelings. Family members and friends can behave in ways that either alleviate or exacerbate the negative effects of social pain. When they see someone being hurt, friends and family can take action to stop the hurtful episode, offer support, stand by passively, or join in on the hurtful behavior. In an effort to explore the tendency of social network members to intervene in hurtful interactions, Brody and Vangelisti (in press) examined people's responses to cyberbullying on Facebook. They found that individuals were more likely to defend a victim in a cyberbullying incident when they had a close relationship with the victim and when they were visible to the victim and to other bystanders. Also, supporting the bystander effect (Darley & Latané, 1968), people were more likely to intervene when there were relatively few bystanders. These findings have interesting implications for other contexts—including situations when members of the social network observe hurtful interactions or when one or both partners involved in a hurtful interaction seek support from network members. Family members may be bystanders to hurtful interactions, or they may be the safe haven individuals turn to after they experience social pain. The ways family members behave as bystanders or sources of support undoubtedly influence the experiences of individuals who are hurt and the behavior of those who hurt them.

REFERENCES

Brody, N., & Vangelisti, A. L. (in press). Bystander intervention in cyberbullying. *Communication Monographs*.

Darley, J. M., & Latané, B. (1968). Bystander intervention in emergencies: Diffusion of responsibility. *Journal of Personality and Social Psychology, 8*, 377–383. http://dx.doi.org/10.1037/h0025589

DeWall, C. N., & Baumeister, R. F. (2006). Alone but feeling no pain: Effects of social exclusion on physical pain tolerance and pain threshold, affective forecasting, and interpersonal empathy. *Journal of Personality and Social Psychology, 91*, 1–15. http://dx.doi.org/10.1037/0022-3514.91.1.1

DeWall, C. N., MacDonald, G., Webster, G. D., Masten, C. L. Baumeister, R. F., Powell, C., ... Eisenberger, N. I. (2010). Acetaminophen reduces social pain: Behavioral and neural evidence. *Psychological Science, 21*, 931–937. http://dx.doi.org/10.1177/0956797610374741

Eisenberger, N. I., Inagaki, T. K., Rameson, L. T., Mashal, N. M., & Irwin, M. R. (2009). An fMRI study of cytokine-induced depressed mood and social pain: The role of sex differences. *NeuroImage, 47*, 881–890. http://dx.doi.org/10.1016/j.neuroimage.2009.04.040

Eisenberger, N. I., & Lieberman, M. D. (2004). Why rejection hurts: A common neural alarm system for physical and social pain. *Trends in Cognitive Sciences, 8*, 294–300. http://dx.doi.org/10.1016/j.tics.2004.05.010

Eisenberger, N. I., Lieberman, M. D., & Williams, K. D. (2003). Does rejection hurt? An fMRI study of social exclusion. *Science, 302*, 290–292. http://dx.doi.org/10.1126/science.1089134

Feeney, J. A. (2004). Hurt feelings in couple relationships: Towards integrative models of the negative effects of hurtful events. *Journal of Social and Personal Relationships, 21*, 487–508. http://dx.doi.org/10.1177/0265407504044844

Feeney, J. A. (2005). Hurt feelings in couple relationships: Exploring the role of attachment and perceptions of personal injury. *Personal Relationships, 12*, 253–271. http://dx.doi.org/10.1111/j.1350-4126.2005.00114.x

Fillingrim, R. B. (2000). Sex, gender and pain: Women and men really are different. *Current Review of Pain, 4*, 24–30.

Folkes, V. S. (1982). Communicating the causes of social rejection. *Journal of Experimental Social Psychology, 18*, 235–252.

Giles, B. E., & Walker, J. S. (2000). Sex differences in pain and analgesia. *Pain Reviews, 7*, 181–193.

Gottman, J. M., & Krokoff, L. J. (1989). Marital interaction and satisfaction: A longitudinal view. *Journal of Consulting and Clinical Psychology, 57*, 47–52. http://dx.doi.org/10.1037/0022-006X.57.1.47

Gottman, J. M., & Levenson, R. W. (1986). Assessing the role of emotion in marriage. *Behavioral Assessment, 8*, 31–48.

Hampel, A. D., & Vangelisti, A. L. (in progress). *Serial hurt*. Manuscript in preparation.

Herman, B. H., & Panksepp, J. (1978). Effects of morphine and naloxone on separation distress and approach attachment: Evidence for opiate mediation of social affect. *Pharmacology, Biochemistry and Behavior, 9*, 213–220. http://dx.doi.org/10.1016/0091-3057(78)90167-3

Johnson, M. P. (1973). Commitment: A conceptual structure and empirical application. *Sociological Quarterly, 14*, 395–406. http://dx.doi.org/10.1111/j.1533-8525.1973.tb00868.x

Johnson, M. P. (1991). Commitment to personal relationships. In W. H. Jones & D. Perlman (Eds.), *Advances in personal relationships* (vol. 3, pp. 117–143). London: Jesssica Kingsley.

Kross, E., Berman, M. G., Mischel, W., Smith, E. E., & Wagner, T. D. (2011). Social rejection shares somatosensory representations with physical pain. *PNAS, 108*, 6270–6275. http://dx.doi.org/10.1073/pnas.1102693108

L'Abate, L. (1977). Intimacy is sharing hurt feelings: A reply to David Mace. *Journal of Marriage and Family Counseling, 3*, 13–16. http://dx.doi.org/10.1111/j.1752-0606.1977.tb00450.x

Leary, M. R., Springer, C., Negel, L., Ansell, E., & Evans, K. (1998). The causes, phenomenology, and consequences of hurt feelings. *Journal of Personality and Social Psychology, 74*, 1225–1237. http://dx.doi.org/10.1037/0022-3514.74.5.1225

Lemay, E. P., Overall, N. C., & Clark, M. S. (2012). Experiences and interpersonal; consequences of hurt feelings and anger. *Journal of Personality and Social Psychology, 103*, 982–1006. http://dx.doi.org/10.1037/a0030064

Levenson, R. W., & Gottman, J. M. (1985). Physiological and affective predictors of change in relationship satisfaction. *Journal of Personality and Social Psychology, 49*, 85–94. http://dx.doi.org/10.1037/0022-3514.49.1.85

MacDonald, G., & Leary, M. R. (2005). Why does social exclusion hurt? The relationship between social and physical pain. *Psychological Bulletin, 131*, 202–223. doi: 10.1037/0033-2909.131.2.202

Malle, B. F., & Knobe, J. (1997). The folk concept of intentionality. *Journal of Experimental Social Psychology, 33*, 101–121. http://dx.doi.org/10.1006/jesp.1996.1314

Markman, H. J. (1979). The application of a behavioral model of marriage in predicting relationship satisfaction of couples planning marriage. *Journal of Consulting and Clinical Psychology, 47*, 743–749.

Markman, H. J. (1981). Prediction of marital distress: A 5-year follow-up. *Journal of Consulting and Clinical Psychology, 49*, 760–762. http://dx.doi.org/10.1037/0022-006X.49.5.760

McLaren, R. M., & Solomon, D. H. (2008). Appraisals and distancing responses to hurtful messages. *Communication Research, 35*, 339–357. http://dx.doi.org/10.1177/0093650208315961

McLaren, R. M., Solomon, D. H., & Priem, J. S. (2011). Explaining variation in contemporaneous responses to hurt in premarital romantic relationships: A relational turbulence model perspective. *Communication Research, 38*, 543–564. http://dx.doi.org/10.1177/0093650210377896

Miller, C. W., & Roloff, M. E. (2005). Gender and willingness to confront hurtful messages from romantic partners. *Communication Quarterly, 53*, 323–337. http://dx.doi.org/10.1080/01463370500101378

Murray, S. L., Holmes, J. G., & Griffin, D. W. (1996a). The benefits of positive illusions: Idealization and the construction of satisfaction in close relationships. *Journal of Personality and Social Psychology, 70*, 79–98. http://dx.doi.org/10.1037/0022-3514.70.1.79

Murray, S. L., Holmes, J. G., & Griffin, D. W. (1996b). The self-fulfilling prophesy of positive illusions in romantic relationships: Love is not blind but prescient. *Journal of Personality and Social Psychology, 71*, 1155–1180.

Panksepp, J. (1998). *Affective neuroscience: The foundations of human and animal emotions.* London: Oxford University Press.

Priem, J. S., McLaren, R. M., & Solomon, D. H. (2010). Relational messages, perceptions of hurt, and biological stress reactions to a disconfirming interaction. *Communication Research, 37*, 48–72. http://dx.doi.org/10.1177/0093650209351470

Rude, S., Gortner, E. M., & Pennebaker, J. (2004). Language use of depressed and depression-vulnerable college students. *Cognition & Emotion, 18*, 1121–1133. http://dx.doi.org/10.1080/026999 30441000030

Shaver, P. R., Mikulincer, M., Lavy, S., & Cassidy, J. (2009). Understanding and altering hurt feelings: An attachment-theoretical perspective on the generation and regulation of emotions. In A. L. Vangelisti (Ed.), *Feeling hurt in close relationships* (pp. 92–119). New York: Cambridge University Press. http://dx.doi.org/10.1017/CBO9780511770548.007

Shaver, P. R., Schwartz, J., Kirson, D., & O'Connor, C. (1987). Emotion knowledge: Further exploration of a prototype approach. *Journal of Personality and Social Psychology, 52*, 1061–1086. http://dx.doi.org/10.1037/0022-3514.52.6.1061

Tausczik, Y. R., & Pennebaker, J. W. (2010). The psychological meaning of words: LIWC and computerized text analysis methods. *Journal of Language and Social Psychology, 29*, 24–54. http://dx.doi.org/10.1177/0261927X09351676

Theiss, J., Knobloch, L. K., Chectron, M. G., & Magsaman-Conrad, K. (2009). Relationship characteristics associated with the experience of hurt in romantic relationships: A test of the relationship turbulence model. *Human Communication Research, 35*, 588–615. http://dx.doi.org/10.1111/j.1468-2958.2009.01364.x

Vangelisti, A. L. (1994). Messages that hurt. In W. R. Cupach & B. H. Spitzberg (Eds.), *The dark side of interpersonal communication* (pp. 53–82). Hillsdale, NJ: Erlbaum.

Vangelisti, A. L., & Crumley, L. P. (1998). Reactions to messages that hurt: The influence of relational contexts. *Communication Monographs, 65*, 173–196. http://dx.doi.org/10.1080/0363775980 9376447

Vangelisti, A. L., & Hampel, A. D. (2010). Hurtful communication: Current research and future directions. In S. W. Smith & S. R. Wilson (Eds.), *New directions in interpersonal communication research* (pp. 221–241). Thousand Oaks, CA: Sage. http://dx.doi.org/10.4135/978148334 9619.n11

Vangelisti, A. L., Maguire, K. C., Alexander, A. L., & Clark, G. (2007). Hurtful family environments: Links with individual, relationship, and perceptual variables. *Communication Monographs, 74*, 357–385. http://dx.doi.org/10.1080/03637750701543477

Vangelisti, A. L., Pennebaker, J. W., Brody, N., & Guinn, T. D. (2014). Reducing social pain: Sex differences in the impact of physical pain relievers. *Personal Relationships, 21*, 349–363. doi: 10.1111/pere.12036

Vangelisti, A. L., & Young, S. L. (2000). When words hurt: The effects of perceived intentionality on interpersonal relationships. *Journal of Social and Personal Relationships, 17*, 393–424. http://dx.doi.org/10.1177/0265407500173005

Vangelisti, A. L., Young, S. L., Carpenter-Theune, K. E., & Alexander, A. L. (2005). Why does it hurt? The perceived causes of hurt feelings. *Communication Research, 32*, 443–477. http://dx.doi.org/10.1177/0093650205277319

Will, G. J., van Lier P. A. C., Crone E. A., & Güroğlu, B. (2015). Chronic childhood peer rejection is associated with heightened neural responses to social exclusion during adolescence. *Journal of Abnormal Child Psychology*. doi: 10.1007/s10802-015-9983-0. http://dx.doi.org/10.1007/s10802-015-9983-0

Williams, K. D., Chung, C. K. T., & Choi, W. (2000). Cyberostracism: Effects of being ignored over the Internet. *Journal of Personality and Social Psychology, 79*, 748–762. http://dx.doi.org/10.1037/0022-3514.79.5.748

Williams, K. D., & Jarvis, B. (2006). Cyberball: A program for use in research on ostracism and interpersonal acceptance. *Behavior Research Methods, Instruments, and Computers, 38*, 174–180. http://dx.doi.org/10.3758/BF03192765

Young, S. L. (2004). Factors that influence recipients' appraisals of hurtful communication. *Journal of Social and Personal Relationships, 21*, 291–303.

Zahn-Waxler, C., & Kochanska, G. (1990). The origins of guilt. In R. A. Thompson (Ed.), *Nebraska symposium on motivation* (pp. 183–258). Lincoln, NE: University of Nebraska Press.

CHAPTER EIGHT

Problematic Intergenerational Communication AND Caregiving IN THE Family

Elder Abuse and Neglect

MEI-CHEN LIN
Kent State University

HOWARD GILES
University of California, Santa Barbara

JORDAN SOLIZ
University of Nebraska – Lincoln

The study of communication and aging is a thriving, multimethod research field that has theoretical and pragmatic implications for personal and family health (e.g., Fisher & Canzona, 2014; Harwood, Rittenour, & Lin, 2012). Scholars of this genre contend that while psychological and physical health mutually influence each other, intergenerational relationships are constituted in the quality of intergenerational communication to and from the old and the young (Giles, Davis, Gasiorek, & Giles, 2013). Putting it another way, intergenerational communication researchers, in the main, conceive of communication playing a central role in the social construction of age and aging, and in ways that can assist in our understanding of successful and unsuccessful aging. One aspect of later-life aging is the health-related changes that necessitate caregiving—a responsibility often carried out by family members.

A constructive caregiving environment is key to successful aging when health issues arise as it is central to physical, psychological, and relational well-being.

Although a majority of caregiving experiences are characterized by a balance of the stressors and rewards associated with this role, issues of elder abuse and neglect in the context of caregiving in the family occur frequently enough to warrant attention by scholars and family practitioners. Our contention is that problematic aspects of caregiving are best understood and, more importantly, ameliorated by attending to the communicative environment that may foster these negative behaviors. Thus, we first turn our attention to the broader landscape of research on problematic intergenerational communication prior to a focused discussion on elder abuse and neglect in the family.

PROBLEMATIC INTERGENERATIONAL COMMUNICATION

Studies have shown that young adults in North America live in an age-segregated society (Hagestad & Uhlenberg, 2005) and have infrequent contact with older adults (see Fox & Giles, 1993; Giles, Ryan, & Anas, 2008). In fact, one of us (HG) found in his communication and aging class that young adults consistently estimate that only 8% of their interactions involve unfamiliar older people, with the number increasing to 12% if family members (or family-like elders) are specified; in other words, intergenerational contact is quite minimal. When evaluating the quality of such infrequent encounters, young adults report that talking to older people is very dissatisfying and problematic, blaming older people for this communicative state of affairs (Williams & Giles, 1996). In addition, many younger people will openly acknowledge that they try and avoid conversations with older adults (Ryan, Kwong See, Meneer, & Trovato, 1992). Such a dismaying communicative landscape is evident even though respect and deference are conveyed (sometimes reluctantly via "biting one's tongue," which is another problematic intergenerational communication by itself).

Studies that have explored the communicative ingredients of these intergenerational conversations—when they do occur—indicate that younger people overaccommodate their elders who, in turn, underaccommodate the younger person (see Williams & Nussbaum, 2001). Overaccommodation (variously termed 'elder-speak' or 'infantilizing' or 'patronizing' talk) is evident in younger people often talking to older people in grammatically simpler ways and more slowly than they would to their same-aged peers (Giles & Gasiorek, 2011); this focus has occupied considerable attention in the domain of intergenerational communication and aging. For cognitively and socially active elders, this, together with overhelping (Ryan, Anas, & Gruneir, 2006), can be interpreted by them as condescending and demeaning, and this speech style is also enacted by older peers (Giles, Fox, & Smith, 1993).

Typically, older folks respond passively to such patronizing approaches, but even when they react assertively—and gain in attributed competence for so doing—they are, then, construed as less respectful and difficult to manage (Harwood & Giles, 1996). Underaccommodative talk is a speech pattern where elders are perceived as failing to attune their message to their conversation partner's needs or wants. Underaccommodative talk is often manifested through verbosity and/or excessive disclosures about hard and painful times they have endured (see Coupland, Coupland, & Giles, 1991). Often, young people respond rather negatively to this kind of talk with discomfort (Bonneson & Hummert, 2002) and attribute negative stereotypes of older adults to these older interlocutors. (Hummert, Garstka, Ryan, & Bonneson, 2004). Indeed, these communicative acts have been labeled painful self-disclosure (PSD) because of the focus on painful experiences regardless of whether or not they are still emotionally "painful" for the older interactant. PSDs have been likened to a "communicative grenade" (Giles, 2014) in that it often comes "out of the blue" in ways that younger people are uncertain how to manage and, as stated, creates or amplifies discomfort and negative affects toward the intergenerational interactions.

Hence, both age groups can be nonaccommodative and, in fact, "miss each other" communicatively (Giles & Gasiorek, 2011), and sometimes in ways that can lead to intergenerational conflict (Zhang & Lin, 2009). The above becomes all the more poignant from studies documenting a relationship between accommodative phenomena; on the other hand, and subjective well-being on the other. The more that older people report feeling that they have not been accommodated to by young people, the lower their self-esteem and life satisfaction, and higher depression may be (Ota, Giles, & Somera, 2007).

The first robust attempt at theorizing about the interfaces of communication, aging, and health was the "communication predicament of aging" model (CPA) (Ryan, Giles, Bartolucci, & Henwood, 1986). This framework, which was inspired by communication accommodation theory, proposes vital relationships between intergenerational communication and subjective well-being. It attends to how negative stereotypes of older people may induce young people to adopt overaccommodative messages that are ideationally simple and exaggerated in intonation (Hummert, 2010). Continued encounters of this nature could lead some older people to wonder if and become anxious about whether they are as truly incompetent as messages to them would indicate. As a result, and in self-stereotypical fashion (e.g., Levy, 2003), older people may assume the very ageist communication characteristics (such as a slowed gait and voice perturbations) implied by a younger person's stance toward them, despite the fact that they may well be quite competent and have independent spirits. The CPA model proposed that poor self-perceptions may cumulatively lead to social withdrawal, a lessened sense of self-worth, and even somatic changes accelerating physical demise.

Much of the research couched in the CPA framework, in general, has focused on institutional settings and/or contexts in which intergenerational encounters are between nonintimates. Yet intergenerational relationships are obviously evident in the family (Dickson & Hughes, 2014). Unfortunately, they are often plagued with some of the same age-based communicative issues in nonintimate intergenerational encounters; at times, with more relational consequences given the expectations and implications associated with familial bonds and identity. For instance, in the context of grandparent-grandchild interactions (Soliz & Lin, 2013), painful self-disclosures engender interactional dissatisfaction, make age overly salient, and detract from family solidarity and a healthy shared family identity (e.g., Harwood, 2000; Soliz & Harwood, 2006), and these effects seem exacerbated in families that do not practice open communication styles (Fowler & Soliz, 2013). Armed with this backdrop, we now move to issues of care of older adults in the family, recognizing that the age stereotypes, negative attitudes toward aging, and problematic aspects of intergenerational communication are central to understanding and, ultimately, avoiding more extreme issues associated with family elder care.

As family members age and begin to experience health issues that drastically alter their lifestyle and independence, younger generations and spouses often assume the informal caregiving role. Building off the seminal works on caregiving burden (Montgomery, Gonyea, & Hooyman, 1985), scholars and practitioners have devoted considerable attention to stressors associated with caregiving (e.g., parent-child role negotiations, financial and time constraints). With appropriate support networks and resources, caregiving can certainly be a rewarding experience for family members (Savundranayagam, 2013), and even with the common burdens associated with caregiving, it is a role that family members willingly accept and uphold in a constructive and functional manner. With that being said, we also recognize that there is a potential very dark-side aspect associated with the responsibility of caring for older family members that is often marginalized in our discourses of problematic family behavior: elder abuse and neglect.

ELDER ABUSE AND NEGLECT: FORMS, PREVALENCE, AND PROFILES

Elder abuse and mistreatment are usually manifested in forms such as physical abuse, emotional/verbal abuse, sexual abuse, financial exploitation, and neglect. Sorenson (2006) introduced *communication neglect*, a form of abuse that is rarely included in the elder abuse research and documents but should be of interest to communication scholars. It is a subtype of neglect in that an elderly victim may be provided with assistance to meet his/her daily needs, but "communicatively" neglected by the caregiver, such as avoiding making social or physical contact with the victim or showing little interest in personable conversations. This, in turn, leads to experiences of emotional abandonment and social isolation and, thus, can be equally detrimental as other forms of abuse. Elder abuse was officially recognized as an offence in the United States in the early 1970s (Stannard, 1973). However, it was not until the 1980s that Congressman Claude Pepper began to label elder abuse as a "hidden problem" and advocated for immediate federal action and funding. To gain attention from Congress, Pepper framed the problem of elder maltreatment as an "aging" issue and in the context of caregiving in order to cast a wider network with interested parties.

The National Center of Elder Abuse estimates that between 1 and 2 million, or 9.5%, of the older adult population, have been victims of abuse in the United States (National Research Council, 2003) although estimates do vary (Laumann, Leitsch, & Waite, 2008), from 7.6% to 11% (Pillemer, Connolly, Breckman, Spreng, & Lachs, 2015). A vast majority (nearly 90% in some estimates) of perpetrators of elder abuse are family members (National Council of Elder Abuse, 2015). The variation in estimates of elder abuse is likely due to the fact that more than half of the cases were not reported, or as other studies suggest, only 1 in 14 cases is ever exposed (National Research Council, 2003). It is possible that the low reporting rate could be due to a lack of training of medical professionals to detect signs of abuse. In many cases, however, the elder victims may choose not to report it to maintain family reputation, protect self from escalating further abuse, and/or fear of being removed from their current home. Further, some victims may be concerned with the social stigma associated with aging and elder abuse, as they may internalize age stereotypes and fear that people may not believe their allegations. In other cases, elderly victims may not be able to recognize the occurrence of abuse when they have mental decline such as dementia or Alzheimer's disease. Like other victims of domestic abuse, it may be that elderly victims are convinced by the abuser that they deserve such mistreatment and, therefore, should endure it (Giles & Helmle, 2011). Whereas victims of elder abuse are typically female, perpetrators are predominantly male spouses or sons. Victims often display signs of depression, agitation, fear, and reticence, whereas a history of behavioral issues often characterizes abusers (Anthony, Lehning, Austin, & Peck, 2009). An overwhelming number of cases of elder abuse take place at home (Teaster et al., 2006), justifying elder abuse and neglect as a pressing concern for family scholars and practitioners.

Even with this evident prevalence of elder abuse and neglect in the U.S. and similar phenomena that have been documented in other countries, such as the UK (Cooper, Selwood, & Livingston, 2008) and China (Dong, Simon, & Gorbien, 2007), this issue has received relatively scant attention from scholars, advocates, and government leadership compared to other family domestic abuse contexts (e.g., child, partner). In 2009, for instance, federal agencies in the USA spent only 11.9 million dollars for all the programs and activities related to elder abuse, while 649 million dollars went into programs on violence against women (Dong, 2014).

We speculate that many of the negative stereotypes toward older adults and aging, to some degree, minimize or ignore the significance of elder abuse and neglect for many.

Another reason for little research in our field is a lack of understanding of the role of communication surrounding the occurrence and continuity of the mistreatment. For instance, in a recent overview of research on elder abuse, and in line with other gerontological and criminological treatises, Dong (2014) affords communicative phenomena, processes, and theories (including a discussion of reporting issues) virtually no attention. Suggestions put forward at the 2015 White House Conference on Aging urged comprehensive research to advance knowledge on elder abuse and neglect but, again, afford no attention to communication (Pillemer et al., 2015). It is with the hopes of addressing this gap that we turn to the role of communication as both a causal and empowering agent for victims and perpetrators of elder abuse and neglect.

COMMUNICATIVE PERSPECTIVE ON ELDER ABUSE AND NEGLECT

Whereas there are various antecedents to elder abuse (e.g., mental health, substance abuse, retribution for childhood neglect), the dominant narrative of elder abuse usually is a "caregiver stress" frame where a caregiver is unable to manage the stress as a result of excessive burdens and, ultimately, "snaps" at the elder person, resulting in violent behavior and/or neglect. This caregiver stress theory and related perspectives focuses solely on the abuser without recognition of the agency of the elder care receiver as well as the general relational and communicative context. Given that the caregiving environment is a reciprocal and communicative process, we should look at the communicative interdependence of both individuals to assess how dysfunctional family communication can escalate conflict and eventually trigger abuse and neglect. One example of this reciprocal caregiving process is captured by Lin and Giles (2013) proposed power-based model of elder abuse and neglect. Based on Bugental and her colleagues' (e.g., 2002) work, this model suggests that the abuser is the one who feels powerless, or a lack of control over the caregiving situation when interpreting the elderly care receiver's behaviors as problematic (e.g., nonresponsive or noncomplying). The caregiver tends to attribute the power to the care receiver and experiences negative emotions such as anxiety, anger or apprehension.

Thus, the caregiver may adopt coercion or abusive behaviors (e.g., physical abuse, verbal abuse, communication neglect) to regain control. In this case, the emerging harm to the elder is a joint effect of nonaccommodation from the elder victim and coercion from the abuser within a power-based schema. Given the limited space available here, we will not review the entire model (see Lin & Giles, 2013). Rather, our goal for the remainder of the chapter is to focus on communicative processes and contexts presented in the Lin and Giles' model and elsewhere that are at the heart of elder abuse and neglect: (a) verbal aggressiveness, (b) the family communication environment, (c) perceived caregiving stress and problematic communication, and (d) the elderly care receiver's communication.

Verbal Aggressiveness

A major dysfunctional family communication pattern is verbal aggression (VA), which Infante and Rancer (1982) conceptualized as a "communication behavior that individuals use to attack another person's self-concept or self-worth in lieu of, or in addition to, arguing against the person's opinions or ideas" (Lin & Giles, 2013, p. 1284). VA is considered a predisposition often triggered by situational stimuli (Rudd, Vogl-Bauer, Dobos, Beatty, & Valencic, 1998) where feelings of frustration and/or anger are elicited. For instance, Wilson and his colleagues (2006, 2008) found that mothers who scored high on verbal aggressiveness also scored high on child abuse potential and were more directive when interacting with their children. They were more likely to view their children as uncooperative, had a rigid expectation of home life and children's behaviors, felt stressed, and attributed problems in life to others. Further, the children whose mothers were verbally aggressive also tended to resist those controlling behaviors (Wilson et al., 2008), which can escalate more verbal aggressiveness from the mother and, hence, an interaction pattern is formed. Repeated exposure to an abusive or violent environment in childhood can have detrimental effects on a child's emotional and psychological development into adolescence (Morimoto & Sharma, 2004). When fathers engage in verbal punishment, this is a strong predictor of the child's verbal and physical aggression toward the father in adolescence (Pagani et al., 2009). Teenagers who displayed verbal and physical aggressiveness toward their mothers had a greater likelihood of having abusive parents growing up (Pagani et al., 2004). Whether the children's aggressiveness toward parents is a result of retaliation or is fostered by drug use, the influence of family violence over time may hinder their communication skills to manage conflicts and, hence, they are likely to resort to aggression later in other intimate relationships when conflicts arise (Theobald & Farrington, 2012).

VA has not been positioned as a central causal factor for elder abuse and neglect. However, the extant research clearly demonstrates a likely connection between VA and potential to engage in abuse toward older family members. First, family caregivers who have a predisposition toward VA could be at risk of mistreating their elderly care receiver, because caregiving is a stressful and/or frustrating situation, particularly when the elderly care receiver is noncooperative or nonaccommodating (see above). Second, VA is likely a joint product of the caregiver's VA trait and the long-term abusive family environment in which the caregiver was raised. Thus, an older family member who was a perpetrator of physical or emotional abuse may now find him- or herself in a victim role. In short, VA, as it relates to the rise of elder abuse and neglect, may be a temporal reciprocal cycle—and this possibility warrants further consideration.

Family Communication Environment

Families typically operate as a collective identity and, as such, develop shared ideologies including perceptions, expectations, and norms of family communication (Koerner & Fitzpatrick, 2002). This is most evident in the theorizing on family communication patterns (FCP), which centers on two salient communication dimensions in the family: conversation orientation and conformity orientation (Schrodt, Witt, & Messersmith, 2008). Briefly, conversation orientation reflects "a concern with open discussion of ideas between parents and children," whereas conformity orientation reflects "the degree to which the family communication climate stresses homogeneity of attitudes, beliefs, and values among all family members." These orientations work in tandem to create the communication environment in the family (i.e., consensual, pluralistic, protective, and laissez-faire families). Ample evidence already supported the utility of FCP in explaining parent-child interactions about different issues, such as politics and advertising, and the FCP is found to be associated with children and/or young adults' levels of aggression and self-disclosure (see Koerner & Schrodt, 2014, for a review).

Potentially harmful effects of a conformity orientation are already suggested in the research such as children's depression, mental health, and maladjustment into adulthood (Koerner & Schrodt, 2014). High-conformity families are more likely to manage conflict in a confrontational manner that normally escalates into further conflict or engage in a demand/withdraw pattern (Sillars et al. 2014). Accordingly, we can reasonably speculate that although not framed explicitly within the family communication patterns framework, research supports the idea that the family environment is associated with abusive behaviors. For instance, Pelcovitz et al. (2000) identified the rigidity of the family (i.e., unwillingness to adapt) as a characteristic of abusive family environments—and this had clear links to conformity orientation. Further, one of the fundamental issues of domestic abuse—including elder abuse—is that victims do not always communicate openly to others in and outside of the family.

Clearly, a family schema that marginalizes the voices of family members, especially when considering protecting family reputation and perceptions of family members, provides a more fertile ground for seeds of abuse. As discussed earlier, the caregiver's level of verbal aggressiveness and a conformity family communication environment could increase the risk of elder abuse in later-life relationships. Putting it differently, caregivers may acquire dysfunctional communication styles or fail to develop healthy communication styles growing up in a high-conformity family environment, and therefore may respond to challenging caregiving situations negatively. Moreover, when role reversal is experienced in the caregiving process, the decades-long parental power can be dismissed or challenged.

Perceived Caregiving Stress and Problematic Communication

As alluded to previously, caregiving can be a satisfying and yet stressful experience. Caregiver stress has been linked to physical pain, as well as depression or anxiety (Cooper, Selwood, Blanchard, & Livingston, 2010; Papastavrou et al., 2011). When caregivers fail to properly manage their stress or, in worse cases, direct their stress outward against others, it could result in elder mistreatment. We should note that caregiving stress is multidimensional, and there are different problems linked with various dimensions of caregiver burden (see Savundranayagam, Montgomery, & Kosloski, 2010). Which communication factors, then, may contribute to perceived caregiving stress? One salient factor is conflict with other family members (Etters, Goodall, & Harrison, 2008), as it often arises during the process of caregiving when a caregiver does not receive support from other family members. Moreover, the burdens associated with caregiving can amplify a long-standing family feud. Obviously, poor family functioning prior to caregiving negatively affects the caregiver-care receiver's relationship and interaction patterns and caregivers' interpretations of the care receivers' behaviors (Steadman, Tremont, & Davis, 2007). Thus, family relationships before and after the caregiving roles emerge should be considered to better understand their potential role as a contextual, enabling factor for elder abuse.

Quality and frequency of communication have also been found to be associated with felt caregiving burden; caregivers who can find positive aspects of caregiving experienced less caregiving burden (Papastavrou et al., 2011). A common misperception is that it is the caregiving recipient who desires more communication when, in fact, some evidence points to older adults preferring less communication. The researchers speculated that older adults prefer less communication because they gradually lose the ability to communicate as their illness progresses. It could also be that older adults prefer less conversation about the illness to avoid having negative emotions (Fried, Bradley, O'Leary, & Byers, 2005). This is potentially problematic, because those caregivers who desire more communication with their older family members may feel more emotionally burdened when this need is not met than those who do not have such a need (Fried et al., 2005).

Communication issues are particularly prevalent for illnesses such as dementia or Alzheimer's disease (Wiglesworth et al., 2010). Elderly care receivers may not be able to comprehend or use words correctly, or they may shift from topic to topic or repeat the same utterance. Diminished communication skills in the elderly care receiver may increase the difficulties of caregiving and, consequently, lead to caregiving burdens. Savundranayagam, Hummert, and Montgomery (2005) found support for communication breakdowns, which can lead to problem behaviors by the caregiving recipient (e.g., agitation, wandering, or irritation). Thus, communication problems may play a role in relationships between the status of the illness and caregiver stress. Communication issues surrounding problematic caregiving interaction are prevalent, in particular, when the path is linked to a demand burden (i.e., perceptions that the elderly care receiver's requests are unreasonable or demanding). The caregiver may feel as though he or she is being taken advantage of or manipulated by the elderly care receiver. As outlined in Lin and Giles' (2013) power-based model, perceived demand burden may be the type of caregiving stress that is likely to prompt the process of elder abuse when the caregiver interprets the elderly care receiver's behavior as ill-intentioned and manipulative.

Elderly Care Receiver's Problematic Communicative Acts

Research on family abuse recognizes an "interactional" approach in that both parties respond to each other's communicative behaviors and contribute to the communicative or relational outcomes (e.g., Bugental et al., 2002). This is not to suggest blame toward the victim of abuse. Rather, it emphasizes the interdependence of family members and the notion that the family environment—which may lead to abuse—is constituted in the communication among and between family members. What may be problematic communicative acts exhibited by the elderly care receiver that may elicit negative caregiving schema, age stereotypes, and in some cases, elder abuse? We borrow from research into intergenerational communication on nonaccommodative behaviors that result (see above) in dissatisfying relationships or conversations and highlight three behaviors from old to young: patronizing talk, painful self-disclosure, and off-target verbosity (see Lin & Giles, 2013) to demonstrate the role of elderly care recipients in creating potentially problematic environments.

Patronizing talk. Older people could be underaccommodative by failing to adjust their speech style or choosing conversation topics that are unfamiliar, inappropriate, or even offensive to the younger person. Giles and Williams (1994) identified three types of patronizing talk from the elderly, *disapproving/disrespecting youth*, *nonlistening* and *overprotective/parental*. They all evoked varying degrees of negative emotions in the younger person. Patronizing talk from the family elderly care receiver can affect caregiving interaction and contribute to caregivers' sense of powerlessness and irritation, particularly in the forms of the disapproving/disrespecting youth and nonlistening.

Painful self-disclosure (PSD). As briefly discussed earlier, older people's painful self-disclosures (PSD) focus on "negative intimate topics" (Bonnesen & Hummert, 2002, p. 276) and emphasizes the discomfort or painfulness incurred for the recipient of such disclosure (Fowler & Soliz, 2010). Research on PSD has placed greater emphasis on the negative influence they have on intergenerational communication than the actual emotions experienced by the elderly person when the disclosure takes place. For instance, younger recipients may find the negative intimate topics such as death, bereavement, or health inappropriate or anxiety provoking and, therefore, find difficulty responding to it. Older interactants may or may not relive the negative emotions when disclosing these experiences, and they may choose to disclose them for various motives (Bonnesen & Hummert, 2002). Older people's PSD is likely to activate a schema of helping or pity in younger people (Harwood, McKee, & Lin, 2000) and may constrain subsequent conversation. In the elder abuse context, it is possible that the caregiver may lose sympathy for or empathy with the elderly person after repeatedly hearing about past painful or unpleasant experiences, such that they are no longer interested in responding to PSD when it occurs. Communication neglect (Sorenson, 2006), as we discussed earlier, may be a likely form of response to discourage PSDs.

Off-target verbosity (OTV). Younger interlocutors may find it difficult to converse with an older person engaging in OTV and may attribute negative stereotypes of aging, such as incompetence and slow thinking, to the older person (Ruscher & Hurley, 2000). It is likely that caregivers may feel frustrated about the communication breakdown when they are unable to obtain information from the elderly care receiver (Fried et al., 2005) and lose the patience to repeat the same questions in conversations seemingly every few seconds.

These underaccommodative communication behaviors incur negative age stereotypes and negative age schema. Limited or unpleasant interaction experiences follow, like a downward spiral. These negative interactions may occur repeatedly on a daily basis and, for some caregivers, they may be exposed to such a climate almost the entire duration in the later stages of their caregiving process. Caregivers may become extremely negative and unable to choose positive coping strategies to alleviate stress, thus opening the door for verbal aggressiveness or other types of abuse. These possible caregiving outcomes, obviously, present challenges for caregivers' family identities. Unlike institutional caregivers, family caregivers have a long relational history with the elderly care receiver. Feelings of anger and agitation may come as strongly as feelings of guilt with caregiving. Caregivers may need to redefine their family identities as a result of these unpleasant interactions. Moreover, they may renegotiate the nature of their multiple roles as a spouse, a child or a family member, in addition to being a caregiver as the elderly care receiver ages and his or her health needs change. Whereas research has recognized the implications of these problematic communication styles for intergenerational relationships, especially for young adults (e.g., negative age stereotypes, dissatisfying intergenerational communication, unwillingness to communicate with older adults), little attention has been paid to consider long-term impacts of these speech styles within the family caregiving context as a potential underlying factor in elder abuse.

CONCLUSION AND FUTURE CONSIDERATIONS

Issues and types of family caregiving vary substantially. Some families have plenty of time and resources to plan for caregiving, and others have to assume caregiver roles rather suddenly (e.g., a stroke or a severe fall) or with constrained resources. As such, a caregiver could be unprepared or unwilling to partake in this role. Miller, Shoemaker, Willyard, and Addison (2008) refer to this scenario as the "unexpected career" (p. 22). The surprising onset of this new responsibility coupled, at times, with an amplified strain on financial, relational, and work responsibilities often increases the stress for the caregiver. The lack of necessary skills and knowledge, whether it be at the beginning stage of the caregiving due to the "new-ness" to this role or later due to the complication of the caregiving needs, places great demands on the caregiver in terms of physical, emotional, financial, and relational resources. While a majority of caregivers manage this stress without a dark turn to elder neglect and abuse, this stress can serve as the seed for this problematic and disheartening behavior. Thus, for family scholars and those interested in later-life relationships and care, understanding factors that allow the stress and burden associated with caregiving to escalate into this dysfunctional and abusive environment is instrumental in reducing the prevalence of this behavior.

Throughout this chapter, we have introduced some of these factors including those that reflect problematic relational histories (e.g., enduring parent-child conflict), dysfunctional or less-than-ideal family communication environments, and individual dispositions (e.g., verbal aggressiveness) that are salient in all contexts of family domestic abuse (e.g., partner and child abuse). We position elder abuse and neglect within a larger intergenerational context, as it is a framework crucial to understanding and potentially minimizing the occurrence of elder abuse and neglect. In the following, we suggest relevant theoretical frameworks and constructs emerging from research on family relations and interactions, coupled with the intergenerational framework, to offer nuanced insight into this dark side of family communication.

Attachment theory. Attachment theory (Ainsworth, Blehar, Waters, & Wall, 1978; Bowlby, 1988) posits that particular attachment styles individuals formed in early childhood become the working model of their intimate relationship in terms of perceptions of others (e.g., trust, dependability) and overall self-concept. Attachment theory has a long history of research on individual and relational development including implications for the caregiving context. For instance, Chen and colleagues (2013) found that a higher score on a secure script of relationships (i.e., a secure attachment style) is associated with less criticism and hostility toward caregiving tasks. This association was significant for the medium- and high-stress-level conditions. The implication, according to Chen et al., is that the ability to access secure-based scripts is important for caregivers when the caregiving tasks are challenging (e.g., dementia). Caregivers will be able to manage their stress better by interpreting problematic behaviors such as agitation and communication difficulties with a more positive frame. Thus, we would benefit from further examination of the relationship between other attachment styles (avoidant, anxious, dismissive) and the occurrence of elder abuse and neglect, especially in cases where caregiving demands are high.

Attribution theory. Another cognitive theory, attribution theory, focuses on the way people assign meanings to their own and others' behaviors. Relevant to the caregiving context, one situation in which we afford meanings is in the attribution of responsibility (Stamp, 2004). Jackson and Hafemeister (2013) interviewed elderly abuse victims and identified a discrepancy between their attributions of the occurrence of the abuse and those of the Adult Protection Services caseworkers. Elderly abuse victims were more likely to find reasons to excuse or dismiss the abuse (e.g., mental health, unemployment of the abuser) rather than placing blame on the personality of the family caregiver. Conversely, caseworkers tended to attribute the abuse to elderly victims' vulnerability and dependency. Attributions both make up and reflect the communication and nature of relationships (Manusov & Spitzberg, 2008) and, as such, may be part of the process linking the intergenerational communicative and relational dynamics discussed in this chapter with the occurrence of elder abuse and neglect. Relatedly, we see opportunities and connection with communication privacy management theory (Petronio, 2002; Petronio & Durham, 2008) to explain elderly abuse victims' attribution of responsibility and decisions to disclose the abuse to others.

Intergenerational ambivalence. A construct used to examine intergenerational relationships within the family, especially applicable to adult children and elderly parents, is intergenerational ambivalence (Lowenstein, 2007; Lüscher, 2004). Simply put, complementary to the intergenerational solidary-conflict model, an intergenerational ambivalence perspective argues that parents and children have inherently contradictory and mixed feelings of this relationship. Lüescher and Pillemer (1998) discussed the ambivalent feelings that may be generated between dependence and autonomy, reciprocity and solidarity, and solidarity and mutual dependency. Intergenerational ambivalence can be manifested by the typical experience described by adult child caregivers. That is, they feel a sense of satisfaction by providing needs for their elderly parent and yet they also express negative emotions towards the parent due to the multiple strains as a result of caregiving. Lowenstein (2010) contends that an elderly care receiver's chronic illness and/ or the adult child's competing obligations and roles may intensify the imbalance of the ambivalent feelings. Such conflicts may arise and result in elder abuse and neglect. As family life in our society today is more pluralistic (e.g., blended families and remarriage), intergenerational relationships within the family may have even higher degrees of mixed feelings of what constitutes shared family norms and expectations. Learning about the subjective feelings and perceptions of the caregiver and elderly care receiver in the context of long-term caregiving, familial resources available, and existing parent-child relationship may help us understand the rise in incidents of elder abuse and neglect.

In conclusion, given that elder abuse is a sensitive family, as well as societal, issue and could be particularly a taboo topic in the family, the severity of the issue can be masked or hidden. The potential implications for family communication research are evident and require further elaboration. Hence, we make an urgent call for family communication scholars to expand family conflict and violence research into the realm of elder mistreatment on the one hand, and on the other, for intergenerational communication scholars to connect with medical practitioners and policy makers to be an integral part of elder abuse detection and prevention endeavors.

REFERENCES

Ainsworth, M. D. S., Blehar, M. C., Waters, E., & Wall, S. (1978). *Patterns of attachment: A psychological study of the strange situation*. Hillsdale, NJ: Erlbaum.

Anthony, E. K., Lehning, A. J., Austin, M. J., & Peck, M. D. (2009). Assessing elder mistreatment: Instrument development and implications for adult protective services. *Journal of Gerontological Social Work, 52*, 815–836. doi: 10.1080/01634370902918597

Bonnesen, J. L., & Hummert, M. L. (2002). Painful self-disclosure of older adults in relation to aging stereotypes and perceived motivations. *Journal of Language and Social Psychology, 21*, 275–301. doi: 10.1177/0261927X02021003004. ISSN: 0261-927X

Bowlby, J. (1988). *A secure base: Parent-child attachment and healthy human development*. New York: Basic Books.

Bugental, D. B., Ellerson, P. C., Lin, E. K., Rainey, B., & Kokotovic, A. (2002). A cognitive approach to child abuse prevention. *Journal of Family Psychology, 16*, 243–258. doi: 10.1037/0893-3200. 16.3.243

Chen, C. K., Waters, H. S., Hartman, M., Zimmerman, S. Miklowitz, D. J., & Waters, E. (2013). The secure base script and the task of caring for elderly parents: Implications for attachment theory and clinical practice. *Attachment and Human Development, 15*, 332–348. doi: I0.1080/14616734.2013. 782658

Cooper, C., Selwood, A., Blanchard, M., & Livingston, G. (2010). Abusive behavior experienced by family carers from people with dementia: The CARD (Caring for Relatives with Dementia) study. *Journal of Neurology, Neurosurgery and Psychiatry, 81*, 592–596. doi: 10.1136/jnnp.2009.190934

Cooper, C., Selwood, A., & Livingston, G. (2008). The prevalence of elder abuse and neglect: A systematic review. *Age and Ageing, 37*, 151–160. doi: 10.1093/ageing/afm194

Coupland, N., Coupland, J., & Giles, H. (1991). *Language, society and the elderly: Discourse, identity, and aging.* Oxford, UK: Blackwell.

Dickson, F. C., & Hughes, P. (2014). Aging families and family communication. In L. H. Turner & R. West (Eds.), *The SAGE handbook of family communication* (pp. 263–275). Thousand Oaks, CA: Sage.

Dong, X. (2014). Elder abuse: Research, practice, and health policy: The 2012 GSA Maxwell Pollack Award Lecture. *The Gerontologist, 54*, 153–162. doi: 10.1093/geront/gnt139

Dong, X., Simon, M. A., & Gorbien, M. (2007). Elder abuse and neglect in an urban Chinese population. *Journal of Elder Abuse and Neglect, 19*, 79–96. doi: 10.1300/J084v19n03_05

Etters, L., Goodall, D., & Harrison, B. E. (2008). Caregiver burden among dementia patient caregivers: A review of the literature. *Journal of the American Academy of Nurse Practitioners, 20*, 423–428. doi: 10.1111/j.1745-7599.2008.00342.x

Fisher, C. L., & Canzona, M. R. (2014). Health care interactions in older adults. In J. F. Nussbaum (Ed.), *Handbook of lifespan communication* (pp. 387–404). New York: Peter Lang.

Fowler, C., & Soliz, J. (2010). Responses of young adult grandchildren to grandparents' painful self-disclosure. *Journal of Language and Social Psychology, 29*, 75–100. doi: 10.1177/0261927X09351680

Fowler, C., & Soliz, J. (2013). Communicative responses to the painful self-disclosures of familial and non-familial older adults. *International Journal of Aging and Human Development, 77*, 163–188. doi: http://dx.doi.org/10.2190/AG.77.3.a

Fox, S., & Giles, H. (1993). Accommodating intergenerational contact: A critique and theoretical model. *Journal of Aging Studies, 7*, 423–451. doi: 10.1016/0890-4065(93)90009-9

Fried, T. R., Bradley, E. H., O'Leary, J. R., & Byers, A. (2005). Unmet desire for caregiver-patient communication and increased caregiver burden. *Journal of American Geriatrics Society, 53*, 59–65. doi: 10.1111/j.1532-5415.2005.53011.x

Giles, H. (2014). Cross-generational health communication. In T. L. Thompson (Ed.), SAGE *Encyclopedia of health communication* (pp. 273–275). Thousand Oaks, CA: Sage.

Giles, H., Davis, S., Gasiorek, J., & Giles, J. (2013). *Successful aging: A communication guide to empowerment.* Barcelona: Editorial Aresta.

Giles, H., Fox, S., & Smith, E. (1993). Patronizing the elderly: Intergenerational evaluations. *Research in Language and Social Interaction, 26*, 129–149.

Giles, H., & Gasiorek, J. (2011). Intergenerational communication practices. In K. W. Schaie & S. Willis (Eds.), *Handbook of the psychology of aging* (7th ed., pp. 231–245). New York: Elsevier.

Giles, H., & Helmle, J. (2011). Elder abuse and neglect: A communication framework. In A. Duszak & U. Okulska (Eds.), *Language, culture and the dynamics of age* (pp. 223–252). Berlin, Germany: Mouton de Gruyter.

Giles, H., Ryan, E. B., & Anas, A. P. (2008). Perceptions of intergenerational communication by young, middle-aged, and older Canadian adults. *Canadian Journal of Behavioral Science, 40*, 121–130. doi: 10.1037/0008-400x.40.1.21

Giles, H., & Williams, A. (1994). Patronizing the young: Forms and evaluations. *International Journal of Aging and Human Development, 39*, 33–53. doi: 10.2190/0LUC-NWMA-K5LX-NUVW

Hagestad, G. O., & Uhlenberg, P. (2005). The social separation of old and young: A root of ageism. *Journal of Social Issues, 61*, 343–360. doi: 10.1111/j.1540-4560.2005.00409.x

Harwood, J. (2000). Communicative predictors of solidarity in the grandparent-grandchild relationship. *Journal of Social and Personal Relationships, 17*, 743–766. doi: 10.1177/0265407500176003

Harwood, J., & Giles, H. (1996). Reactions to older people being patronized: The roles of response strategies and attributed thoughts. *Journal of Language and Social Psychology, 15*, 395–422. doi: 10.1177/0261927X960154001

Harwood, J., McKee, J., & Lin, M.-C. (2000). Younger and older adults' schematic representations of intergenerational communication. *Communication Monographs, 67*, 20–41. doi: 10.1080/03637750009376493

Harwood, J., Rittenour, C. E., & Lin, M.-C. (2012). Family communication in later life. In A. Vangelisti (Ed.), *Handbook of family communication* (2nd ed., pp. 112–126). London: Routledge.

Hummert, M. L. (2010). Age group identity, age stereotypes, and communication in a life span context. In H. Giles, S. A. Reid, & J. Harwood (Eds.), *The dynamics of intergroup communication* (pp. 41–52). New York: Peter Lang.

Hummert, M. L., Garstka, T. L., Ryan, E. B., & Bonnesen, J. (2004). The role of age stereotypes in interpersonal communication. In J. F. Nussbaum & J. Coupland (Eds.), *Handbook of communication and aging research* (pp. 91–115). Mahwah, NJ: Lawrence Erlbaum.

Infante, D. A., & Rancer, A. S. (1982). A conceptualization and measure of argumentativeness. *Journal of Personality Assessment, 46*, 72–80. doi: 10.1207/s15327752jpa4601_13

Jackson, S. L., & Hafemeister, T. (2013). Differences in causal attributions of caseworkers and elderly clients in the USA: Impact on case resolution and cessation of abuse. *The Journal of Adult Protection, 15*, 246–257. doi: 10.1108/JAP-12-2012-0029

Koerner, A. F., & Fitzpatrick, M. A. (2002). Toward a theory of family communication. *Communication Theory, 12*, 70–91. doi: 10.1111/j.1468-2885.2002.tb00260.x

Koerner, A. F., & Schrodt, P. (2014). An introduction to the special issue on family communication patterns theory. *Journal of Family Communication, 14*, 1–15. doi: 10.1080/15267431.2013.857328

Laumann, E. O., Leitsch, S. A., & Waite, L. J. (2008). Elder mistreatment in the United States: Prevalence estimates from a nationally representative study. *Journal of Gerontology: Psychological Science, 63B*, 248–254.

Levy, B. R. (2003). Mind matters: Cognitive and physical effects of aging self-stereotypes. *Journals of Gerontology: Psychological Sciences, 58B*, 203–211. doi: 10.1093/geronb/58.4.P203

Lin, M.-C., & Giles, H. (2013). The dark side of family communication: A communication model of elder abuse and neglect. *International Psychogeriatrics, 25*, 1275–1290. doi: 10.1017/S1041610212002347

Lowenstein, A. (2007). Solidarity-conflict and ambivalence: Testing two conceptual frameworks and their impact on quality of life for older family members. *Journal of Gerontology Series B: Psychological Sciences and Social Sciences, 62*, S100–S107.

Lowenstein, A. (2010). Caregiving and elder abuse and neglect: Developing a new conceptual perspective. *Aging International, 35*, 215–227. doi: 10.1007/s12126-010-9068-x

Lüscher, K. (2004). Conceptualizing and uncovering intergenerational ambivalence. In K. Pillemer & K. Lüscher (Eds.), *Intergenerational ambivalence: Perspectives on parent-child relations in later life* (pp. 23–62). New York: Elsevier.

Lüescher, K., & Pillemer, K. (1998). Intergenerational ambivalence: A new approach to the study of parent-child relations in later life. *Journal of Marriage and the Family to Journal of Marriage and Family in 2000, 60*, 413–425. doi: 10.2307/353858

Manusov, V., & Spitzberg, B. (2008), Attribution theory. In D. O. Braithwaite & L. A. Baxter (Eds.), *Engaging theories in interpersonal communication* (pp. 37–50). Thousand Oaks, CA: Sage.

Miller, K. I., Shemaker, M. M., Willyard, J., & Addison, P. (2008). Providing care for elderly parents: A structurational approach to family caregiver identity. *Journal of Family Communication, 8*, 19–43. doi: 10.1080/15267430701389947

Montgomery, R. J. V., Gonyea, J. G., & Hooyman, N. R. (1985). Caregiving and the experience of subjective and objective burden. *Family Relations, 34*, 19–26. doi: 10.2307/583753

Morimoto, Y., & Sharma, A. (2004). Long-term outcomes of verbal aggression: The role of protective factors. *Journal of Emotional Abuse, 4*, 71–99. doi: 10.1300/J135v04n02_04

National Council of Elder Abuse. (2015). *Statistics/Data*. Retrieved from National Center on Elder Abuse, Administration on Aging. http://http://www.ncea.aoa.gov/Library/Data/

National Research Council. (2003). *Elder mistreatment: Abuse, neglect, and exploitation in an Aging America*. Washington, DC: National Academies Press.

Ota, H., Giles, H., & Somera, L. (2007). Beliefs about intra- and intergenerational communication in Japan, the Philippines, and the United States: Implications for older adults' subjective well-being. *Communication Studies, 58*, 173–188. doi: 10.1080/10510970701341139

Pagani, L., Tremblay, R. E., Nagin, D., Zoccolillo, M., Vitaro, F., & McDuff, P. (2004). Risk factor models for adolescent verbal and physical aggression toward mothers. *International Journal of Behavioral Development, 28*, 528–537. doi: 10.1080/01650250250444000243

Pagani, L., Tremblay, R. E., Nagin, D., Zoccolillo, M., Vitaro, F., & McDuff, P. (2009). Risk factor model for adolescent verbal and physical aggression toward fathers. *Journal of Family Violence, 24*, 173–182. doi: 10.1007/s10896-008-9216-1

Papastavrou, E., Tsangari, H., Karayiannis, G., Papacostas, S., Efstathiou, G., & Sourtzi, P. (2011). Caring and coping: The dementia caregivers. *Aging and Mental Health, 15*, 702–711. doi: 10.1080/13607863.2011.562178

Pelcovitz, D., Kaplan, S. J., Ellenberg, A., Labruna, V., Salzinger, S., Mandel, F., & Weiner, M. (2000). Adolescent physical abuse: Age at time of abuse and adolescent perception of family functioning. *Journal of Family Violence, 15*, 375–389. doi: 10.1023/A:10075063136630.1023/A:1007506313663

Petronio, S. (2002). *Boundaries of privacy: Dialectics of disclosure*. Albany, NY: SUNY Press.

Petronio, S., & Durham, W. (2008), Communication privacy management theory. In D. O. Braithwaite & L. A. Baxter (Eds.), *Engaging theories in interpersonal communication* (pp. 309–322). Thousand Oaks, CA: Sage.

Pillemer, K., Connolly, M.-T., Breckman, R., Spreng, N., & Lachs, M. S. (2015). Elder mistreatment: Priorities for consideration by the White House Conference on Aging. *The Gerontologist, 55*, 320–327. doi: 10.1093/geront/gnu180

Rudd, J. E., Vogl-Bauer, S., Dobos, J. A., Beatty, M. J., & Valencic, K. M. (1998). Interactive effects of parents' trait verbal aggressiveness and situational frustration on parents reported anger. *Communication Quarterly, 46*, 1–11. doi: 10.1080/01463379809370080

Ruscher, J. B., & Hurley, M. M. (2000). Off-target verbosity evokes negative stereotypes of older adults. *Journal of Language and Social Psychology, 19*, 141–149. doi: 10.1177/0261927X00019001007

Ryan, E. B., Anas, A. P., & Gruneir, A. J. S. (2006). Evaluations of overhelping and underhelping communication: Do old age and physical disability matter? *Journal of Language and Social Psychology, 25*, 97–107. doi: 10.1177/0261927X05284485

Ryan, E. B., Giles, H., Bartolucci, G., & Henwood, K. (1986). Psycholinguistic and social psychological components of communication by and with older adults. *Language and Communication, 6*, 1–24. doi: 10.1016/0271-5309(86)90002-9

Ryan, E. B., Kwong See, S., Meneer, W. B., & Trovato, D. (1992). Age-based perceptions of language performance among young and older adults. *Communication Research, 19*, 423–443. doi: 10.1177/009365092019004002

Savundranayagam, M. Y. (2013). Receiving while giving: The differential roles of receiving help and satisfaction with help on caregiver rewards among spouses and adult-children. *International Journal of Geriatric Psychiatry, 29*, 41–48. doi: 10.1002/gps.3967

Savundranayagam, M. Y., Hummert, M. L., & Montgomery, R. J. V. (2005). Investigating the effects of communication problems on caregiver burden. *Journal of Gerontology: Social Sciences, 60B*, s48–s55. doi: 10.1093/geronb/60.1.S48

Savundranayagam, M. Y., Montgomery, R. J. V., & Kosloski, K. (2010). A dimensional analysis of caregiver burden among spouses and adult children. *The Gerontologist, 51*, 321–331. doi: 10.1093/geront/gnq102

Schrodt, P., Witt, P. L., & Messersmith, A. (2008). A meta-analytical review of family communication patterns and their associations with information processing, behavioral, and psychosocial outcomes. *Communication Monographs, 75*, 248–269. doi: 10.1080/03637750802256318

Sillars, A., Holman, A. J., Richards, A., Jacobs, K. A., Koerner, A., & Reynolds-Dyk, A. (2014). Conversation and conformity orientations as predictors of observed conflict tactics in parent-adolescent discussions. *Journal of Family Communication, 14*, 16–31. doi: 10.1080/15267431.2013.857327

Soliz, J., & Harwood, J. (2006). Shared family identity, age salience, and intergroup contact: Investigation of the grandparent-grandchild relationship. *Communication Monographs, 73*, 87–107. doi: 10.1080/03637750500534388

Soliz, J., & Lin, M.-C. (2013). Friends and allies: Communication in grandparent-grandchild relationships. In K. Floyd & M. Mormon (Eds.), *Widening the family circle: New research on family communication* (2nd ed., pp. 35–50). Thousand Oaks, CA: Sage.

Sorenson, H. (2006). Verbal abuse and communication neglect in the elderly. In R. W. Summers & A. M. Hoffman (Eds.), *Elder abuse: A public health perspective* (pp. 117–129). Washington, DC: American Public Health Association.

Stamp, G. H. (2004). Theories of family relationships and a family relationship theoretical model. In A. L. Vangelisti (Ed.), *Handbook of family communication* (pp. 1–30). Mahwah, NJ: Erlbaum.

Stannard, C. I. (1973). Old folks and dirty work: The social conditions for patient abuse in a nursing home. *Social Problems, 20*, 329–342.

Steadman, P. L., Tremont, G., & Davis, J. D. (2007). Premorbid relationship satisfaction and caregiver burden in dementia caregivers. *Journal of Geriatric Psychiatry and Neurology, 20*, 115–119. doi: 10.1177/0891988706298624

Teaster, P. B., Otto, J. M., Dugar, T. D., Mendiondo, M. S., Abner, E. L., & Cecil, K. A. (2006). The 2004 survey of state adult protective services: Abuse of adults 60 years of age and older. *Report to the National Center on Elder Abuse*, Administration on Aging, Washington, DC.

Theobald, D., & Farrington, D. P. (2012). Child and adolescent predictors of male intimate partner violence. *Journal of Child Psychology and Psychiatry, 53*, 1242–1249. doi: 10.1111/j.1469-7610.2012.02577.x

Wiglesworth, A., Mosqueda, L., Mulnard, R., Liao, S., Gibbs, L., & Fitzgerald, W. (2010). Screening for abuse and neglect of people with dementia. *Journal of the American Geriatrics Society, 58*, 493–500. doi: 10.1111/j.1532-5415.2010.02737x

Williams, A., & Giles, H. (1996). Retrospecting intergenerational conversations: The perspective of young adults. *Human Communication Research, 23*, 220–250.

Williams, A., & Nussbaum, J. F. (2001). *Intergenerational communication across the lifespan*. Mahwah, NJ: Erlbaum.

Wilson, S. R., Hayes, J., Bylund, C. E., Rack, J. J., & Herman, A. P. (2006). Mother's trait verbal aggressiveness and child abuse potential. *Journal of Family Communication, 6*, 279–296. doi: 10.1207/s15327698jfc0604

Wilson, S. R., Roberts, F., Rack, J. J., & Delaney, J. E. (2008). Mother's trait verbal aggressiveness as a predictor of maternal and child behavior during playtime interactions. *Human Communication Research, 34*, 392–422. doi: 10.1111/j.1468-2958.2008.00326.x

Zhang, Y. B., & Lin, M.-C. (2009). Conflict initiating factors in intergenerational relationships. *Journal of Language and Social Psychology, 28*, 343–363. doi: 10.1177/0261927X09341836

CHAPTER NINE

Is Love Blind TO Abuse?

Factors Affecting Victims' Preferences for Love-Communication from Abusive Romantic Partners

JESSICA J. ECKSTEIN
Western Connecticut State University

For many families, love and suffering are not mutually exclusive. In 2010, the National Intimate Partner and Sexual Violence Survey predicted that over 34.27 million women and more than 11.21 million men will be victimized by a romantic partner in the context of intimate partner violence (IPV) (Black et al., 2011). In addition to physical forms of violence, the psychological abuse experienced within families is projected to be much higher, as *poly-victimization*, or the overlapping occurrence of different forms of abusive behavior, is common in these contexts (Basile & Hall, 2011). IPV prevalence, combined with its severe outcomes for individuals (Rogers & Follingstad, 2014; Sillito, 2012), families (Kitzmann, Gaylord, Holt, & Kenny, 2003; Rhodes, Cerulli, Dichter, Kothari, & Barg, 2010), and society (Kruse, Sorensen, Bronnum-Hansen, & Helweg-Larsen, 2011), necessitates further examination of the motives and experiences of family members within a communication context.

A commonly held belief is that abuse victims stay in IPV relationships because of love, received from and felt for abusive family members during the dark moments of family communication (Eckstein, 2011; Towns & Adams, 2000). Indeed, in the early days of studying IPV, both victim and practitioner/provider reports included frequent mention of love or romantic commitment as a primary motivator of women's reasons for staying with abusive partners (e.g., Snell, Rosenwald, & Robey, 1964). Decades later, love remains a central theoretical part of many IPV studies but is largely included in name only. Love as a distinct variable is rarely examined by IPV researchers and appears to never have been explored as a communicative act among abusive couples.

To examine the role of this love and commitment feature, often claimed by victims as central to their relational experiences, I begin by framing multiple IPV contexts and operationalizing varied components of love as traditionally studied in nonviolent contexts. This foregrounding is followed by presentation of a study of love-communication as reported by IPV victims.

INTERPERSONAL LOVE

Human interaction, filial affection, and/or intimacy are arguably necessary for people's well-being and interpersonal competency (Horan & Booth-Butterfield, 2010). Intimate relational partners are the primary source of social support for individuals in both normative and stressful life situations (Collins & Feeney, 2000). Partners' expressions of intimacy involve making people feel personally validated by (i.e., *transactional affirmation benefit*) and close to (i.e., *interactional reliance benefit*) their relational partners (Lemieux & Hale, 2000). These features of affect-based intimacy are central to understandings of "love" in many family contexts. Considering these components of relational intimacy, Sternberg and Grajek (1984) conceptualized love as "generally" consistent across relational contexts (i.e., romantic, family, friendship). Their view of a general love experience may encapsulate—and be supported by—research on intimacy at large, but most love research has tended to differentiate "types" based on varied components.

Typological and Thematic Frameworks

Beginning with transactional exchange conceptualizations (e.g., Blau, 1964) and progressing to a more "communal" framing approach (e.g., Clark & Mills, 1979), the study of interpersonal love eventually took the form of typological research that distinguished between the levels and kinds of emotion, physiological reactions, and goals unique to each purported love type. Rubin's (1970) distinction between liking and loving (see Hatfield & Rapson's 1993 "passionate" versus "companionate" love) was a basis for more nuanced typologies.

Used in many social psychology studies to date (e.g., Hendrick & Hendrick, 1986, 1988), Lee's (1976) model conceived of three primary and three secondary types of love based on mixtures of each paired primary type. The primary types include *Eros* ("romantic, passionate"), *Ludus* ("game-playing"), and *Storge* ("friendship"). A subtype that pairs Eros and Ludus characteristics is that of *Mania* ("possessive, dependent"). *Pragma* ("logical, shopping list") is a Storge-Ludus subtype, and *Agape* ("all-giving, selfless") illustrates an Eros-Storge combination. Lee's model is believed to encompass the many other theories of love. For example, Storge and Agape embody companionate and communal love, respectively (e.g., Walster & Walster, 1978).

In Western culture, the ideal for romantic relational love has been framed as a passionate love similar to Eros. Even though passionate love is unlikely to sustain and/or be the sole impetus for lasting, long-term relationships (Sprecher, 1999), the ideology of romantic love maintains a stronghold on couples' beliefs and marital ideals in popular imagination as well as a focus of research for many relational scholars (Hefner & Wilson, 2013; Huston, 2009). Indeed, Aron and Westbay (1996) showed that these love types corresponded with other operationalizations of love, such as that of a prototype approach.

A prototypical approach to love, whereby we define or label aspects or types of love according to what they most resemble from our experiences, provides an alternative way to frame love as a relational concept. Aron and Westbay's (1996) research using this approach uncovered three factors comprising an overall love construct. These factors, uncovered via factor analysis and confirmed in subsequent studies, closely aligned with Sternberg's (1986) triangular theory of love, in which love is revealed by three components: *passion* (physical or cognitive romantic or sexual drives), *intimacy* (affectional closeness or connection experiences), and *commitment* (short-term decision or long-term choices to maintain pursuit/involvement). These features of love mirror attachment perspectives (i.e., sexuality-attachment-caregiving systems) for explaining family-affect and communication (Shaver, Schwartz, Kirson, & O'Connor, 1987). For example, according to attachment theory, relational communication behaviors (usually labeled *caregiving behaviors*) both predict and result from different attachment styles—theoretically attributed to intimacy and commitment experienced from primary caregivers at an early age (e.g., Birnbaum, 2010; Collins & Ford, 2010).

Both typological (Hendrick, Hendrick, & Adler, 1988; Lee, 1976) and thematic prototype (Sternberg, 1986) approaches to love can serve to describe the motives for love internalized by family members. However, because of their focus on cognitive-emotional and psychological factors, the way in which they operate externally—or are *communicated*—is missing from these theories. In the systemic world of families and dyadic partnerships, external indicators of purported love felt for another are necessary and indicate love experiences distinct from relational constructs typically used as primary indicators of romantic love (Marston, Hecht, & Robers, 1987). In other words, the communication of love not only reveals to the recipient its existence but also shapes its actual experience (Ackerman, Griskevicius, & Li, 2011). Certainly, love is communicated in a variety of ways (Honeycutt, Cantrill, Kelly, & Lambkin, 1998).

Communication of Love

Scholars have labeled dimensions or facets of internalized love as "styles" or "types" of love. To distinguish between those cognitive-emotional labels and the interpersonal communication of this feeling, I delineate *love languages*—a term from Chapman (2014), whose contributions are discussed later—as the strategies used to display felt-love for others. Although the method and outcomes may overlap, love languages (LLs) are distinct from typical relational maintenance behaviors (e.g., Stafford, 2010) or "intensification strategies" (e.g., Levine, Aune, & Park, 2006) in that the motive for performing LLs is primarily to express a sentiment regarding an individual, not necessarily to care for or further a relationship for its own sake. From a communication approach, language in general is merely a symbolic way to show our meanings to others in external ways (Hayakawa, 1972); the specific words chosen to represent our internal cognitions and emotions not only show the receiver our intentions but also convey certain identities. Thus, *love languages*, in all their diverse possibilities, are the means by which individuals reveal aspects of themselves and their relational love intent to others. Although LLs are used to convey love in any relationship, for current purposes, I focus on their use in romantic relationships. LLs can be directly or indirectly verbal as well as nonverbal in nature.

Scholars have examined the direct/explicit verbal communication of love in platonic (Morman & Floyd, 1998), familial (Floyd, 2005; Keeley, 2004; Kostelecky & Bass, 2004; Myers, Byrnes, Frisby, & Mansson, 2011), and romantic (Ackerman et al., 2011; Dillow, Goodboy, & Bolkan, 2014; Horan & Booth-Butterfield, 2010) relationships. However, communication of love or romantic affection is also demonstrated through indirect verbal messages such as compliments or affirmations and expressions of appreciation (Olson, 2003), provision of emotional support (Collins et al., 2014), and public revelation (e.g., telling others of love/attraction/pride for partner; O'Leary, Acevedo, Aron, Huddy, & Mashek, 2011).

Nonverbally, love is communicated via facial expressions or kinesics (Hafner & Ijzerman, 2011), vocalics (Farley, Hughes, & LaFayette, 2013), companionate physicality (i.e., nonsexual touch; Dainton, Stafford, & Canary, 1994), sexual physicality (Hendrick & Hendrick, 2002), gift giving or financial support (Cheal, 1987), shared activities or time spent together (Huston, 2009), loyalty/trust or embodied respect for a shared commitment (Hendrick & Hendrick, 2006), tie-signs (i.e., external indicators of relational status), favors/acts or instrumental support (Reis, Maniaci, & Rogge, 2014), and self-modification (e.g., to please or attract a partner) (Levine et al., 2006).

Whereas most research focuses on one or a few of many love-communication possibilities, a few scholars have explicitly considered them as plural and overlapping. There are distinct positive associations between particular love languages and a variety of variables. For example, people prefer to send and receive different "languages" (Marston et al., 1987). Men and women may use different languages (Schoenfeld, Bredow, & Huston, 2012); diverse motivations (i.e., self versus other) exist for men expressing love for their wives (Olson, 2003). Further, different types of languages may be associated with varying levels of reported love intensity (O'Leary et al., 2011) and satisfaction and success (Huston, 2009) in long-term marriages. Finally, perceived equity of love-tactics used (Williams, 2012) and perceived levels of intimacy escalation (Honeycutt et al., 1998) can affect relational satisfaction and relationship development/escalation, respectively. Incorporation of multiple LLs in tandem suggests typological variety in the means and outcomes of each language. However, systematic inclusion of the full variety of love communication possibilities in relational research is lacking, with most scholars focusing on one or a few forms at a time. Methodical examination of LLs has largely been left to trade-specific and lay practitioners. To begin to explore such typological frameworks in more detail, I turn to a popular counseling perspective on LLs that has received much attention to date.

Chapman's 5 love languages. Chapman (2014) designed a typology of five LLs based on more than 40 years as a minister and relationship counselor. The original formulation (Chapman, 2010) has gone through multiple editions, with separate versions tailored specifically for singles, men, parents of children and teens, and members of the military. Chapman's texts have outsold their previous annual sales almost every year for over two decades and are extremely pervasive in pop culture (Casey, 2011; Feiler, 2011; Podrazik, 2013).

The basic premise of Chapman's typology is that individuals typically use five types of behaviors to communicate love to someone. Each of the languages includes various "dialects" or personal ways of conveying those languages. Research on LLs found distinct, expected factor loadings for Chapman's items ascribed to each LL (Goff, Goddard, Pointer, & Jackson, 2007).

First, the *words of affirmation* language includes verbal expressions of appreciation, compliments, or encouragement communicated with "kindness" (p. 42) (i.e., nonverbally consistent with a loving message) and humility (i.e., "requesting" as opposed to "demanding"; Chapman, 2010). Words of affirmation can be directly conveyed to the target or indirectly conveyed to others about the target.

Quality time consists of total distraction-free attention given to the target. One dialect of quality time is "shared activities" in which one or both parties have interest, the target is willing to perform, and both parties know the love-communication goal at the time; a secondary purpose is the relational maintenance strategy of shared memories or common experiences on which to draw at a future date. Another dialect is that of "quality conversation" involving standard verbal and nonverbal "effective listening" techniques. Words of affirmation differ from quality conversation in that the former focuses on the message or "what we are saying," whereas the latter involves the meta-message or "what we are hearing" (Chapman, 2010, p. 61).

The giving and receiving of *gifts* or "visible symbols of love" (Chapman, 2010, p. 77), includes tangible objects provided for the sole purpose of conveying affection. Gifts may be bought, found, or created by the giver and thus are not limited to those with funds. Indeed, one dialect is the "gift of self" or mere presence used to indicate love (e.g., showing up at an event solely to support another in their interests or a time of crisis).

Acts of service involve "doing things you know your spouse would like you to do" (Chapman, 2010, p. 91). As an LL, the act of serving another is distinct from chore performance or responsible daily labor in that it involves conscious thought, advance consideration, and time/effort. Chapman notes that to truly perform acts of service in romantic relationships—where roles are often culturally pre-assigned—couples must often first challenge their stereotypes about traditional sex role expectations. Even scholarly research must struggle against these norms when measuring LLs. For example, in the study by Goff et al. (2007), this LL was broken by gender role norms into the "feminine" Domestic Service and the "masculine" Manual Service; this was maintained, despite the fact that eigenvalues for each loaded on their own factors such that it appears there was no reason not to collapse them into one Acts category in final analyses.

Finally, the *touch* LL is the activation of person-specific pleasurable physiological receptors to indicate affection. It may be performed using one's own body or objects and, for couples, can be platonic or sexual in nature; it must adhere to a couple's agreed-upon norms for appropriate time and place of occurrence. Both "implicit" momentary, passing touches and "explicit" time-consuming touches require conscious thought as an LL.

Comparing the LLs to various tactics used by interpersonal dyads, it is clear they match up with much of the scientific literature on communication by families and romantic partners. However, Chapman (2010) was arguably the first to propose a model of these relational communication strategies that (a) is "comprehensive" in nature, (or at least attempts to be), (b) ties their use to the specific goal-directed behavior of love communication, and (c) includes testable claims as to LL use across different contexts; this latter distinction I now detail.

Although not explicitly detailed by Chapman (2010) as such, his work implicitly included multiple axioms that serve as a working model of LL communication. First, he proposed that each individual possesses a primary and a secondary LL he/she prefers to receive and a primary/secondary LL he/she prefers to give. Next, the nature or dialect of each LL received is purported to differ according to a variety of factors. For example, a person may prefer to get quality time from a fiancé but prefer gifts or words of affirmation from parents to feel maximally loved. Similarly, provision preferences may be (a) individualistic, with a person's preference differing from others' generally used cross-situationally, (b) relationship-specific, with a person preferring diverse LLs based on affiliation type (e.g., touch for husband/wife, gift for parents), and/or (c) contextual, with a different LL tailored to or preferred for each specific individual encountered. Finally, the amount of felt-love (and, implicitly, relational satisfaction) reported by relational members will be directly associated with the extent to which they perceive their partner communicating via their primary/secondary LLs. To date, none of these suppositions have been empirically tested. However, due to the frequency with which "love" is cited as a motive for positive and negative behaviors, exploration of LLs seems particularly important in the presence of intimate partner violence (IPV), a context to which I now turn.

LOVE AND FAMILY VIOLENCE

A fundamental assumption of family contexts is that they involve love among members, particularly in partnerships to which individuals have made conscious commitments. IPV couples have reported the simultaneous presence of love both during and after abusive encounters, and love (both for and from their abuser) has been cited as a reason for staying in abusive relationships (Borochowitz & Eisikovits, 2002; Browne, 1991). However, despite its prevalence as an explanatory mechanism for IPV, no actual evidence exists of a predictive link between romantic love and IPV (Yuste, Serrano, Girbés, & Arandia, 2014). Instead, victims, abusers, and the practitioners who directly work with them may continue to perceive romantic love as a factor in their violence—which may reaffirm cultural impressions of this same phenomenon (Halket, Gormley, Mello, Rosenthal, & Mirkin, 2014). Despite the assumption by many scholars that love is implicit in IPV contexts (for a summary of these beliefs, see Yuste et al., 2014), little attention has been devoted by scholars to the "seemingly paradoxical phenomenon of the existence of positive emotions in violence-ridden relationships" (Borochowitz & Eisikovits, 2002, p. 477).

In a few studies that operationalized "romantic love" *and* studied its role in IPV contexts, scholars uncovered nuanced roles of the construct of love, its performance by partners, and associated relational functioning. Certainly, romantic love can be seen as both an impetus for and/or existing despite violence in relationships. As found by Borochowitz and Eisikovits (2002), those who viewed love and IPV as distinct, separate occurrences in their relationship tended to minimize the impact of violence, normalize its role in relationship conflict, and emphasize the overpowering role of love in their IPV relationship. Those who instead viewed love and IPV as mutually functional in their relationship emphasized the role of violence as arising from the complexity of misunderstandings about love; a tool to maintain love; and indicative of overwhelming needs of love from the victim.

If, as noted by Borochowitz and Eisikovits (2002), "acts of meaning, rather than violent behavioral acts alone … delimit the boundaries of life in violence" then couples must create "meaning … constructed in a manner that allows for a quality of relationship conducive to ['continuous coexistence']" (p. 492). Basically, they argue that love in IPV contexts must occur in ways that perceptually (at least for victims) outweigh the violence. Specific aspects of a larger romantic love discourse may be drivers for abused women seeking to cement and/or invest further in IPV contexts (Power, Koch, Kralik, & Jackson, 2006). As such, the same behaviors that indicate romantic love in non-IPV contexts (e.g., sharing physical warmth, spending time with or monitoring a partner) provide ideal covers for perpetrators to contextualize their use of abusive behaviors within a framework of love. It is this potential overlap between the specific acts of love-performance and the perpetration of IPV that has yet to be examined. To explore the manner of this love performance in IPV contexts for both male and female victims, I proposed the following research questions:

RQ1: Which love languages do IPV victims report made them feel "most loved" when communicated by an abusive romantic partner?

RQ2: What differences, if any, exist between male and female IPV victims' preferences for love languages communicated by abusive romantic partners?

Varying abuse types (e.g., physical, psychological), severity and outcomes, and corresponding relationship types (e.g., *situational couple violence*, *intimate terrorism*) have been found to be predictive of the types of communication occurring in those relationships (Johnson & Leone, 2005; Olson, 2004). Correspondingly, it is likely that patterns in partner communication preferences are also present in IPV contexts. There is a clear positive association between the extent of psychological and physical victimization and negative personal and relational outcomes (Leone, 2011); more (and severer) abuse relates to negative perceptions and experiences within and outside the relationship (Sullivan, Schroeder, Dudley, & Dixon, 2010). For example, Eckstein (2012b) found that greater physical and psychological victimization were tied to victims' higher levels of relational uncertainty about their partner and the relationship as a whole. More frequent and severe abuse victimization was also connected to victims' stay-rationalizations during the course of their relationship, such that fear and externally directed reasons were more likely for those with high levels of victimization (Eckstein, 2012a). Thus, it was expected that communication preferences related to love would also differ corresponding to abuse experienced. To test this supposition, I proposed the following hypotheses:

H1:   Abuse will be negatively related to LLs, such that higher levels of physical victimization will result in victims reporting lower preference/s for: (a) acts of service, (b) words of affirmation, (c) quality time, (d) gifts, and (e) touch.

H2:   Abuse will be negatively related to LLs, such that higher levels of psychological victimization will result in victims reporting lower preference/s for: (a) acts of service, (b) words of affirmation, (c) quality time, (d) gifts, and (e) touch.

METHODS

Participants and Procedures

Men and women were recruited for participation via targeted Internet sampling in general and violence-specific forums as well as convenience word-of-mouth methods. Postings included study information, the online survey link, victim resource information, and researcher contact information. Due to safety concerns, people currently "in" an abusive relationship were instructed not to participate in this study. Given inclusion parameters both prior to and on accessing the survey, uncompensated participants self-selected as "having experienced physically or psychologically abusive behavior from a past romantic partner." Twenty-nine people (5.9%) reported on a same-sex relationship (with 94.1%, n = 466 differently sexed), but—similar to most research on hetero-/homosexual relationship differences (Frankland & Brown, 2014; Kurdek, 2004)—no significant differences between sexual relationship types emerged on any of the results in this study. Further, eliminating homosexual relationships from the study only marginally reduced variability of the overall results, with no changes in significance found for the main analyses. Therefore, groups were collapsed and results include all individuals.

Excluding substantially incomplete surveys (n = 13) from final analyses in an effort to respect participants' desires to discontinue the study, 495 people (338 females, 157 males) self-identified as IPV victims for this study. Partners/perpetrators of participants were 32.3% (n = 160) female and 67.7% (n = 335) male. Participants ranged from 18 to 74 years of age (M = 36.68, SD = 13.61), were mostly White (85.9%), and had completed some college (34.9%) or earned a bachelor's degree (25.9%). Further demographics are available from the author.

An Internet web service with SSL data-encrypted server settings hosted the survey. Respondents began by clicking a link agreeing with the informed consent terms. Collector settings deleted IP addresses and survey web history from a participant's computer on exiting the survey and from the composite database when sending the results to the researcher; randomly assigned participant numbers were the only record of participant identification.

Measures

Demographic items assessed personal and relationship characteristics of each participant. Additionally, measures included items operationalizing (a) physical and (b) psychological abuse victimization and (c) love language communication.

The physical assault subscale of the Conflict Tactics Scales 2 (CTS2; Straus, Hamby, & Warren, 2003) was supplemented for comprehensiveness with the Partner Abuse Scale-Physical (PASPH; Hudson, 2000). Participants assessed the frequency (0 = *Never* to 6 = *Always*) of physical tactics used by a former partner via 19 items spanning types and severity levels of physical victimization (e.g., *twisted skin; beat up badly, tried to choke or strangle*) calculated as mean frequencies of tactics reported (M = 2.13, SD = 1.10, α = .94).

A sex-modified version of the Index of Psychological Abuse (IPA; Sullivan, Parisian, & Davidson, 1991) measured ridicule (e.g., *tried to humiliate*), harassment (e.g., *harassed family in some way*), criticism (e.g., *criticized parts of which I was proud*), and emotional withdrawal (e.g., *withheld approval, appreciation, or affection as punishment*). Participants reported frequencies (1 = *Never* to 7 = *Always*) of 25 psychological behaviors experienced from the former partner, with mean scores calculated for analyses (M = 4.15, SD = 1.24, α = .93).

To measure the communication victims preferred as "most effective" in conveying love when used by their former abusive partner, twenty-four items comprised five subscales measuring: Acts of Service, Words of Affirmation, Quality Time, Gifts, and Touch (using five items for each, except for Touch, which used four items) (Brule, 2002). Psychometric properties for all subscales and items are provided in Table 1. Participants read the following: "People often feel loved as a result of different behaviors from those closest to us. The following are statements about behaviors others do to make us feel loved. While all of these actions may make us feel loved, we are interested in knowing what made you feel MOST LOVED by your FORMER PARTNER. Remember—while all of these statements may be true—indicate which ones made you feel MOST LOVED when they happened." Thus, mean scores for each LL subscale were used to indicate victims' perceived efficacy of receiving the combination of specific behaviors, or the extent to which items, in comparison to all potential possibilities, made them most feel loved when used by the former partner (1 = *Never true for me* to 5 = *Always true for me*).

RESULTS

In preliminary analyses conducted to ascertain relationships among LLs, bivariate correlations indicated that each LL was significantly positively related to all others and was negatively related to both physical and psychological abuse victimization. Physical and psychological abuse victimization were positively related to each other (see Table 2).

The first research question asked which LLs victims would report made them feel most loved by a former abusive partner. Results of paired samples t-tests comparing the five LLs showed that Touch was preferred more than: Acts [t (484) = 13.60, $p < .001$], Quality Time [t (485) = 8.12, $p < .001$], Words [t (486) = 7.21, $p < .001$], and Gifts [t (484) = 12.97, $p < .001$]. Words of affirmation were rated as more desired than were Acts [t (484) = 8.41, $p < .001$] and gifts [t (483) = 8.05, $p < .001$]. Words and Quality Time did not significantly differ from one another in perceived effectiveness at communicating love, but Quality Time was preferred over Acts [t (484) = 2.79, $p < .001$] and Gifts [t (483) = 7.28, $p < .001$]. Finally, Gifts and Acts of service did not significantly differ from one another. Sample means and standard deviations for each love language scale are provided in Table 1.

The second research question asked about differences between male and female preferences for LLs received. Five one-way analyses of variance (ANOVAs) were used to test the role of victims' sex in predicting their preference for particular LLs. The ANOVA examining Acts produced a main effect for sex, such that men were more likely than women to prefer this LL, $F (1, 484) = 8.54, p < .01$, $\eta^2 = .02$. Additional main effects showed that men were more likely than women to prefer Touch, $F (1, 486) = 5.46, p < .05, \eta^2 = .01$, and Quality Time, $F (1, 484) = 5.28, p < .05, \eta^2 = .01$. No significant main effects for sex emerged for Words of affirmation or Gifts.

Hypotheses predicted that people who reported low levels of felt-love efficacy from, or preferences for, each LL would have experienced more abuse (physical in H1, psychological in H2) than those with high efficacy preferences on each LL. These results were predicted for Acts (Ha), Words (Hb), Quality Time (Hc), Gifts (Hd), and Touch (He). I first calculated tertile groupings, whereby participants were categorized independently for each LL, based on their indicated preference for a particular language. Participants were considered "high" on receipt-preference for a LL if they scored ≥3.00 for Acts ($n = 176$), ≥3.40 for Words ($n = 169$), ≥3.20 for Quality Time ($n = 187$), ≥3.00 for Gifts ($n = 176$), and ≥3.75 for Touch ($n = 171$). People were considered to have a "low" preference for receiving an LL if they scored ≤2.00 for Acts ($n = 190$), ≤2.20 for Words ($n = 175$), ≤2.40 for Quality Time ($n = 208$), ≤1.80 for Gifts ($n = 151$), and ≤2.67 for Touch ($n = 174$). Preliminary support for these hypotheses was found via bivariate correlations (see Table 2), showing both physical and psychological abuse as negatively related to each preferred LL.

Independent samples t-tests further revealed that greater physical abuse was experienced by "low" raters of an LL than by "high" raters of that same LL. This finding was significant for all five LLs, such that significant mean differences in

Table 1. Victims' Preferred Love Languages as Used by Former Abusive Partners.

Subscale Items	Overall Sample Mean (SD)	Men Mean (SD)	Women Mean (SD)	t (df)
Acts of Service (α = .84)	2.54 (1.02)	2.74 (0.95)	2.45 (1.04)	2.92 (484)**
Did something for me like make me dinner		3.26 (1.14)	2.62 (1.28)	5.47 (339.12)***
Did something for me like clean the house so I didn't have to		2.50 (1.17)	2.18 (1.25)	2.68 (481)**
Did something unexpected to surprise me like washing my car for me or cleaning the kitchen		2.29 (1.22)	2.21 (1.30)	0.61 (475)
Did things for me just to show me he/she cared		3.16 (1.38)	2.96 (1.45)	1.45 (477)
Did a chore or errand for me so I didn't have to		2.42 (1.21)	2.25 (1.32)	1.38 (474)
Words of Affirmation (α = .90)	2.85 (1.17)	2.87 (1.13)	2.84 (1.20)	0.29 (485)
Complimented me on my appearance		2.98 (1.25)	3.17 (1.32)	1.52 (481)
Praised me in front of friends or family		2.77 (1.37)	2.52 (1.47)	1.77 (479)
Told me I was beautiful or handsome		2.85 (1.26)	3.06 (1.38)	1.59 (476)
Encouraged me verbally		3.01 (1.29)	2.74 (1.45)	2.02 (331.64)*
Often told me how special I was		2.75 (1.29)	2.67 (1.43)	0.62 (329.13)
Quality Time (α = .88)	2.84 (1.17)	3.02 (1.12)	2.76 (1.18)	2.30 (484)*
Spent time doing something with me like going for a walk		3.20 (1.33)	2.98 (1.39)	1.64 (478)
Simply spent time alone with me in the same room, even though we were doing separate activities		2.94 (1.22)	2.61 (1.36)	2.64 (330.86)**
Looked me in the eyes and listened to my thoughts/feelings		2.95 (1.46)	2.81 (1.59)	0.93 (322.75)
Spent a lot of quality time with me		3.11 (1.35)	2.81 (1.42)	2.23 (477)*
Met me some place to talk and spend time together		2.88 (1.36)	2.52 (1.42)	2.62 (477)**

	Total M (SD)	M (SD)	M (SD)	t/F (df)
Gifts (α = .85)	2.57 (1.09)	2.53 (1.07)	2.59 (1.09)	0.55 (483)
Gave me an unexpected gift		2.78 (1.27)	2.83 (1.31)	0.35 (479)
Bought me dinner or a movie		2.39 (1.29)	2.75 (1.27)	2.82 (477)**
Gave me funny or sweet cards or notes for no reason		2.85 (1.37)	2.56 (1.45)	2.10 (311.31)*
Did something like pick a flower to give to me		2.22 (1.32)	2.54 (1.46)	2.43 (322.04)*
Did something like bring me a small surprise from a trip		2.41 (1.32)	2.25 (1.35)	1.24 (477)
Touch (α = .87)	3.11 (1.17)	3.29 (1.17)	3.03 (1.16)	3.03 (1.16)
Gave me an unexpected hug or kiss		3.31 (1.33)	3.22 (1.33)	0.64 (482)
Sat and cuddled with me		3.38 (1.34)	3.06 (1.44)	2.32 (474)*
Touched me in some way		3.30 (1.30)	2.79 (1.28)	3.99 (480)***
Held my hand		3.19 (1.40)	3.00 (1.40)	1.40 (481)

Note: N = 482 participants (n = 155 men, n = 331 women).
*p < .05. **p < .01. ***p < .001

Table 2. Bivariate Correlations Among Reports of Love Language Preferences and Abuse Victimization.

Love Language	Acts of Service	Words of Affirmation	Quality Time	Gifts	Touch	Physical Abuse
Acts of Service	—					
Words of Affirmation	.71***	—				
Quality Time	.72***	.82***	—			
Gifts	.75***	.78***	.75***	—		
Touch	.66***	.77***	.81***	.69***	—	
Physical Abuse	-.15**	-.18***	-.20***	-.12**	-.19***	—
Psychological Abuse	-.14**	-.14**	-.20***	-.12**	-.16***	.55***

Note: *p < .05. **p < .01. ***p < .001.

physical abuse existed for Low (M = 2.40, SD = 1.24) and High (M = 1.96, SD = 0.99) raters of Acts' efficacy, t (357.42) = 3.73, p < .001; for Low (M = 2.38, SD = 1.18) and High (M = 1.91, SD = 1.00) raters of Words' efficacy, t (336.49) = 4.02, p < .001; for Low (M = 2.39, SD = 1.17) and High (M = 1.87, SD = 0.99) raters of Quality Time's efficacy, t (391.91) = 4.74, p < .001; for Low (M = 2.37, SD = 1.18) and High (M = 2.02, SD = 1.08) raters of Gifts' efficacy, t (325) = 2.86, p < .01; and for Low (M = 2.39, SD = 1.19) and High (M = 1.89, SD = 1.03) raters of Touch's efficacy, t (337.50) = 4.19, p < .001. When looking at high versus low raters of particular LLs, H1a-e was each supported.

Similar results for psychological abuse (H2) showed that those "low" in an LL preference were significantly more likely than "high" raters to have experienced greater psychological victimization. Significant high- versus low-group mean differences in psychological victimization were found for all five LLs: Acts (Low M = 4.39, SD = 1.33; High M = 3.92, SD = 1.21), t (364) = 3.55, p < .001; Words (Low M = 4.46, SD = 1.30; High M = 4.04, SD = 1.19), t (342) = 3.09, p < .01; Quality Time (Low M = 4.47, SD = 1.27; High M = 3.92, SD = 1.17), t (393) = 4.48, p < .001; Gifts (Low M = 4.45, SD = 1.28; High M = 4.07, SD = 1.21), t (325) = 2.73, p < .01; and Touch (Low M = 4.44, SD = 1.31; High M = 3.95, SD = 1.18), t (343) = 3.69, p < .001. When looking at high versus low raters of particular LLs, H2a-e were each supported.

The relationships between abuse types and all five LLs were established in the preliminary analyses, and differences in physical and psychological abuse between "low" and "high" raters of LLs were established in H1 and H2. Nonetheless, when coupled with LL-preference sex differences (RQ2), findings that women (M = 2.25, SD = 1.16) experienced greater physical victimization than men (M = 1.86, SD = 0.90; t (384.49) = 4.09, p < .001) suggest that the negative relationships between victimization and LLs may vary by victims' sex. To see whether sex-victimization interactions affected the sex differences found in LL-preferences or if LL-preferences were truly different among men and women regardless of victimization effects, hierarchical regression analyses were employed to test these options; each LL was run as the dependent variable in separate models. On the first step, victims' sex (dummy coded as men = 0, women = 1) was entered into the model. The second step included the independent variable of psychological abuse, entered separately and prior to physical abuse because sex differences were not found for psychological victimization in this sample. Step three included physical abuse. The fourth step included two-way interaction terms of the product of the first three variables paired with one another. Finally, a three-way interaction term was tested (see Table 3).

Hierarchical regression effects indicated that sex in the first step predicted preferences for Acts, Words, Quality Time, and Touch (see Table 3), with men reporting higher preferences for these LLs. On the second step, psychological

Table 3. Hierarchical Regression of Sex and IPV Victimization Predicting Love Languages Preferred from Former Abusive Partners.

Model Steps	ΔR	f^2	Sex	Psych.	Phys.	Sex × Psych.	Sex × Phys.	Psych. × Phys.	Sex × Psych. × Phys.
Acts of Service									
1	.02**	.02	-.13**	-.12**					
2	.02**	.03	-.12**	-.07	-.10				
3	.01	.04	-.11*	.06	.37	.04	-.20	-.45	
4	.01	.05	-.01	.15	.58	-.18	-.57	-.74	.43
5	.00	.06	.20						
Words of Affirmation									
1	.02**	.00	-.01**	-.14**					
2	.02**	.02	-.00	-.06	-.16**				
3	.02**	.04	.02	.06	.06	-.08	-.03	-.26	
4	.00	.04	.11	-.00	-.10	.08	.25	-.04	-.32
5	.00	.04	-.05						
Quality Time									
1	.01*	.01	-.10*	-.19***					
2	.04***	.05	-.09	-.12*	-.12*				
3	.01*	.06	-.07	.01	.11	-.08	-.01	-.30	
4	.00	.07	-.00	-.01	.07	-.04	.05	-.25	-.07
5	.00	.07	-.04						
Gifts									
1	.00	.00	.03	-.12**					
2	.01**	.02	.04	-.07	-.10				
3	.01	.02	.05	.00	.05	-.04	-.02	-.18	
4	.00	.02	.09	.02	.09	-.07	-.08	-.22	.07
5	.00	.02	.12						
Touch									
1	.01*	.01	-.11*	-.15**					
2	.02**	.04	-.09*	-.08	-.13*				
3	.01*	.05	-.08	.06	.27	.00	-.12	-.43	
4	.01	.06	-.00	.15	.49	-.22	-.51	-.73	.44
5	.00	.06	.21						

Note: Cell entries are β coefficients except in the first two columns.

*p < .05. **p < .01. ***p < .001.

victimization predicted all LL preferences, such that greater abuse experienced reflected lower reports of each LL. Thus, H2 was further supported when viewing LL preference as a continuous variable in the presence of sex as a separate model component. Physical victimization, in the third step, predicted only Words, Quality Time, and Touch, with greater physical abuse reflecting lower preferences for those LLs. This lent additional support to H1b, H1c, and H1e; however, for Acts (H1a) and Gifts (H1d), physical abuse failed to reach significance when sex was also included in the model. On the fourth step, none of the two-way interaction terms predicted any LLs. Finally, the three-way interaction term of psychological and physical abuse and sex did not predict any LLs. Therefore, the interactions of abuse types and sex did not additionally add to the predictive ability of the models. Victims' sex and type of abuse experienced operated independently in predicting different LL scores.

DISCUSSION

For IPV victims, it appears that the ways they preferred their former abusive partner to communicate love were determined by the type and extent of victimization they experienced, as well as by sex identification. These results have implications for theorizing models of violent and nonviolent family functioning. I discuss these aspects by incorporating discussion of this study's limitations alongside proposed avenues for future research. Further, practitioner applications of these findings will also be considered.

What We Know: Similarities With Nonviolent Love Communication

Individuals can identify myriad ways they feel love when communicated by family members and often express preferences for some ways of communicating over others. Replicating previous research by Goff et al. (2007), all LLs were positively related to one another. In this study, significant differences were found in preferences for certain LLs compared to others (RQ1). Overall, the sample indicated they felt "most loved" when their partner used Touch to express love for them. In Goff et al.'s (2007) survey with college students, the most common preference for LL expression was Quality Time, followed by Touch and Words of Affirmation. Although similar in that these were mostly top preferences in this study, the current sample's preference for expressions of love via Touch is consistent with notions of romantic love associated with physical intimacy, particularly in Western culture relationships and when used as a form of maintenance in established relationships (Dainton et al., 1994). In that respect, these IPV victims do not appear to differ from the larger population.

What We Are Learning: Violent Nuance in Love Communication

Individual applications. When looking at the distinctions between types of abuse experiences, however, a different story emerges. For example, male victims expressed higher preferences than did women for Acts, Touch, and Quality Time (RQ2). One interpretation may be that men simply expressed stronger preferences for LLs overall.

A more contextual explanation may be that women's preferred LLs were tied to the manner and extent of abuse they received. On average, women in this sample reported significantly more physical victimization than did men. Further, higher levels of physical victimization were predictive of lower preferences for LLs. The same finding held for psychological victimization, such that greater abuse predicted lower preferences for each LL when used by a partner. One interpretation of this finding could be that, contrary to popular perceptions of victims staying passionately in love with their abusive partner (Halket et al., 2014), remaining in severe IPV situations is more likely to be for practical considerations outside their control than because of positive emotions (Eckstein, 2011, 2012a; Rhodes et al., 2010).

Although results from the hierarchical models suggest that sex and IPV victimization operate independently in predicting LL preferences (as no significant additional variance was explained by an interaction between the variables in the overall model tests), a societal understanding of IPV as it occurs for women versus men—in both experiences and outcomes—suggests a more complex story than captured by the current study (e.g., Williams & Frieze, 2005). For example, Eckstein (2012b) found that victims' gender was more important than biological sex in predicting IPV experiences and outcomes. It is a particular type of *masculinity*, not a sex in particular, that is situated as the "causal" factor in most feminist IPV models (e.g., Braithwaite & Daly, 1994). As such, future research should thus consider the role of gender (as opposed to sex) nuance in reporting LLs and IPV in general.

Theory and research implications. IPV is often theorized as a gendered occurrence in domestic contexts (Johnson, 2005; Langhinrichsen-Rohling, 2009). Anecdotally, particular LLs are often affiliated with sex roles (Chapman, 2010). However, research has yet to *consistently* find sex differences. Models of IPV victimization differ according to the theoretical approach taken (e.g., family violence and feminist models often contradict on findings related to sex differences), and Chapman's model of LLs is simply untested as an area of study. To clarify the influence of sex (and, correspondingly or not, gender style) in the communication by men and women in violent families, future research must articulate the ways in which tactics used to outwardly demonstrate emotions—positive and negative—are received by their targets.

To clarify these factors, basic issues in the measure of LLs must first be addressed. The construct validity of LLs, as measured by Chapman's scale (which uses participants' dichotomous choice of random pairings of the five LLs for each item), is currently potentially problematic, because (a) there is no one accepted measure of these constructs as of yet and (b) those using different scales often fail to report complete psychometric properties of their instrument. Thus, the convergent and divergent validity of the items used to measure each LL remains unknown. In addition to fine-tuning our explanatory (and predictive) models of emotions and family functioning (in violent and nonviolent contexts), such research would also have practical applications for enhancing coping strategies, emotion- and conflict-management tactics, and advice to third-party family members. Future work should consider both the validity of each language and the proposed axioms across myriad family and relationship contexts, as their prescriptive nature may serve as an empirically legitimate (as opposed to intuitive) recommendation for practitioners.

Also untested are some of Chapman's (2010) other claims regarding the ways LLs are used, received, and operate to affect relationship outcomes. As yet, the predictive validity of LL axioms as applied in the general population (as opposed to case examples) has not been determined. For example, do LLs change as we age? At what age do LLs become primary/secondary—that is, preferred over others? To what extent are they dominant culture versus family constructed? Do differences exist in LL preferences or social display norms across cultures and/or generations? And finally, as was examined in this study, what other types of life experiences (e.g., sex- and gender-specific wording/themes of specific tactics) shape preferences for different LLs and in what ways? Knowing the answers to these types of questions not only would aid our understanding of communication in violent relationships but would also contribute to the study of love-communication in general family research.

CONCLUSION

The pervasiveness of the five LLs and their overlap with established research on relational communication styles (albeit ones yet unformulated systematically in a love-communication context) suggest potential for examining the communication of love. This study provides an initial step in examining LLs in a particular family context—intimate partner violence. Knowing that men and women abused by romantic partners have overall lower preferences for love expressed in any manner by their abusive partner lends support to the notion that love as sole motivator for staying in IPV relationships may indeed be a societal myth. "I love you" may be easy to say, but for those living with daily communication to the contrary, love is not blind to abuse.

REFERENCES

Ackerman, J. M., Griskevicius, V., & Li, N. P. (2011). Let's get serious: Communicating commitment in romantic relationships. *Journal of Personality and Social Psychology, 100*(6), 1079–1094. doi: 10.1037/a0022412

Aron, A., & Westbay, L. (1996). Dimensions of the prototype of love. *Journal of Personality and Social Psychology, 70*(3), 535–551.

Basile, K. C., & Hall, J. E. (2011). Intimate partner violence perpetration by court-ordered men: Distinctions and intersections among physical violence, sexual violence, psychological abuse, and stalking. *Journal of Interpersonal Violence, 26*(2), 230–253. doi: 10.1177/0886260510362896

Birnbaum, G. E. (2010). Bound to interact: The divergent goals and complex interplay of attachment and sex within romantic relationships. *Journal of Social and Personal Relationships, 27*(2), 245–252. doi: 10.1177/0265407509360902

Black, M. C., Basile, K. C., Breiding, M. J., Smith, S. G., Walters, M. L., Merrick, M. T., … Stevens, M. R. (2011). *The National Intimate Partner and Sexual Violence Survey (NISVS): 2010 summary report*. National Center for Injury Prevention and Control, Centers for Disease Control and Prevention. Retrieved from www.cdc.gov/violenceprevention/pdf/nisvs_report2010-a.pdf

Blau, P. M. (1964). *Exchange and power in social life*. New York: Wiley.

Borochowitz, D. Y., & Eisikovits, Z. (2002). To love violently: Strategies for reconciling love and violence. *Violence Against Women, 8*(4), 476–494. doi: 10.1177/10778010222183170

Braithwaite, J., & Daly, K. (1994). Masculinities, violence and communitarian control. In T. Newburn & E. A. Stanko (Eds.), *Just boys doing business?: Men, masculinities, and crime* (pp. 189–213). New York: Routledge.

Browne, A. (1991). The victim's experience: Pathways to disclosure. *Psychotherapy, 28*(1), 150–156.

Brule (Eckstein), N. J. (2002, November). *"You don't bring me flowers anymore": An analysis of the five love languages through various stages of the life span*. Paper presented at the annual conference of the National Communication Association, New Orleans, LA.

Casey, E. (2011, April 10th). Love language. *Success*. Retrieved from www.success.com/article/love-language

Chapman, G. (2010). *The five love languages: The secret to love that lasts* (4th ed.). Chicago, IL: Northfield Publishing; Moody.

Chapman, G. (2014). *The 5 love languages*. Retrieved from http://www.5lovelanguages.com/

Cheal, D. (1987). "Showing them you love them": Gift giving and the dialectic of intimacy. *The Sociological Review, 35*(1), 150–169. doi: 10.1111/j.1467-954X.1987.tb00007.x

Clark, M. S., & Mills, J. (1979). Interpersonal attraction in exchange and communal relationships. *Journal of Personality and Social Psychology, 37*, 12–24.

Collins, N. L., & Feeney, B. C. (2000). A safe haven: An attachment theory perspective on support seeking and caregiving in intimate relationships. *Journal of Personality and Social Psychology, 78*(6), 1053–1073. doi: 10.1037/0022.3514.78.6.1053

Collins, N. L., & Ford, M. B. (2010). Responding to the needs of others: The caregiving behavioral system in intimate relationships. *Journal of Social and Personal Relationships, 27*(2), 235–244. doi: 10.1177/0265407509360907

Collins, N. L., Kane, H. S., Metz, M. A., Cleveland, C., Khan, C., Winczewski, L., ... Prok, T. (2014). Psychological, physiological, and behavioral responses to a partner in need: The role of compassionate love. *Journal of Social and Personal Relationships, 31*(5), 601–629. doi: 10.1177/0265407514529069

Dainton, M., Stafford, L., & Canary, D. J. (1994). Maintenance strategies and physical affection as predictors of love, liking, and satisfaction in marriage. *Communication Reports, 7*(2), 88–98.

Dillow, M. R., Goodboy, A. K., & Bolkan, S. (2014). Attachment and the expression of affection in romantic relationships: The mediating role of romantic love. *Communication Reports, 27*(2), 102–115. doi: 10.1080/08934215.2014.900096

Eckstein, J. J. (2011). Reasons for staying in intimately violent relationships: Comparisons of men and women and messages communicated to self and others. *Journal of Family Violence, 26*, 21–30. doi: 10.1007/s10896-010-9338-0

Eckstein, J. J. (2012a). Reasons for staying in abusive relationships: A resource for understanding identities. In A. Browne-Miller (Ed.), *Violence and abuse in society: Understanding a global crisis* (Vol. 4: Faces of intimate partner violence, pp. 53–75). Santa Barbara, CA: Praeger.

Eckstein, J. J. (2012b). Sex, gender, and relationship type in the relational uncertainty of victims of partner violence. *Partner Abuse, 3*(1), 22–42. doi: 10.1891/1946-6560.3.1.22

Farley, S. D., Hughes, S. M., & LaFayette, J. N. (2013). People will know we are in love: Evidence of differences between vocal samples directed toward lovers and friends. *Journal of Nonverbal Behavior, 37*, 123–138. doi: 10.1007/s10919-013-0151-3

Feiler, B. (2011, November 19th). Can Gary Chapman save your marriage? *New York Times*. Retrieved from www.nytimes.com/2011/11/20/fashion/can-gary-chapman-save-your-marriage-this-life.html?pagewanted=all&_r=0

Floyd, K. (2005). Fathers' and sons' reports of fathers' affectionate communication: Implications of a naive theory of affection. *Journal of Social and Personal Relationships, 22*(1), 99–109. doi: 10.1177/0265407505049323

Frankland, A., & Brown, J. (2014). Coercive control in same-sex intimate partner violence. *Journal of Family Violence, 29*(1), 15–22. doi: 10.1007/s10896-013-9558-1

Goff, B. G., Goddard, H. W., Pointer, L., & Jackson, G. B. (2007). Measures of expressions of love. *Psychological Reports, 101*, 357–360. doi: 10.2466/PR0.101.2.357-260

Hafner, M., & Ijzerman, H. (2011). The face of love: Spontaneous accommodation as social emotion regulation. *Personality and Social Psychology Bulletin, 37*(12), 1551–1563. doi: 10.1177/0146167211415629

Halket, M. M., Gormley, K., Mello, N., Rosenthal, L., & Mirkin, M. P. (2014). Stay with or leave the abuser?: The effects of domestic violence victim's decision on attributions made by young adults. *Journal of Family Violence, 29*(1), 35–49. doi: 10.1007/s10896-013-9555-4

Hatfield, E., & Rapson, R. L. (1993). *Love, sex, and intimacy: Their psychology, biology, and history.* New York: Harper Collins.

Hayakawa, S. I. (1972). *Language in thought and action* (3rd ed.). New York: Harcourt Brace Jovanovich, Inc.

Hefner, V., & Wilson, B. J. (2013). From love at first sight to soul mate: The influence of romantic ideals in popular films on young people's beliefs about relationships. *Communication Monographs, 80*(2), 150–175. doi: 10.1080/03637751.2013.776697

Hendrick, C., & Hendrick, S. (1986). A theory and method of love. *Journal of Personality and Social Psychology, 50*(2), 392–402.

Hendrick, C., & Hendrick, S. S. (1988). Lovers wear rose colored glasses. *Journal of Social and Personal Relationships, 5*(2), 161–183. doi: 10.1177/026549758800500203

Hendrick, S. S., & Hendrick, C. (2002). Linking romantic love with sex: Development of the perceptions of love and sex scale. *Journal of Social and Personal Relationships, 19*(3), 361–378. doi: 10.1177/0265407502193004

Hendrick, S. S., & Hendrick, C. (2006). Measuring respect in close relationships. *Journal of Social and Personal Relationships, 23*(6), 881–899. doi: 10.1177/0265407506070471

Hendrick, S. S., Hendrick, C., & Adler, N. L. (1988). Romantic relationships: Love, satisfaction, and staying together. *Journal of Personality and Social Psychology, 54*(6), 980–988.

Honeycutt, J. M., Cantrill, J. G., Kelly, P., & Lambkin, D. (1998). How do I love thee? Let me consider my options: Cognition, verbal strategies, and the escalation of intimacy. *Human Communication Research, 25*(1), 39–63.

Horan, S. M., & Booth-Butterfield, M. (2010). Investing in affection: An investigation of affection exchange theory and relational qualities. *Communication Quarterly, 58*(4), 394–413. doi: 10.1080/01463373.2010.524876

Hudson, W. W. (2000). *The WALMYR assessment scales scoring manual.* Tallahassee, FL: WALMYR Publishing.

Huston, T. L. (2009). What's love got to do with it?: Why some marriages succeed and others fail. *Personal Relationships, 16*, 301–327. doi: 10.1111/j.1475-6811.2009.01225.x

Johnson, M. P. (2005). Domestic violence: It's not about gender—or is it? *Journal of Marriage and Family, 67*, 1126–1130.

Johnson, M. P., & Leone, J. M. (2005). The differential effects of intimate terrorism and situational couple violence: Findings from the National Violence Against Women Survey. *Journal of Family Issues, 26*(3), 322–349. doi: 10.1177/0192513X04270345

Keeley, M. (2004). Final conversations: Messages of love. *Qualitative Research Reports in Communication, 5*, 34–40.

Kitzmann, K. M., Gaylord, N. K., Holt, A. R., & Kenny, E. D. (2003). Child witnesses to domestic violence: A meta-analytic review. *Journal of Consulting and Clinical Psychology, 71*(2), 339–352. doi: 10.1037/0022-006x.71.2.339

Kostelecky, K. L., & Bass, B. L. (2004). Grandmothers and their granddaughters. *Journal of Intergenerational Relationships, 2*(1), 47–61. doi: 10.1300/J194v02n01_04

Kruse, M., Sorensen, J., Bronnum-Hansen, H., & Helweg-Larsen, K. (2011). The health care costs of violence against women. *Journal of Interpersonal Violence, 26*(17), 3494–3508. doi: 10.1177/0886260511403754

Kurdek, L. A. (2004). Are gay and lesbian cohabiting couples *really* different from heterosexual married couples? *Journal of Marriage and Family, 66*, 880–900.

Langhinrichsen-Rohling, J. (2009). Controversies involving gender and intimate partner violence in the United States. *Sex Roles, 62*(3–4), 179–193. doi: 10.1007/s11199-009-9628-2

Lee, J. A. (1976). *The colors of love.* Englewood Cliffs, NJ: Prentice-Hall.

Lemieux, R., & Hale, J. L. (2000). Intimacy, passion and commitment among married individuals: Further testing of the triangular theory of love. *Psychological Reports, 87*(3), 941–948.

Leone, J. M. (2011). Suicidal behavior among low-income, African American female victims of intimate terrorism and situational couple violence. *Journal of Interpersonal Violence, 26*(13), 2568–2591. doi: 10.1177/0886260510388280

Levine, T. R., Aune, K. S., & Park, H. S. (2006). Love styles and communication in relationships: Partner preferences, initiation, and intensification. *Communication Quarterly, 54*(4), 465–486. doi: 10.1080/01463370601036515

Marston, P. J., Hecht, M. L., & Robers, T. (1987). "True love ways": The subjective experience and communication of romantic love. *Journal of Social and Personal Relationships, 4*(4), 387–407. doi: 10.1177/0265407587044001

Morman, M. T., & Floyd, K. (1998). "I love you, man": Overt expressions of affection in male-male interaction. *Sex Roles, 38*(9/10), 871–881.

Myers, S. A., Byrnes, K. A., Frisby, B. N., & Mansson, D. H. (2011). Adult siblings' use of affectionate communication as a strategic and routine relational maintenance behavior. *Communication Research Reports, 28*(2), 151–158. doi: 10.1080/08824096.2011.565276

O'Leary, K. D., Acevedo, B. P., Aron, A., Huddy, L., & Mashek, D. (2011). Is long-term love more than a rare phenomenon?: If so, what are its correlates? *Social Psychological and Personality Science, 3*(2), 241–249. doi: 10.1177/1948550611417015

Olson, L. N. (2003). "From lace teddies to flannel PJ's": An analysis of males' experience and expressions of love. *Qualitative Research Reports in Communication, 4*, 38–44.

Olson, L. N. (2004). Relational control-motivated aggression: A theoretically-based typology of intimate violence. *Journal of Family Communication, 4*(3&4), 209–233.

Podrazik, J. (2013, February 14). '5 love languages': Oprah takes Dr. Gary Chapman's 'love language' quiz. *Huffington Post.* Retrieved from www.huffingtonpost.com/2013/02/14/love-languages-oprah-gary-chapman-love-language_n_2671852.html

Power, C., Koch, T., Kralik, D., & Jackson, D. (2006). Lovestruck: Women, romantic love and intimate partner violence. *Advances in Nursing and Interpersonal Violence, 21*, 174–185.

Reis, H. T., Maniaci, M. R., & Rogge, R. D. (2014). The expression of compassionate love in everyday compassionate acts. *Journal of Social and Personal Relationships, 31*(5), 651–676. doi: 10.1177/0265407513507214

Rhodes, K. V., Cerulli, C., Dichter, M. E., Kothari, C. L., & Barg, F. K. (2010). "I didn't want to put them through that": The influence of children on victim decision-making in intimate partner violence cases. *Journal of Family Violence, 25*(5), 485–493. doi: 10.1007/s10896-010-9310-z

Rogers, M. J., & Follingstad, D. R. (2014). Women's exposure to psychological abuse: Does that experience predict mental health outcomes? *Journal of Family Violence, 29*(6), 595–611. doi: 10.1007/s10896-014-9621-6

Rubin, Z. (1970). Measurement of romantic love. *Journal of Personality and Social Psychology, 16*, 265–273.

Schoenfeld, E. A., Bredow, C. A., & Huston, T. L. (2012). Do men and women show love differently in marriage? *Personality and Social Psychology Bulletin, 38*(11), 1396–1409. doi: 10.1177/0146167212450739

Shaver, P. R., Schwartz, J., Kirson, D., & O'Connor, C. (1987). Emotion knowledge: Further exploration of a prototype approach. *Journal of Personality and Social Psychology, 52*(6), 1061–1086.

Sillito, C. L. (2012). Physical health effects of intimate partner abuse. *Journal of Family Issues, 33*(11), 1520–1539. doi: 10.1177/0192513x12448742

Snell, J. E., Rosenwald, R. J., & Robey, A. (1964). The wifebeater's wife: A study of family interaction. *Archives of General Psychiatry, 11*, 107–113.

Sprecher, S. (1999). "I love you more today than yesterday": Romantic partners' perceptions of changes in love and related affect over time. *Journal of Personality and Social Psychology, 76*(1), 46–53.

Stafford, L. (2010). Measuring relationship maintenance behaviors: Critique and development of the revised relationship maintenance behavior scale. *Journal of Social and Personal Relationships, 28*(2), 278–303. doi: 10.1177/0265407510378125

Sternberg, R. J., & Grajek, S. (1984). The nature of love. *Journal of Personality and Social Psychology, 47*, 312–329.

Sternberg, R. J. (1986). A triangular theory of love. *Psychological Review, 93*, 25–37.

Straus, M. A., Hamby, S. L., & Warren, W. L. (2003). *The Conflict Tactics Scales handbook: Revised Conflict Tactics Scales (CTS2), CTS: Parent-Child Version (CTSPC).* Los Angeles, CA: Western Psychological Services.

Sullivan, C. M., Parisian, J. A., & Davidson, W. S. (1991). *Index of psychological abuse: Development of a measure.* Paper presented at the annual conference of the American Psychological Association, San Francisco, CA.

Sullivan, T. P., Schroeder, J. A., Dudley, D. N., & Dixon, J. M. (2010). Do differing types of victimization and coping strategies influence the type of social reactions experienced by current victims of intimate partner violence? *Violence Against Women, 16*(6), 638–657. doi: 10.1177/1077801210370027

Towns, A., & Adams, P. (2000). "If I really loved him enough, he would be okay": Women's accounts of male partner violence. *Violence Against Women, 6*(6), 558–585. doi: 10.1177/10778010022182038

Walster, E., & Walster, G. W. (1978). *A new look at love.* Reading, MA: Addison-Wesley.

Williams, M. L. (2012). *Romantic love communication: Examination of equity and effects on relational, sexual, and communication satisfaction.* (Doctor of Philosophy dissertation), Kent State University. Retrieved from http://rave.ohiolink.edu/etdc/view?acc_num=kent1332191567

Yuste, M., Serrano, M. A., Girbés, S., & Arandia, M. (2014). Romantic love and gender violence: Clarifying misunderstandings through communicative organization of the research. *Qualitative Inquiry, 20*(7), 850–855. doi: 10.1177/1077800414537206

Social, Cultural, AND Historical Structures AND Processes

CHAPTER TEN

"You say you love me, but you don't support me"

Coming-Out Communication within Religious Family Contexts

CHANA ETENGOFF

"Authentic liberation—the process of humanization—is not another deposit to be made in men [sic]. Liberation is a praxis: the action and reflection of men and women upon their world in order to transform it."

—PAULO FREIRE (*PEDAGOGY OF THE OPPRESSED*, 1968)

Disclosing one's sexual identity [coming out] to family can be challenging for both parties, with some suggesting it triggers parental mourning and other relational challenges, particularly for religious families (Savin-Williams & Dube, 1998; Schnoor, 2003). However, Orthodox Jewish and conservative Christian families report diverse reactions to their relatives' sexual orientation disclosure—while some use God as a manipulative weapon of reproach, others employ religious values of love and acceptance (Etengoff & Daiute, 2014, 2015a). In a similar vein, there are conflicting reports regarding whether religious values adversely impact the coming-out process (e.g., D'Augelli 2005; Serovich, Skeen, Walters, & Robinson, 1993). Yet despite such variations, little is known about the family communication patterns that can foster post–coming-out resilience and familial acceptance amid potential religious conflicts (D'Augelli, 2005; Lee & Lee, 2006; Willoughby, 2008). Alternatively, religious conflicts are often approached as the defining and determining characteristic of negative familial reactions to the coming-out event and the exploration of general communication styles and family system health is largely reserved for understanding non-religious families' responses (Etengoff, 2013). However, recent research suggests that family systems can successfully use religious texts and values to negotiate cultural and familial conflicts *or* to promote familial estrangement and hostility (Etengoff & Daiute, 2014). In which case, it becomes imperative to explore the larger communication patterns surrounding and contributing to diverse family reactions.

The need for further communication-centered inquiry is indisputable, as the sexual orientation disclosure process is interpersonal in nature, reflecting "families' communication routines and fault lines" (Bigner, 2013, p. 137). For example, Adams (2011) writes of how early childhood family communications (or lack thereof) regarding sexuality contribute to the creation of the metaphoric "closet"— the sociocultural designation of a non-heterosexual identity as a hidden, stigmatized, and shameful status. Whether it be targeted physical abuse, heteronormative assumptions, homophobia, or the silencing of conversations about sexual and gender identity, Adams (2011) asserts that familial communication plays a powerful role in one's decision to suppress and/or reveal his or her sexual or gender minority identity. Building upon this body of work, the present chapter argues that the process of emerging from this secretive state of suppression also hinges upon the family's general communication patterns and conflict-resolution strategies—as do most family secrets (Afifi & Olson, 2005).

In an effort to answer the question of why some religious family members are able to successfully negotiate conflicting religious beliefs while others employ darker communication strategies, the present chapter explores the communication patterns associated with and/or preceding conservative Christian and Orthodox Jewish family members' religious responses to their relative's sexual orientation disclosure. By using an applied sociocultural method of analysis (Etengoff & Daiute, 2015), this inquiry focuses on how family power dynamics impact religious families' relationally productive (e.g., responding with unconditional love and asking to meet the child/sibling's partner) and repressive communication patterns (e.g., telling a child he or she is sinning and asking him or her to change his or her sexual orientation). The following research questions guided this inquiry: What are the underlying communication themes that contribute to relationally productive vs. repressive responses to a relative's sexual orientation disclosure? How do power dynamics contribute to religious relative's responses to their gay relative's disclosure? In an effort to address these questions, the chapter begins by discussing the relational role of religion as well as the major family frameworks that have been applied to familial coming-out analyses. The chapter then continues with an analysis of 23 gay men's and their 15 religious family allies' accounts of relational dynamics and coming-out communication.

DISTINGUISHING BETWEEN RELIGIOUS TOOLS AND DETERMINISTIC SCRIPTS

Within the lens of cultural historical activity theory (Vygotsky, 1978), culture is formed at the intersection of individual and community activity. In this vein, religion is a relationally performative activity the enactment of which varies based on individuals' choices and social contexts (Day, 2002). Individuals appropriate religious values and scriptural passages as cultural tools—agentively negotiating conflicts and relationships (Etengoff & Daiute, 2011, 2014, 2015b). In other words, religious experience is largely dependent upon the practitioner's sociorelational goals. For example, scriptural justifications have been used throughout the centuries to support both discrimination and equality, depending upon individuals' and communities' social visions (Frontain, 1997; Miller, 1998). Moreover, while Christian and Jewish communities focus on similar cultural artifacts, there are different post-biblical traditions within and between communities (for a full review see Etengoff, 2013). This means that although Orthodox Jewish and Christian communities share Leviticus 18:22—"Thou shalt not lie with mankind, as with womankind: it is an abomination (*to'evah*)"—interpretations may vary depending upon individuals' and communities' relational goals. In summary, the variability within and between religious families' responses to the disclosure event supports the perspective that religion is not a deterministic relational script (e.g., D'Augelli 2005; Etengoff & Daiute, 2014; Serovich et al., 1993; Tremble, Schneider, & Appathurai, 1989). In which case, researchers must go beyond merely conducting correlational analyses and utilize psychological, familial, and communication paradigms to further explore the nexuses among religion, family, and sexual orientation. Instead of continuing to reaffirm our understanding that these various factors are related, it is imperative to understand *how* the interrelationship among religion, family and sexual orientation is negotiated by family systems.

THEORETICAL APPROACHES TO FAMILY DISCLOSURE DYNAMICS

Child and family development models have rarely been applied to the study of sexual minorities and their families of origin/birth (Willoughby, Doty, & Malik, 2008). While emerging research spans multiple fields of study (e.g., sociology, psychology, and communication studies), family stress (e.g., Baioco et al., 2014; Willoughby et al., 2008) and attachment theories (e.g., Carnelley, Hepper, Hicks, & Turner, 2011) have largely dominated recent psychological research. Although each theory assists researchers in conceptualizing the relation between the coming-out event and general family responses, the theories do not simultaneously offer a comprehensive analysis of the associated family communication patterns. Therefore, after reviewing the above theoretical perspectives, a critical sociocultural framework for exploring family communication is presented.

Family Stress Theory

Coming out to family is a stressor that often shifts family values, roles, expectations, and boundaries (Willoughby et al., 2006). Given this context, a number of sexual minority scholars have applied Family Stress Theory (Hill, 1958) to further understand familial response variability (e.g., Baioco et al., 2014; Willoughby et al., 2006). Drawing on a social systems approach, Family Stress Theory suggests that family reactions to traumatic and/or stressful events are dependent upon a) family stress management resources such as cohesion, adaptability, warmth, and flexibility; b) family cognitions regarding the meaning of the event—cost/benefit analyses, beliefs, values, attributions, and expectations; c) presence or absence of co-occurring stressors such as social pressure (Baioco et al., 2014; Crosbie-Burnett, Foster, Murray, & Bowen, 1996; Green, 2000; Hill, 1958; Willoughby et al., 2008). In other words, extant family resources may be a primary differentiating factor between families that defer to community homophobia and those that give precedence to the family (Willoughby et al., 2006). Similarly, the Family System Model of Resilience suggests that families can adapt to a crisis as a functional unit if they enter into the stressful event with social competency, problem solving skills, autonomy, optimism, and the ability to recruit social support (Lee & Lee, 2006). While the sociorelational breadth of such theories is essential to understanding complex events involving sexual orientation, family, and community systems, communication-focused research is needed to move from theoretical paradigms to practice-based interventions.

Attachment Theory

As an alternative to Family Stress Theory (Hill, 1958), researchers have applied Attachment Theory (Bowlby, 1969) to further understand the parent-child relationship dynamics proceeding and affecting the coming-out event (e.g., Carnelley et al., 2011; Willoughby et al., 2006). Attachment Theory suggests that adult relationship patterns are largely determined by early childhood experiences with a primary caregiver (Bowlby, 1969). These initial experiences with a caregiver influence children's perceptions of adults' relational behavior and often lead to the replication of these communication patterns into adulthood (Olson, Baoicchi-Wagner, Wilson Kratzer, & Symonds, 2012). Utilizing this lens, research indicates that the coming-out experience is more difficult for sexual-minority individuals raised by authoritarian parents who value obedience over warmth as compared to those raised by authoritative parents who are accepting of their child's independence and exploration (Carnelley et al., 2011; Willoughby et al., 2006). In a similar vein, researchers report that pre-existing levels of parent-child closeness/conflict, time spent together, sensitive childhood parenting, and parental social support can lead to positive sexual orientation disclosures (Heatherington & Lavner, 2008; Mohr & Fassinger, 2003). Moreover, adult family patterns of attachment may influence whether there will be a sexual orientation disclosure to family or whether it will remain a secret (Boon & Miller, 1999; Holtzen, Kenny, & Mahalik, 1995). Although this body of work begins to address the relational components involved in families' reactions to a relative's coming out, further research is needed to understand the power dynamics that impact family communication norms, closeness, commitment, and concealment (Afifi & Olson, 2007).

A Critical Sociocultural Framework of Family Communication

Over a decade ago, Savin-Williams and Dube (1998) stated that it may be more important to understand the factors leading to a healthy *long-term* family relationship post-disclosure than it is to predict the *initial* disclosure response. Critical family communication scholars attempt to answer such questions by approaching the family as a sociohistorical creation of contemporary power struggles vying to determine whose norms are legitimated and whose are silenced (Braithwaite & Baxter, 2006, p. 6). Some of the power dynamics that come into play for gay men and their religious families are situated within parent-child relations, heteronormative cultural expectations, and socioreligious concerns regarding sexual morality (Etengoff, 2013).

Within a critical communication framework, family communication is understood to be a "joint activity shaped by the individual characteristics of the participants and the social groups to which they belong" (Harwood, Soliz, & Lin, 2006, p. 19). Daiute's (2012) theory of relational complexity offers a starting point for critical communication scholars interested in developing applied narrative analysis strategies. Relational complexity is "the ability to interact meaningfully and flexibly with diverse others, in terms of their differing understandings, influence (power), expectations, and to adjust one's expression with them in terms of goals and needs" (Daiute, 2012, p. 6). Daiute's (2012) construct facilitates the transition from Vygotsky's (2012) emphasis on *understanding* the affective-volitional bases of others' thoughts to the process of *modifying* interpersonal communications based on this knowledge. In addition, this framework expands beyond traditional perspective-taking paradigms by shifting the focus from relational anticipation to relational modification (e.g., Batson, Early, & Salvarani, 1997).

Building on this foundation, the present study operationalizes relational complexity as a humanizing process that alters power and oppression dynamics by promoting relational attachment (Bell & Khoury, 2011; Hidalgo, 2011). Prior research defines humanization as the "experience of having one's experiences, desires, and feelings recognized" by an empathic audience and the "opportunity for personal agency and self-actualization" (Bell & Khoury, 2011, p. 168). In the case of gay men and their religious families, a humanizing response may focus on unconditional love and empathy for their gay relative (e.g., *"I know how J. [son] feels and what he goes through—I, if, if anything, I just feel compassion."*). Contrastingly, a lack of relational complexity may be manifested in dehumanizing discursive violence—"words, gestures, tones, images, presentations, and omissions used to differentially treat, degrade, pathologize, and represent lesbian and gay subjectivity and experience (Yep, 2003, p. 23)."

PRESENT STUDY

Familial sexual orientation acceptance is associated with positive mental and physical health outcomes (Ryan, Russel, Huebner, Diaz, & Sanchez, 2010). However, there is limited research on the protective factors facilitating positive family responses and the sociocultural contexts of those responses (D'Augelli, 2005; Elizur & Ziv, 2004; Goodrich, 2009). The present study therefore explores how power dynamics and communication patterns impact conservative Christian and Orthodox Jewish families' responses to the coming-out event.[1] Other religious groups with homoprohibitive laws based on alternative religious texts (e.g., Quran) were not sampled in an effort to reduce cultural cohort differences such as differing *contemporary* implementations of scriptural punishments ranging from social exclusion to extreme cases of religiously sanctioned death (for a full review, see Etengoff, 2013).

As sexual-minority research largely focuses on only sexual minorities' perspectives regarding familial relationships (personological perspectives), the present study's sampling of both gay men *and* their religious family allies explores an additional facet of the family system (Carnelley et al., 2011; D'Augelli, 2005; Savin-Williams & Dube, 1998). However, given the known difficulties of recruiting gay men's relatives for participation, the present study only approached family allies as they were viewed as being more likely to consent to participate (Ben-Ari, 1995; Savin-Williams & Dube, 1998).

In addition, lesbians and their families were not recruited, as sexual orientation disclosure and religious identity conflict frequently differ between gay men and lesbians (Rodriguez & Ouellette, 2000). For example, while many scholars argue that the Bible's heteronormativity impacts both gay men and lesbians, others note that scriptural passages in Leviticus (18:22, 20:13) regarding same-sex intercourse are historically interpreted as relating specifically to men, with lesbian sanctions often viewed as being more permeable social constructions (Etengoff & Daiute, 2014; Greenberg, 2004). Moreover, it was important to select the sexual minority group with the more explicit/literal biblical prohibition in light of the present study's focus on how families communicate about *conflicts* between religion and sexuality (e.g., "If a man lies with a male as with a woman, both of them have committed an abomination; they shall surely be put to death; their blood is upon them," Leviticus, 20:13).

METHODS

Participants

Ten gay men from Orthodox Jewish backgrounds and seven of their key family allies participated (four sisters, one brother, two mothers). In addition, 13 gay men from Christian backgrounds and eight of their key family allies participated (one sister, six mothers, one father). The rate of family ally participation was similar for the two groups (70% Jewish; 62% Christian). Due to possible cohort effects related to changing sociopolitical attitudes, gay male participants were required to be within the range of 18–35 years of age. The mean age for gay men from Jewish and Christian backgrounds was 25 (Jewish *SD* = 5, Christian *SD* = 3), 42 years of age for Jewish family members (*SD* = 17), and 52 for Christian family members (*SD* = 12). On average, gay men from Jewish backgrounds were interviewed five years after their first familial disclosure (*SD* = 4), and gay Christian men were interviewed four years after their first familial disclosure (*SD* = 2.5). All participants identified as White, although this was not a criterion for inclusion (for further demographic information, see Etengoff, 2013).

Initial participant recruitment efforts focused on Catholics given the Catholic Church's recent statements regarding homosexuality. However, due to recruitment difficulties, inclusion criteria expanded to include gay men from all Christian subgroups. Gay participants who self-identified as being raised within Christian families reported a past/present affiliation with: Mormon (seven), Catholic (two), Methodist (two), Evangelical (one), and Seventh-Day Adventist (one) communities. Participating Christian family allies identified as: Mormon (four), Catholic (one), Methodist (one), Evangelical (one), and Seventh-Day Adventist (one). While the religious groups included in this sample are diverse, both in terms of between- and within-group variation, this diversity was viewed as acceptable given that participants' religious affiliation descriptions were consistent with conservative or fundamentalist religious values.

Eighty-six percent of Jewish family allies and 75% of Christian family allies identified as strictly observant. Fifty-seven percent of Jewish family allies attended services weekly, 29% monthly, and 14% for High Holidays and celebratory events. Eighty-eight percent of Christian family allies reported attending services weekly, and 12% did not attend services at all due to a lack of availability. Thirty percent of gay participants from Jewish backgrounds identified as currently Orthodox, 10% as agnostic, and 60% as non-practicing believers. Similarly to gay men from Jewish backgrounds, 38% of gay men from Christian backgrounds identified as practicing and observant. However, a greater percentage of gay men from Christian backgrounds identified as agnostic or atheist (38%), and a lower percentage reported being non-practicing believers (23%).

Recruitment

Gay participants were recruited either directly (n = 13), by participant referral (n = 6), or organizational membership, blogs, and listservs. (n = 4). While this sampling technique is not representative of all gay men from religious homes, this sampling strategy was a deliberate aspect of the design, as it focuses upon gay men already engaged in negotiation strategies. After informed consent was obtained, gay participants were asked if they felt comfortable encouraging their most supportive family member—their key family ally—to participate. Ninety-two percent of all family unit dyads were recruited via this referral process, and the remaining family allies contacted the researcher based on peer or community referrals.

Measures

Semi-structured interviews were employed, as this method flexibly allows for culturally sensitive adaptations that engage the diversity and heterogeneity between and within religious groups (Lee & Lee, 2006; Wengraf, 2001). Interviews were based on 21 questions addressing participants' demographics, socioreligious activities and practices, family system dynamics, and related experiential history (see Etengoff, 2013, for a complete listing). Gay men's and their family allies' interviews were conducted separately, with 31 interviews conducted by phone and 4 conducted in person over a period of 8 months (M *Interview Time* = 74 min., SD = 20 min.). Although the initial research design aimed to have all participant interviews conducted in person, phone interviews were conducted as well due to recruitment difficulties. It should also be noted that clarifying correspondence initiated by participants is additionally included in the analysis when relevant.

Method of Analysis

In light of Olson et al.'s (2012) recommendation to explore dark family communication utilizing a combination of quantitative and qualitative methodologies, the present study reports both frequency and narrative analyses in order to provide both a broad overview and an in-depth exploration of gay men's and their families' lived experiences, strengths and solutions (e.g., Lee & Lee, 2006). Furthermore, as prior research has established the applicability of descriptive and pattern coding techniques to this population (e.g., Lee & Lee, 2006), the analysis initially focused on identifying broad concept narratives regarding relational complexity and de/humanization. More specific codes and power dynamic categories were then conceptualized after a line-by-line examination of the broad concept narratives as per Daiute's (2014) work regarding sociocultural methods of narrative analysis. Given this multilayered method of narrative analysis and the complexity of relational communication, narrative codes were not viewed as mutually exclusive.

Following this protocol, dehumanizing discursive violence was initially conceptualized as post-disclosure assertions of authority via conflicts, disbelief, intolerance, and rejection (Savin-Williams & Dube, 1998). Power struggles and conflicts were identified based upon participants' responses to specific questions focusing on possible familial tensions (e.g., Is there someone in your family who is experiencing "the most difficulty" in this process? If so, can you describe your relationship with them? Were there any activities or people that made the disclosure process more difficult for you?). In addition, the complete interview was read for conflicts and difficulties that participants labeled as being a *"challenge," "hard," "difficult," "upsetting," "a fight/battle/argument,"* and *"terrible,"* etc. (Etengoff & Daiute, 2014). Line-by-line analysis then yielded the following dehumanization codes: (a) undermining sexual orientation status: denial, desire for orientation change, communicating to gay relative that they are a sinner; (b) rejection/disownment: physical, emotional, spiritual; (c) viewing the relative's sexual orientation as interpersonal rebellion/intentional desire to hurt relative; (d) shame focused on community ramifications/social status changes; and (e) grief response centered on personal loss (see Table 1).

Contrastingly, religious family members' humanization of their gay relative is operationalized as: (a) expressing unconditional love and support for gay relative; (b) expressing sympathy for gay relative's difficulties; (c) viewing a gay relative as the same person pre and post-disclosure; (d) redefining power dynamics by focusing on the relative's needs and shifting relational roles; and (e) hoping for the gay relative's personal happiness (see Table 2).

In addition, in an effort to explore the association between relationally productive (e.g., God/faith invoked constructively to mediate conflict) and destructive uses of religion and de/humanization (e.g., God/faith positioned as an ally against other party), narratives were additionally coded for relational uses of religion (Butler & Harper, 1994; Etengoff & Daiute, 2014). Given that previous work explores religious family members' post-disclosure uses of religion in great depth (Etengoff & Daiute, 2014), the present study does not replicate this endeavor and instead explores the association between relational religious frequencies and productive/repressive communication styles.

The primary research questions that will be addressed below are: 1) How do family communication patterns contribute to relationally productive and repressive religious coming-out responses? 2) What types of power dynamics play a role in both positive and negative coming-out communications between gay men and their religious relatives? The primary power dynamics that will be explored are related to relational roles (*"God can take care of everything on the other side. My job as his mother is just to love my son."* vs. *"If it wasn't about it breaking the commandment of God, I [father] would've dropped this long ago"*), the premise that the LGBTQ individual is the author/protagonist of the coming-out experience (*"... my [mother's] pain never mattered. It was his pain that came first"* vs. *"... part of her [mother's] concern is that I did this to hurt her."*), and post-disclosure character judgments (*"it [being gay] doesn't lessen him at all as ... a person ... he will always be my son."* vs. *"I would rather have you dead [than gay]"*). Power dynamic themes were developed after reviewing all of the de/humanization codes for commonalities. After exploring the overarching association between general communication styles and religious responses to the coming-out event, a qualitative comparison of the contributing power dynamics is presented.

RESULTS

General Communication Patterns and Religious Coming-Out Responses

Relatives' relationally repressive and productive religious responses to the coming-out event were associated with two distinct communication patterns: discursive violence and communication challenges vs. productive, relationally complex interactions. In this vein, all 17 (74%) gay participants who spoke of their religious relatives' relationally destructive uses of religion also recounted a general history of discursive violence and/or familial communication challenges (See Table 1 for frequency percentages and narrative examples). For example, a gay Jewish participant reported that while it was painful to be told by his father that his life's purpose as a gay man is to be dedicated to *"the Orthodox Jewish community and just do Chessed* [acts of kindness] *and be celibate"*—his father's hostility was not surprising given their relational history. In the participant's words, *"I never had a close relationship with my father growing up. And it was never anything about the gay thing, it was just*

Table 1. Frequency and Examples of Gay Men's Reports of Family Members' Discursive Violence.

Discursive Violence/ Dehumanization Code	Narrative Example	Participant Frequency: Jewish Gay Men's Reports	Participant Frequency: Christian Gay Men's Reports
Undermining Sexual Orientation Status: Denial, Desire for Orientation Change, Communicating to Gay Relative That They Are a Sinner	*...It* [coming out], *it didn't go fabulously, and it, it was just, you know, it just was hard ... they* [parents] *did sort of provide me with some, like, ex-gay literature ... Exodus ... I did a lot of research into them, and then, just through pretty much horror story after horror story after horror story, I realized that they were just not, not viable options.* —Gay Evangelical Participant	60%	63%
Rejection/ Disownment: Physical, Emotional, Spiritual	*He* [father] *sat in the rocking chair in the living room and said, "I would rather have you dead," and I told him, "Go get your shotgun." ... And that was a rather intense moment.* —Gay Mormon Participant	30%	15%
Viewing Relative's Sexual Orientation as Interpersonal Rebellion/ Intentional Desire to Hurt Relative	*My father thinks that I am gay to rebel against him ... I ... want to just apologize to them* [parents] *just for being gay, because you know, that's kinda really hard on them and the community that they are in and the hopes that they have ...* —Gay Jewish Participant	20%	8%
Shame Focused on Community Ramifications/ Social Status Changes	*My mother is more concerned with her social status within the Church and how she is perceived, more than what the truth really is—and that having a gay son looks bad in the Mormon church ... As far as she's concerned, we're just going to pretend like the family is the typical Mormon family.* —Gay Mormon Participant	20%	33%
Grief Response Centered on Personal Loss	*When we finally did have the discussion he* [father] *... said ... "I'm sad that you'll never have the experience of ...* [a] *normative family structure."* —Gay Jewish Participant	20%	23%

because my father's life style was working all day and being in Beis Medrish [A Torah studies learning group] *all night … the only connection I really had with my father was disciplinarian … he would come home … and start, like, yelling … I would get into fights with my father a lot."* Ultimately, this harmful relational pattern and absence of positive religious family experiences later contributed to the participant being disowned by his father through a religious mourning ritual usually reserved for the dead (*shiva*). In total, five gay men (three Jewish, two Christian) reported that their relatives rejected them post-disclosure in physical, emotional or financial terms—resulting in both relational stress and conflict.

While religious contexts clearly play an important role in familial responses, relationally destructive uses of religion were not universal, highlighting the inter-action between relational uses of religion and familial communication capabilities (see Table 2). For example, an Orthodox religious mother shared the following sentiment: *"I would sooner choose my child over my religion … I can't imagine … that the religion should have such power over me that it could force me to think about my child in such a, in such a negative way … I wouldn't allow that to happen."* Indeed, all 15 participating religious family allies either reported that they maintained their unconditional love for their gay relative, chose not to employ religious evaluations (e.g., *"that's* [being gay] *just something that is just between him and God and I can't judge."*), or that they coupled relationally complex responses with productive uses of religion (e.g., *"J. always lived his life to please God. He didn't seek this … I don't think that God loves him any less … God knew from the beginning; He created him."*). For many parents, these productive responses were facilitated by their awareness of maturing relational dynamics between parents and adult children (e.g., *"level of acceptance and tolerance that comes from being a parent to adult children"*). In addi-tion, while the initial disclosure may have been personally challenging for reli-gious allies, many chose not to communicate that in an effort to maintain focus on their relative's coming-out experience (e.g., *"I'm scared to say too many things, 'cause I don't ever want him to feel bad about himself."*). Below, narrative analyses explore the power dynamics contributing to variations in dys/functional family communica-tion around the coming-out event: relational roles, coming-out authorship/focus, and character judgments.

The Darker Side of Disclosure Discourse

One of the primary power dynamics involved in the disclosure event is the rela-tional role of the family confidant—does the confidant view him or herself as an authority figure, religious guide, judge, or evaluator of "reality"? For example, 11 (6 Jewish, 5 Christian) gay men reported that their religious relatives under-mined their sexual orientation by denying their homosexuality (e.g., *"it's just a phase"*), suggesting they change their sexual orientation ("reparative therapy"), or communicating that homosexuality was an intentional sin (e.g., *"gay people are going to hell."*). Moreover, such assertions of authority are particularly challenging as they are often contested by the other party—leading to relational tension and distance. For example, a 24-year-old nonactive Mormon participant is still estranged from his parents 5 years after his disclosure due to their demand that he *"marry someone of the opposite sex … because homosexual relationships … do not fit God's description of marriage and family."* This relational dynamic becomes further complicated, as religious siblings and parents often do not view their judgments as being separate from their love for their relative—indeed, some even view their stance as an outgrowth of their care for their gay relative's soul. However, gay participants often viewed this juxtaposition of love and judgment as harmful. For example, a 21-year-old gay Orthodox Jewish participant shared that his older sister's initial attempt to maintain unconditional love while condemning his sexual orientation as *"unnatural"* resulted in him feeling *"very awkward … being with her, talking to her."* Moreover, the participant believed that he was responsible for his sister's response and the loss of *"one of his best friends"* (e.g., *"… I just ruined a relationship—like what did I just do? Maybe it was better if I didn't tell anybody."*)—and he has resultantly not yet disclosed to any other family members. While the relationship between them has improved with time, with the brother even identifying his sister as an ally, his sister still struggles with her role as an older sister and judge (e.g., *"Is he just saying this, is it just a phase? Like, is it real? Is there anything biological to it?"*). Similarly, a gay participant from a Mormon background shared that his older brother responded to his suicide attempt by stating, *"I love you and that's never going to change, but, I definitely still believe what I believe."* Although the participant was not expecting his brother to change his religious beliefs or affiliation, his brother's active assertion of his faith as a counterpoint to his love undermined the participant's own struggles with his religious and sexual identity (e.g., *"I struggled on a cyclical basis … just being die-hard button-down Mormon and then being full-blown gay … it got to a point when I ended up in the hospital because I had tried to commit suicide."*). Similarly, a no-longer-religious Jewish gay participant reported that while his parents have said that they love him unconditionally, he does not know if he has ever *"experienced unconditional love,"* as they will not financially support his LGBTQ pride college programs on moral grounds (*"Torah condemns such acts"*) or allow him to express his sexual or gender orientation at home or synagogue. In the participant's words: *"you say you love me, but, you don't, like, you don't support me … If I don't feel, like, accepted around you … I don't feel that you love me."* Alternatively, the Orthodox Jewish mother shared in her ally interview that she tries to *"support him and love him,"* hoping that her son's happiness and well-being won't be compromised by his sexual orientation. This tension between the mother's attempts to communicate her love and her son's alternative interpretation of her behavior highlights the challenges posed when a parent loves his or her child *"despite"* his or her sexual orientation. Such ongoing relational tensions between parents and children as well as older and younger siblings emphasize the difficulty of applying previously established communication patterns and power dynamics to the coming-out event.

An additional power dynamic contributing to the discursive violence surrounding the coming-out period is related to the issue of event and narrative authorship: Whose story is it? Who is the protagonist of the coming-out event—and can/should there be more than one? Many of the gay participants expressed that these disputes were often implied although not explicitly stated. For example, gay men reported that their religious relatives focused on their own shame ($n = 6$) and grief ($n = 5$) instead of shifting focus to their gay relative's experience (e.g., *"My mother is more concerned with her social status within the Church."*) In a similar vein, three gay men reported that their religious relatives viewed their sexual orientation as an interpersonal rebellion aimed at hurting their relatives (e.g., *"... part of her* [mother's] *concern is that I did this to hurt her ... she won't talk about it and she won't, like, understand it as part of who I am."*). While a number of gay participants acknowledged that their sexual orientation disclosure may impact their religious relatives in a variety of ways, including their community standing (e.g., *"I was waiting for him* [brother] *to get married* [before coming out]*"*), the expectation was that these concerns would not take center stage during the coming-out event. For example, a gay participant from an Orthodox Jewish background shared his disappointment that his sister's *"first question ... was, like, "how are my kids going to find a shidduch* (spouse)*?" ... that was her first question."* Moreover, the participant reported that his sister subsequently *"never talk*[ed] *about the gay thing"* again. This act of redirecting ("othering") and then silencing the coming-out narrative is inherently an act of discursive violence—as it strips the author of ownership as well as their ability to engage their own experience. Indeed, the participant's closing statement to his sister was *"*[my nephew] *is 3 years old, in 20 years when he is shidduch dating* [religious dating facilitated by a matchmaker], *maybe this won't be a problem."* With this last statement, the participant's own experience becomes subsumed by his relative's self-concerns and the question of how this cultural narrative of heteronormativity may be impacting his own life remains unaddressed.

Gay men's reports of their religious relatives' discursive violence seem to be situated in a lack of relational complexity—their relatives' inability to modify their response based on an understanding of their loved one's experience within challenging power dynamics. The goal of relationally complex interactions is not to ignore cultural challenges but rather to integrate these tensions into a larger empathic understanding of the *discloser's* experience (e.g., *"... to see him* [gay brother] *going through something so painful ..."*). While religious relatives may encounter a number of personal faith challenges (e.g., *"How could God do this?"*), the way in which religious conflicts contribute to coming-out discourse is largely overshadowed by whether the relative views him or herself as a judge versus a supportive confidant as well as his or her ability to focus on the discloser as the primary protagonist. However, when religious relatives are unable to engage these forms of relational complexity, they often "simplify" the coming-out event by retaliating with negative character judgments about their gay relative. Once a gay relative is labeled as acting *"against God,"* being *"unnatural"* or an *"abomination,"* religious relatives' previous perceptions of their brother/son as a moral and loving family member are viewed as irrelevant, and they can excuse themselves from further relational responsibility. Unfortunately, negative character judgments coupled with relational disassociation are often related to adverse mental health outcomes—with 87% (seven of eight) of gay participants with depressive disorders also reporting familial difficulties and a history of discursive violence.

Into the Light: Countering Discursive Violence with Humanizing Communication

Deficit models have dominated sexual-minority research for some time, and far more is known about failed and destructive disclosures than the features of relationally successful coming-out experiences (e.g., D'Augelli & Hershberger, 1993). Therefore, the present study expands upon the humanization methods religious allies used to avoid or repair post-disclosure discursive violence. Moreover, the section below is relevant to the discussion of dark family communication, as the present study suggests that it is the absence of the humanization strategies discussed below that often provokes relational dysfunction.

Unconditional Love and Support

Fourteen family allies (eight Christian, six Jewish) discussed their unconditional love for their gay relative (see Table 2 for frequencies and examples), with four of seven Christian participants situating their unconditional love within religious values (e.g., *"God is love, and if you don't love your children, you don't love God."*). For example, an allied Mormon father explained that his primary relational role and *"reason for being should be to accept and to love and to lift up … those in need, no matter who they are … he is still my son …"* Moreover, the father's multifaceted efforts to maintain a positive and loving relationship with his son were acknowledged and appreciated by his son (e.g., *"hugs from my dad are like hugs from on high; they are just full of unconditional love."*). This form of mutual appreciation and admiration was expressed by a number of dyads in the study, indicating that humanization strategies successfully foster positive relationships amid complex socioreligious contexts. Moreover, this positive appropriation of religious values illustrates the sociocultural assertion that religious experiences are individually and contextually created—in other words, relational strength and health determines whether divine and brotherly love is pushed to the background or featured in the foreground.

While Christian allies used religion in relationally supportive ways, Jewish allies discussed religion as an obstacle to be overcome in order to maintain their unconditional love for their gay relative. For example, an allied Jewish sister stated that while homosexuality is *"unnatural"* as *"it's a mitzvah* [commandment] *to have kids … at the end of the day, I still love him and I'm gonna be there for him."* Similarly, another Jewish sister shared, *"I love him no matter what … it didn't matter if I was at a different place, you know, umm, religiously … because I loved him for who he is as a person, and his struggles."* Within this last narrative, the participant explicitly draws the connection between her choice to unconditionally love her brother and her recognition of *"who he is as a person,"* illustrating the link between humanization and unconditional love. However, as discussed in the previous section, many gay participants believe that their family ally relationships would be further improved if their religious relatives recognize that sexual orientation acceptance is a key feature of unconditional love (e.g., *"my sister told me she would not … support a relationship that I would have with another man, even though she would still love me. I'm not okay with that—and that will cause a strain in our relationship."*)

Sympathy for Gay Relative's coming-out Challenges

Thirteen family members (five Jewish, eight Christian) recognized their relative's authorship of the coming-out narrative by discussing their sympathy for their gay relative's challenges. This experience was discussed by eight mothers, one father, and three siblings. When participants spoke of their own difficulty, it was often linked to the process of watching their gay relative experience pain related to community and religious leader reactions, dating challenges, family reactions, self-acceptance difficulties, and the generally *"harder road"* of being gay (see Table 2 for further information).

Participants' sympathy narratives were particularly relationally complex, as they referenced the social dimensions of power intertwined with their relative's pain and interpersonal relations. In the words of a Methodist mother, *"this is society's um problem that you have to deal with … God didn't say he was gonna make it easy."* This sentiment was similarly echoed by a Mormon mother, who shared, *"We've gotta be clear as the difficulty is not in accepting him, the difficulty is worrying about what he has to deal with … society."* This mother's interview narrative 6 years postdisclosure is particularly meaningful, as her immediate response to her son was that his coming out was *"a mother's worst nightmare."* Unfortunately, her meaning that *"this was a nightmare for a mother to have a son that would be facing things she could not protect him from"* was not understood by her son, who instead interpreted her statement to mean that it was her *"worst nightmare to have him*

Table 2. Frequency and Examples of Family Allies' Humanization of Gay Relative.

Humanization Code	Narrative Example	Participant Frequency: Jewish Family Allies	Participant Frequency: Christian Family Allies
Unconditional Love & Support	*I just care so much about him* [gay brother] *and you know, I love him no matter what, and I wanted to be there for him as much as I could be, and I wanted to understand what he was going through. We were just, we were just very close.* —Jewish Sister	86%	100%
Sympathy for Gay Relative's coming-out Challenges	*...to see him* [gay brother] *going through something so painful and knowing that just by all my worldly experience that I'd had that ... like I could do NOTHING for him. I could not say one word of comfort. There's nothing I could do or say to make it an ounce better.* —Mormon Sister	71%	88%
Viewing Gay Relative as the Same Person Pre and Post-disclosure	*And it doesn't matter what others think of me. My son, is a good man ... he's a-a-, works hard, he's a kind person, so there- fore, you know, I don't know what they're thinking, but that's- that's- so that's kind of how I navigate it.* —Catholic Mother	43%	63%
Redefin- ing Power Dynamics by Focusing on Relative's Needs and Shifting Rela- tional Roles	*I can choose to, um, to, to dislike him, to hate him, to, you know, disown him, or I can choose to accept him and to love him, and to embrace him, um, no matter, so, you know, those choices I make ... He is still my son, um, so someday I will under- stand, but, you know, it's not my position to condemn ...* —Mormon Father	43%	75%
Hoping for Gay Relative's Happiness	*And quite honestly, I'm really delighted, [Laugh.] I'm very happy that he's not observant. I just, it's just the, the* [Jewish] *Orthodox community does not, it's just, it's not a, it's just not a comfortable place for somebody who is- Gay. So why put that on yourself?* —Jewish Mother	71%	50%

gay." Although the mother has apologized for her word choice since, this is still a salient icon in both of their disclosure stories, perhaps due to the inherently negative tone of the term "nightmare" as well as their disparate views regarding whether there are social consequences to being gay that require maternal protection. Similarly, an allied Jewish mother shared that even at 5 years after her son's disclosure, she needs to be careful with *"missing words"* in her *"intellectual game of chess"* with her son. Such narratives highlight the pivotal role that conscious relationally complex communication plays in re/establishing healthy familial relationships post-disclosure.

Seeing the Same Person Post-Disclosure

Eight participants (five Christian, three Jewish) shared that their perception of their gay relative was unchanged by their sexual orientation disclosure. This strategy was self-initiated for most participants, with only one Jewish sister referencing this as her therapist's recommendation. Family members discussed that they maintained a multifaceted view of their relative that extended beyond the dimension of sexuality, allowing them to recognize that their gay relative's character remained unchanged. For example, a Mormon father shared that *"it wasn't a case of, of me, you know, thinking any less of him, um, or kicking him out, or disowning him, or anything like that. 'Cause … he's an incredible individual. He is very talented, and he is very capable with people … it doesn't lessen him at all as, you know, as, as a person. Um, and it's, he, he is my son, he will always be my son."* By referring to his son as both an *"individual"* and a *"person,"* the father affirmed his son's humanity and human potential. Similarly, an allied Orthodox Jewish mother shared that she and her husband *"really treasure"* and *"really respect"* their gay son post-disclosure—as his coming out did not change anything she *"felt about him at all."*

Redefining Power Relations

Eight family members—five mothers, one father, and two sisters (three Jewish, six Christian)—indicated that they shifted relational power dynamics with their gay relative. Four participants (three Christian, one Jewish) discussed their relative's sexuality as being *"just between him and God"* (e.g., *"God can take care of everything on the other side. My job as his mother is just to love my son."*). This strategy is pivotal as it enables religious family allies to retain their faith without morally demanding that they impose their religious perspectives on their gay relative. In other words, humanization does not require that conflicting or dissonant personal perspectives be reconciled, changed, or ignored but rather that familial and emotional needs be engaged as the primary and immediate concern.

In the same vein, four participants (two Jewish, two Christian) shifted power dynamics by noting that their gay relative's disclosure was about their relative's experience (e.g., *"it wasn't really my process; it was more my brother's process."*). For example, a Methodist mother shared that *"… it's not my story. It's his story. And my story is to support him if he needs support and I'll be there for that. And I've told him that I could love anybody that he could love."* Similarly, a Mormon mother acknowledged that while she had struggled post-disclosure, she retained her relationship with her son by focusing on her son's pain (*"… my pain never mattered. It was his pain that came first. So, it didn't matter what I was going through, I was gonna be there for my son."*). In addition, a Jewish mother shared that her son recommended this strategy to her as she struggled with her concerns *"about telling certain people or sharing this information."* With time, the mother came to the conclusion that *"This is not about me, or my husband, or our family. It's really about my son … I was misguided in thinking that it was about me. It was not about me, it was more about him, and it was about his life and his choices—and it was important for us to be supportive of him … cuz it really is not about me."* This communication strategy seemed to yield mutual relational benefits, as the son noted that his mother *"was very emotionally supportive and wanted it to only be known that I was loved, and that it was not something that would be an impediment to our relationship. And that whoever I'd brought home, would be acceptable and loved."* In addition, these dyad narratives of mutual respect are particularly meaningful given that the Orthodox Jewish family is currently navigating the complex dynamics of their relative seriously dating a Christian-Arab man.

Hoping for Happiness

Nine family allies (five Jewish, four Christian) focused on their gay relative as the disclosure protagonist by hoping that their gay relative would find happiness, often in the context of a romantic relationship. In addition, this strategy was at times paired with other relationally complex responses such as unconditional love and shifting power dynamics (e.g., *"… I want him to be happy. And I just care and love him so much, and I just feel like that's just something that is just between him and God and I cant judge."*). Moreover, allies' hopes for their relative's happiness were often used to help allies cope with their gay relative's religious choices. For example, an allied Orthodox Jewish mother spoke of her joy that her son is no longer religiously observant as *"the Orthodox Community does not, it's just, it's not a, it's just not a comfortable place for somebody who is gay"* (see Table 2 for full narrative). This narrative illustrates the importance of recognizing the power contexts of individual experience—parents that were unable to do so often only expressed pain regarding their gay relative's nonobservance (e.g., *"… our son started distancing himself from um, from the practical aspects uh, of observance. That makes it* [his being gay] *uh quite painful."*).

DISCUSSION

Coming out is an inherently relational act, as the speaker demands that others acknowledge their gayness and join them in their disavowal of negative stereotypes (Chirrey, 2003). Given this context, this chapter utilized a critical communication perspective and sociocultural theory of relational complexity to further understand family communications as a mediating construction of reality and power (Daiute, 2012; Harwood et al., 2006; Langellier & Peterson, 1993). Drawing on this interdisciplinary foundation, analyses indicate that it is the in/ability to communicate in relationally complex ways that directs religious responses to a relative's sexual orientation rather than a uniformly binding religious script. For example, while some religious relatives used religion to justify their lack of relational engagement with their gay relative, others restructured relational power dynamics and left the job of judgment to God. In light of such disparate uses of religion, it is likely that religious values are a fig leaf for other family communication challenges.

The present study's response variability echoes Schnoor's (2003) findings that while some religious families respond negatively to their gay relative, others are religiously motivated to reconcile and maintain cohesion. Moreover, exploratory clinical research with this population supports the therapeutic relevance of humanization interventions, particularly the strategies of maintaining unconditional love and recognizing that a relative's character remains unchanged by his sexual orientation (Etengoff & Daiute, 2015a). Given this initial line of clinical inquiry, further research regarding humanization interventions within applied clinical settings may prove to be particularly helpful in developing family members' relationally complex communication skills. Furthermore, additional research is needed to understand how cognitive and personality factors impact communication capabilities and choices (Olson et al., 2012).

Limitations

Results presented here provide one of the first multilayered descriptions of how a sample of gay men *and* their religious relatives engage in relationally productive (e.g., humanization) and nonproductive (e.g., discursive violence) communication strategies during the disclosure period. However, the results must be interpreted in light of the associated sampling and data collection limitations. Firstly, the limited sample size ($N = 38$) may have restricted the reported range of participant responses. In addition, all participants identified as White, and a majority of Christian respondents identified as Mormon, limiting the generalizability of the present study's results. Moreover, the comparisons between conservative Christian and Orthodox Jewish families' responses should be viewed with caution given the limited sample size as well as the oversampling of Mormon participants within the Christian sample. However, despite such limitations, a sample of this size was viewed to be best suited to meet the goal of pioneering a sociocultural framework for understanding coming-out communications within religious families. It is therefore the author's hope that future research will apply this framework to other communities and larger sample sizes. In addition, it would be beneficial to longitudinally explore family members' communication development, as the present study only provides a brief snapshot. Furthermore, while recruitment may prove to be difficult, it would be most beneficial to interview a complete family unit—comprised of both allies and nonallies—in order to develop a more complete family systems framework.

CONCLUSION

While research on familial coming-out responses continues to grow, a notable gap in sexuality-focused communication research remains—limiting researchers' understanding of the associated relational dynamics (Yep, 2003). This chapter therefore aims to begin addressing this gap by applying a critical sociocultural framework to explore how religion and family communications are used as a tool to negotiate coming-out conflicts. Narrative analyses suggest that the majority of reported conflicts stem from religious relatives' inability to understand their gay relative's experience within complex power dynamics and/or modify their behavior based on this knowledge. Alternatively, the religious allies that successfully negotiated the relational interplay between religion and sexuality demonstrated a keen awareness of their relative's human experience of sociocultural and relational pressures. Such analyses support the need for further inquiry into the individual and systemic factors contributing to relationally complex capabilities. It is therefore the author's hope that the present study offers an applied critical communication model for future sociocultural explorations of familial disclosures.

REFERENCES

Adams, T. E. (2012). *Narrating the closet: An autoethnography of same-sex attraction.* Walnut Creek, CA: Left Coast Press.

Afifi, T. D., & Olson, L. (2005). The chilling effect in families and the pressure to conceal secrets. *Communication Monographs, 72*(2), 192–216. **doi:** 10.1080/03637750500111906

Batson, C. D., Early, S., & Salvarani, G. (1997). Perspective taking: Imagining how another feels versus imaging how you would feel. *Personality and Social Psychology Bulletin, 23*(7), 751–758. doi: 10.1177/0146167297237008

Bell, C. M., & Khoury, C. (2011). Organizational de/humanization, deindividuation, anomie, and in/justice. In S. W. Gilliland, D. D. Steiner, & D. P. Skarlicki (Eds.), *Emerging perspectives on organizational justice and ethics* (pp. 167–197). Charlotte, NC: IAP Information Age Publishing.

Ben-Ari, A. T. (1995). The discovery that an offspring is gay: Parents', gay men's, and lesbians' perspectives. *Journal of Homosexuality, 30*(1), 89–112. doi: 10.1300/J082v30n01_05

Bigner, J. J. (2013). *An introduction to GLBT family studies.* New York: Routledge.

Boon, S. D., & Miller, R. J. (1999). Exploring the links between interpersonal trust and the reasons underlying gay and bisexual males' disclosure of their sexual orientation to their mothers. *Journal of Homosexuality, 37*(3), 45–68. doi: 10.1300/J082v37n03_04

Bowlby, J. (1969). *Attachment and loss: Vol. 1. Attachment.* New York: Basic Books.

Braithwaite, D. O., & Baxter, L. A. (Eds.). (2006). *Engaging theories in family communication: Multiple perspectives.* Thousand Oaks, CA: Sage Publications.

Butler, M. H., & Harper, J. M. (1994). The divine triangle: God in the marital system of religious couples. *Family Process, 33,* 277–286. doi: 10.1111/j.1545-5300.1994.00277.x

Carnelley, K. B., Hepper, E. G., Hicks, C., & Turner, W. (2011). Perceived parental reactions to coming out, attachment, and romantic relationship views. *Attachment & Human Development, 13*(3), 217–236. doi: 10.1080/14616734.2011.563828

Chirrey, D. A. (2003). "I hereby come out": What sort of speech act is coming out?. *Journal of Sociolinguistics, 7*(1), 24–37. doi: 10.1111/1467-9481.00209

Crosbie-Burnett, M., Foster, T. L., Murray, C. I., & Bowen, G. L. (1996). Gays' and lesbians' families of origin: A social–cognitive–behavioral model of adjustment. *Family Relations: Journal of Applied Family and Child Studies, 45,* 397–403. http://dx.doi.org/10.2307/585169

D'Augelli, A. R. (2005). Stress and adaptation among families of lesbian, gay, and bisexual youth: Research challenges. *Journal of GLBT Family Studies, 1*(2), 115–135. doi: 10.1300/J461v01n02_07

D'Augelli, A. R., & Hershberger, S. L. (1993). Lesbian, gay, and bisexual youth in community settings: Personal challenges and mental health problems. *American Journal of Community Psychology, 21*(4), 421–448. doi: 10.1007/BF00942151

Daiute, C. (2012, May 31–2 June). *Relational complexity.* Paper presented at the 42nd Annual Meeting of the Jean Piaget Conference, Vancouver, Canada.

Day, J. M. (2002). Religious development as discursive construction. In C. A. M. Hermans, A. de Jong, & J. van der Lans (Eds.), *Social constructionism and theology* (pp. 63–89). Leiden, the Netherlands: Brill.

Elizur, Y., & Ziv, M. (2001). Family support and acceptance, gay male identity formation, and psychological adjustment: A path model. *Family Process, 40*(2), 125–144. doi: 10.1111/j.1545-5300.2001.4020100125.x

Etengoff, C. (2013). *Gay men's and their religious relatives' negotiation of sexual orientation, religion, family values, and homophobia* (doctoral dissertation). New York, NY: Graduate Center of the City University of New York. Retrieved from ProQuest Dissertations and Theses. (Accession Order No. 3561270)

Etengoff, C., & Daiute, C. (2013). Sunni-Muslim American religious development during emerging adulthood. *Journal of Adolescent Research, 28*(6), 690–714. doi: 10.1177/0743558413477197

Etengoff, C., & Daiute, C. (2014). Family members' uses of religion in post–coming out conflicts with their gay relative. *Psychology of Religion and Spirituality, 6*(1), 33. http://dx.doi.org/10.1037/a0035198

Etengoff, C. & Daiute, C. (2015b). Online coming out communications between gay men and their religious family allies: A family of choice and origin perspective, *Journal of GLBT Family Studies, 11*(13), 278–304. doi: 10.1080/1550428X.2014.964442

Etengoff, C., & Daiute, C. (2015a). Clinicians' perspective of the relational processes for family and individual development during the mediation of religious and sexual identity disclosure. *Journal of Homosexuality, 62*(3), 394–426. doi: 10.1080/00918369.2014.977115

Frontain, R. (1997). Introduction: Reclaiming the sacred: The Bible in gay and lesbian culture. *Journal of Homosexuality, 33*(3–4), 1–23. doi: 10.1300/J082v33n03_01

Freire, P. (2000). *Pedagogy of the oppressed.* New York, Bloomsbury Publishing.

Goodrich, K. M. (2009). Mom and dad come out: The process of identifying as a heterosexual parent with a lesbian, gay, or bisexual child. *Journal of LGBT Issues in Counseling, 3*(1), 37–61. doi: 10.1080/15538600902754478

Green, R. J. (2000). "Lesbians, gay men, and their parents": A critique of LaSala and the prevailing clinical "wisdom." *Family Process, 39*(2), 257–266. doi: 10.1111/j.1545-5300.2000.39208.x

Greenberg, S. (2004). *Wrestling with God & men: Homosexuality in the Jewish tradition.* Madison, WI: The University of Wisconsin Press.

Harwood, J., Soliz, J., & Lin, M. C. (2006). Communication accommodation theory. In D. O. Braithwaite & L. A. Baxter (Eds.), *Engaging theories of family communication* (pp. 19–34). Thousand Oaks, CA: Sage.

Heatherington, L., & Lavner, J. A. (2008). Coming to terms with coming out: Review and recommendations for family systems-focused research. *Journal of Family Psychology, 22*(3), 329–343. http://dx.doi.org/10.1037/0893-3200.22.3.329

Hidalgo, B. E. (2011). *Opportunities for humanization in the relationship between service providers and their homeless clients* (doctoral dissertation). University of Illinois at Urbana-Champaign. Retrieved from http://hdl.handle.net/2142/18359

Hill, R. (1958). Generic features of families under stress. *Social Casework. 39*, 139–150.

Holtzen, D. W., Kenny, M. E., & Mahalik, J. R. (1995). Contributions of parental attachment to gay or lesbian disclosure to parents and dysfunctional cognitive processes. *Journal of Counseling Psychology, 42*(3), 350. http://dx.doi.org/10.1037/0022-0167.42.3.350

Langellier, K. M., & Peterson, E. E. (1993). Family storytelling as a strategy of social control. In D. Mumby (Ed.), *Narrative and social control* (pp. 49–76). Newbury Park, CA: Sage.

Lee, M. M., & Lee, R. E. (2006). The voices of accepting and supportive parents of gay sons: Towards an ecosystemic strengths model. *Journal of GLBT Family Studies, 2*(2), 1–27. doi: 10.1300/J461v02n02_01

Miller, K. D. (1998). *Voices of deliverance: The language of Martin Luther King Jr. and its sources.* Athens, Georgia: University of Georgia.

Mohr, J. J., & Fassinger, R. E. (2003). Self-acceptance and self-disclosure of sexual orientation in lesbian, gay, and bisexual adults: An attachment perspective. *Journal of Counseling Psychology, 50*(4), 482. http://dx.doi.org/10.1037/0022-0167.50.4.482

Olson, L. N., Baoicchi-Wagner, E., Wilson Kratzer, J., & Symonds, S. (2012). *The darkside of family communication.* Cambridge, UK: Polity Press.

Rodriguez, E. M., & Ouellette, S. C. (2000). Gay and lesbian Christians: Homosexual and religious identity integration in the members and participants of a gay-positive church. *Journal for the Scientific Study of Religion, 39*(3), 333–347. doi: 10.1111/0021-8294.00028

Ryan, C., Russell, S. T., Huebner, D., Diaz, R., & Sanchez, J. (2010). Family acceptance in adolescence and the health of LGBT young adults. *Journal of Child and Adolescent Psychiatric Nursing, 23*(4), 205–213. doi: 10.1111/j.1744-6171.2010.00246.x

Savin-Williams, R. C., & Dube, E. M. (1998). Parental reactions to their child's disclosure of a gay/lesbian identity. *Family Relations,* 7–13. doi: 10.2307/584845

Schnoor, R. (2003). *Finding one's place: Ethnic identity construction among gay Jewish men* (doctoral dissertation). Montreal: Canada: McGill University. Retrieved January 6, 2011, from Dissertations & Theses: Full Text. (Publication No. AAT DC52836).

Serovich, J. M., Skeen, P., Walters, L. H., & Robinson, B. E. (1993). In-law relationships when a child is homosexual. *Journal of Homosexuality, 26*(1), 57–76. doi: 10.1300/J082v26n01_05

Tremble, B., Schneider, M., & Appathurai, C. (1989). Growing up gay or lesbian in a multicultural context. *Journal of Homosexuality, 17*(3–4), 253–267. doi: 10.1300/J082v17n03_03

Vygotsky, L. S. (2012). *Thought and language*. Cambridge, MA: MIT Press.

Vygotsky, L. (1978). *Mind in society*. (Trans. M. Cole). Cambridge, MA: Harvard University Press.

Wengraf, T. (2001). *Qualitative research interviewing: Biographic narrative and semi-structured methods*. Thousand Oaks, CA: Sage.

Willoughby, B. L., Doty, N. D., & Malik, N. M. (2008). Parental reactions to their child's sexual orientation disclosure. A family stress perspective. *Parenting: Science and Practice, 8*(1), 70–91. doi: 10.1080/15295190701830680

Willoughby, B. L., Malik, N. M., & Lindahl, K. M. (2006). Parental reactions to their sons' sexual orientation disclosures: The roles of family cohesion, adaptability, and parenting style. *Psychology of Men & Masculinity, 7*(1), 14–26. http://dx.doi.org/10.1037/1524-9220.7.1.14

Yep, G. A. (2003). The violence of heteronormativity in communication studies: Notes on injury, healing, and queer world-making. *Journal of Homosexuality, 45*(2–4), 11–59. doi: 10.1300/J082v45n02_02

NOTE

1. The present inquiry is part of a larger sociocultural study of gay men's and their religious family allies' diverse negotiations of familial and community conflicts during the coming-out period (for a broad project review, see Etengoff, 2013).

CHAPTER ELEVEN

Violence AS Gendered Communication IN Families

KRISTIN L. ANDERSON

Violence and abuse are today viewed as illegitimate forms of communication in which family members use emotional or physical tactics to coerce other family members to comply with their demands. However, violence was viewed as a legitimate form of communication within families throughout much of human history. Men's physical violence against their wives was legally and culturally sanctioned in the United States and Europe until the 19th and 20th centuries. The belief that husbands and fathers have a right to use violence against family members is held by a majority of people in many places throughout the world today (Pierotti, 2013).

Cultural ambivalence about men's right to use violence against family members characterizes most places today. The legitimacy of men's use of violence against wives has been challenged over the past 200 years by a global feminist movement (Htun & Weldon, 2012). Although the use of violence against wives is increasingly viewed as illegitimate and illegal, cultural ideologies also justify violence. Qualitative interviews conducted with adolescents in one large U.S. city found that although adolescent boys and girls reported that dating violence was unacceptable in the abstract, actual incidents of boys' violence against girlfriends were deemed appropriate because the victim "asked for it" (Miller, 2008). In a study of attitudes towards intimate partner violence in Tanzania, Jakobsen (2014) found that both women and men support the position that "a good beating" is sometimes necessary for husbands to use against wives who step outside of the boundaries of appropriate wifely behavior. Ambivalence about the legitimacy of violence is also displayed through cultural ideologies that abuse is a "private family matter" that should not be reported or discussed (Kelly, 2003).

Abuse is prevalent within intimate relationships around the world. A World Health Organization multicountry study found that the lifetime prevalence rate of physical domestic violence victimization among women in the nations studied ranged between 23% and 49% (García-Moreno, Jansen, Ellsberg, Heise, & Watts, 2005). Recent studies find that 25% of women and 14% of U. S. men report experiencing domestic violence in their lifetime (Breiding, Black, & Ryan, 2008). In a study of 16 countries, Straus (2004) found that between 17% and 45% of university students reported perpetrating physical violence against a dating partner during the past year.

CIVIL PROTECTION ORDERS

Legislation intended to challenge cultural perceptions that men's violence against women partners is acceptable was enacted, beginning in the 1970s, in the United States and many other nations. A key component of the legislation is civil protection orders (CPOs) that are explicitly designed to provide protections to victims of domestic abuse. CPOs are available to victims of domestic violence within all U.S. states. The person seeking the order (the petitioner) submits a written statement to the courts that describes the domestic violence perpetrated against her and the type of protection she seeks from the courts. The orders can prevent the person who is alleged to have committed domestic violence (the respondent) from abusing, contacting, or coming within a specified distance of the petitioner. They can also grant the petitioner temporary custody of children and pets and access to a shared vehicle or residence. After reviewing the petition to determine whether acts of domestic violence have occurred, a judge may grant a temporary order and schedule a hearing to determine whether a permanent order should be granted. The respondent is served with copies of the petition, the temporary order, and/ or notice of the hearing. The respondent can attend the hearing to challenge the evidence presented in the petition.

The number of CPOs sought by victims of abuse increased during the 1990s and the first decade of the 21st century (Durfee, 2011). In this chapter, I use data from CPO petitions filed with the court in a small city in the Pacific Northwest of the United States to examine the types of violence experienced in relationships, the connections between types of violence victimization, and the ways that gender influences domestic violence. CPO petitions provide first-person accounts of abuse experienced in intimate relationships from the standpoint of the alleged victim. These data are useful for an analysis of the gendered communication dynamics that occur in relationships involving violence because the petitions submitted to the court require that the document "Describe <u>specific acts</u> of domestic violence and their <u>approximate dates</u>, beginning with the <u>most recent act</u>." Petitioners often describe the details of the interaction with the respondent that preceded the most recent act of domestic violence, including statements made by the respondents. The petition form also asks petitioners to describe any threats of harm, violence toward children, and suicidal behavior of the respondent. However, it is important to note that only a small percentage of people who experience domestic violence seek protection from the civil courts. A study focusing on cases in which police were called out for domestic violence found that approximately 20% of female victims seek CPOs (Holt, Kernic, Lumley, Wolf, & Rivara, 2002).

ABUSE AS GENDERED COMMUNICATION

Although the prevalence and dynamics of abuse within families are shaped by societal inequalities related to gender, race, social class, and sexuality, I focus on abuse as a gendered form of communication. I focus on gender in part because CPO data do not provide identifying details about social class and race, and there are not enough cases of same-sex violence to enable comparative analysis by sexuality. Additionally, it is important to focus on gender because existing research and theory indicate that the dynamics and consequences of domestic violence are gendered such that women and men experience different types of victimization and suffer divergent consequences (Anderson, 2002, 2005; Miller, 2008). Sociologists and communication scholars define gender as a multilevel social construction; it is a form of identity that people adopt due to socialization, a set of behavioral practices for which people are held accountable, a structural basis for the assignment of labor and the distribution of rewards, and a set of cultural ideologies (Krolokke & Sorensen, 2006; Ridgeway & Correll, 2004).

Domestic violence is linked to gender because cultural ideologies and the structural division of labor by gender make women more vulnerable to domestic abuse than men (Anderson, 2005). Cultural beliefs that link aggression to masculinity and the historical notion that men have greater rights to control of and deference from their partners than women influence the meaning attributed to violence when it occurs within heterosexual pairings. Men's violence often leads to their women partners' compliance with the abuser's wishes, whereas women's violence is often defined as trivial or amusing by their male partners and does not result in deference or compliance (Anderson & Umberson, 2001; Miller, 2008). The social structural division of labor by gender creates a society in which boys and men are physically advantaged in conflicts with their wives or girlfriends. In general, boys and men receive more training in how to fight physically and defend themselves than do girls and women. Men are also physically advantaged because the norms for heterosexual relationships encourage pairings between couples in which the man is physically taller and larger than the woman. These societal-level gender practices influence the way abuse plays out in heterosexual relationships.

However, the connection between gender and intimate partner violence is controversial because substantial evidence indicates that men also experience violence victimization at the hands of their wives and girlfriends (Breiding et al., 2008; Straus, 2004). The percentage of women among those arrested for domestic violence increased over the last 30 years (Henning & Feder, 2004). Men also seek CPOs from the courts to protect them from abusive female partners, although women make up the majority of those who request protection (Durfee, 2011).

This chapter examines how gender influences the experiences of domestic violence victimization reported by men and women who seek CPOs. The analysis is guided by two research questions about the gendered dynamics of abuse. First, I examine the types of abuse described in petitions written by female and male petitioners to examine whether the tactics of abuse vary by gender. Second, I analyze how female and male petitioners communicate about the violence they experience, focusing on the words they use to define their victimization and how they frame their experiences of abuse. Theories of gender propose that women and men construct gendered identities through self-presentation, including their narrative descriptions of their experiences of abuse (Anderson & Umberson, 2001; Gubrium & Holstein, 2000; West & Zimmerman, 1987). Thus, I examine how cultural ideologies of femininity and masculinity are conveyed or resisted in petitioners' framing of abuse.

DATA AND METHODS

Data for this chapter are drawn from the full population of 153 civil protection order petitions filed during the first nine months of 2010 in a small city in the Pacific Northwest region of the U.S. The majority of the petitions (79%) were filed by people seeking protection from a current or former intimate partner. The other 21% of the petitions were filed by parents against children, children against parents, or roommates. For this analysis, I use the subsample of petitions filed by those seeking protection from current or former intimate partners. Two cases filed by people seeking protection from same-sex intimate partners were dropped from the sample because the number of these cases is too small to enable analyses. Of the 120 petitions filed against heterosexual partners, 109 (91%) were filed by women seeking protection from men, and 11 (9%) were filed by men seeking protection from women. In order to provide a larger sample of cases of male petitioners, I use nine additional petitions from the end of 2010 and the first half of 2011 that were filed by men seeking protection from current or former intimate heterosexual partners.

The final sample for quantitative analysis consists of 129 cases: 109 filed by women seeking protection from men and 20 filed by men seeking protection from women.

The narrative for each petition was quantitatively coded to identify the types of domestic violence described in the petition. Categories included physical violence, verbal abuse, and sexual violence; petitions were coded 1 if the narrative described this type of violence and 0 if the narrative did not describe the type of violence. Petitions were also coded (yes/no) to identify whether the narrative described any injuries to the petitioner, threats to use a weapon against the petitioner (e.g., holding a gun or knife to him), child abuse, reflected in physical or sexual violence towards children, and behavior that would endanger a child (such as driving under the influence of drugs or alcohol with children as passengers in the vehicle).

I conducted qualitative analysis of the petition narratives for a subsample of 40 petitions. I randomly selected 20 of the 109 petitions filed by women seeking protection from men partners to compare to the population of 20 petitions filed by men seeking protection from women partners. I read the narratives for each petition multiple times and coded them thematically using procedures outlined by Corbin and Straus (1990). Initially, I used a variety of codes to identify patterns in how petitioners described abuse. During additional stages of focused coding, I refined the codes to identify the most common and theoretically productive patterns.

I used the general concept of framing, defined by Goffman as "the schemata of interpretation," to guide the coding process (1974, p. 21). Frames organize the presentation of information to suggest particular meanings (Borah, 2011; Entman, 1993). I focused on how petitioners presented the violence they experienced, including the types of abuse that were emphasized and minimized. I was also guided by theoretical work on gender as performance during the qualitative coding process. That is, I examined the narratives to identify whether women and men described abuse in ways that are consistent with cultural ideologies of gender (West & Zimmerman, 1987). After the primary themes emerged, I reexamined the petition narratives to explicitly compare the similarities and differences across the petitions authored by women and men. Quotations from the petitions are deidentified by the use of pseudonyms and nonspecific dates but otherwise reproduced in the original language.

FINDINGS

Quantitative Results: Types of Abuse Reported by Male and Female Petitioners

Some types of violence victimization reported by petitioners vary by gender, whereas others are reported by both women and men at similar rates. Figure 1

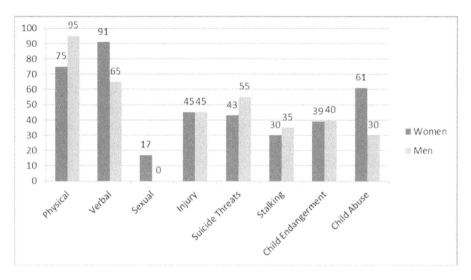

Fig 1. Percentage of Petitions Including Types of Violence, by Sex of Petitioner (N = 129).

presents the percentage of petitions authored by women and men that include each type of violence. Male petitioners are more likely than female petitioners to describe physical violence victimization (95% of men and 75% of women, X^2 = 3.89, df = 1, p ≤ .05). Women are significantly more likely than men to include verbal and sexual abuse and to describe the respondent as physically abusive towards children. For example, 61% of women's petitions versus 30% of men's petitions describe the respondents' physical or sexual abuse of children (X^2 = 6.40, df = 1, p ≤ .01). Petitions written by men and women do not significantly differ in the inclusion of stalking, injury from violence, threats of suicide, or behavior that might endanger a child.

Recent studies find that the experience of multiple forms of abuse, or polyvictimization, is important because victims of more than one type of abuse suffer greater negative outcomes as compared to people who experience only one type of abusive victimization (Finkelhor, Ormrod, & Turner, 2007; Sabina & Straus, 2008). Figure 2 presents the combinations of types of abuse included in petitions filed by women, and Figure 3 presents the combinations of abuse described in petitions written by men. As indicated by the comparison of Figures 2 and 3, women are more likely than men to be polyvictims of verbal, sexual, and physical assaults. Almost 12% of women report victimization by all three types of abuse, whereas no male petitioners report physical/sexual/verbal abuse victimization (X^2 = 2.65, df = 1, p ≤ .10). Men petitioners are slightly more likely than women petitioners to report victimization by a combination of verbal and physical assaults (65% of men and 55% of women), but this difference is not statistically significant. Chi-square

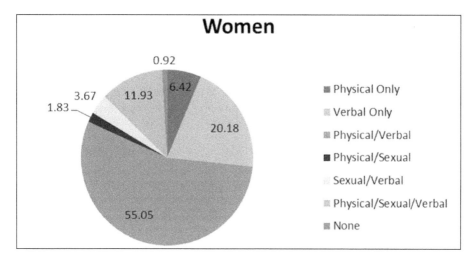

Fig 2. Percentage of Types of Violence in Civil Protection Order Petitions, Women Petitioners (*N* = 109).

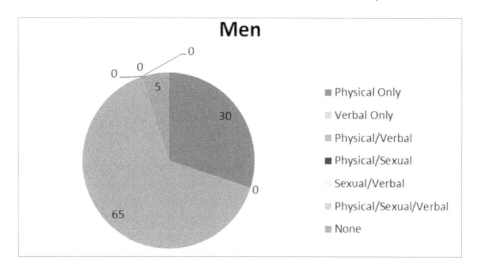

Fig 3. Percentage of Types of Violence in Civil Protection Order Petitions, Men Petitioners (*N* = 20).

tests show that women petitioners are significantly more likely than men petitioners to report experiencing only verbal-abuse (20% of women and 0% of men; X^2 = 4.87, df = 1, $p \leq .05$). Men petitioners are significantly more likely than women petitioners to report physical-only abuse (30% of men versus 6.4% of women; X^2 = 10.37, df = 1, $p \leq .001$).

These quantitative results show that female and male petitioners include different types of violence victimization in the petitions. Male petitioners focus on physical violence victimization, in isolation or combined with verbal abuse, whereas female petitioners include physical violence less frequently and are more likely to emphasize threats and verbal abuse. Women petitioners also describe sexual violence victimization, alone or in combination with other forms of abuse.

Qualitative Findings: Gender and the Framing of Abuse

Quantitative findings indicate that men and women report different forms of violence victimization. Yet CPO petitions are more than direct statements of fact. They are narrative stories of abuse in which the authors choose what to include and what to leave out. It is possible that women and men frame the violence they experience differently by choosing to emphasize or downplay certain aspects of the abuse they experience. The qualitative analysis focused on the similarities and differences in how female and male petitioners frame the violence they experience in CPO petitions using the subsample of 20 petitions filed by women seeking protection from men and 20 petitions filed by men seeking protection from women.

Sociological theories of gender propose that gender shapes human experience in multiple ways (Ridgeway & Correll, 2004; Schrock & Schwalbe, 2009). First, gender is an identity—a way of thinking about and understanding who we are. Gender socialization encourages boys and men to self-identify as strong, stoic, and capable. Men who petition for protection from women partners may feel that their identity as *men* is challenged if they describe themselves as suffering from abuse victimization. In contrast, gender socialization encourages women to self-identify as nurturing and vulnerable. Women are thus less likely to feel that they are *unwomanly* by describing their victimization. Second, sociologists theorize gender as a performance for which we are held accountable (West & Zimmerman, 1987). Boys and men learn to "do masculinity" in their interactions with others because they are expected to act in masculine ways (Schrock & Schwalbe, 2009). Women learn to enact femininity, which often involves caretaking, supportive, and deferential behaviors. Finally, gender serves as the basis for organizing a division of labor and distributing economic and status rewards. Women are encouraged to take on supportive and nurturing tasks, whereas men are encouraged to seek physical, technological, and leadership roles. These patterns might influence how individual women and men describe their victimization when they seek protection from the courts from abuse they have experienced from an intimate partner. Men who petition for CPOs as victims of domestic violence may attempt to maintain masculine identities, downplaying their vulnerability and victimization even as they seek protection from the courts. Women who petition for CPOs may feel shame and embarrassment about identifying as victims of violence, but they may be less likely to feel that their gender identities are relevant due to cultural constructions of women as vulnerable to abuse.

Comparative qualitative analysis of CPOs filed by heterosexual women and men indicates four gendered patterns in the way that petitioners describe their victimization. First, female petitioners emphasize polyvictimization. They describe the mutually reinforcing ways that different types of abuse impact their lives. They are also more likely than male petitioners to describe verbal abuse in detail, including specific information about what the respondent said or did that caused them emotional harm. In contrast, male petitioners emphasize physical abuse victimization. Second, women are much more likely than men to express fear of their partners and to describe the emotional impact of the violence. Third, men downplay their vulnerability to abuse and their partners' ability to harm them by stating that although their partners or others "try to" attack, they are able to defend themselves and avoid harm. The fourth gendered pattern is that male petitioners are more likely than female petitioners to state that their partners threaten them by telling them that they will have other men attack the petitioner.

Gendered polyvictimization and the importance of verbal abuse. A key difference in petitions filed by women and men is that women emphasize the interconnections between the physical, verbal, and sexual abuse that they experience, whereas men emphasize physical abuse. Polyvictims suffer multiplicative negative consequences because the effects of each form of abuse are exacerbated when the victim is also experiencing other forms of abuse (Finkelhor, Ormrod, & Turner, 2007). For example, the experience of being threatened is enhanced when a domestic violence victim has also experienced physical and sexual assaults because the threats may remind victims of previous assaults and because victims know from experience that the threats are real. Bailey, a female petitioner, wrote that the respondent's verbal abuse led her to fear that she would be physically assaulted at a court hearing: "Ed started calling me foul names under his breath as soon as he spotted me. He was quite agitated. He pushed past us and as he went into the elevator he said, 'Oh, that bitch is here, they need to kick her fucking ass out of here now.' I was afraid he might go after me the way he did last time." The verbally abusive messages are reinforced by physical assaults, which convey to the victim that verbal threats are real. Similarly, physical assaults reinforce verbal insults by conveying to victims that they are worthless to the perpetrator (Kirkwood 1993).

Diana emphasized her husband's use of emotional abuse to punish her if she did not comply with his demands that she engage in sexual behavior that she did not like: "If I didn't comply with or meet Rob's standard of 'sexual performance,' he would get angry, short tempered, sulky, ignore me, slam doors, and use intimidating looks, actions, or gestures." After Rob slapped Diana when she accidentally bumped his chin with her head when they were in bed, she "was scared and didn't know how many times he would hit me, or if he was done. I was absolutely stunned and emotionally devastated. I curled up in a ball and started sobbing, which only annoyed him." For Diana, the combination of physical, sexual, and emotional abuse was important; her husband used emotionally abusive tactics to punish her if she resisted the sexual abuse, and his addition of physical violence compounded her fear and suffering.

In contrast, male petitioners were less likely to experience polyvictimization, and their narratives did not emphasize the interconnections between types of abuse. Men described the physical abuse perpetrated by their partners against them using brief, straightforward language. Aiden began his petition with the statement, "Lacy June Pedersen threw a wooden chair at me, which hit me in my ankle." Similarly, Brody's petition starts with the statement, "Elaine Jones struck me (Brody Wilson) in the face knocking my glasses off my face."

Women petitioners were also more likely than male petitioners to provide detailed information about verbal and emotional abuse. Only 3 out of 20 men petitioners (15%) included specific quotations of the respondents' verbal abuse, whereas 13 out of 20 (65%) women petitioners included quotations. Men petitioners who mention verbal abuse typically do so in general terms. Nathan said, "Alicia Evans became loud and aggressive towards my children." Jordan noted that "I have been mentally and verbally abused by her and her daughter for the last two years." Only one man petitioner, Rafael, emphasizes the words his partner used to denigrate him: "We were at a friend Entman's house and we were arguing about disagreements about our parenting and she yelled 'you're a dead beat', you're a black nigger' and kept saying it over and over." Rafael describes both racialized and gendered insults. The term "deadbeat" mocks a man's ability to provide for his children and his failure to live up to the cultural ideal that men should be good providers for their families. Moreover, Rafael's partner explicitly denigrates his race, perhaps with the goal of reminding him of the historical and current disenfranchisement of black men in U.S. society.

As does Rafael, the majority of women petitioners describe verbal abuse directed toward them in explicit detail, including the names they were called and the words that their partners use in an effort to harm them. Women petitioners describe several forms of verbal abuse that are seldom described in petitions authored by men, including gendered insults, silencing or controlling statements, and statements designed to attack the petitioner's self-worth. Insults that are explicitly gendered include calling petitioners names like "bitch" or "whore" or questioning their ability to care for their children. Three women describe this form of verbal abuse in detail. Kylee writes that the respondent, Jared, kept their child Tyler "in the house and wouldn't let me get Tyler. Jared told me that I didn't deserve him and that I was a bad mom. Jared often called me a 'bitch' and an 'unfit mom.'"

Three petitions authored by women, but none of the petitions authored by men, described their partners' demands that they "shut up" or "get home." Gianna quoted her partner's statement: "He said, 'If you don't shut your fucking mouth I'm going to bash your face in.'" Olivia described this type of abuse in more general terms: "He was yelling at me and telling me to get home." This pattern is consistent with gender ideologies that suggest men have the *right* to control the behavior of female partners. Men petitioners did not include information about efforts made by their partners to enforce their silence or movements outside of the home.

A final type of verbal abuse that was described more often by women petitioners was statements made by their partners about the petitioner's insufficiencies. Three women included detailed descriptions of the words used by their partner to tear down and devalue the petitioners. Chiara writes that "He said I was worthless and stupid." Mia states, "Randy verbally abused me by always telling me I never did things right." Jasmine included the following details:

> He started to become upset and told me he was not going to hurt me. To me that comment seemed out of place and it put me on alert. Then he became angry and told me I was crazy, hateful and cruel, that I was uncaring and [he] was very agitated. He was marching in and out of the house saying "this is my house" and he would open and shut cupboards, digging through them.

The level of detail reported by Jasmine about the respondent's words and behaviors is characteristics of petitions written by women, whereas male petitioners rarely include this level of detail about forms of abuse other than physical violence.

Overall, female petitioners were more likely than men petitioners to emphasize the interconnections between different types of abuse and to provide detailed accounts of their partner's verbally abusive tactics, including efforts to control their behavior and denigrate their worth. Men petitioners emphasized physical abuse they experienced, and they did not provide detailed accounts of verbal and emotional abuse.

Fear and the emotional impact of violence. A second gender difference is the inclusion of statements about fear in the petition narratives. The legal definition of domestic violence for the civil protection order process includes "fear of imminent physical harm, bodily injury or assault between family or household members." This definition appears on the petition document, thus encouraging petitioners to describe their fear. However, male and female petitioners differ in the degree to which they write about fear in the petitions. Eighty percent of the narratives written by women (16/20) include explicit statements that the petitioner is afraid of the respondent:

> He looked like he was going to hurt me. At this point I was panicking. I wanted to get to my keys that were in my car. I was terrified so I screamed. (Faith)

> I was staying at a friend's when around 11:15 p.m. on 9/12/10 Alec could be heard knocking on neighbor's doors. I was scared that he had found me. I cracked open the door, told him we were safe and tried to close the door. He pushed his way into the house & pushed me across the room . ... I had severe anxiety after this incident and kept hyperventilating. (Gianna)

> I'm afraid he will retaliate against me and harm me again. (Chiara)

> In November 2010 Simon Anderson came to my residence carrying a large K knife with gang emblems dangling next to it. He had come to pick up our children from me, although while in my home Simon took the knife with a 7.5 inch blade out and held it a foot from me moving it around with his hand. I asked Simon what the knife was for and he stated, "It is to protect my family." I felt extremely threatened and afraid. (Piper)

These female petitioners emphasize the feelings of terror and anxiety that they experience due to their fear of their abusive partners. In contrast to the 80% of women who describe fear, 25% of petitions written by men (5/20) mention that the petitioners are afraid of their partners. Only one man, Daniel, described experiencing negative consequences from his fear of his partner: "I've been hospitalized from anxiety panic attacks from stress from her."

Typically, men who mentioned fear did so without describing fear of violence or injury at the hands of their partner:

> My wife scares me. She has lied before and had me thrown in jail for something I didn't do, this is why I was scared to leave and continued to take the abuse. She is the most evil person I have ever met, and I am afraid that she will continue to torment me. (Ethan)

> I'm scared to be in her presence and need to feel safe again knowing that we are not near each other. (Ian)

These male petitioners mention fear, but unlike female petitioners, they do not state that they are explicitly afraid that their partners might physically assault them. An additional three men mention fear in their petitions, but they state that they are afraid for the safety of their children or another person rather than for their own safety. For example, Kevin wrote, "The kids are terrified of her. I fear for them all the time because I don't even know what she's capable of doing." Unlike female petitioners, who describe their fear of their partners as a cause of panic and anxiety, male petitioners do not emphasize their fear of the abuse that their partners perpetrated.

"Trying to" abuse. The third pattern of gender difference in the narratives is that men were more likely than women to write that their partner attempted to physically abuse them but was unsuccessful. Thirty percent (6/20) of the male petitioners describe incidents in which the respondent "tried to" abuse them or in which they were able to successfully defend themselves from their partner's ineffectual attempts to assault them:

She has said she would hunt me down and take care of me as in try to beat me. (Fernando)

About 6–7 months ago she actually tried to slap me while intoxicated while I was holding our daughter. (Zion)

We had words in the past. But no violence until last night. We had words, she went up the stairs. I went up a short time later to find her on the floor past out. I went to pick her up to put her in bed and she started throwing punches pushing shoving, breaking pitchers on the wall knocking over bottles. I protected myself by holding her back. She soon left the house in her truck. (Michael)

These statements position the female respondent as motivated to harm the male petitioner but as ineffective. The phrase "try to" implies that the actor is not successful in the attempt. Michael states that, despite his partner's multiple punches, pushes, and shoves, he is able to hold her back and remain unharmed. This framing allows male petitioners to describe the respondent's behavior as abusive and illegitimate without presenting themselves as vulnerable to the attack (Anderson & Umberson, 2001).

Women petitioners use the phrase "tried to" just as frequently as men (7/20, or 35% of petitions), but in a different context. Two women used this phrase to describe how they tried to escape from the abuser. Faith wrote that,

"Alan started to verbally harass me. I said that [I] was no longer able to deal with his verbal abuse, and can no longer handle it. He wouldn't stop, so I tried to get to my car. As I open the door, he shut it. This made me frightened."

Ivy began her petition with the claim that "Over the last month, I've tried to leave." These statements frame the petitioner as vulnerable to abuse. Only one woman petitioner frames her male abuser as unsuccessfully attempting to use physical abuse, and she does so only after describing multiple incidents in which the respondent successfully assaulted her. Serenity noted that, "He hit me when I would do something wrong and always yelled at me." She goes on to describe an incident in which "I thought he was going to tell me something. But instead he kicked me in my chest with his leg really hard." At the end of the petition, she notes that on one occasion when she was ill, "He ran in and tried hitting me."

Fifteen percent (3/20) of women petitioners use the phrase "tried to" to describe the respondents' efforts to force them into sexual contact or to talk about reconciling. Ruby states that "He was trying to get close to me and kiss me and I was resisting." Olivia described a similar incident: "On August 15 Eric tried to get me to have sex with him and I refused. He became very angry and started to go through my personal belongings."

Men thus frame their female partners as "trying to" physically assault them, without success. In contrast, women depict their partner's physically abusive behavior as successful, resulting in their physical harm and feelings of fear and intimidation. This pattern suggests that male and female petitioners view their vulnerability to physical abuse differently; men see themselves as targets of abuse but not as vulnerable to harm, whereas women feel threatened and vulnerable.

Threats from other men. A final pattern of gender difference in the petition narratives is that women petitioners consistently describe their abuser as their current or former intimate partner, whereas men petitioners claim that they are at risk of harm from physical assaults by other men. Eight men petitioners (40%) and zero female petitioners describe instances when their partners threatened to have other people attack the petitioner:

> Rebecca pulled a knife on me and threatened to have me killed by her new boyfriend. (Sebastien)

> Then this afternoon Lisa came home for lunch and said that if I didn't have all my stuff out of the house she was going to bring her brother with her and they were going to kick my ass if my stuff wasn't gone by the time she got home from work. (Jordan)

> At approximately 1:30 a.m. three men came to the house, assaulted me, broke my windshield and tried to steal my car. As they were leaving they said my wife Ellen had sent them. (Ethan)

By claiming that they are at risk from other men's violence, men petitioners avoid having to present themselves as in need of protection from women. Yet this strategy is problematic for the courts, which define domestic violence as acts that occur between co-residents of a household and/or people involved in an intimate dating, cohabiting, or marital relationship. CPOs cannot restrain the boyfriend of the respondent from coming near the petitioner because the relationship between the petitioner and the boyfriend of the respondent does not meet the legal definition of domestic violence.

This pattern also suggests that some of the women respondents described by men petitioners adhere to gendered notions of men's violence as more threatening and damaging than women's violence. They seek the aid of other men to physically-assault their partners, or they threaten their partners with violence from other men:

> Susanna called yesterday and told me that if I didn't call the school and tell them to her pick up our son early from school, that she would have Eddie (her boyfriend) come over and kick my ass. She has been calling every couple of days threatening to have Eddie "take care of the problem" or "clean up the mess," if I don't give in to her demands in regard to our son. I take these threats seriously because Eddie has assaulted me in the recent past. (Thomas)

> The Respondent continues to text message, email and make frequent calls. For example, on 07/30/10 she called 7 times in 8 minutes from 10:08 to 10:16. The texts, calls and messages are aggressive and intimidating. These include threatening to have "friends break your legs." Due to previous assaults, these phone calls are uncomfortable and unwanted. (Liam)

Here, Thomas and Liam express their feelings of fear and intimidation at the threat of violence from other men who could attack them at their abusive partners' request. These statements frame violence as masculine; the threat becomes credible when it is at the hands of another man.

CONCLUSIONS

Although there is a global social movement to redefine domestic violence as an illegal and illegitimate use of power within intimate relationships, abusive behavior remains a prevalent tactic used by partners in intimate relationships. There is extensive scholarly debate about how gender shapes the experience of domestic violence. Some scholars propose that women and men are equally likely to use abuse to "get their way" in intimate relationships, whereas other scholars propose that abuse is a gendered social phenomenon (Jakobsen, 2014; Straus, 2008). This chapter examines the questions of how abuse described by men and women who seek protection from the civil courts is gendered. Findings indicate that both the types of abusive behavior described in the petitions and how the abuse is framed vary by gender. A quantitative comparison of the types of abuse included in CPO petitions found that the larger majority of male petitioners describe only physical abuse victimization, whereas female petitioners emphasize their polyvictimization, or concurrent experience of physical, emotional, verbal, and sexual abuse. These patterns replicate research findings of gender differences in the perpetration of abusive behavior that have been documented across multiple studies. Previous studies find that women and men perpetrate physical violence at similar rates but that women are more likely than men to be polyvictims (Black et al., 2010; Sabina & Straus, 2008; Straus, 2004).

The qualitative analysis of how male and female petitioners frame the abuse they experience identified several gender differences. First, the findings indicate that men petitioners emphasize physical acts and that women emphasize the multiple and interconnected forms of abuse they experience. Female petitioners are much more likely than male petitioners to describe verbal abuse with detailed narrative accounts that explain the specific words used by their partners to abuse them and the impact that this form of abuse has on their lives. This pattern suggests that women and men petitioners construct gender through their written accounts of abuse (Anderson & Umberson, 2001; Jakobsen, 2014). Gender socialization that encourages boys and men to show stoicism and regulate their emotional displays, whereas women are encouraged to display emotion, may shape the decisions that petitioners make when deciding what to include in CPO petitions (Schrock & Schwalbe, 2009). Women may feel more justified in seeking protection from the courts on the basis of verbal threats alone because of cultural constructions of men's violence as dangerous or lethal, whereas men may believe that they should not be affected by verbal abuse due to norms of masculine stoicism in the face of danger.

Moreover, research on indirect or relational aggression suggests that girls and women are socialized to use verbal forms of aggression toward others rather than physical violence (Underwood, 2003). This socialization may encourage women to pay more attention to verbal insults than men. Women may also have greater recall of the verbal abuse they experienced because women learn to pay attention to the hurt feelings of others (and of themselves). Additionally, cultural images of men as stoic and unconcerned about "mere words" may encourage men petitioners to minimize the details of verbal abuse they experience.

Narrative analysis of how women and men petitioners frame their victimization showed that women were more likely than men to describe feelings of fear, panic, and emotional harm that they suffered as a consequence of the abuse. This pattern is consistent with the finding from previous research that men's violence against women engenders fear in the victim, whereas women's violence against men is viewed as trivial and ineffectual (Anderson & Umberson, 2001; Miller, 2008). Gendered cultural ideologies that men are naturally aggressive and dangerous when provoked, whereas women are vulnerable and weak, influence the meanings attached to threats and physical abuse such that men's violence is viewed as more damaging and menacing—more worthy of fear—than women's violence. The complexity here is that this gender difference is both an ideology that shapes perceptions of violence and a structural reality—previous studies consistently find that women are more likely than men to be injured in a domestic violence incident (Breiding et al., 2008).

In writing CPO petitions, both women and men frame abuse to suggest that men's violence is effective and powerful, reinforcing cultural ideologies that link masculinity to aggression. Women describe men's violence as having a powerful impact on their physical and emotional well-being, whereas men downplay the emotional and physical consequences of their victimization at the hands of women. Men who seek protection from the courts for heterosexual domestic violence must position themselves as victims of women, which may be emasculating in the context of stereotypes that men are physically strong and in control (Anderson, 2005). These findings replicate Durfee's (2011) study of 48 protection order petitions written by men seeking protection from women partners. Durfee (2011) finds that the majority of male petitioners do not express fear of their partners and that they describe their power and control over their intimate partners rather than their experience of being controlled.

Gender ideologies and identities also shape people's perceptions of their ability to use physical violence against others. Men petitioners framed their women partners as "trying to" abuse them, unsuccessfully, and as seeking the aid of other men to physically attack the petitioner. Because training and practice at violence are shaped by the gendered social structure, it is likely that the women respondents described by male petitioners are untrained and unpracticed in using physical violence. Some of these women may threaten their men partners with other men's violence because they feel the threat will be taken more seriously by the respondent.

Female petitioners describe men as unsuccessfully "trying to" abuse them in the context of unwanted sexual advances. Cultural messages about women's right to refuse unwanted sexual encounters such as the "NO Means NO" campaign may influence women's beliefs that they can resist the respondents' sexual overtures, whereas women are not given similar messages about their ability to resist physical assaults (Cermele, 2010; Gidycz et al., 2001; Hollander, 2009). In contrast, men receive cultural messages that they should "stand their ground" when assaulted and be able to defend themselves from physical attacks. The framing of women as "trying to" physically assault them allows men petitioners a way to position their partners as physically violent without having to depict themselves as damaged from the abuse. This gendered pattern in which men who petition the courts for protection frame themselves as invulnerable to assaults by their partners, whereas women frame themselves as fearful and vulnerable, reflects and recreates gender ideologies that link masculinity to physical power and dominance and femininity to weakness and submission.

The ways that gender shapes domestic violence victimization and victims' framing of their experiences of violence matter. Previous studies of the CPO process have often focused solely on petitions filed by women under the assumption that women are more vulnerable to abuse than men and because women are more likely than men to seek CPOs (Holt et al., 2002; Logan, Cole, Shannon, & Walker, 2007). This approach assumes that violence within families is gendered rather than examining the complex ways that gender matters in the experience of intimate partner violence (Anderson, 2005; Jakobsen, 2014). In order to explicate how violence is a gendered form of communication, we need studies that compare women's and men's experiences of perpetration and victimization.

REFERENCES

Anderson, K. L. (2002). Perpetrator or victim? Relationships between intimate partner violence and well-being. *Journal of Marriage and Family*, *64*(4), 851–863. http://doi.org/10.1111/j.1741-3737.2002.00851.x

Anderson, K. L. (2005). Theorizing gender in intimate partner violence research. *Sex Roles*, *52*(11–12), 853–865. http://doi.org/10.1007/s11199-005-4204-x

Anderson, K. L., & Umberson, D. (2001). Gendering violence: Masculinity and power in men's accounts of domestic violence. *Gender & Society*, *15*(3), 358–380. http://doi.org/10.1177/089124301015003003

Black, M. C., Basile, K. C., Breiding, M. J., Smith, S. G., Walters, M. L., Merrick, M. T., & Stevens, M. R. (2011). *The National Intimate Partner and Sexual Violence Survey (NISVS): 2010 summary report*. Atlanta, GA: National Center for Injury Prevention and Control, Centers for Disease Control and Prevention.

Borah, P. (2011). Conceptual issues in framing theory: A systematic examination of a decade's literature. *Journal of Communication, 61*(2), 246–263. http://doi.org/10.1111/j.1460-2466.2011.01539.x

Breiding, M. J., Black, M. C., & Ryan, G. W. (2008). Prevalence and risk factors of intimate partner violence in eighteen U.S. states/territories, 2005. *American Journal of Preventive Medicine, 34*(2), 112–118. http://doi.org/10.1016/j.amepre.2007.10.001

Cermele, J. (2010). Telling our stories: The importance of women's narratives of resistance. *Violence Against Women, 16*(10), 1162–1172. http://doi.org/10.1177/1077801210382873

Corbin, J., & Strauss, A. (1990). Grounded theory research: Procedures, canons, and evaluative criteria. *Qualitative Sociology, 13*(1), 3–21. http://doi.org/10.1007/BF00988593

Durfee, A. (2011). "I'm not a victim, she's an abuser": Masculinity, victimization, and protection orders. *Gender & Society, 25*(3), 316–334. http://doi.org/10.1177/0891243211404889

Entman, R. M. (1993). Framing: Toward clarification of a fractured paradigm. *Journal of Communication, 43*(4), 51–58. http://doi.org/10.1111/j.1460-2466.1993.tb01304.x

Finkelhor, D., Ormrod, R. K., & Turner, H. A. (2007). Poly-victimization: A neglected component in child victimization. *Child Abuse & Neglect, 31*(1), 7–26. http://doi.org/10.1016/j.chiabu.2006.06.008

García-Moreno, C., Jansen, H. A. F. M., Ellsberg, M., Heise, L., & Watts, C. (2005). *WHO multi-country study on women's health and domestic violence against women: Initial results on prevalence, health outcomes and women's responses*. Geneva, Switzerland: World Health Organization.

Gidycz, C. A., Layman, M. J., Rich, C. L., Crothers, M., Gylys, J., Matorin, A., & Jacobs, C. D. (2001). An evaluation of an acquaintance rape prevention program impact on attitudes, sexual aggression, and sexual victimization. *Journal of Interpersonal Violence, 16*(11), 1120–1138. http://doi.org/10.1177/088626001016011002

Goffman, E. (1974). *Frame analysis: An essay on the organization of experience*. Cambridge, MA: Harvard University Press.

Gubrium, J. F., & Holstein, J. A. (2000). The self in a world of going concerns. *Symbolic Interaction, 23*, 95–115. http://doi.org/10.1525/si.2000.23.2.95

Henning, K., & Feder, L. (2004). A comparison of men and women arrested for domestic violence: Who presents the greater threat? *Journal of Family Violence, 19*(2), 69–80. http://doi.org/10.1023/B:JOFV.0000019838.01126.7c

Hollander, J. A. (2009). The roots of resistance to women's self-defense. *Violence against Women*. http://doi.org/10.1177/1077801209331407

Holt, V. L., Kernic, M. A., Lumley, T., Wolf, M. E., & Rivara, F. P. (2002). Civil protection orders and risk of subsequent police-reported violence. *JAMA, 288*(5), 589–594. http://doi.org/10.1001/jama.288.5.589

Htun, M., & Weldon, S. L. (2012). The civic origins of progressive policy change: Combating violence against women in global perspective, 1975–2005. *American Political Science Review, 106*(03), 548–569. http://doi.org/10.1017/S0003055412000226

Jakobsen, H. (2014). What's gendered about gender-based violence? An empirically grounded theoretical exploration from Tanzania. *Gender & Society*, 0891243214532311. http://doi.org/10.1177/0891243214532311

Kelly, K. A. (2003). *Domestic violence and the politics of privacy.* Ithaca, NY: Cornell University Press.

Kirkwood, C. (1993). *Leaving abusive partners: From the scars of survival to the wisdom for change.* Thousand Oaks, CA: Sage.

Krolokke, C., & Sorensen, A. S. (2006). *Gender communication theories and analyses: From silence to performance.* Thousand Oaks, CA: Sage.

Logan, T. K., Cole, J., Shannon, L., & Walker, R. (2007). Relationship characteristics and protective orders among a diverse sample of women. *Journal of Family Violence, 22*(4), 237–246. http://doi.org/10.1007/s10896-007-9077-z

Miller, J. (2008). *Getting played: African American girls, urban inequality, and gendered violence.* New York: NYU Press.

Pierotti, R. S. (2013). Increasing rejection of intimate partner violence: Evidence of global cultural diffusion. *American Sociological Review, 78*(2), 240–265. http://doi.org/10.1177/0003122413480363

Ridgeway, C. L., & Correll, S. J. (2004). Unpacking the gender system: A theoretical perspective on gender beliefs and social relations. *Gender & Society, 18*(4), 510–531. http://doi.org/10.1177/0891243204265269

Sabina, C., & Straus, M. A. (2008). Polyvictimization by dating partners and mental health among U.S. college students. *Violence and Victims, 23*(6), 667–682. http://doi.org/10.1891/0886-6708.23.6.667

Schrock, D., & Schwalbe, M. (2009). Men, masculinity, and manhood acts. *Annual Review of Sociology, 35*(1), 277–295. http://doi.org/10.1146/annurev-soc-070308-115933

Straus, M. A. (2004). Prevalence of violence against dating partners by male and female university students worldwide. *Violence against Women, 10*(7), 790–811. http://doi.org/10.1177/1077801204265552

Underwood, M. K. (2003). *Social aggression among girls.* New York: Guilford Press.

West, C., & Zimmerman, D. (1987). Doing gender. *Gender & Society, 1*(2), 125–151. http://doi.org/10.1177/0891243287001002002

The Effects OF Economic Pressure ON Couple Communication, Parenting, AND Child Cognitive Development

TRICIA K. NEPPL

Department of Human Development and Family Studies, Iowa State University

JENNIFER M. SENIA

Department of Human Development and Family Studies, Iowa State University

M. BRENT DONNELLAN

Department of Psychology, Texas A & M University

This research is currently supported by grants from the Eunice Kennedy Shriver National Institute of Child Health and Human Development, the National Institute of Mental Health, and the American Recovery and Reinvestment Act (HD064687, HD051746, MH051361, and HD047573). The content is solely the responsibility of the authors and does not necessarily represent the official views of the funding agencies. Support for earlier years of the study also came from multiple sources, including the National Institute of Mental Health (MH00567, MH19734, MH43270, MH59355, MH62989, and MH48165), the National Institute on Drug Abuse (DA05347), the National Institute of Child Health and Human Development (HD027724), the Bureau of Maternal and Child Health (MCJ-109572), and the MacArthur Foundation Research Network on Successful Adolescent Development Among Youth in High-Risk Settings. Correspondence regarding this manuscript should be addressed to Tricia K. Neppl, Department of Human Development and Family Studies, Iowa State University, 4380 Palmer, Suite 2358, Ames, IA 50011-4380; tneppl@iastate.edu.

Extensive research indicates that economic hardship has an adverse effect on the well-being of children and families. Theoretical work suggests that couple inter-action and parenting behaviors may play a critical role in mediating the effects of economic disadvantage on child outcomes. For example, the Family Stress Model (FSM; Conger & Conger, 2002) proposes that economic hardship leads to eco-nomic pressure, which is defined as the perceived inability to pay for basic needs, the inability to make ends meet, and having to cut back on necessary expenses. The model predicts that when economic pressure is high, parents are at increased risk for emotional distress, which, in turn, leads to disruptions in the couple rela-tionship including harsh and unsupportive interactions and maladaptive parent-ing. According to the FSM, parents who are distracted by emotional and marital distress demonstrate less effective parenting practices and this impairs child out-comes. Thus, the FSM provides one way to understand how economic problems facing families undermine the well-being of children.

A complementary perspective is the Investment Model (IM), which focuses on the advantages that financial wealth and prosperity offer to children and fam-ilies. The model proposes that parents with higher incomes invest more resources in their children, which results in greater educational opportunities and long-term educational, economic, and social success (Becker, 1981; Conger & Donnellan, 2007; Mayer, 1997). According to the IM, the impact of family economics on children is mediated through parental investments of limited resources like time and money rather than couple interactions and disrupted parenting.

Several studies have examined predictions from both the FSM and IM. Although the results are somewhat preliminary, there is an apparent pattern in the literature. Previous studies tend to find that family stress processes consistent with the FSM are better predictors of child behavioral problems, whereas dimin-ished parental investments consistent with the IM are better predictors of child cognitive development (Linver, Brooks-Gunn, & Kohen, 2002; Yeung, Linver, & Brooks-Gunn, 2002). For example, Gershoff and colleagues (2007) used a nationally representative sample of parents and their 6-year-old children to con-duct a joint test of both the FSM and IM. Consistent with the FSM, they found that material hardship was associated with increased parental stress and decreased positive parenting. This, in turn, was associated with diminished social develop-ment of children. In addition, they found an association between family income and child cognition that was mediated by parental investments such as the pur-chase of cognitively stimulating materials for the child. Similarly, Mistry, Biesanz, Chien, Howes, and Benner (2008) found that language stimulation mediated the relation between socioeconomic status (SES) and child cognitive outcomes, whereas parental stress mediated the impact of SES on child aggressive behavior. Thus, causal pathways proposed by the FSM predicted child outcomes related to social development, whereas pathways consistent with the IM predicted cognitive outcomes.

However, important elements of the FSM such as couple interaction were omitted from many previous investigations focused on cognitive versus social emotional outcomes. Therefore, it is important to test the family pathways of the FSM to ascertain whether family stress processes help explain children's cognitive skills (Conger, Conger, & Martin, 2010). Thus, following the pathways consistent with the FSM, the present investigation examined the effect of economic pressure on children's cognition. Specifically, we evaluated the impact of family economic pressure, parental emotional distress, observed couple communication and interpersonal interactions, and observed positive parenting on children's cognitive development as assessed during early childhood.

FAMILY STRESS FRAMEWORK

The FSM (Conger & Conger, 2002) was originally developed to help explain how financial adversity impacted families going through the downturn in the agricultural economy in the late 1980s. The FSM proposes that perceived economic pressure in the family can impact parent psychological functioning, as well as critical relationships within the family system. Parents who are distressed by their economic situation are less able to engage in positive communication patterns with their partner and supportive parenting practices with their children. These kinds of impaired parenting behaviors, in turn, have a detrimental consequence for the development of the child.

Empirical evidence supporting the FSM was first demonstrated with the first two generations from the present study. Since then, findings have been replicated in a number of studies drawing from different populations using a wide array of measures reflecting either positive or harsh behavioral interactions or competent or problematic child development to operationalize the constructs in the model (see Conger et al., 2010). For example, in a study of African-American couples, it was reported that economic pressure increased emotional distress for both partners in the relationship. Emotional distress, in turn, increased conflict between the partners (Conger et al., 2002). Similarly, Sobolewski and Amato (2005) reported that pathways consistent with the FSM predicted children's psychological adjustment into the adult years. More recently, Neppl, Jeon, Schofield, and Donnellan (2015) examined the FSM in the context of parental positivity, positive parenting, and the development of positive youth outcomes. They found that economic pressure was negatively associated with parent positivity, which facilitated adolescent positive adaptation into young adulthood.

THE INVESTMENT MODEL

The FSM emphasizes couple communication and interactions as well as the interpersonal and affective elements of parenting, and the investment model (IM) focuses on limited resources drawing on an economic framework. The IM proposes that parents with higher incomes have the ability to invest more time and financial resources in their children, which enhances their children's educational opportunities (Becker, 1981; Conger & Donnellan, 2007; Mayer, 1997). These investments can include learning materials available in the home, parent stimulation of learning through support of specialized training, the family's standard of living (i.e., adequate food, medical care, etc.), as well as social address variables such as residing in a location that nurtures a child's competent development. For example, wealthier parents often reside in areas that promote a child's association with conventional friends, access to good schools, and involvement in neighborhood activities. In short, the basic approach to the IM is to focus on resources that facilitate child development.

A number of studies have confirmed the basic proponents of the investment model. For example, it has been found that family income affects the types of investments parents make in their children (Bradley & Corwyn, 2002; Bradley, Corwyn, McAdoo, & García Coll, 2001; Davis-Kean, 2005; Mayer, 1997). It was also found that a stimulating home environment where children experience verbal stimulation and access to educational materials is associated with higher levels of child school readiness (Wagmiller, Lennon, Kuang, Alberti, & Aber, 2006). Similarly, Forget-Dubois et al. (2009) reported that children's language skills during early childhood mediated the association between home characteristics and children's readiness to learn. In addition, family income during childhood is positively related to academic, financial, and occupational success in adulthood (Bradley & Corwyn, 2002; Corcoran & Adams, 1997; Mayer, 1997; Teachman, Paasch, Day, & Carver, 1997). Moreover, several studies have found an association between family income and child cognitive development largely explained by the educational investments parents made in their children (Gershoff et al., 2007; Linver et al., 2002; Mistry et al., 2008; Yeung et al., 2002). More recently, Conger et al. (2012) found a significant association between family economic hardship during adolescence and educational attainment during adulthood, with parental investments as one potential mediating mechanism. Thus, there is support for the mediating processes between income and child cognition proposed by the IM.

THE PRESENT INVESTIGATION

The present study investigated how observed couple communication processes and parenting processes can be incorporated into the Family Stress Model (FSM) to potentially explain the association between family economic pressure and child cognitive development. Specifically, family economic pressure, parental emotional distress, observed couple interaction, observed parenting, and child cognition were assessed when the child was between the ages of 3 and 5 years old (see Figure 1). Accordingly, the current study contributes to the body of literature by prospectively examining how economic distress influences child cognitive skills within a family stress framework. Based on the pathways of the FSM (Conger & Conger, 2002), it is hypothesized that parents experiencing economic pressure will show higher levels of emotional distress, which will lead to a negative association with both observed couple communication patterns and positive parenting, behavior. In turn, couple interaction will be associated with parenting, which will be related to children's cognition. True to the model, it is expected that couple communication will be associated with parenting, which will lead to child development. It is not expected that couple communication will directly influence child cognitive skills.

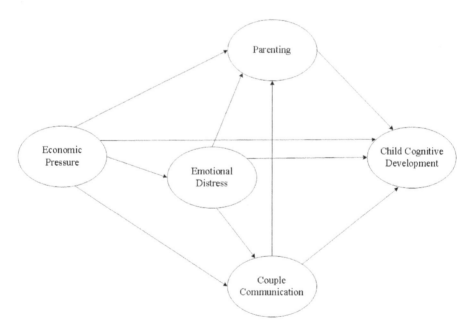

Fig 1. Conceptual Model.

In order to ensure that any relationships found could not be better accounted for by social or background characteristics, the present investigation also controlled for parent per capita income, age for both parent and child, and gender for parent and child. Previous research has shown that these control variables may be related to parenting behaviors. For example, income and socioeconomic status are both related to factors such as parenting and problems in adolescents (Conger & Donnellan, 2007; Conger & Simons, 1997). In terms of age and gender, research shows that younger mothers are at increased risk of negative life outcomes. In a study of children born to mothers younger than 19 years of age, sons were more likely than daughters to experience externalizing problems (Pogarsky, Thornberry, & Lizotte, 2006). Moreover, mothers with older compared to younger boys showed less effective parenting, and older sons showed an increase in antisocial behavior (Bank, Forgatch, Patterson, & Fetrow, 1993).

METHOD

Participants

Data come from the Family Transitions Project (FTP), a longitudinal study of 559 target youth and their families. The FTP represents an extension of two earlier studies: the Iowa Youth and Families Project (IYFP) and the Iowa Single Parent Project (ISPP). In the IYFP, data from the family of origin (N = 451) were collected annually from 1989 through 1992. Participants included the target adolescent, their parents, and a sibling within 4 years of age of the target adolescent (217 females, 234 males). These families (451 mothers, 451 fathers) were originally recruited for a study of family economic stress in the rural Midwest. When interviewed in 1989, the target adolescent was in seventh grade (M age = 12.7 years; 236 females, 215 males). Participants were recruited from schools in eight rural Iowa counties. Due to the rural nature of the sample, there were few minority families (approximately 1% of the population); therefore, all participants were Caucasian. Seventy-eight percent of eligible families agreed to participate in the study. Families were primarily lower middle or middle class with 34% residing on farms, 12% living in nonfarm rural areas, and 54% living in towns with fewer than 6,500 residents. In 1989, parents averaged 13 years of schooling and had a median family income of $33,700. Fathers' mean age was 40 years, while mothers' mean age was 38.

The ISPP began in 1991 when the target adolescent was in ninth grade (M age = 14.8 years), the same year of school for the IYFP target youth. Participants included the target adolescents, their single-parent mothers, and a sibling within 4 years of age of the target adolescent (N = 108). Families were headed by a mother who had experienced divorce within 2 years prior to the start of the study. All but three eligible families agreed to participate. The participants were Caucasian, primarily lower middle- or middle-class, one-parent families that lived in the same general geographic area as the IYFP families. Measures and procedures for the IYFP and ISPP studies were identical.

In 1994, families from ISPP were combined with families from IYFP to create the FTP. At that time, adolescents from both studies were in 12th grade. In 1994, target youth participated in the study with their parents as they had during earlier years of adolescence. Beginning in 1995, the target adolescent (1 year after completion of high school) participated in the study with a romantic partner or friend. In 1997, the study was expanded to include the first-born child of the target adolescent, now a young adult. The target's child was at least 18 months of age. By 2005, children in the FTP ranged in age from 18 months to 13 years old. Thus, the FTP has followed the target youth from as early as 1989 through 2005 (M target age = 25.7 years), with a 90% retention rate.

The present chapter reports data from 222 target adults, representing one member from each couple, who had an eligible child participating in the study at least once by 2005. We also include the target's romantic partner (spouse, cohabiting partner, or boy/girlfriend) who was either the other biological parent, stepparent, or parental figure to the target's child. The data were analyzed from the first assessments of each child between the ages of 3 and 5 years of age. Because the same child could participate at age 3 to 5, we include data only from the first time a child was assessed during that time period to assure that the same child is not counted multiple times within the limited age range. Age at first assessment varied somewhat because not all participants were available to be interviewed when the child first participated. Children averaged 3.2 years of age at first assessment, with 120 boys and 102 girls. There were 187 3-year-olds, 27 4-year-olds, and 8 5-year-old children. The parents averaged 26.3 years of age (89 men and 133 women) at the first assessment of their child. Of the 222 parents, 88% were married to or cohabiting with a romantic partner at the time of the visit.

Procedures

From 1997 through 2005, each target parent, his or her romantic partner, and the target's first-born child were visited in their home each year by a trained interviewer. During the visit, the target parent and his/her romantic partner completed a number of questionnaires, some of which included measures of parenting and individual characteristics. In addition to questionnaires, the target parent and his or her child participated in two separate videotaped interaction tasks. These tasks included a parent-child puzzle completion task and a clean-up task. Observational codes derived from the puzzle completion task were used for this study. Target parents and their children were presented with a puzzle that was too difficult for children to complete alone. Parents were instructed that children must complete the puzzle alone, but they could provide any assistance necessary. The task lasted 5 minutes. Puzzles varied by age group so that the puzzle slightly exceeded the child's skill level. The interaction task created a stressful environment for both parent and child, and the resulting behaviors indicated how well the parent handled the stress and how adaptive the child was to an environmental challenge. Trained observers coded aspects of harsh parenting from video recordings of the puzzle task using the Iowa Family Interaction Rating Scales (Melby et al., 1998).

Also during the visit, the target adult and his or her romantic partner participated in a videotaped 25-minute discussion task. This interaction task allowed for the discussion of various topics such as childrearing, employment, and other life events. Trained observers rated the quality of interactions during these tasks using the Iowa Family Interaction Rating Scales (Melby et al., 1998). The project observers were staff members who had received training on rating family interactions and specialized in coding one of the interaction tasks. Additional details regarding each interaction task are provided in the following discussion of study measures.

Measures

The means and standard deviations for study variables are provided in Table 1.

Economic pressure. Economic pressure was measured as a latent construct with three indicators: unmet material needs, can't make ends meet, and cutbacks. Unmet material needs included six items asking the target parent whether they had enough money to afford their home, clothing, furniture, car, food, and medical expenses. Each item ranged from *1 = strongly agree* to *5 = strongly disagree*. Scores on all items were summed together with an alpha coefficient of .89.

The second indicator was not being able to make ends meet. This included asking the target parent whether he or she had difficulty paying bills (1 = a great deal of difficulty to 5 = no difficulty at all) and how much money they have left at the end of each month (1 = more than enough money left over to 4 = not enough to make ends meet). The first item was recoded, and then both items were standardized and summed together. The correlation between the two items was .71.

The last indicator, cutbacks, consisted of 29 items that asked the target parent whether he or she had made significant financial cutbacks in the past 12 months. Questions included items such as postponing medical or dental care, changing food shopping or eating habits to save money, and taking an extra job to help meet expenses. Each item was answered on a *1 = yes* or *0 = no* scale. All items were summed together with adequate internal consistency (alpha = .83).

Emotional distress. Emotional distress was assessed through target self-report using the depression, anxiety, and hostility subscales from the SCL-R-90

(Derogatis, 1994). Items from each subscale were summed and used as a separate indicator for the latent construct. Response categories assessed how distressed the parent felt during the past week, ranging from *1 = not at all* to *5 = extremely*. For the depression scale, target parents were asked 13 questions regarding depressive symptoms such as crying easily or feelings of worthlessness. The anxiety subscale included 10 questions assessing behavior such as nervousness or shakiness inside, suddenly feeling scared for no reason, and feeling fearful. Finally, hostility included six items asking questions related to feeling easily annoyed or irritated, having temper outbursts that you could not control, and having the urge to break or smash things. The alpha coefficients for each subscale were .89, .92, and .82, respectively.

Couple communication. Six observer ratings were used to assess the target's communication and interaction toward his or her romantic partner during the discussion task. A high score indicates high positivity and low anger or hostility in observed interactions. Communication (CO) measures one's ability to positively express oneself in a clear and appropriate way while demonstrating consideration of the other person's view. Prosocial (PR) measures acts of helpfulness, sensitivity, and cooperation. Assertiveness (AR) measures one's ability to express oneself using a straightforward, nonthreatening style. Hostility (HS; reverse-coded) measures hostile, angry, critical, disapproving, and/or rejecting behavior. Antisocial (AN; reverse-coded) is the demonstration of socially irresponsible behavior, including resistance, defiance, and insensitivity. Angry coercion (AC; reverse-coded) is the attempt to control or change the behavior of another in a hostile manner. It includes demands, hostile commands, refusals, and threats. Each observer rating was scored on a nine-point scale, ranging from low (no evidence of the behavior) to high (the behavior is highly characteristic of the parent). The positive-valence dimensions and reverse-coded negative-valence dimensions of couple communication were combined into three parcels (Kishton & Widaman, 1994; Little, Rhemtulla, Gibson, & Schoemann, 2013). The first parcel combined CO and HS (reversed). The second parcel combined PR and AN (reversed). The third parcel combined AR and AC (reversed). Each of the three parcels was used as separate indicators for the latent construct (see also Spilman, Neppl, Donnellan, Schofield, & Conger, 2013).

During the romantic partner discussion task, couples discussed questions from a series of cards. Each person took turns reading questions related to subjects such as household responsibilities, each other's family, and raising a child. The person reading the card was instructed to read each question out loud and give his or her answers first. The other person was instructed to give her or his answer next, and then the couple talked together about the answers that were given. They were to go on to the next card once they felt as though they had said everything they wanted to about each question. Scores were averaged across data collected during time 1. The observational ratings were internally consistent (alpha = .88) and inter-rater reliability was high (.93).

Positive parenting. Direct observations assessed target parenting behaviors to their child during the videotaped puzzle task. Trained observers rated the same behaviors as for couple communication. Communication, prosocial, assertiveness, hostility (reverse-coded), antisocial (reverse-coded), and angry coercion (reverse-coded) were rated by observers on a nine-point scale. The positive-valence dimensions and reverse-coded negative-valence dimensions of parenting were combined into the same three parcels as for couple communication. Each parcel was used as a separate indicator for the latent construct. The scores for the parenting construct were internally consistent (alpha = .86), and interrater reliability was substantial (.94).

Child cognition. The Peabody Picture Vocabulary Test-Revised (PPVT-R; Dunn & Dunn, 1997) was used to measure child cognition at age 3, 4, or 5. The PPVT-R consists of a series of words for which respondents are required to select a picture from four drawings that best represents the word. This process is continued with matching the best picture to the word until they get 8 or more incorrect in a single 12-item block. The PPVT-R has good psychometric properties (Williams, 1997; Williams & Wang, 1997). The standardized score was used in the analyses.

Control variables. The control variables were measured when the child was 3, 4, or 5 years old. Target and romantic partner self-reports of family per capita income were included and log transformed to correct for positive skewness. Targets reported on their gender and their child's gender (1 = male, 2 = female), as well as the age of their child (3, 4, or 5 years old).

RESULTS

Correlations Among Measures of the Constructs

Table 1 shows the zero-order correlations among the measures of the theoretical constructs. Consistent with theoretical predictions, economic pressure was significantly correlated with parental emotional distress (r = .38), parenting behaviors (r = -.18), and with child's cognition between the ages of 3 and 5 years old (r = -.18). Parental emotional distress was also significantly correlated with parenting (r = -.28) and couple interaction (r = -.18). Couple interaction was significantly correlated with parenting (r = .44), which, in turn, was significantly

Table 1. Correlations, Means, and SD for Variables Used in Analyses.

Variable	1	2	3	4	5	6	7	8	9	10
1. Economic Pressure										
2. Emotional Distress	.38***									
3. Couple Communication	-.07	-.18*								
4. Parenting	-.17*	-.28***	.44***							
5. Child Cognitive Development	-.18*	-.11	.18*	.35***						
6. Family Income	-.30***	-.19*	.31***	.24**	.13†					
7. Parent Age	-.17*	-.08	.39***	.37***	.29***	.33***				
8. Parent Relation- ship Status	.22**	.00	.06	-.07	-.11	-.13†	-.21**			
9. Parent Gender	.06	.17*	-.12	-.00	.03	-.07	-.12†	.15*		
10. Child Gender	-.06	.07	.04	.06	.20**	.03	.14*	-.11	.04	
Mean	5.81	1.29	5.82	6.92	96.05	16772.38	26.31			
SD	2.97	0.38	1.43	1.16	15.56	13337.46	2.42			

Note. †$p < .10$. *$p < .05$. **$p < .01$ ***$p < .001$.

related to child's cognition ($r = .35$). The patterns of associations were gen-erally supportive of the theoretical model and justified the formal test of the model.

Structural Equation Analyses

Structural equation models (SEMs) were analyzed using the AMOS 22.0 software package and full information maximum likelihood (FIML) estimation procedures (Arbuckle, 2003). FIML procedures are recommended for handling missing data in longitudinal research (Arbuckle, 2003). Economic pressure, parental emotional distress, couple interaction, and parenting were specified as latent variables. Child cognition was examined as a manifest variable. The SEMs were estimated in two ways. First, models were estimated with all of the control variables in the analyses: family per capita income, target relationship status, target age, and gender for both target parent and child. Second, the models were refigured to exclude these control variables. Separate analyses generated similar findings; therefore, we present the results without the inclusion of the control variables in the final model.

Several types of indicators were used when evaluating the fit of structural models to the data. First, the standard chi-square index of statistical fit that is routinely provided under maximum likelihood estimation of parameters was evaluated. Two indices of practical fit, the root mean square error of approximation (RMSEA; Browne & Cudeck, 1993) and the comparative fit index (CFI; Bentler, 1990), were also used. RMSEA values under .05 indicate close fit to the data, and values between .05 and .08 represent reasonable fit (Bentler, 1990). For the CFI, fit index values should be greater than .90, and preferably greater than .95, to consider the fit of a model to data to be acceptable. This model showed an acceptable fit, χ^2 (56) = 95.88, p < .001, CFI = .976, RMSEA = .057, and was the model used for our primary analyses. Economic pressure had standardized loadings of λ = .73 or higher. Parental emotional distress had standardized loadings of λ = .77 or higher. Couple communication had standardized loadings of λ = .81 or higher. Parenting had standardized loadings of λ = .85 or higher. Standardized coefficients from the final model that reached statistical significance are presented in Figure 2.

Consistent with theoretical predictions, economic pressure was significantly associated with higher parental emotional distress (β = .38, SE = .01). Parental emotional distress was significantly associated with lower levels of couple communication (β = -.18, SE = .29) and lower levels of parenting (β = -.20, SE = .20). Couple communication was significantly associated with higher levels of parenting (β = .40, SE = .06), which, in turn, was significantly associated with higher cognition in

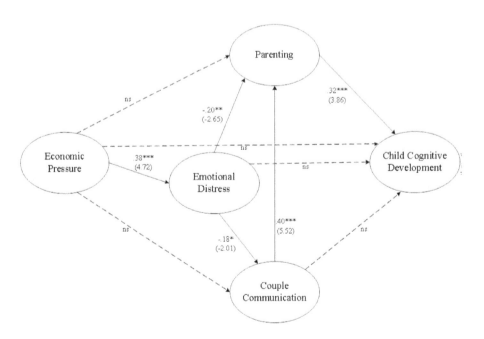

Fig 2. Statistical Model
Note: *p < .05, **p < .01, ***p < .001.

children between the ages of 3 and 5 (β = .32, SE = 1.13). Also true to the model, results demonstrated that economic pressure was not associated with couple communication, parenting, or cognition in early childhood. In addition, couple communication did not directly predict cognition; rather it was related through parenting.

DISCUSSION

The present investigation evaluated connections among economic adversity, family processes, and child cognitive development in ways consistent with the Family Stress Model (FSM). Specifically, we examined how economic pressure was related to disrupted communication patterns between couples and their communication and parenting to their child. These family processes were related to child cognition in early childhood. This study adds to the existing literature by prospectively evaluating how economic stress is associated with child cognitive skills within a family stress framework. Results showed support for the model in that economic pressure influenced parental emotional distress, which was negatively associated with observed communication patterns between the couple. This couple interaction, in turn, was associated with observed parenting, which was directly related to later childhood cognition. These results suggest that economic pressure and disrupted couple communication patterns may undermine effective parenting, which contributes to child cognitive development. In other words, couple interaction and communication processes appear to be one conduit through which economic conditions are related to cognitive outcomes in children.

Altogether, the results replicate and extend previous studies by suggesting that economic influences on children's cognition may be mediated through couple communication processes and parenting behavior. For example, using an IM framework, Sohr-Preston et al. (2013) found that parental income and education predicted responsive communication patterns between parent and adolescent, which, in turn, was associated with offspring educational attainment. Similarly, it has been found that socioeconomic status relates to parenting processes, which are then associated with child cognitive outcomes (Mistry et al., 2008). These findings are important, as they suggest that the FSM might have relevance to cognitive development as well as social/emotional development. While the results in the current study provide a first step in examining these processes through a stress framework, future research should continue to investigate pathways consistent with both the FSM and IM within the same study. That way, we can further our understanding of whether causal pathways consistent with the IM better predict cognitive development, and the FSM better predicts social development in young children. In addition, future studies should extend the model from early childhood to the later adolescent years.

It should be acknowledged that there are alternative explanations for some of the present findings. For example, it could be that shared genetic factors passed from parent to child help explain some of the relations. It may also be that genetically influenced individual differences in children might elicit certain parenting practices. Thus, future research should examine genetic factors within the pathways of both the FSM and IM. There are also limitations of this study worthy of comment. The sample was primarily white and came from the rural Midwest, which could limit generalizability of the findings; however other research has shown similar findings using more diverse samples. For instance, initial findings from the FSM have been replicated in a sample of immigrant, low-income families (Mistry et al., 2008), as well as a nationally represented study of families with young children (Gershoff et al., 2007). Another limitation is that the current study was cross-sectional. However, it is important to note that the study used an observational design, thus eliminating reporting biases inherent in self-report measures of couple interactions and parenting. Future studies should certainly use a longitudinal design to provide more causally informative results.

In sum, the present results suggest that couple communication processes can be embedded within a theoretically grounded approach for evaluating how economic pressure is associated with child cognitive development. Results suggest that economic conditions contribute to interpersonal distress, which is negatively associated with positive communication patterns. Communication patterns marked by hostility and interpersonal antagonism seem to undermine parenting behaviors, thereby pointing to the potential dark side of couple interactions within a family context. Thus, couple communication patterns might reflect a distressed marital relationship, which is associated with children's cognitive development through parenting. This is a potentially important finding that could have applied implications. For example, this result may illustrate the importance of effective preventive interventions designed to promote positive communication. For example, family-based programs that focus on increasing positive communication patterns between couples and decreasing harsh parenting may be effective in promoting child cognitive development. Thus, findings underscore the usefulness of evaluating how efforts to promote interpersonal processes in families may facilitate positive child developmental outcomes.

REFERENCES

Arbuckle, J. L. (2003). *AMOS 5.0 update to AMOS user's guide.* Chicago: Small Waters.

Bank, L., Forgatch, M., Patterson, G., & Fetrow, R. (1993). Parenting practices of single mothers: Mediators of negative contextual factors. *Journal of Marriage and the Family, 55,* 371–385. http://dx.doi.org/10.2307/35280

Becker, G. S. (1981). *A treatise on the family.* Cambridge, MA: Harvard University Press.

Bentler, P. M. (1990). Comparative fit indexes in structural models. *Psychological Bulletin, 107*, 238–246. http://dx.doi.org/10.1037/0033-2909.107.2.238

Bradley, R. H., & Corwyn, R. F. (2002). Socioeconomic status and child development. *Annual Review of Psychology, 53*, 371–399. http://dx.doi.org/10.1146/annurev.psych.53.100901.135233

Bradley, R. H., Corwyn, R. F., McAdoo, H. P., & García Coll, C. (2001). The home environments of children in the United States: Part I. Variations by age, ethnicity, and poverty status. *Child Development, 72*, 1844–1867. http://dx.doi.org/10.1111/1467-8624.t01-1-00382

Browne, M. W., & Cudeck, R. (1993). Alternative ways of assessing model fit. In K. A. Bollen & J. S. Long (Eds.), *Testing structural equation models* (pp. 136–162). Newbury Park, CA: Sage.

Conger, K. J., Martin, M. J., Reeb, B. T., Little, W. M., Craine, J. L., Shebloski, B., & Conger, R. D. (2012). Economic hardship and its consequences across generations. In V. Maholmes & R. B. King (Eds.), *Oxford handbook of child development and poverty*, (pp. 37–53). New York: Oxford University Press.

Conger, R. D., & Conger, K. J. (2002). Resilience in Midwestern families: Selected findings from the first decade of a prospective, longitudinal study. *Journal of Marriage and Family, 64*, 361–373. http://dx.doi.org/10.1111/j.1741-3737.2002.00361.x

Conger, R. D., Conger, K. J., & Martin, M. J. (2010). Socioeconomic status, family processes, and individual development. *Journal of Marriage and Family, 72*, 685–704. http://dx.doi.org/10.1111/j.1741-3737.2010.00725.x

Conger, R. D., & Donnellan, M. B. (2007). An interactionist perspective on the socioeconomic context of human development. *Annual Review of Psychology, 58*, 175–199. http://dx.doi.org/10.1146/annurev.psych.58.110405.08555

Conger, R. D., & Simons, R. (1997). Life-course contingencies in the development of adolescent antisocial behaviors: A matching law approach. In T. P. Thornberry (Ed.), *Advances in criminological theory: Vol. 7. Developmental theories of crime and delinquency* (pp. 55–99). New Brunswick, NJ: Transaction.

Conger, R. D., Wallace, L., Sun, Y., Simons, R. L., McLoyd, V. C., & Brody, G. (2002). Economic pressure in African American families: A replication and extension of the family stress model. *Developmental Psychology, 38*, 179–193. http://dx.doi.org/10.1037/0012-1649.38.2.179

Corcoran, M., & Adams, T. (1997). Race, sex, and the intergenerational transmission of poverty. In G. J. Duncan & J. Brooks-Gunn (Eds.), *Consequences of growing up poor* (pp. 461–517). New York: Russell Sage Foundation.

Davis-Kean, P. E. (2005). The influence of parent education and family income on child achievement: The indirect role of parental expectations and the home environment. *Journal of Family Psychology, 19*, 294–304. http://dx.doi.org/10.1037/0893-3200.19.2.294

Derogatis, L. R. (1994). *Symptom checklist-90-R (SCL-90-R): Administration, scoring and procedures manual.* Minneapolis, MN: National Computer Systems.

Dunn, L. M., & Dunn, L. M. (1997). *Peabody picture vocabulary Test* (3rd ed.). Bloomington, MN: Pearson Assessments.

Forget-Dubois, N., Dionne, G., Pascal-Lemelin, J., Pérusse, D., Tremblay, R. E., & Boivin, M. (2009). Early child language mediates the relation between home environment and school readiness. *Child Development, 80*, 736–749. http://dx.doi.org/10.1111/j.1467-8624.2009.01294.x

Gershoff, E. T., Aber, J. L., Raver, C. C., & Lennon, M. C. (2007). Income is not enough: Incorporating material hardship into models of income associations with parenting and child development. *Child Development, 78*, 70–95. http://dx.doi.org/10.1111/j.1467-8624.2007.00986.x

Kishton, J. M., & Widaman, K. F. (1994). Unidimensional versus domain representative parceling of questionnaire items: An empirical example. *Educational and Psychological Measurement, 54,* 757–765. http://dx.doi.org/10.1177/0013164494054003022

Linver, M. R., Brooks-Gunn, J., & Kohen, D. E. (2002). Family processes as pathways from income to young children's development. *Developmental Psychology, 38,* 719–734. http://dx.doi.org/10.1037/0012-1649.38.5.719

Little, T. D., Rhemtulla, M., Gibson, K., & Schoemann, A. M. (2013). Why the items versus parcels controversy needn't be one. *Psychological Methods, 18,* 285–300. http://dx.doi.org/10.1037/a0033266

Mayer, S. E. (1997). *What money can't buy: Family income and children's life chances.* Cambridge, MA: Harvard University Press.

Melby, J., Conger, R., Book, R., Rueter, M., Lucy, L., Repinski, D., & Scaramella, L. (1998). *The Iowa family interaction rating scales* (5th ed.). Ames: Iowa State University, Institute for Social and Behavioral Research.

Mistry, R. S., Biesanz, J. C., Chien, N., Howes, C., & Benner, A. D. (2008). Socioeconomic status, parental investments, and the cognitive and behavioral outcomes of low-income children from immigrant and native households. *Early Childhood Research Quarterly, 23,* 193–212. http://dx.doi.org/10.1016/j.ecresq.2008.01.002

Neppl, T. K., Jeon, S., Schofield, T. J., & Donnellan, M. B. (2015). The impact of economic pressure on parent positivity, parenting, and adolescent positivity into emerging adulthood. *Family Relations, 64,* 80–92. http://dx.doi.org/10.1111/fare.12098

Pogarsky, G., Thornberry, T., & Lizotte, A. (2006). Developmental outcomes for children of young mothers. *Journal of Marriage and Family, 68,* 332–344. http://dx.doi.org/10.1111/j.1741-3737.2006.00256.x

Sobolewski, J. M., & Amato, P. R. (2005). Economic hardship in the family of origin during childhood and psychological well-being in adulthood. *Journal of Marriage and Family, 67,* 141–156. doi: 10.1111/j.0022-2445.2005.00011.x

Sohr-Preston, S. L., Scaramella, L. V., Martin, M. J., Neppl, T. K., Ontai, L., & Conger, R. (2012). Parental socioeconomic status, communication, and children's vocabulary development: A third-generation test of the family investment model. *Child Development, 84,* 1046–1062. doi: 10.1111/cdev.12023

Spilman, S. K., Neppl, T. K., Donnellan, M. B., Schofield, T. J., & Conger, R. D. (2013). Incorporating religiosity into a developmental model of positive family functioning across generations. *Developmental Psychology, 49,* 762–774. doi: 10.1037/a0028418

Teachman, J. D., Paasch, K. M., Day, R. D., & Carver, K. P. (1997). Poverty during adolescence and subsequent educational attainment. In G. J. Duncan & J. Brooks-Gunn (Eds.), *Consequences of growing up poor* (pp. 382–418). New York: Russell Sage Foundation.

Wagmiller, R. L., Lennon, M. C., Kuang, L., Alberti, P. M., & Aber, J. L. (2006). The dynamics of economic disadvantage and children's life chances. *American Sociological Review, 71,* 847–866.

Williams, K. T. (1997). *Expressive vocabulary test.* Circle Pines, MN: American Guidance Service.

Williams, K. T., & Wang, J. (1997). *Technical references to the Peabody Picture Vocabulary Test–Third Edition (PPVT-III).* Circle Pines, MN: American Guidance Service.

Yeung, W. J., Linver, M. R., & Brooks-Gunn, J. (2002). How money matters for young children's development: Parental investment and family processes. *Child Development, 73,* 1861–1879. http://dx.doi.org/10.1111/1467-8624.t01-1-00511

PART FOUR

Methodological
Considerations

Complicating THE Dark Side OF Family Communication through Postpositivist, Interpretivist, AND Critical Perspectives

SHARDÉ DAVIS, ABD, TAMARA D. AFIFI, PHD
Department of Communication Studies, University of Iowa

Every family, couple, and individual experiences stress and difficulties that bring about negative aspects of their communication and personalities. This "dark side" reveals itself in a multitude of complex ways, however, that are often difficult to capture in current research. The dark side of family communication involves the "synchronic or diachronic production of harmful, morally suspect, and/or socially unacceptable messages, observed and/or experienced at one or multiple interlocking structures of interaction, that are the products or causes of negative effects (temporary or long term) within the family system" (Olson, Baiocchi-Wagner, Wilson-Kratzer, and Symonds, 2012, p. 9). Using this definition, even extremely healthy families have dark moments of communication that are "harmful, morally suspect, and/or socially unacceptable." In fact, anyone who has ever had a sibling might think that this is typically the way siblings communicate with each other! As pointed out by Olson and colleagues (2012), there are various shades of "dark" in families, and sometimes the dark is fleeting and sometimes it is long lasting. Some families, however, have more harmful communication patterns that have the potential for long-term detrimental consequences. In order to help families come through the darkness, we need to focus on the co-occurrence of the light and dark sides of family communication and how the two inform each other. In particular, researchers need to more closely examine the shades of gray in the ways that family members interact with each other. Families are nuanced in their structure and their communication patterns, and researchers need to analyze families in ways that can capture this complexity.

One way scholars can explore the complexity of the dark side of family life is to use multiple epistemological and methodological orientations. When a concept is explored from multiple vantage points, its essence can be more completely understood. Researchers can then create more sound interventions to help families communicate in ways that foster health and resiliency. The purpose of this chapter is to examine the messiness of family communication from multiple methodological and epistemological angles—from postpositivist, interpretive, and critical perspectives. We first provide a brief overview of these three traditions and provide examples of scholarship that explore the dark side of family communication from each tradition. We also discuss several ethical implications of this work. Finally, we conclude the chapter by setting forth a new agenda for adding more depth to the way scholars study the dark side of families.

META-THEORETICAL APPROACHES

Epistemology, methodology, and method are three fundamental aspects of research design (Carter & Little, 2007), which collectively create a framework for the implementation and evaluation of dark-side family communication research. The epistemological arm of the larger meta-theory umbrella is a philosophy of knowledge or how people come to know what they know. Identifying one's philosophical approach to research is an important scholarly endeavor because it concerns the assumptions and methods employed in one's research. Although some scholars may not staunchly identify with one philosophical tradition, researchers often construct research questions and employ research studies grounded in a particular meta-theoretical approach. Epistemology by itself does not translate into a practical set of research behaviors. Rather, it informs researchers' methodology and methods (see Harding, 1987). Methodology and methods are often discussed interchangeably, but they are indeed different aspects of research. Methodology is the study, explanation, and justification of one's method (i.e., quantitative, qualitative), whereas method is the practical techniques of research (i.e., sampling, data collection and analysis, reporting) (Carter & Little, 2007). Epistemology, methodology, and method collectively undergird all research, whether they are explicitly reported or implied. Thus, all scholars should ensure these three facets cohere in their research so that the meta-theoretical assumptions and commitments are internally consistent. In this chapter we discuss ways that dark-side family communication research can be approached from multiple epistemological and methodological orientations to enable an exploration of the dark and light shades of family communication. We begin with a postpositivist approach.

Postpositivist Approach

When most people today think of quantitative social scientific research, they are adopting a postpositivist approach. Even though reality is understood through the perception of the researcher, postpositivists believe that there is a larger, objective "Truth" with a capital "T" that exists across a population (Phillips & Burbules, 2000). This truth can be measured, tested, and then hopefully generalized to the larger population. The researcher creates causal-like hypotheses or explanations among variables to explain and predict why something occurs (see also Baxter & Braithwaite, 2008, for further explanation). For example, a postpositivist might argue that abusive parenting has a negative effect on children's attachments (e.g., Sousa et al., 2011). The researcher could show that this is the case, on average, for the population being studied, even though there will probably be some people who had abusive parents whose attachments were not disrupted. Postpositivists also argue that warrants or arguments created by researchers are falsifiable through repeated tests of the assumptions they hold to be true. This orientation assumes a quantitative methodology whereby hypotheses are generated and tested. The goal is to be able to predict and, ultimately, to explain behavior. Experimental designs, longitudinal data analysis, and randomly selected samples are often ideal because they can best test causality and generalizability. Nevertheless, postpositivists use a variety of data collection methods, including surveys, content analysis, observational coding, and physiological measurements.

A significant amount of the dark-side work in family studies uses a postpositivist approach. For example, the research on hurtful messages in families has relied almost exclusively on this orientation. Vangelisti, Young, McLaren, and colleagues (McLaren & Solomon, 2008; Vangelisti & Young, 2000) have identified the messages that people perceive as hurtful in their families and other close relationships and then used these messages to predict relational distancing and other outcomes of relational quality. They have also shown that messages that are perceived as more intentional are deemed more hurtful. This research has used hypothetical scenarios in surveys, diary methods, and observational research to assess attributions of hurt. Similarly, Horan's research (e.g., Horan & Booth-Butterfield, 2010, 2013) on deceptive affection has shown that affection can also have a dark side. His work has shown that feeling affectionate and communicating affection are separate entities. Romantic partners routinely deceive the partner by engaging in affection that does not match their true feelings (e.g., kissing, hugging, or having sex with one's romantic partner when one does not feel like it). These behaviors may actually help support and maintain relationships by saving the face of the partner, encouraging positive emotions, managing conflict, and promoting the relationship satisfaction of the partner (Horan & Booth-Butterfield, 2013). Deceptive affection has also been found to not be any more physiologically arousing (e.g., heart rate, blood pressure) compared to honest affection or common communication (Horan & Booth-Butterfield, 2013). This might be due to the fact that people use deceptive affection with their romantic partners on a regular basis. At the same time, however, they can sometimes be used to hide negative feelings about the relationship, which might be indicative of deeper relational issues. Likewise, the vast amount of research on family secrets uses a postpositivist approach. This research tends to examine different types of secrets and their functions in families and the impact of perceptions of family secrecy on relationship satisfaction and closeness (e.g., Afifi & Olson, 2005; Vangelisti, 1994; Vangelisti & Caughlin, 1997). While the majority of the research on family secrecy is quite dark, scholars also point out that withholding information from loved ones is not always deceptive and/or harmful to a person or her or his relationships with others.

Many dark-side topics, such as those identified above, present ethical considerations regarding epistemology and research design. For instance, most research on hurtful messages only involves individuals recalling a hurtful message he/she has experienced rather than examining individuals discussing the hurtful message they experienced with a relational partner or other family members. A notable exception would be the research by McLaren and colleagues (e.g., McLaren & Sillars, in press), who have had adult children discuss a hurtful message they received from a parent with the parent in a laboratory setting and asked each person to recall their attributions about the hurtful messages. This research is groundbreaking in the sense that it is the first to examine hurtful messages in real conversations between the person who was hurt and the person who inflicted the hurt. This scholarship simultaneously poses numerous ethical implications for researchers. For example, what if participants are asked to talk about something hurtful that they are sincerely uncomfortable sharing but do not feel like they can tell the researcher to end their study participation (e.g., due to legitimate power differences between the participant and the researcher)? What if discussing the hurtful messages makes the relationship between the parent and child worse? Even after debriefing the family members, what if the relationship is permanently damaged because of what is said in the conversation? Sometimes people avoid discussing hurtful messages because they are afraid that discussing them will significantly disrupt the state of the relationship.

The research on secrecy poses similar ethical implications. Most of the research on secrecy has also used cross-sectional and longitudinal survey data to gather information because of ethical concerns with revealing secrets unbeknownst to others. For instance, it would probably be unethical to have someone reveal a secret to another person in a study and gauge the impact of the revelation of the secret on personal and relational health. Yet one of the critiques of the research on secrecy is that it is too psychological in nature and does not focus enough on the relational and dynamic nature of secrecy. How can researchers study the dyadic nature of secrecy when the phenomenon under investigation is a secret? These issues pose ethical implications for researchers from any epistemological orientation but are particularly relevant for postpositivist scholars because of the nature of the research methodologies commonly used to conduct this type of research.

There is an abundance of dark-side research from a postpositivist tradition; however, the area lacks well-tested theories that delve into the dark, light, and gray shades of family life shades of family life. We recently developed a postpositivist theory of stress and resilience in families and other intimate relationships (e.g., romantic couples) called the Theory of Resilience and Relational Load (TRRL; Afifi, Merrill, & Davis, 2014). The theory captures both the dark and light sides of stress in intimate social relationships. In the TRRL we adapt the idea of allostatic load (see McEwen, 1998) to couples and families but in a way that captures the wear and tear of stress on relationships. When the body is stressed, it has natural ability to physiologically respond to the stress and restore homeostasis. This process is typically healthy and adaptive. It can become maladaptive, however, when chronic stress occurs. Too much chronic stress can wear and tear on multiple stress-response systems in the body, resulting in allostatic load (McEwen, 1998). Allostatic load, in turn, can make the body more susceptible to disease (see Miller, Chen, & Zhou, 2007). We argue that relationships can become fatigued and experience "relational load" due to repeated stress and depletion of one's emotional, cognitive, and relational resources. This depletion, especially if it occurs long term can negatively affect one's stress levels (perceived and biological) and individual and relational health unless people continually invest in their relationships. Relational load reveals itself in dark communication patterns, like negative emotions and detrimental conflict patterns, because people's emotional and relational resources are depleted and they do not have any reserves from which to draw in stressful circumstances.

The TRRL also examines the "light" side of resilient communication patterns that prevent relational load and facilitate recovery if it occurs. The TRRL extends ideas proposed in the Theory of Emotional Capital (Feeney & Lemay, 2012; see also Gottman, Driver, & Tabares, 2002), which states that when couples build emotional capital over time by investing emotional resources in the relationship, this protects the relationship from relational threats. We contend that couples that have more of a communal orientation toward stress, and life in general, are likely to invest in their relationships and build emotional reserves through repeated communicative maintenance strategies. These emotional reserves, in turn, make it likely that relational partners and family members perceive and communicate with each other in secure ways when they are stressed. Their goal when they are stressed is to preserve the relationship and turn toward their partner for strength. Couples who lack a communal orientation, who have a lack of reserves, and/or whose standards on these dimensions are unmet are likely to engage in more threatening perceptions and conflict behaviors when they are stressed. Their goal in stressful situations, which often reveals itself in conflict, is to defend and preserve the self—even if it means attacking one's partner. These threatening perceptions and behaviors can deplete one's cognitive, emotional, and relational resources. Relationships have their own homeostasis that is continually being calibrated in response to stress and communicative responses to that stress. Partners must repeatedly invest in their relationships to adapt successfully to stress that affects their relationships. Couples who adapt successfully are generally more resilient and even thrive when faced with stressful situations.

Our theory is an example of a way to examine the complexity of the dark side of family communication from a postpositivist perspective. Most families are shades of gray—with some dark and many light moments. The TRRL should explain why it is that some families experience more dark than light moments and how those moments can turn into repeated patterns of behavior. It is also an example of a postpositivist theory, given that it is based upon a certain set of propositions or beliefs about associations between variables. These propositions set the foundation from which hypotheses can be generated and tested. The theory is very predictive in nature in that if people invest in their marriages on a regular basis, they should experience less stress and more resilience in their family. The ultimate value of a postpositivist approach is that it gives the researcher predictive power. Postpositivist approaches, however, have been critiqued for being too superficial in their testing of human behavior. Indeed, human beings are incredibly complex. An important component of postpositivist research is measurement—that researchers measure the construct the best way possible and test their ideas in a way that maps onto their hypotheses. To provide a more holistic assessment of human behavior, researchers often combine a postpositivist approach with an interpretive approach, which is discussed next.

Interpretivist Approach

Interpretivism is another framework within the social sciences that is rooted in philosophical and methodological ways of understanding social reality (Given, 2008). In this approach scholars interrogate the meaning-making process of communication phenomena from the family member's point of view. Unlike a postpositivist orientation, the goal of an interpretivist orientation is not to predict behavior. The goal is to explain and better understand it. For example, the researcher goes into a study attempting to understand something from the participants' perspective, drawing upon the richness of their experiences (Creswell, 1998; Moustakas, 1994). Whereas postpositivists believe there is more of an objective truth, interpretivists believe in a subjective truth and that everyone has their own truth or perspective (truth with a small "t"). At the same time, interpretivists often try to look across participants to generate themes that can capture ideas in one's sample. In this sense, there is generalizability, but within one's sample and not to the larger population outside it. Interpretivists also know they are biased and try to set aside these biases going into the study. In addition, whereas postpositivists make every attempt to separate themselves from the participants, interpretivists realize that they are often intimately connected to their participants and may become quite close to the participants as the research process unfolds. In this sense, the participant and the researcher become an integral part of the research process. In many interpretivist studies, the researcher explicitly states her/his biases or personal position in the manuscript and may even integrate it throughout the manuscript.

A large amount of the research on the dark side of family life has been interpretive in nature. The research on divorce and stepfamilies within the field of communication, for example, has been either postpositivist or interpretive (see Schrodt's work for an example of a postpositivist orientation; e.g., Schrodt et al., 2007). Braithwaite and colleagues' research (e.g., Baxter, Braithwaite, Bryant, & Wagner, 2004; Golish, 2003) on communicative challenges in stepfamilies has largely involved interviewing members of stepfamilies to discover the struggles in stepfamilies and the ways family members manage them. For example, Baxter et al. (2004) interviewed stepchildren about their perceptions of the contradictions with their stepparent in their family of residence. They identified three dialectical tensions that revolved around the larger contradiction of expression in which both candor and discretion were necessary and opposed each other. Another line of work with excellent examples of interpretive research is family violence (e.g., Eckstein, 2004). For instance, Eckstein interviewed 20 parents whose adolescents had verbally and physically abused them. She uncovered themes regarding the escalation of the abuse and the parents' role within and outside the family. Eckstein's study is a good example of the value of interpretive work. Her study is incredibly novel and involves a relatively unexplored topic, and it would have been nearly impossible to gather a sample and garner the richness of the subject with a postpositivist approach. With all of the aforementioned research, the emphasis is on describing people's experiences with a particular phenomenon in an in-depth manner.

Similar to a postpositivist approach, interpretive approaches also pose ethical implications for researchers. The beauty of interpretive research is that scholars can access the richness of participants' experiences, allowing for a deep and complex understanding of a phenomenon. While interpretive methods enable this richness, they also expose researchers to situations where various types of abuse and other ethical issues reveal themselves. For example, even if the topic of an interview with a family is seemingly unrelated to abuse, the interview itself could prompt a child to indicate that he/she is being abused. The researcher then has an ethical obligation to report this abuse to the proper authorities and the institutional review board. Postpositivist research often (but certainly not always) involves methods where participants are asked a predetermined set of questions. While it is highly possible that participants can disclose abuse or other extremely harmful circumstances in a discussion task in the lab or in the field, it is probably more likely that this type of disclosure occurs in a setting where the researcher is interviewing the participant on a sensitive, dark-side topic, a relationship with the participant is established, and the researcher is allowed to probe private information.

Critical Approach

Thus far, the postpositivist and interpretive orientations serve as general approaches to illuminate and explain dark communication patterns in families. One lingering criticism of both orientations is that they overlook power differentials between groups of people (e.g., family communication patterns are privileged for some at the expense of others) and lack an explicit deconstruction of the status quo (Morrow & Brown, 1994). Power, as a construct, can be approached from each meta-theoretical orientation. For example, a postpositivist can test power as an independent variable predicting certain family communication outcomes, while an interpretivist can understand power as a shared system of meaning among a family unit (Baxter & Asbury, 2015). In contrast, critical research moves beyond predictive and explanatory approaches to the social world adopted by postpositivists and interpretivists (Morrow & Brown, 1994). Being critical of the social world means researchers are pointedly detecting and unmasking forms of social/cultural domination in everyday communication practices (e.g., Usher, 1996) or in this case everyday family situations. Critical family researchers assume systems of power must be re-structured so that social systems are free of privilege and domination. Power restructuration is a catalyst for positive social change where people can equally engage in the world around them (Morrow & Brown, 1994). Understanding the ways power, domination, and oppression imbue everyday family interactions is a gateway to emancipate structurally oppressed persons and groups (Morrow & Brown, 1994).

Similar to interpretivism and postpositivism, there is not a universal understanding of critical meta-theory. Some scholars challenge the traditional postpositivist, interpretive, and critical meta-theoretical tripartite because no approach is all embracing. Rather, each approach represents a cluster of approaches that bear some resemblance to each other. Critical meta-theory, then, has many strands within it that constitute the larger meta-theoretical perspective. For example, critical organizational communication scholars Deetz (2001) and Mumby (1997) distinguish the critical modern tradition from the critical postmodern tradition, with respect to their conceptualizations of power and envisioning of social change.

Since then, other family studies scholars have followed suit (e.g., Baxter & Asbury, 2015; Baxter & Braithwaite, 2008). Each approach within critical meta-theory is unique and could easily be discussed on its own. But, for the sake of succinctness and clarity, this chapter speaks about the critical approach as one comprehensive framework.

Methods from the broad critical orientation are largely consistent with those of interpretive research, some including ethnography, open-ended interviews, and case studies. The difference between the two orientations lies in the analytic approach; critical family scholars are in the business to critique rather than describe or explain social phenomena. This can be done using critical discourse analysis, critical textual analysis or even phenomenology. Though qualitative analyses are common in this research tradition, critical scholars of a certain strand, such as critical realists, also embrace quantitative methods (i.e., lab interaction, survey, quantitative content analysis). Using methods commonly employed by postpositivists can be embraced and not disowned because quantitative methods are powerful and enable ways to document inequality. Although the critical orientation comes in many shapes and sizes, critical family researchers are universally invested in one general goal, which is to identify discourses that reinforce the structural domination of one group by another within families so that a new system of social interaction can be instituted.

The critical perspective is an underutilized approach within family and interpersonal communication. In fact, according to Baxter and Braithwaite (2008), 83.2% of interpersonal communication scholarship published between 1990 and 2005 was submitted from a normative tradition, dominating the mere 13.9% of interpretive scholarship and a meager 2.9% using a critical/cultural perspective. The critical approach is common in family communication research, but it is still extremely underutilized (Stamp, 2004). Needless to say, critical research on dark-side family communication is scant. Nevertheless there are a few noteworthy studies to review.

For the most part, a critical approach to dark-side family research entails a heightened awareness of power differentials and their embeddedness in the family unit as well as the larger social structure. Metts and Asbury (2014) concluded that the family system and larger society have a bidirectional relationship: the family shapes social systems, but the social systems also structure the family. A host of research examines the latter relationship to expose the omnipresence of dominant family discourses diffused from a greater social structure into the family unit. The dominant discourses reward families who adhere to its strict standards and, conversely, harm families who do not. A common way to interrogate this relationship is to study how "nonnormative" families challenge the superiority of dominant family discourses. For example, Baxter, Norwood, Asbury, and Scharp (2014) analyzed online stories of domestic adoption narrated by adoptive parents.

From these stories, they identified four discourses of adoption challenging the idea that adoption is secondary to biological reproduction. Many families in the study legitimated their family identity and negated and countered the dominant discourse by embracing alternate family discourses. In accordance with the critical perspective, this research exposed the social reality that not all family discourses are equally valued and legitimated in U.S. American culture. Thus some families face more challenges to establish a strong family identity than others.

In a related study using online adoption stories, Baxter, Scharp, Asbury, Jannusch, and Norwood (2012) explored the construction of birth mother identity for women who relinquished their children for adoption. The researchers examined birth mother identity against the pervasive "intensive mother ideology." The intensive mothering discourse set conditions under which women were considered an ideal or good mother. These traits included selflessness, intense displays of unconditional love for the child, a source for material resources (e.g., clothing, education), and member of a nuclear family. With this in mind, the researchers were interested in whether one of the dominant discourses was privileged in the birth mother's identity construction. The researchers found that birth mothers co-opted the conditions of an intensive mothering ideology and transformed the mother discourse so that they could construct their own positive mother identity. Similar to the first study, the researchers from the second study used a form of inductive discourse analysis to expose the tension and inequality between these two competing discourses. According to the critical perspective, the differential privilege some families received over other families was a consequence of the unjust power structures imbedded in U.S. culture. The findings illustrate that families facing external hostilities can communicatively resist in the short term and potentially build resilience in the long term.

Family scholars have also used quantitative methodologies to critically explore the dark side of family life. For example, DePaulo has crafted a long-standing research program devoted to the study of people who are not married, have no children, and/or experience long-term singleness (DePaulo & Morris, 2005). In one of her studies, DePaulo and colleagues conducted a series of experiments that evidenced housing discrimination against singles compared to married and cohabitating couples (Morris, DePaulo, Hertel, & Taylor, 2008; Morris, Sinclair, & DePaulo, 2007). Singlehood, similar to adoption, is a nonnormative family form in the U.S. In fact, DePaulo wrote that single people are often described with shorthand words and colloquialisms, such as "alone," "unattached," and "with no one" because the common way of thinking is that single people have no family (DePaulo, 2012). Even though DePaulo's work is not explicitly critical, it does expose and challenge existing systematic power differentials that operate to unjustly discriminate against men and women who live a single life. Quantitative research methods not only allow her to understand the dark sides of single life but also expose the light sides. She has demystified the negative untruths about singlehood as well as enlightened people's perceptions of the overall benefits of singlehood. For instance, DePaulo (2011) openly critiqued a multitude of research studies establishing marriage as a healthy and advantageous life experience. She warns that scholars should not let their cultural presumptions about marriage influence the way they conduct and interpret the research; research should not be biased toward married—or even single—people, "but should be based on the highest scientific standards" (DePaulo 2011, p. 435). Her line of quantitative research interrogates the unpleasant picture of singleness and exposes the possibility that people can live a healthy and full life as a single person. The qualitative and quantitative studies discussed above exemplify the ways critical research can expose the dark and light hues of family realities.

Conducting dark-side family research from a critical perspective can pose its own ethical challenges that are distinct from postpositivist and interpretive work. Many critical family scholars advocate for a more reflexive and relational approach to knowledge building. Unlike scholars from other methodological perspectives, critical family scholars are more inclined to saturate every aspect of the research process with their personal morals, values, feelings, and experiences. This particular axiological commitment enables critical family researchers to reconstruct the normative research tradition by highlighting the concerns of family members that are typically silenced and ignored, such as the elderly, mentally unstable, and single. Engaging vulnerable groups like the ones mentioned adds more depth and complexity to dark-side family research but also provides an arena for informants to confide in a nonthreatening and non–family-related entity.

The potential benefits are, however, accompanied by serious risks for the researcher and participants. For instance, this line of work might enhance the emotional labor that is already associated with dark family research. We encourage scholars from this tradition to be more thoughtful and reflexive about their close positionality to the families. There are also emotional challenges for the participants. For example, research on family incest, intimate partner violence, corporal punishment, and elder abuse might examine the way power dynamics are enacted in family interactions between systemically privileged and disenfranchised family members. Asking participants to discuss the harmful and unjust treatment they experience at the hand of a "loved" one might place them in a precarious position with the abuser after the study concludes. At minimum, participants are reliving negative experiences that might cause them anguish and distress. With this in mind, critical scholars have to consider the calculation of harm when exploring these sensitive topics. One important way to protect the participants from undue harm is to provide counseling and debriefing resources and enhance the anonymity and confidentiality of their responses. In most instances, scholars should consult their human subjects board, as well as local family counselors who are knowledgeable about the issue under investigation, to protect the participant's safety and general well-being. This line of research is certainly risky but also proves to be advantageous for furthering our knowledge on family dynamics and facilitating new research that can improve family interactions.

Existing dark-side research has effectively studied family life from the post-positivist, interpretive, and critical traditions, but there are opportunities to extend this research in new ways. The second half of this chapter discusses the potential of using *multiple* frameworks to study the shades of family life.

EXPLORING THE SHADES OF GRAY OF FAMILY COMMUNICATION WITH A NEW APPROACH

Each meta-theoretical orientation comes with unique ontological, epistemological, and axiological commitments that guide the types of questions posed and therefore the types of conclusions that can be drawn. When the dark side is studied from only one perspective, then the conclusions and implications are one dimensional. But dark communication may actually have shades of gray or even beams of light. These complexities might go unnoticed in family research because scholars are only using one meta-theoretical approach to study one end of the dark-light spectrum. For example, work from the postpositivist tradition may test whether certain communication strategies are unhealthy for a person or relationship. This approach, however, might miss the inherent power structures that shape how a destructive message is delivered or received. Interpretive work, for example, may capture the ways in which people attach similar meanings to a communication exchange, but the research cannot predict which families will (not) be resilient in the situation. The two approaches ask different kinds of questions but are equally necessary. Researchers should understand the context of the communication environment while also revealing the conditions under which people fare better after an interaction. This multiparadigmatic approach can allow researchers to develop practical strategies that help families emerge from the darkness.

Admittedly, this approach is not new to family research. There are a number of family studies scholars who adopt two or more theoretical perspectives in their work. But researchers studying the dark side of family life rarely utilize this approach. We argue that studying dark-side family communication from multiple perspectives allows scholars to highlight the potentiality to brighten grim family realities. The following sections discuss existing studies from one perspective to explore the possibility of extending the research with an additional approach.

Combining Postpositivist and Interpretive Approaches

Researchers sometimes combine postpositivist and interpretivist approaches in their research. In fact, both of our (the authors') scholarly identities are firmly situated in the idea that triangulated approaches can provide incredible richness to a topic. The triangulation of multiple methods, however, tends to be more common in data collection than it is in the publication of the manuscripts that emerge from that data collection. Space limitations in journals often prevent the ability to present both quantitative and qualitative results in one article. As a result, the "true" picture regarding the data often lies in multiple manuscripts that are published off of a data set. Researchers also tend to assume that qualitative research is a first step to quantitative research. But qualitative research is an end in and of itself and can also be used to help explain quantitative results. For example, Afifi, Olson, and Armstrong (2005) examined the chilling effect of family secrets. They used data from 170 families with parents and siblings and examined how family members' reasons for withholding information influenced their decisions to reveal or continue to conceal secrets from other members of their family. Part of their statistical model, however, was not significant, and they wondered why. So the researchers interviewed a small subset of participants from their sample about their secret keeping to further explore the paths in the model. The qualitative results revealed other variables that played a prominent role in family members' decisions to conceal or reveal secrets that were not included in the original path model. Not only did the interpretive work follow and enhance the postpositivist work in the same manuscript, but it provided heuristic potential for future research.

Many dark-side family research studies use one approach but could be adapted to incorporate other approaches. For example, a study by Braithwaite and Baxter (2006) used relational dialectics theory to understand the relational complexities between college-aged stepchildren and the children's nonresidential parents (parent living outside of the stepfamily boundary). The researchers used an interpretive approach because it allowed the children to construct their own meanings of the relationship. Results suggested that two interlocking contradictions—parenting/not parenting and openness/closedness—animated stepchildren's perceptions of the relationship. More specifically, the children wanted a close relationship with their nonresidential parent but had divided loyalties between the residential and nonresidential parent. The children's desire for a close parent-child relationship was accompanied by a competing perception that the nonresidential parents were unavailable and a source of disruption in the children's lives. Both contradictions illuminated the difficulties, awkwardness, and challenges of communication in a stepfamily living arrangement. Adding empirical tests to studies like Braithwaite and Baxter (2006) could further substantiate the authors' claims and also allow them to advance communication strategies that help stepfamilies. Braithwaite and Baxter discussed practical applications for stepfamilies at the end of their study. They proposed that nonresidential parents and stepfamily members dually support and encourage stepchildren through their transition from an intact to a stepfamily structure. Adding an intervention from a postpositivist perspective is a great way to test which behaviors are catalysts for positive change in the family. The researchers could ask the stepchildren to list behaviors they think are helpful, supportive, and encouraging and train the children's parents and other stepfamily members to do those behaviors at home. After a week, the children could complete a survey with items on relational closeness and satisfaction with the nonresidential parent, level of comfort when communicating with their nonresidential parent, and feelings of being caught in between both parents. The interpretive and postpositivist approaches combined extend knowledge in this area of research while also helping families realize behaviors *they* consider healthy and beneficial.

Interpretive work provides an important foundation that postpositivists can extend with empirical tests. Both approaches show families how to be resilient in ways that are meaningful to them. In other instances, postpositivist research makes initial claims about (un)helpful family communication patterns that interpretivists can extend. For example, Suter and Ballard (2009) investigated remarks international adoptive families (child adopted from China) receive from outsiders about their family identity. The study surveyed a national sample of international adoptive families, who answered a variety of open-ended questions. These included ways families responded to remarks from outsiders (defined by the family and not the researchers), the decision-making criteria underlying their responses, and changes to their responses over time. The results illuminated fundamental criteria that influence how parents respond to others' identity-challenging remarks. The study focused on the verbal response, but families may respond nonverbally or even dismiss the comment altogether. A useful interpretive slant to this body of research could ask international adoptive families to define what a successful response means to them in this situation. Success may carry different meanings for different families. It could also be helpful for adoptive families to generate example responses they consider successful to enhance knowledge of communication experiences in adoptive families. A later study could use those data to test which messages foster more family resilience to external hostilities.

Most studies examine families from one meta-theoretical approach, and the reasons for doing so are stated explicitly by the researchers. But adding a second theoretical component to the study might enrich the conclusions and practical implications for the types of families being studied. Postpositivist and interpretive approaches cohere with each other in studies because inductive data can provide a more complete picture of a complex empirical phenomenon. Other approaches, however, like a postpositivist and critical approach, may not closely align and are often in direct opposition to one another. In the section that follows, however, we demonstrate how and why they might be able to inform each other in the same body of work.

Combining Postpositivist and Critical Approaches

Abuse in the family is a common topic studied in dark-side research, and it offers a useful set of scholarship to illustrate a dual postpositivist and critical approach. Many dark-side communication researchers use a postpositivist approach to study abuse in the family, such as corporal punishment and elder abuse, but few scholars approach abuse from a critical lens. A few studies, however, uncover communication processes saturated with power dynamics and ripe for a critical analysis. As such, critical and postpositivist approaches could be paired to enhance dark-side family research collectively.

Early research stated that corporal punishment can be harmful to children and the parent-child relationship. Grounded in the communication skills deficiency model, earlier researchers believed that people get physically and verbally aggressive when they lack the skills necessary to diffuse a conflict situation Infante, Sabourin, Rudd, & Shannon, 1990; Infante & Wigley, 1986; Sabourin, Infante, & Rudd, 1993). More recent research has established that parents with high levels of perceived and self-reported verbal aggression tend to use more corporal punishment on their children (e.g., Roberto, Carlyle, & Goodall, 2007; Roberto, Carlyle, & McClure, 2006). Child and family research also indicates that a history of parental maltreatment during childhood also heightens the likelihood for perpetuating maltreatment on future generations. When people received high levels of corporal punishment during their childhood, they report having higher levels of anger and assault tendencies and are more likely to use corporal punishment on their own children (e.g., Kassing, Pearce, Infante, & Pyles, 1999; Toth, Pickrign, & Gravener, 2009).

Not to negate the validity of these results, but the findings illuminate surface-level relationships that veil deeply structured inequalities. In some instances, harmful corporal punishment practices can be intentionally used as a parent's response to institutional racism (e.g., Ispa & Halgunseth, 2004) and other social realities in a child's future (Taylor, Hamvas, & Paris, 2011). Scholars researching this topic could think more critically about the social position of some parents and why certain parenting strategies are used rather than others. For instance, research suggests that some Black American parents support the use of nonabusive corporal punishment for disciplining their children (e.g., Ispa & Halgunseth, 2004). In a qualitative study, Ispa and Halgunseth (2004) noted that the Black mothers relied on strict, controlling parenting styles to teach their children that there are negative consequences for poor behavior. According to the mothers, their Black sons and daughters must know the inevitable reality that they will encounter external hostilities at higher rates than children of other races. Some Black mothers in the study avowed to use corporal punishment because they "see little room for error" concerning their children's future in a racist society. They may even continue to

278 | SHARDÉ DAVIS AND TAMARA D. AFIFI

discipline their children in this manner knowing that it positively predicts aggressive behavior problems and cognitive development difficulties in their children (Berlin et al., 2009). According to this research, institutional structures necessitate Black parents' use of disciplinary strategies that U.S. culture deems negative but the parents find helpful. It would be useful for abuse research to recognize that children are not faced with the same life circumstances, and families adopt behaviors that befit their unique situations. This is not to say a study should establish that corporal punishment is good or healthy for families. Rather, future studies could reveal inherent power differentials saturating parents' disciplining practices. One way to extend the traditional (post)positivist research is to add a critical component. Doing so begins to dismantle the good-bad binary in dark family research that privileges the behaviors of certain families (e.g., nuclear, white, high socioeconomic status) over others (e.g., poor families of color). For instance, Black mothers could identify specific nonabusive corporal punishment behaviors they use, enact and researchers could determine the effectiveness of those culturally sensitive discipline strategies. Perhaps their forms of physical discipline are ineffective parenting strategies but serve as a powerful agent for racial socialization for their children. This idea does not, in any way, legitimize abuse. Instead, researchers could interrogate the functions of physical discipline in Black families to devise more effective and less abusive discipline strategies that Black mothers are inclined to implement in their households. Examining dialectical tensions such as this is one way to situate communication experiences in their power-laden contexts.

Similar to the child abuse and corporal punishment research, the small but notable elder abuse research tests the prevalence, forms, and predictors of elder abuse accounts (see Giles & Helmle, 2011). More recently, Lin and Giles (2012) advanced a power-oriented communication model integrating dyadic influences between the elder care receiver and family caregiver that ignite the elder abuse (see Lin, Giles, & Soliz in this volume for a review). The model posits that family caregivers with certain profiles (e.g., history of substance abuse, mental health issues) will enact abusive behaviors when the person receiving care displays nonaccommodative behaviors. The noncompliance of the elder can trigger the caregiver's threat-oriented schema, predicting perceived powerlessness and lack of control in the situation. The nonaccommodation incites negative emotions and consequently an abusive response style. The model explicitly identifies power in that it emphasizes the abusers' perceived powerlessness. The researchers' postpositivistic approach enabled the discovery of a holistic elder abuse process, in which they considered the direct and indirect role of multiple factors.

Indeed, Lin and Giles's (2012) power-based model extends elder abuse research by focusing more on the types of people that enact abuse and less on the prevalence of abuse in families. A critical component could be added to uncover the classist underpinnings of elder abuse that the research may have overlooked. That is, people from a lower socioeconomic status may be more likely to display the background characteristics of an abuser: history of substance abuse and poor mental health, verbal aggressiveness, and overly distressed. These behaviors might have biological or social explanations, but they can also spring from class inequalities imbedded in their everyday lives. For example, they can experience high levels of stress from class-related life strains that compound caregiving stress. They can also have limited access to mental and psychological treatment yet easy access to drugs and alcohol in their living environment. All of these reasons contribute to poor mental health and aggressive behaviors. Future scholars could also conduct a critical ethnography in a low-income neighborhood. Adding rich ethnographic data to the elder abuse study uncovers structural factors underlying abuse for certain disenfranchised groups. Family caregivers may be more willing to embrace new solutions that reduce abuse incidents when the perpetrator is more accurately defined as being embedded in a flawed social structure rather than a flawed individual or group of people.

A new meta-theoretical approach not only extends theorizing and empirical tests of these communication topics but also extends an opportunity to explore the light side of these situations in productive ways. For example, research recognizing that mothers use corporal punishment to socialize their children enables future tests of Black family resilience and positive child development in a culturally accurate manner. Consequently, the research can help families move past the darkness and into the light.

Challenges and Benefits of a New Approach

Engaging in a new way of doing research is daunting and risky. One of the most glaring challenges to this new approach is addressing two sets of theoretical assumptions in one dark-side family research study. Approaching dark-side communication from one meta-theory poses its own challenges because it requires consistency between the research design and the underlying theoretical assumptions. Thus, dark-side research approached from two perspectives necessitates much more attention to internal consistency. In some instances, assumptions of both meta-theoretical perspectives do not cohere. For example, some traditional interpretivists emphasize the local participant's subjective perceptions of the social world and are concerned with understanding the meaning that an individual attaches to surrounding social phenomena. On the other hand, some postpositivist researchers are interested in studying social phenomena objectively in order to advance generalizable claims about group (rather than individual) behavior. This presents a challenge to conducting one study that meets all assumptions.

There are also execution challenges with a multilevel approach. Studies of this kind require a large-scale research design with elaborate methods and data collection protocol. As such, the researchers must be familiar with various research designs, methods, analyses, and reporting styles. Fourth, journal editors institute strict page limits to the manuscripts that can make it difficult to report results that involve triangulated data. Considering the magnitude of data produced from multilevel studies, researchers may not have enough page space to outline the study in an exhaustive manner. As such, scholars might be discouraged from taking multiple approaches. Finally, there are challenges with the acceptance of multi–meta-theoretical research. Scholars hope their colleagues will evaluate their research favorably, but combining certain approaches, such as postpositivism and critical cultural approaches, might initially result in rejection from peers and journal reviewers. Researchers across academic fields do not agree on all matters of meta-theory and philosophy. In fact, readers might well scrutinize the claims posed in this chapter because they push traditional approaches to research. But if researchers do not journey down unchartered territory, then they miss opportunities for new discoveries that extend current thinking and theory. We encourage family studies scholars to experiment with multiple approaches or co-author with people who are experts in another area to increase their research's appeal and legitimacy over time.

Indeed, this new approach requires some risks (some of which are noted above). But there is an overflow of benefits for dark-side family research if it is done well. As it was aforementioned, dark-side family research is complex because there are many shades to the darkness. Researchers should approach the phenomenon in various ways to elucidate people's experiences in their entirety. Revealing all aspects of the dark side enables scholars to gain a holistic picture of family interaction, in turn helping families in need. One way to make this approach more accessible is to use two theoretical approaches that align to some degree. For instance, postpositivism and critical realism may cohere because both approaches are committed to an external world existing beyond human knowledge. The types of information that come from both traditions are equally valuable and, when combined, could illuminate more about dark and light shades of communication than they do independently. Interpretivists and critical postmodernists also privilege the shared-meaning making process within the family and agree that the social world is discursively constituted in communication. Perhaps the critical realist and critical postmodernist could extend postpositivist and interpretivist work by overlaying their respective sensitivities to power.

This approach also lends an opportunity for collaboration in all fields interested in the study of families. Approaching one's research from an entirely different perspective is a hefty task. Consequently, family scholars across fields should collaborate with each other to approach the same dark-side phenomena in different yet equally meaningful ways. In fact, family studies scholars in the field of Communication have expressed the need for more critical research and made strides to conduct this type of research with family scholars in other areas. Loreen

Olsen raised this issue in her introduction to the 2012 volume of *Journal of Family Communication* and even invited family studies scholars Few-Demo, Lloyd, and Allen (2014) to write an essay applying critical feminist perspectives to the study of family interaction and communication in this book. More recently, Leslie Baxter (2014) published an edited book exploring the ways postnuclear families are communicatively constructing alterative meanings of "family." Also, special issue co-editors Elizabeth Suter and Sandra Faulkner are devoting one issue for critical approaches to family communication research in the *Journal of Family Communication*. Redressing the underrepresentation of critical work in family studies will extend new opportunities for more dark-side family research from critical, feminist, postmodern/structuralist and other nondominant perspectives. Moreover, it will open the door for scholars to explore dark side family communication from multiple perspectives concurrently. Altogether, the benefits are abounding for researchers across multiple research traditions to come together to study the dark, gray, and light sides of family communication.

REFERENCES

Afifi, T. D., Merrill, A., & Davis, S. M. (2015). The theory of resilience and relational load (TRRL). Manuscript revised and resubmitted for publication at *Personal Relationships*.

Afifi, T. D., & Olson, L. N. (2005). The chilling effect in families and the pressure to conceal secrets. *Communication Monographs, 72*, 192–216. doi: 10.1080/03637750500111906

Afifi, T. D., Olson, L., & Armstrong, C. (2005). The chilling effect and family secrets: Examining the role of self protection, other protection, and communication efficacy. *Human Communication Research, 31*, 564–598. doi: 10.1093/hcr/31.4.564

Baxter, L. A. (2014). *Remaking "family" communicatively*. New York, NY: Peter Lang Publishing.

Baxter, L. A., & Asbury, B. (2015). Critical approaches to interpersonal communication: Charting a future. In D. O. Braithwaite & P. Schrodt (Eds.), *Engaging theories in interpersonal communication* (2nd ed., pp. 189–201). Thousand Oaks, CA: Sage Publications.

Baxter, L., & Braithwaite, D. (2008). Introduction: Metatheory and theory in interpersonal communication research. In L. Baxter & D. Braithwaite (Eds.), *Engaging in theories of interpersonal communication: Multiple perspectives* (pp. 1–18). Thousand Oaks, CA: Sage Publications.

Baxter, L., Braithwaite, D., Bryant, L., & Wagner, A. (2004). Stepchildren's perceptions of the contradictions in communication with stepparents. *Journal of Social and Personal Relationships, 21*, 447–467. doi: 10.1177/0265407504044841

Baxter, L. A., Norwood, K. N., Asbury, B., & Scharp, K. M. (2014). Narrating adoption: Resisting adoption as "second best" in online stories of domestic adoption told by adoptive parents. *Journal of Family Communication, 14*(3), 253–269. doi: 10.1080/15267431.2014.908199

Baxter, L. A., Scharp, K. M., Asbury, B., Jannusch, A., & Norwood, K. N. (2012). "Birth mothers are not bad people": A dialogic analysis of online birth mother stories. *Qualitative Communication Research, 1*(1), 53–82.

Berlin, L. J., Ispa, J., Fine, M. A., Malone, P. S., Brooks-Gunn, J., Brady-Smith, C., Ayoub, C., & Bai, Y. (2009). Correlates and consequences of spanking and verbal punishment for low-income

White, African American, and Mexican American toddlers. *Child Development, 80*(5), 1403–1420. doi: 10.1111/j.1467-8624.2009.01341.x

Braithwaite, D. O., & Baxter, L. A. (2006). "You're my parent but you're not": Dialectical tensions in stepchildren's perceptions about communicating with the nonresidential parent. *Journal of Applied Communication Research, 34*(1), pp. 30–48. doi: 10.1080/00909880500420200

Carter, S. M., & Little, M. (2007). Justifying knowledge, justifying method, taking action: Epistemologies, methodologies, and methods in qualitative research. *Qualitative Health Research, 17,* 1316–1328. doi: 10.1177/1049732307306927

Creswell, J. W. (1998). *Qualitative inquiry and research design: Choosing among five traditions.* Thousand Oaks, CA: Sage Publications.

Deetz, S. (2001). Conceptual foundations. In F. M. Jablin & L. L. Putnam (Eds.), *The new handbook of organizational communication: Advances in theory, research, and methods* (pp. 3–46). Thousand Oaks, CA: Sage Publications.

DePaulo, B. (2011). Living single: Lightening up those dark, dopey myths. In W. R. Cupach & B. H. Spitzberg (Eds.), *The dark side of close relationships II* (pp. 409–439). New York, NY: Routledge.

DePaulo, B. (2012). Single, no children: Who is your family? In A. Vangelisti (Ed.), *Routledge handbook of family communication* (2nd ed., pp. 190–204). New York, NY: Routledge.

DePaulo, B. M., & Morris, W. L. (2005). Singles in society and in science. *Psychological Inquiry, 16*(2–3), 57–83. doi: 10.1080/1047840X.2005.9682918

Eckstein, N. (2004). Emergent issues in families experiencing child-to-parent abuse. *Western Journal of Communication, 68,* 365–388. doi: 10.1080/10570310409374809

Feeney, B. C., & Lemay, E. P. (2012). Surviving relationship threats: The role of emotional capital. *Personality and Social Psychology Bulletin, 38,* 1004–1017. doi: 10.1177/0146167212442971

Few-Demo, A. L., Lloyd, S. A., & Allen, K. R. (2014). It's all about power: Integrating feminist family studies and family communication. *Journal of Family Communication, 14,* 85–94. doi: 10.1080/15267431.2013.864295

Giles, H., & Helmle, J. (2011). Elder abuse and neglect: A communication framework. In A. Duszak & U. Okulska (Eds.), *Language, culture and the dynamics of age* (pp. 223–252). Berlin, Germany: Mouton de Gruyter.

Given, L. M. (2008). *The encyclopedia of qualitative research.* Thousand Oaks, CA: Sage Publications. doi: http://dx.doi.org/10.4135/9781412963909

Golish, T. D. (2003). Stepfamily communication strengths: Understanding the ties that bind. *Human Communication Research, 29,* 41–80. doi: 10.1111/j.1468-2958.2003.tb00831.x

Gottman, J. M., Driver, J., & Tabares, A. (2002). Building the sound marital house: An empirically derived couple therapy. In A. S. Gurman & N. S. Jacobson (Eds.), *Clinical handbook of couple therapy* (3rd ed., pp. 373–399). New York, NY: Guilford.

Harding, S. (1987). *Feminism and methodology.* Milton Keynes: Open University Press.

Horan, S., & Booth-Butterfield, M. (2010). Is it worth lying for? Physiological and emotional implications of recalling deceptive affection. *Human Communication Research, 37,* 78–106. doi: 10.1111/j.1468-2958.2010.01394.x

Horan, S., & Booth-Butterfield, M. (2013). Understanding the routine expression of deceptive affection in romantic relationships. *Communication Quarterly, 61,* 195–216. doi: 10.1080/01463373.2012.751435

Infante, D. A., Sabourin, T. C., Rudd, J. E., & Shannon, E. A. (1990). Verbal aggression in violent and nonviolent marital disputes. *Communication Quarterly, 38,* 361–371. doi: 10.1080/01463379009369773

Infante, D. A., & Wigley, C. J. (1986). Verbal aggressiveness: An interpersonal model and measure. *Communication Monographs, 53*, 61–69. doi: 10.1080/03637758609376126

Ispa, M., & Halgunseth, L. C. (2004). Talking about corporal punishment: Nine low-income African American mothers' perspectives. *Early Childhood Research Quarterly, 19*, 463–484. doi: 10.1016/j.ecresq.2004.07.002

Kassing, J. W., Pearce, K., Infante, D., & Pyles, S. (1999). Exploring the communicative nature of corporal punishment. *Communication Research Reports, 16*(1), 18–28. doi: 10.1080/08824099909388697

Lin, M., & Giles, H. (2012). The dark side of family communication: A communication model of elder abuse and neglect. *International Psychogeriatrics, 25*(8), 1275–1290. doi: 10.1017/S1041610212002347

McEwen, B. S. (1998). Protective and damaging effects of stress mediators. *New England Journal of Medicine, 338*, 171–179. doi: http://dx.doi.org/10.1016/S0079-6123(08)62128-7

McLaren, R. M., & Sillars, A. (in press). Hurtful episodes in parent-adolescent relationships: How accounts and attributions contribute to the difficulty of talking about hurt. *Communication Monographs.*

McLaren, R. M., & Solomon, D. H. (2008). Appraisal and distancing responses in response to hurtful messages. *Communication Research, 35*, 339–357. doi: 10.1177/0093650208315961

Metts, S., & Asbury, B. (2014). Theoretical approaches to family communication. In L. H. Turner & R. West (Eds.), *The Sage handbook of family communication* (pp. 41–57). Thousand Oaks, CA: Sage Publications.

Miller, G., Chen, E., & Zhou, E. (2007). If it goes up, must it come down? Chronic stress and the hypothalamic-pituitary-adrenocortical axis in humans. *Psychological Bulletin, 133*, 25–45. http://dx.doi.org/10.1037/0033-2909.133.1.25

Morris, W. L., DePaulo, B. M., Hertel, J., & Taylor, L. C. (2008). Singlism—another problem that has no name: Prejudice, stereotypes, and discrimination against singles. In M. A. Morrison & T. G. Morrison (Eds.), *The psychology of modern prejudice* (pp. 165–194). New York, NY: Nova Science Publishers.

Morris, W. L., Sinclair, S., & DePaulo, B. M. (2007). No shelter for singles: The perceived legitimacy of marital status discrimination. *Group Processes & Intergroup Relations, 10*(4), 457–470. doi: 10.1177/1368430207081535

Morrow, R. A., & Brown, D. (1994). *Critical theory and methodology.* Thousand Oaks, CA: Sage Publications.

Moustakas, C. (1994). *Phenomenological research methods.* Thousand Oaks, CA: Sage Publications.

Mumby, D. K. (1997). Modernism, postmodernism, and communication studies: A rereading of an ongoing debate. *Communication Theory, 7*, 1–28. doi: 10.1111/j.1468-2885.1997.tb00140.x

Olson, L. N., Baiocchi-Wagner, E. A. Wilson-Kratzer, J. M., & Symonds, S. E. (2012). *The dark side of family communication.* Cambridge, MA: Polity Press.

Philips, D. C., & Burbules, N. C. (2000). *Postpositivism and educational research.* Lanham & Boulder: Rowman & Littlefield Publishers.

Roberto, A., Carlyle, K., & Goodall, C. (2007). Communication and corporal punishment: The relationship between self-reported parent verbal and physical aggression. *Communication Research Reports, 24*(2), 103–111. doi: 10.1080/08824090701304741

Roberto, A. J., Carlyle, K. E., & McClure, L. (2006). Communication and corporal punishment: The relationship between parents' use of verbal and physical aggression. *Communication Research Reports, 23*(1), 27–33. doi: 10.1080/17464090500535848

Sabourin, T. C., Infante, D. A., & Rudd, J. E. (1993). Verbal aggression in marriages: A comparison of violent, distressed but nonviolent, and nondistressed couples. *Human Communication Research, 20*, 245–267. doi: 10.1111/j.1468-2958.1993.tb00323.x

Schrodt, P., Braithwaite, D., Soliz, J., Tye-Williams, S., Miller, A., Normand, E. A., & Harrigan, A. A. (2007). An examination of everyday talk in stepfamily systems. *Western Journal of Communication, 71*, 216–234. doi: 10.1080/10570310701510077

Sousa, C., Herrenkohl, T., Moylan, C., Tajima, E., Klika, J., Herrenkel, R., & Russo, M. (2011). Longitudinal study on the effects of child abuse and children's exposure to domestic violence, parent-child attachments, and antisocial behavior in adolescence. *Journal of Interpersonal Violence, 26*, 111–138. doi: 10.1177/0886260510362883

Stamp, G. H. (2004). Theories of family relationships and a family relationships theoretical model. In A. L. Vangelisti (Ed.), *The handbook of family communication* (pp. 1–30). Mahwah, NJ: Lawrence Erlbaum Associates.

Suter, E. A., & Ballard, R. L. (2009). "How much did you pay for her?": Decision-making criteria underlying adoptive parents' responses to inappropriate remarks. *Journal of Family Communication, 9*(2), 107–125. doi: 10.1080/15267430902773253

Taylor, C. A., Hamvas, L., & Paris, R. (2011). Perceived instrumentality and normativeness of corporal punishment use among black mothers. *Family Relations, 60*(1), 60–72. doi: 10.1111/j.1741-3729.2010.00633.x

Toth, S., Pickrign, E., & Gravener, J. (2009). Child abuse and neglect. In H. Reis & S. Sprecher (Eds.), *Sage encyclopedia of human relationships* (pp. 207–211). Thousand Oaks, CA: Sage Publications.

Usher, R. (1996). A critique of the neglected epistemological assumptions of education research. In D. Scott & R. Usher (Eds.), *Understanding educational research* (pp. 9–32). London, UK: Routledge.

Vangelisti, A. L. (1994). Family secrets: Forms, functions, and correlates. *Journal of Social and Personal Relationships, 11*, 113–135. doi: 10.1177/0265407594111007

Vangelisti, A. L., & Caughlin, J. P. (1997). Revealing family secrets: The influence of topic, function, and relationship. *Journal of Social and Personal Relationships, 14*, 679–705. doi: 10.1177/0265407597145006

Vangelisti, A. L., & Young, S. L. (2000). When words hurt: The effects of perceived intentionality on interpersonal relationships. *Journal of Social & Personal Relationships, 17*, 393. doi: 10.1177/0265407500173005

CHAPTER FOURTEEN

Foucault, Poststructural Feminism, AND THE Family

Posing New Questions, Pursuing New Possibilities

LYNN M. HARTER, CHAREE M. THOMPSON, &
RAYMIE E. MCKERROW***

Family communication scholars are concerned with processes that shape, maintain, and shift familial relationships. Though scholars adopt divergent approaches to the study of family communication, they generally define and theorize about family from a social constructionist standpoint (Turner & West, 2014; Vangelisti, 2013). A social construction orientation considers interactions between individuals as the defining qualities of family relationships. Since family communication coalesced as a distinct field of study in the 1970s (Galvin & Braithwaite, 2014), a burgeoning literature has yielded a greater understanding of how families navigate the development, maintenance, and dissolution of their relationships through communication. Existing literature has elucidated the complexities of family life, including difficult experiences such as partner violence, jealousy and envy, and parent-child abuse. Although attention has been paid to "the darker side" of relationships, the discipline remains stymied with the question, "How does one theorize—comprehensively—the dark side of communication within the family?" (Olson, Baiocchi-Wagner, Kratzer, & Symonds, 2012, p. ix).

Olson and colleagues (2012) developed the Darkness Model of Family Communication to explore interconnections between the "what" (i.e., dark messages, dark outcomes) and the "how" (i.e., meaning-making processes) of morally suspect,

---

*** The authors share equal responsibility for and authorship of this chapter.

socially unacceptable, and even harmful family patterns. In the original presentation of their model, Olson et al. urged critical communication scholars to join the conversation driven heretofore by a focus on topics (e.g., teasing, bullying, sexual aggression) rather than process. Others have made similar calls (e.g., Few-Demo, Lloyd, & Allen, 2014; Olson, 2012; Suter & Faulkner, 2014), and so we accepted the invitation to pen this chapter. Generally, critical scholars are theoretically equipped to explore the situated, interrelated, and multivocal discourses through which power relations are continually constructed, masked, and contested (Dow & Condit, 2005). In this chapter, we rely on critical theory to recast three major approaches to the study of family communication: storytelling; privacy management; and stress, coping, and support. We selected privacy management and storytelling because theorizing about them originated in the field of communication studies (Braithwaite & Baxter, 2006; Galvin & Braithwaite, 2014). We include stress, coping, and support because much theorizing among communication studies scholars and those in allied fields centers on the experiences and consequences of crisis and change in families, including implications for stress, coping, and support (Maguire, 2012). In doing so, we offer a fresh perspective for exploring perennial concerns of interest to family communication scholars.

This chapter unfolds in three parts. First, we articulate a critical communication framework inspired by the work of Michel Foucault. Foucault's work is complex and multifaceted, and a thorough review is beyond the scope of this chapter. Here our focus rests with his discussions of modernity, particularly his insights into the production of individuals and relationships by the prevailing language and structures of power. Next, we chart how contemporary poststructural feminists employ Foucault's work to explore the discursive nature of social control. Building from this foundation, we "widen the circle" of family communication research by posing questions that merit scholarly and practical attention (see Floyd & Morman, 2013). We do not claim that a Foucauldian and poststructural feminist lens can address all issues of importance to family communication scholars. Instead, we offer these conceptual ideas as a productive framework for exploring how control and resistance play out amid historically informed subjectivities.

FOUCAULT AND COMMUNICATION STUDIES

Critical studies take diverse forms guided by various theoretical approaches. A thorough review of critical traditions is beyond the scope of this chapter and is available elsewhere (e.g., Malpas & Wake, 2013; Ono, 2011). Although scholars (i.e., critics) differ in theory and methods of inquiry, generally they investigate exploitation, repression, social injustice, power relations, and distorted communication. In this section, we develop a critical framework informed by key principles in the works of Michel Foucault. This framework considers families, like other cultural institutions, to be composed of normalized patterns of behavior that discipline members. Generally speaking, we develop an orientation that requires courage on the part of the critic to challenge assumptions behind dominant and often taken-for-granted ways of perceiving, conceiving, and acting.

To begin, there is a duality in Foucault's orientation to the relationship between power and the subject. On the one hand, his critique challenges the constraining influences of power in subjecting individuals to normalized conventions of conduct. We are "effects of practices" that have preceded our being in the world. Within a world not of our own making, we are governed in large part by our own docile acceptance of what appear as normal "taken-for-granted" rules of conduct within society. In particular, the limits of the "sayable" condition us with respect to who might say what to whom under what circumstances with what consequences. On the other hand, none of these constraints or limits on what may be done or what may be said is written in stone—they are creations that may have preceded us but are vulnerable to critique and the possibility of change. As subjects, we also have freedom to become other than we are. While this may not be a limitless, all-encompassing freedom, it nonetheless permits one to, in Foucault's orientation, engage in practices of "care for the self." Such practices not only offer openings for a "new normal" but also may impact our ability to influence the conduct of others.

The tension between these orientations toward the subject defines human existence. As Foucault suggested, with respect to techniques of domination, of relations of power that engage one in governing the other, we must attend to those relations that "permit one to determine the conduct of individuals, to impose certain wills on them, and to submit them to certain ends or objectives" (Foucault, 1993, p. 203). Governing the conduct of others is not his sole concern. The personal care one engages in mandates an application of "techniques which permit individuals to affect, by their own means, a certain number of operations on their own bodies, on their own souls, on their own thoughts, on their own conduct, and this in a manner so as to transform themselves, modify themselves" (Allen, 2013, p. 346). Conceiving of subjects in this fashion permits a twin critique beginning with modernity's penchant for engaging in repressive tactics in controlling populations (juridical power is oriented toward punishing transgressions against the state or individual in accordance with normative guidelines for proper conduct). The second critique is more individualized—it permits one to assess the limits placed on personal conduct and determine which of these might need remediation in improving one's own self.

Foucault's critique of modernity provides an entrée into the possibilities for transformation in family relations. In particular, as McKerrow (1998) has noted, the traditional binaries that dominate the modern landscape—male/female, mind/body, reason/emotion, nature/culture, public/private—perpetuate a Western, white, male-dominant set of values that function to limit the possibilities of freedom for anyone not already part of the elite. Women, in particular, have historically been relegated the "weaker" of the binaries as their lot in life—their perceived reliance on emotion and their relegation to the private realm are key attributes, among others, positioning them as handmaidens to history. Adopting a "philosophical ethos" that he "characterized as a limit attitude," Foucault sought, through his own historical investigations, to unpack and potentially undermine the influence of "limits" (see Simons, 2013, pp. 301–302). His primary approach was:

> to analyze the process of "problematization" which means: how and why certain things (behavior, phenomena, processes) became a *problem*. Why, for example, certain forms of behavior were characterized and classified as "madness" while other similar forms were completely neglected at a given historical moment; the same thing for crime and delinquency, the same question of problematization for sexuality. (Foucault, 2001, p. 191; italics in original)

In assuming this approach, one asks why things are the way they are at a given point in time and across time and, in the process, challenges conventional understanding. For example: How did marriage come to be defined in spiritual terms? When and under what conditions is it possible to re-define and govern marriage from a secular standpoint? How did we come to define homosexuality as a sin rather than as an act of love toward another? What changed in permitting women to speak in public—how did their sense of a freedom to resist contribute to a fundamental shift in power relationships between men and women?

Although Foucault rejected the label, his perspective moves us into a postmodern world, wherein totalizing or universal "truths" are scrutinized and found lacking as groundings for belief or action. Instead of relying on truths external to human experience, Foucault's conviction is that truths are constructed through interaction with others. Hence, their presumed role as a "regime" or "game" of truth is open to question. These terms represent what he earlier referenced as "discursive formations," functioning as constellations within which normative judgments constrain or facilitate the process of governing oneself and others. In his view, "Truth is a thing of this world. … Each society has its regime of truth, its 'general politics' of truth: that is, the types of discourses which it accepts and makes function as true" (Foucault, 1980c, p. 131). This generalization applies to specific entities within society, such as a family unit; as we delineate later in this chapter, family discourse engages with truths in the same fashion. In essence, we authorize actions of control, as well as engagement with care of the self, through the language we employ in submitting to, or critiquing, "relations of power" (Foucault, 1980b, p. 291).[1]

Power, in and of itself, is not the key term—as power is neither a substance nor a possession. It rather exists in the "in-between" spaces that link one with others (Foucault, 1997, p. 291). In a move that reconceptualizes power as something more than a repressive force, he noted:

> If power were never anything but repressive, if it never did anything but to say no, do you really think one would be brought to obey it? What makes power hold good, what makes it accepted, is simply the fact that it doesn't only weigh on us as a force that says no, but that it traverses and produces things, it induces pleasure, forms knowledge, produces discourse. It needs to be considered as a productive network which runs through the whole social body, much more than as a negative instance whose function is repression. (Foucault, 1980b, p. 119)[2]

Conceived in this manner, power relations between manager and employee or between "husband and wife" are circumscribed by tradition. For example, the "husband/wife" phrase in wedding ceremonies permits the male to keep his subject status, while transforming the female's with a term of subordination. In similar fashion, the expression "don't tell your mother!" reflects an act of resistance to a mother's normative rule for allowing/disallowing certain behaviors on the part of children in the family. This is an example of the productive form a power relationship may take between father and son or daughter in establishing possibilities for "breaking the rules." When then encountering the mother, the child's immediate revelation ("Dad let us. …") changes the power dynamics once again, illustrating the ongoing, fluid nature of these patterns within lived experience.

Language does matter in understanding and critiquing the power "roles" that tradition dictates to society. It should be noted that in "unmasking" these relations, it is not the case that they are "hidden" from view; instead, they exist in plain sight but may not be "seen" as they have become conventional practices that people embrace without conscious awareness. Nor is it the case that these relations, once made salient, cannot be changed. As McKerrow (2011) noted:

> Power depends on freedom for its existence. In pure domination, there is no relationship possible, if one means by a relational tie the possibility of reversal. One cannot reverse power in an instance of pure domination. Power also demands the possibility, given some "margin of freedom," of resistance. (p. 264)

There is an old expression—"Seeing is believing"—that may assist in explaining the role that a perception of freedom engages: once one "sees" power relations in terms of their function to either inhibit or, in their productive sense, to enable, the possibility for change becomes real. It is not for Foucault to say what that change should be—only to suggest its possibility. We live resistance on a daily basis, whether it is ignoring our partner's request that we pay attention to our diet (while living the life of a couch potato eating chips) or in refusing to follow the dictates of a command. As Simons (2013) pointed out, Foucault "claims that resistance occurs because power relations do not solidify into states of domination so complete that they become physical determinations and subject people to the point of impotence" (p. 311).

Being within a power relation "does not [necessarily] mean one is trapped" and thus without the option of changing perceived "limits" on freedom to be otherwise engaged with a social other (Foucault, 1980a, p. 142). At the same time, this does not mean that resistance is going to be successful. It is possible that a person feels "imprisoned" by the relations of power within which one exists. The sense of being constrained by what one can do or not do may take the form of "any time I ignore my partner I may be verbally abused." This is the "repressive" sense in which "power over" another constitutes domination; the converse sense of power as "productive" of new and hopefully improved relations within a family unit does not get as much attention within studies of family relations. Hopefully, all is not lost with respect to a possible change in power relations over time. How one relates to practices of freedom, of engaging the possibility of change in one's subjectivation, can be outlined in Foucault's delineation of strategies for remaking oneself:

> (1) refusal, that is, refusing "to accept as self-evident the things that are proposed to us";
> (2) curiosity, "the need to analyze and to know, since we can accomplish nothing without reflection and knowledge"; and (3) innovation, "to seek out in our reflection those things that have never been thought or imagined." (Taylor, 2013, p. 411)

Thus, we have the possibility of personal agency even while recognizing that our everyday existence is conditioned by a set of normative prescriptions "to do this rather than that." Our social existence is not so constrained by "limits" that it is impossible to function in ways we have yet to imagine.

In Table 1, we articulate critical questions raised by Foucault's work that serve as a backdrop for the remaining discussion.

FOUCAULT AND POSTSTRUCTURAL FEMINISM

Poststructural feminists, drawing inspiration in large part from Foucault, explore the historically contingent nature of gendered power relations. As indicated earlier, Foucault offers an understanding of power not as a possession but as a process—dispersed and evident in discourses and inscribed in social practices. In his words, "There are manifold relations of power which ... cannot themselves be established, consolidated nor implemented without the production, accumulation, circulation and functioning of a discourse" (1980d, p. 93). Discourses make possible and deter relational patterns (e.g., sexual division of labor), arrangements that come to be perceived as natural and incontestable. In taking a discursive turn, we focus specifically on "the range of symbolic activities by which members of a

Table 1. Questions Inspired by Foucault and Poststructural Feminism.

- How do discourses order the world in particular ways? (e.g., gendered, sexed, classed, raced)
- How do discourses make possible particular forms of organizing?
- How do discourses shape possibilities for practice?
- How do discourses challenge men and women to intersubjectively (re)construct their identities and agency?
- How are different subject positions called into being in discourse?
- How does discursive closure solidify, shield, restrict participation and the exercise of agency?
- How do texts work to fix meaning in particular ways, and with what consequences?
- What are the visible and hidden costs of asymmetrical power relations?
- How do identities shift in varied and conflicting ways, with what implications for agency?
- How do individuals exert agency, shift meanings, resist hegemonic subject positions?
- What are the practical implications of particular theoretical standpoints, arguments, assumptions?
- Under what conditions is human agency possible?
- How is the body inscribed by a range of cultural beliefs and practices?
- How can our scholarship reckon with institutions and discourses as *contested terrains*? What does it mean for the way we engage in inquiry?
- How can sociocultural awareness of discourses and imagery contribute to alternative ways of seeing and being? How can discursive analyses call publics into being by raising consciousness?
- How do relations of power enable/constrain who can enact agency in a particular setting?
- How do relations of power condition the limits of the sayable?
- Given that power is not only repressive but productive, how does our use of language influence the possibility of productive outcomes within specific relations of power?

culture name, legitimize, and establish meanings for social organization" (Wood, 1994, p. 123). Contemporary poststructural feminists explore power relations of everyday life by focusing on connections between signifying practices, subject positions, and subjugated knowledges (e.g., Ashcraft & Mumby, 2005; Buzzanell & Liu, 2005; Fixmer & Wood, 2005). From this perspective, power is present in every family, unavoidable, and productive as well as repressive.

A poststructural feminist standpoint explores how discursive practices construct beliefs, inform communication practices, and contest social orders. To participate in family life, members depend on a general knowledge of shared signifying systems. Over time, routines develop and understandings solidify about "how things are done" and "what things mean." Importantly, though, scholars guided by Foucauldian sensibilities acknowledge that familial and cultural stocks of knowledge are not static or fixed. Discourse does not stand still. Thus, sense making remains an indeterminate process. Rather than representing the inner state of an individual, meaning is co-constructed between people. A poststructural feminist perspective challenges us to move beyond a message-production perspective (i.e., "the what" and "by whom") to recognize the co-constructed and processual nature of meaning making achieved in particular contexts (i.e., "the how" and "the when"). In short, a poststructural feminism acknowledges the contingency of human relations. How discourse operates is shaped by the social or communication situations out of which humans act. What do families, organizations, and/or communities accept as prevailing social relations at a given point in time? In answering this question, critics shift attention away from a fixed set of individuals or institutions exerting agency toward the routine and contested discursive processes through which gendered subjectivities become hegemonic.

Discourses (re)produce identifiable subjects around which particular systems of possibilities and power relations materialize among men and women (Acker, 1990). In other words, discourse functions as a textual guide that directs the formation of individual identities (e.g., husbands as breadwinners). Poststructural feminists ask questions like: How do certain definitions of masculinity (e.g., husband as breadwinner) come to hold sway over other competing definitions, and how do they shift in tandem with discourses of race, class, and other differences that matter? Issues of women's rights, for instance, cannot fully be understood in isolation from masculinity(s). Just as there cannot be one standpoint of "woman" that feminists embrace, Mumby (1998) cautioned feminists against painting masculinity in monolithic strokes. Instead, he urged scholars to explore the "ways in which different (and in some ways opposing) conceptions of masculinity are socially constructed through mundane organizing practices" (p. 171).

Finally, poststructural feminists stretch beyond symbols and texts to engage the materiality of discourse (e.g., Fraser, 1989; McKerrow, 1998). Institutions of all sorts, including families, take form in and through symbolic interactions and situated within (and shaped by) material circumstances. Discourse endows human experience with meaning by connecting (however unstably) parts in a configuration of relationships composed of symbolic, institutional, and material practices. As such, Ashcraft and Mumby (2005) reminded us that symbols are not the only things that matter. In similar fashion, Cheney (2000) argued that interpretive communication scholars too often have suffered from a case of "symbol worship" and suggested, "interpretive scholars need to *come to terms with the material world*" (p. 44, emphasis in original). Of course, symbols do matter. Discourses have material consequences and serve material interests (McKerrow, 1998).

In sum, critical scholarship inspired by Foucault and poststructural feminism assumes that humans are subjects—descendants of time and inhabitants of space. Explorations of present family relations and conditions demand a socio-historical attentiveness. As O'Grady (2005) suggested, "emancipatory ideas do not come from a point beyond history or culture but are present or have their potential in existing social discourses" (p. 111). In Table 2, we synthesize these theoretical musings in the form of questions to "widen the circle" of family communication scholarship (see calls by Floyd & Morman, 2013). We then turn our attention to perennial concerns of family communication scholarship, engaging these processes from a Foucauldian and poststructural feminist standpoint.

Table 2. Salient Questions for Family Communication Scholarship.

- What are the key processes of producing and circulating meanings about families? What (and whose) values, beliefs, and concepts are espoused? What pre-established knowledge or belief systems are drawn upon to create meaning?
- What narrative structures, tropes, metaphors recur in autobiographical and social representations of families? How do such discourses make possible particular forms of relationships and shape possibilities for role enactment?
- How have linguistic and iconographic representations of family life shifted in concert with wider sociocultural and political shifts in understanding and organizing the social world?
- How does a given set of ideas play out in human affairs? Contribute to human well-being?
- How do webs of interwoven forces (corporeal experiences, symbolic interactions, market patterns, legislation) enable, justify, constrain, mask and mystify the interests of particular individuals? What sociohistorical, political, and economic factors shape a culture's responses to and concepts of violence and abuse in the family?
- How can we acknowledge and explore the materiality and corporeality of people's lives from a discursive perspective? How can we avoid what Lupton dubbed discursive determinism?
- How can our scholarship offer accounts that acknowledge relations between individuals and social processes/structures?
- How are different subject positions/identities (e.g., wife, husband, partner) made possible through discourse? How do cultural practices (e.g., artistic forms, commodities, everyday activities) challenge men and women to intersubjectively (re)construct their identities?
- How do families function as social control and/or empowerment?
- How do individuals, in concert with others, exercise agency in families? How do individuals resist hegemonic subject positions?
- Why are "alternative" families the target of intense public discussion and scrutiny?

POSING NEW QUESTIONS ABOUT PERENNIAL CONCERNS IN FAMILY COMMUNICATION SCHOLARSHIP

Commonly studied family communication processes include (1) storytelling; (2) managing private information (e.g., disclosure, privacy, secrecy, topic avoidance); and (3) stress, social support, and coping. We selected storytelling and privacy management because theorizing about them originated in the field of communication studies (Baxter & Braithwaite, 2006; Galvin & Braithwaite, 2014). We include stress, coping, and support because much theorizing among communication studies scholars and those in allied fields centers on the experiences and consequences of change in families, including implications for stress, coping, and support (Maguire, 2012). These processes foster individual and relational resiliency under some conditions, and in other circumstances hostility and secrecy ensues. In this section, we leverage Foucauldian and poststructural feminist concepts to explore the productive and repressive potential of typical family communication processes.

Family Stories and Storytelling

A growing body of literature explores family stories and storytelling processes (see Koenig Kellas, 2015, for a review). Narrative plots are event centered and temporally and spatially depict human action and agency (Harter, 2013). As symbolic resources, narratives allow individuals to size up circumstances and judge actions and outcomes. Storytelling in families creates and passes on defining moments and events, plots, archetypal characters, values, and pathways to action (Jorgenson & Bochner, 2004; Langellier, 2006). As such, narratives instruct members about what to notice and in turn how to judge outcomes and actions.

Narratives serve a variety of functions: they help families make sense of and organize their experiences (mundane to extraordinary moments); they maintain and uphold individual and family identities; they socialize family members into particular values and beliefs; they help families cope; they provide a sense of security and belonging; and they help families heal in the midst of traumatic events (see Koenig Kellas & Kranstuber Horstman, 2014, and Koenig Kellas & Trees, 2013, for reviews). Even so, scholars interested in family stories have not explored in depth how storytelling creates or upholds disadvantage, inequity, or privilege. A case in point: In her discussion of the future of narrative research about interpersonal relations including familial ties, Koenig Kellas (2015) urged scholars to "examine the ways stories disconfirm, belittle, reject, reify stereotypes, or hurt individual and relational members" (p. 263). In this section, we draw on Foucault and poststructural feminist ideas to problematize existing scholarship and chart directions for research on family stories and storytelling.

The process of storytelling both affects and reflects family life (Koenig Kellas, 2010). Family life is composed of narrative scripts that summon multiple forms of privilege and exclusion through their tenacious familiarity (e.g., aging as decline). Poststructural feminists encourage attention to how relational lives are embedded in larger narrative landscapes, temporal moments and spaces that shape our lives and how we story them (e.g., Trethewey, 2001). Storytelling is not a benign process—narratives are inherently partial and reflect cultural values and struggles. Poststructural feminists agree that narratives constitute primary rhetorical resources through which some subject positions or identities are legitimized and privileged (e.g., to be a woman is to be a mother), while others are disqualified or denied expression (e.g., to be childless is abnormal) (Weedon, 1987). In turn, feminists rely on storytelling to raise consciousness about lived inequities and emphasize that the personal is political. In doing so, they acknowledge that personal experience is inescapably social and political. We challenge family scholars to delve more fully into the processes through which storytelling simultaneously reveals and obscures, disrupts and reifies power relations that guide everyday life. By problematizing the ideological nature of stories, scholars can identify the social, political, corporeal, and economic consequences of storytelling.

Importantly, stories unfold as fragments that are challenged and shifted to meet individual, familial, and institutional needs. Stories evolve across time as individuals take up and play out others' stories. Family members inherit and restory legacies with deep roots spanning generations, acting out what Gladwell (2008) termed *inherited ethos* (see also Thompson, Koenig Kellas, Soliz, Thompson, Epp, & Schrodt, 2009). Both a Foucauldian perspective on the function of discourse and poststructural feminism provide robust frames for engaging questions such as: Which family narratives endure? Which stories are sequestered? Who functions as primary storytellers—individuals Langellier (2006) described as *keepers of the kin*? What are the consequences produced by family legacies? Whose material interests are (not) served by storytelling? What stories are told to justify actions and relationships? How do family members manage narrative discrepancies and conflicting versions of experiences and events? Who serves as *intergenerational buffers* (see Kotre & Kotre, 1998), individuals who protect younger generations from distressing storylines? We urge family scholars to explore how "needs" are defined and negotiated, by whom and for whom and with what consequence.

The aforementioned questions inspired White and Epson (1990) to re-envision family therapy as a storytelling process (see also White, 2007, 2011). How family members attribute meanings to events maintains and/or disrupts social orders. Family narratives can "inadvertently contribute to the 'survival' of, as well as the 'career' of, the problem" (p. 3). Understood from this perspective, storytelling can function as "life support" that sustains a problem—narratives can distort voices, mask interests, disconnect individuals, and even justify violence. A key task of the therapist, then, is to help family members generate alternative stories that open up different and desirable possibilities. A Foucauldian and poststructural feminist approach to therapy works to mitigate the stultifying effects of a therapy that privileges the objective knowledge of a therapist (i.e., "this is good for you") and ignores the contingent nature of family relations (O'Grady, 2005). Meanwhile, in their work with veterans and survivors of natural disasters, some therapists use patients' reconstructed autobiographies for human rights advocacy (Schauer, Neuner, & Elbert, 2011). The burgeoning literature on narrative-based therapy coupled with public witnessing of survivors' testimonies illustrate the capacity of Foucauldian and poststructural feminist frameworks to pursue novel research and activist agendas about family storytelling.

In sum, we encourage family scholars to explore the storytelling process and how it shifts or maintains familial and societal power relations. Poststructural feminists, inspired by Foucault, position storytelling as a vital resource for relational and social change. Individuals can account for their experiences, adjust personal expectations, re-identify priorities, and envision alternative futures through storytelling.

Managing Private Information

Within family communication literature, a great deal of contemporary work centers on how individuals make decisions to disclose (or not) private information to members within and outside of the family and how disclosure, openness, avoidance (e.g., Guerrero & Afifi, 1995), and secrecy (e.g., Vangelisti, 1994) affect family relationships (see Caughlin, Petronio, & Middleton, 2013, for a review). Evolving from a rich history of self-disclosure research in interpersonal relationships, this line of inquiry is broadly influenced and represented by Communication Privacy Management Theory, hereafter referred to as CPM (see Petronio, 2002). CPM outlines the rules of disclosure, the boundaries that define who is within or outside of information privileges, the experience of and expectations for owning information, and the boundary turbulence possible when coordinating disclosures go awry (e.g., a family member shares private information with someone who should not be privy to such information).

Family communication scholars view disclosure as a complex decision and experience (Caughlin et al., 2009; Goldsmith, Miller, & Caughlin, 2008), and scholarly beliefs about disclosure have moved away from an ideology that espouses unequivocal openness in relationships as good and avoidance as detrimental (Bochner, 1982; Parks, 1982). Yet, what "openness" (and consequentially, avoidance) means in relationships remains an important and unanswered question for family communication scholars (Goldsmith & Domann-Scholz, 2013). That is, some view openness as a pattern of and schema for family interactions (e.g., Koerner & Fitzpatrick, 2002); many take a functional approach and view avoidance and secrecy as necessary to maintaining relationships (e.g., Caughlin & Afifi, 2004); others find that openness (paradoxically) includes both rigid and flexible (contextual) rules for disclosure in relationships (e.g., Roggensack & Sillars, 2014); and some conceive of disclosure and avoidance as goal-driven processes bound by contextual factors (e.g., Caughlin, Mikucki-Enyart, Middleton, Stone, & Brown, 2011). We suggest that one way to approach the question, "What does it mean to be open in families?" is to shift the question slightly to consider from where our ideals and expectations about disclosures in family relationships come. We might ask how societal discourse of openness shapes meanings of disclosure and avoidance (Goldsmith et al., 2008). Who determines what information is considered private within families? How can we think about the ownership of information as not only a source of power but also a process of power? How do discourses of openness and privacy get used, and by whom, to (re)produce power relations in families that may silence (Afifi, Olson, & Armstrong, 2006), coerce, and manipulate some family members' disclosures? Why do some individuals feel compelled to account for their identity through disclosures more (often) than others (e.g., GLBTQ identities; Denes & Afifi, 2014)? The principle being advocated here is drawn from a primary critical question: "In whose name is this practice being legitimated or authorized?" In Foucauldian terms, the focus of attention is on the relations of power that exist within a family unit to authorize one behavior rather than another.

Moreover, a significant and largely unchallenged assumption of the privacy management research is that individuals have a sense of agency or free will to decide who and when to tell their private information, though they may feel vulnerable in doing so (Petronio, 2002). In today's information age, privacy is a major concern, yet institutions and businesses seemingly have uninhibited access to people's private information, which includes their communication with their families. We contend that an important question to revisit through a critical lens is "Who has control over individuals' private information?" And whose interests are served when a family's information (e.g., health records, such as a family history of illness and disease) and interactions (e.g., via social networking) are collected and monitored by these institutions? A related assumption concerning control is that individuals have the ability to manage their private information. However, a growing body of literature concerning health communication reminds us that illness touches every family member (see Peccioni, Overton, & Thompson, 2014). Thus, we propose greater consideration of the taken-for-granted assumptions concerning how individuals' abilities to communicate (and in what ways) shape the processes of disclosure and avoidance.

Stress, Coping, and Social Support

Families experience a great deal of stress both within (e.g., sibling conflict; Pawlowski, Myers, & Rocca, 2000) and outside (e.g., work "spillover"; Krouse & Afifi, 2007) of the family. Most family scholars assume that family members respond to stress by coping (Lazarus & Folkman, 1984) and providing social support (MacGeorge, Feng, & Burleson, 2011). Generally, the social support literature focuses on the resources families have to cope (e.g., emotional support; Fisher, 2010), the strategies individuals and families use to cope (e.g., protective buffering; Joseph & Afifi, 2010), and the outcomes of coping (e.g., resolution of stressor, well-being; Matsunaga, 2009). Coping differs to the extent that it is undertaken individually, dyadically, and communally, and recent theorizing about family coping stresses the fluid and interdependent nature of coping, as well as the importance of family norms and beliefs about responsibility for family coping (see Afifi, Hutchinson, & Krouse, 2006). In times of stress and need, research has found that the most comforting and supportive messages are those that are sophisticated to the extent that they are person centered; these messages help the target articulate feelings and place them in a broader context (for a review, see MacGeorge, Feng, & Burleson, 2011). Some research has focused on not only the risk factors associated with poorer outcomes in stressful situations or environments but also the resilience possible through family communication (Lucas & Buzzanell, 2012; Wilson, Wilkum, Chernichky, MacDermid Wadsworth, & Broniarczyk, 2011).

In sum, over the past 20 years, family communication scholars have usefully developed typologies of social support and explored perceptions of how support buffers individuals from the negative effects of stress. Yet social support in families does not always facilitate coping nor does it uniformly benefit recipients or their relationships. After all, advice can be seen as impositional and intrusive (e.g., Petronio & Jones, 2006), and providing support can strip individuals of their autonomy (e.g., overparenting; Givertz & Segrin, 2014). As noted by Goldsmith and Fitch (1997), the utility of social support is a rhetorical matter. "By *rhetorical* we mean that situations in which social support is communicated involve multiple goals and outcomes," argued Goldsmith and Fitch, "and that effective interactants are those who deploy discursive resources in ways that are adapted to these demands" (p. 455, emphasis in original). Ten years later, Goldsmith (2004) critiqued literature on stress, coping, and social support for its attention to "the what" of social support to the neglect of "the how." In her words, *"many of the problems and disappointments researchers have encountered in studying enacted support have come about because we have tried to understand communicative phenomena without attention to communication processes"* (p. 24, emphasis in original). Foucault and poststructural feminism offer a framework for acknowledging the rhetorical enactment of social support.

The seeking, giving, and receiving of support occur in conversational, situational, and sociohistorical contexts. Thus, the provision of social support, like other communicative acts, needs to be understood in light of cultural assumptions about personhood and prevailing power relations. Goldsmith and Fitch (1997) provided an insightful example: "advice will be evaluated differently in a speech community that frames directing others' behavior as an intrusion on autonomy than in a community in which directing behavior is heard as involvement and caring" (p. 456). A critical approach toward social support problematizes the cultural ideologies and power relations that shape how support is enacted and understood and toward what ends (i.e., material and corporeal consequences).

Why do some individuals who experience life stressors succumb to negative physical and psychological effects whereas others do not? How and when does access to coping resources matter? Under what circumstances does social support protect or buffer individuals from negative outcomes like illness? What discourses give rise to the feminization of caregiving and social support? What discourses and practices devalue caring? Whose lives and bodies are more susceptible to the burdens of providing social support (e.g., burnout and fatigue)? These questions merit the attention of family scholars and can be usefully engaged from a critical standpoint. A Foucauldian and poststructural feminist lens directs attention toward the sociocultural environment and power relations that shape family members' ability to seek, give, and receive support through discursive interactions.

CONCLUDING REFLECTIONS

Family members give meaning to their lives by drawing on available discourses in their surroundings. Foucauldian and poststructural feminist frameworks emphasize the constitutive power of discourse in normalizing some experiences while subjugating other ways of knowing. Even so, all discourses are partial and indeterminate and subject positions necessarily vulnerable and open to change. In reflecting on the communication processes family communication scholars nurture most, we are energized by the possibilities afforded by adopting a Foucauldian and poststructural feminist approach. Specifically, we urge family communication scholars to explore both the "what" and the "how" of managing private information, coping amid stress, and fostering storytelling in families. For example, the historically and culturally specific discursive resources available to families shape members' understanding of *what* counts as "public" and "private" and *how* to manage information disclosures. Likewise, the communication of social support and storytelling are processes enacted amid normative expectations and social relations.

Foucauldian and poststructural feminists focus on sociohistorical structures of signification and, as such, are equipped to answer Olson et al.'s (2012) call to theorize the darker sides of family communication. Various crises and the ensuing aftermath (e.g., societal reintegration of veterans and posttraumatic stress disorder, cyberbullying, sexual orientation discrimination, natural disasters and displacement) present unique communication challenges (see Dickson & Webb, 2012). Irrespective of the plight, families do not experience predicaments in a vacuum. When narrating one's experience, disclosing information, and providing social support, the communication process is enabled and constrained by normative standards and power relations. Critical scholars can and should problematize these discursive processes.[3] Critical scholarship can and should become recognizable and relevant to the study of family communication.

REFERENCES

Acker, J. (1990). Hierarchies, jobs, bodies: A theory of gendered organizations. *Gender & Society, 4*, 130–158. doi: 10.1177/089124390004002002

Afifi, T. D., Hutchinson, S., & Krouse, S. (2006). Toward a theoretical model of communal coping in postdivorce families and other naturally occurring groups. *Communication Theory, 16*, 378–409. doi: 10.1111/j.1468-2885.2006.00275.x

Afifi, T. D., Olson, L. N., & Armstrong, C. (2006). The chilling effect and family secrets: Examining the role of self protection, other protection, and communication efficacy. *Human Communication Research, 31*, 564–598. doi: 10.1093/hcr/31.4.564

Allen, A. (2013). Power and the subject. In C. Falzon, T. O'Leary, & J. Sawicki (Eds.), *A companion to Foucault* (pp. 337–52). Malden, MA: Blackwell.

Ashcraft, K. L., & Mumby, D. (2005). *Reworking gender: A feminist communicology of organization.* Thousand Oaks, CA: Sage.

Baxter, L. A., & Braithwaite, D. O. (2006). Introduction: Metatheory and theory in family communication research. In D. O. Braithwaite & L. A. Baxter (Eds.), *Engaging theories in family communication: Multiple perspectives* (pp. 1–15). Thousand Oaks, CA: Sage.

Bochner, A. P. (1982). On the efficacy of openness in close relationships. In M. Burgoon (Ed.), *Communication yearbook 5* (pp. 49–78). New Brunswick, NJ: Transaction Books.

Buzzanell, P. M., & Liu, M. (2005). Struggling with maternity leave policies and practices: A poststructuralist feminist analysis of gendered organizing. *Journal of Applied Communication Research, 33*, 1–25. doi: 10.1080/0090988042000318495

Caughlin, J. P., & Afifi, T. D. (2004). When is topic avoidance unsatisfying? Examining moderators of the association between avoidance and dissatisfaction. *Human Communication Research, 30*, 479–513. doi: 10.1093/hcr/30.4.479

Caughlin, J. P., Brashers, D. E., Ramey, M. E., Kosenko, K. A., Donovan-Kicken, E., & Bute, J. J. (2008). The message design logics of responses to HIV disclosures. *Human Communication Research, 34*, 655–684. doi: 10.1111/j.1468-2958.2008.00336.x

Caughlin, J. P., Mikucki-Enyart, S. L., Middleton, A. V., Stone, A. M., & Brown, L. E. (2011). Being open without talking about it: A rhetorical/normative approach to understanding topic avoidance in families after a lung cancer diagnosis. *Communication Monographs, 78,* 409–436. doi: 10.1111/j.1468-2958.2008.00336.x

Caughlin, J. P., Petronio, S., & Middleton, A. V. (2013). When families manage private information. In A. L. Vangelisti (Ed.), *The Routledge handbook of family communication* (2nd ed., pp. 321–337). New York: Routledge.

Cheney, G. (2000). Interpreting interpretive research: Toward perspectivalism without relativism. In S. R. Corman & M. S. Poole (Eds.), *Perspectives on organizational communication theorizing* (pp. 17–45). New York: The Guilford Press.

Cole, C. E. (2010). Problematizing therapeutic assumptions about narratives: A case study of storytelling events in a post-conflict context. *Health Communication, 12,* 650–60. doi: 10.1080/10410236.2010.521905

Denes, A., & Afifi, T. D. (2014). Coming out again: Exploring GLBQ individuals' communication with their parents after the first coming out. *Journal of GLBT Family Studies, 10,* 298–325. doi: 10.1080/1550428x.2013.838150

Dickson, F. C., & Webb, L. M. (Eds.). (2012). *Communication for families in crisis: Theories, research, strategies.* New York: Peter Lang.

Dow, B. J., & Condit, C. M. (2005). The state of the art in feminist scholarship in communication. *Journal of Communication, 55,* 448–478. doi: 10.1093/joc/55.3.448

Few-Demo, A. L., Lloyd, S. A., & Allen, K. R. (2014). It's all about power: Integrating feminist family studies and family communication. *Journal of Family Communication, 14*(2), 85–94. doi: 10.1080/15267431.2013.864295

Fisher, C. L. (2010). Coping with breast cancer across adulthood: Emotional support communication in the mother-daughter bond. *Journal of Applied Communication Research, 38,* 386–411. doi: 10.1080/00909882.2010.513996

Fixmer, N., & Wood, J. T. (2005). The personal is still political. Embodied politics in third wave feminism. *Women's Studies in Communication, 28,* 235–257. doi: 10.1080/07491409.2005.10162493

Floyd, K. W., & Morman, M. T. (Eds.). (2013). *Widening the family circle: New research on family communication.* Thousand Oaks, CA: Sage Publications.

Foucault, M. (1997). The ethics of concern for the self as a practice of freedom. In M. Foucault, *Ethics, Subjectivity and truth/essential works of Foucault,* Vol. 1 (pp. 281–302). Trans. R. Hurley. Ed. Rabinow, P. New York: The New Press.

Foucault, M. (1980a). Powers and strategies. In C. Gordon (Ed. & Trans.), *Power/knowledge* (pp. 134–145). New York: Pantheon Books.

Foucault, M. (1980b). The confession of the flesh. In C. Gordon (Ed. & Trans.), *Power/knowledge* (pp. 194–228). New York: Pantheon Books.

Foucault, M. (1980c). Truth and power. In C. Gordon (Ed. & Trans.), *Power/knowledge* (pp. 109–133). New York: Pantheon Books.

Foucault, M. (1980d). Two lectures. (A. Fontana & P. Pasquino, Trans.). In C. Gordon (Ed.), *Power/knowledge* (pp. 78–108). New York: Pantheon Books.

Foucault, M. (1989). The concern for truth. (A J. Johnston, Trans.). In M. Foucault, *Foucault live: Interviews 1964–1984* (pp. 293–308). S. Lotringer, Ed. New York: Semiotext(e).

Foucault, M. (1993). About the beginnings of the hermeneutics of the self: Two lectures at Dartmouth. *Political Theory, 21,* 197–227. Transcript, M. Blasius and T. Keenan.

Foucault, M. (2001). *Fearless speech.* Ed. J. Pearson. Los Angeles, CA: Semiotext(e).

Fraser, N. (1989). *Unruly practices. Power, discourse and gender in contemporary social theory.* Minneapolis: University of Minnesota Press.

Galvin, K. M., & Braithwaite, D. O. (2014). Theory and research from the communication field: Discourses that constitute and reflect families. *Journal of Family Theory & Review, 6,* 97–111. doi: 10.1111/jftr.12030

Givertz, M., & Segrin, S. (2014). The association between overinvolved parenting and young adults' self-efficacy, psychological entitlement, and family communication. *Communication Research, 41,* 1111–1136. doi: 10.1177/0093650212456392

Gladwell, M. (2008). *Outliers. The story of success.* New York: Little, Brown and Company.

Goldsmith, D. (2004). *Communicating social support.* Cambridge: Cambridge University Press.

Goldsmith, D. J., & Domann-Scholz, K. (2013). The meanings of "open communication" among couples coping with a cardiac event. *Journal of Communication, 63,* 266–286. doi: 10.1111/jcom.12021

Goldsmith, D., & Fitch, K. (1997). The normative context of advice as social support. *Human Communication Research, 23,* 454–476. doi: 10.1111/j.1468-2958.1997.tb00406.x

Goldsmith, D. J., Miller L. E., & Caughlin, J. P. (2008). Openness and avoidance in couples communicating about cancer. In C. Beck (Ed.), *Communication yearbook 31* (pp. 62–115). Malden, MA: Blackwell.

Guerrero, L. K., & Afifi, W. A. (1995). Some things are better left unsaid: Topic avoidance in family relationships. *Communication Quarterly, 43,* 276–296. doi: 10.1080/01463379509369977

Harter, L. M. (2013). The poetics and politics of storytelling in health contexts. In L. M. Harter and Associates (Ed.), *Imagining new normals: A narrative framework for health communication* (pp. 3–28). Dubuque, IA: Kendall Hunt.

Hecht, M. L., & Miller-Day, M. (2007). The Drug Resistance Strategies Project as translational research. *Journal of Applied Communication Research, 35,* 343–349. doi: 10.1080/00909880701611086

Jorgenson, J., & Bochner, A. P. (2004). Imagining families through stories and rituals. In A. L. Vangelisti (Ed.), *Handbook of family communication* (pp. 513–538). Mahwah, NJ: Erlbaum.

Joseph, A. L., & Afifi, T. D. (2010). Military wives' stressful disclosures to their deployed husbands: The role of protective buffering. *Journal of Applied Communication Research, 38,* 412–434. doi: 10.1080/00909882.2010.513997

Koenig Kellas, J. (2010). Narrating family: Introduction to the special issue on narratives and storytelling in the family. *Journal of Family Communication, 10,* 1–6. doi: 10.1080/15267430903401441

Koenig Kellas, J. (2015). Narrative theories: Making sense of interpersonal communication. In Braithwaite, D. O., & Schrodt, P. (Eds.), *Engaging theories in interpersonal communication: Multiple perspectives* (2nd ed., pp. 253–266). Thousand Oaks, CA: Sage.

Koenig Kellas, J., & Kranstuber Horstman, H. (2014). Communicated narrative sense-making: Understanding family narratives, storytelling, and the construction of meaning through a communicative lens. In L. H. Turner & R. West (Eds.), *The Sage handbook of family communication* (pp. 76–90). Thousand Oaks, CA: Sage.

Koenig Kellas, J., & Trees, A. (2013). Family stories and storytelling: Windows into the family soul. In A. L. Vangelisti (Ed.), *The Routledge handbook of family communication* (2nd ed., pp. 76–90). New York: Routledge.

Koerner, A. F., & Fitzpatrick, M. A. (2002). Toward a theory of family communication. *Communication Theory, 12,* 70–91. doi: 10.1093/ct/12.1.70

Kotre, J., & Kotre, K. B. (1998). Intergenerational buffers: The damage stops here. In D. P. McAdams & E. de St. Aubin (Eds.), *Generativity and adult development* (pp. 367–389). Washington, DC: APA Press.

Krouse, S. S., & Afifi, T. D. (2007). Family-to-work spillover stress: Coping communicatively in the workplace. *Journal of Family Communication, 7,* 85–122. doi: 10.1080/15267430701221537

Langellier, K. (2006). Family storytelling as communication practice. In L. H. Turner & R. West (Eds.), *The Sage family communication handbook* (pp. 109–128). Thousand Oaks, CA: Sage.

Lazarus, R. S., & Folkman, S. (1984). *Stress, appraisal, and coping.* New York, NY: Springer.

Lucas, K., & Buzzanell, P. M. (2012). Memorable messages of hard times: Constructing short- and long-term resiliencies through family communication. *Journal of Family Communication, 12,* 189–208. doi: 10.1080/15267431.2012.687196

MacGeorge, E. L., Feng, B., & Burleson, B. R. (2011). Supportive communication. In M. L. Knapp & J. A. Daly (Eds.), *The handbook of interpersonal communication* (4th ed., pp. 317–354). Thousand Oaks, CA: Sage.

Maguire, K. (2012). *Stress and coping in family relationships.* Cambridge, UK: Polity Press.

Malpas, S., & Wake, P. (Eds.). (2013). *The Routledge companion to critical and cultural theory* (2nd ed.). New York, NY: Routledge.

Matsunaga, M. (2009). Parents don't (always) know their children have been bullied: Child-parent discrepancy on bullying and family-level profile of communication standards. *Human Communication Research, 35,* 221–247. doi: 10.1111/j.1468-2958.2009.01345.x

McKerrow, R. E. (1998). Corporeality and cultural rhetoric: A site for rhetoric's future. *Southern Communication Journal, 63,* 315–328. doi: 10.1080/10417949809373105

McKerrow, R. E. (2011). Foucault's relationship to rhetoric. *Review of Communication, 11,* 253–271. doi: 10.1080/15358593.2011.602103

Mumby, D. K. (1998). Organizing men: Power, discourse, and the social construction of masculinity(s) in the workplace. *Communication Theory, 8,* 164–182. 10.1111/j.1468-2885.1998.tb00216.x

O'Grady, H. (2005). *Woman's relationship with herself: Gender, Foucault and therapy.* London: Routledge.

Olson, L. N. (2012). Editor introduction: Pushing the boundaries. *Journal of Family Communication, 12*(1), 1–3. doi: 10.1080/15267431.2012.653941

Olson, L. N., Baiocchi-Wagner, E. A., Kratzer, J. M. W., & Symonds, S. E. (2012). *The dark side of family communication.* Cambridge, England: Polity Press.

Ono, K. A. (2011). Critical: A finer edge. *Communication and Critical/Cultural Studies. 8,* 93–96. doi: 10.1080/14791420.2011.543332

Parks, M. R. (1982). Ideology in interpersonal communication: Off the couch and into the world. In M. Burgoon (Ed.), *Communication yearbook 6* (pp. 79–107). Beverly Hills, CA: Sage.

Pawlowski, D. R., Myers, S. A., & Rocca, K. A. (2000). Relational messages in conflict messages among siblings. *Communication Research Reports, 17,* 271–277. doi: 10.1080/08824090009388774

Pecchioni, L. L., Overton, B. C., & Thompson, T. (2014). Families communicating about health. In L. H. Turner & R. West (Eds.), *The Sage handbook of family communication* (pp. 306–319). Thousand Oaks, CA: Sage.

Petronio, S. (2002). *Boundaries of privacy: Dialectics of disclosure.* Albany, NY: SUNY Press.

Petronio, S., & Jones, S. (2006). When "friendly advice" becomes a privacy dilemma for pregnant couples: Applying communication privacy management theory. In L. Turner & R. West (Eds.), *The family communication sourcebook* (pp. 201–219). Thousand Oaks, CA: Sage Publications, Inc. doi: http://dx.doi.org/10.4135/9781452233024.n11

Roggensack, K. E., & Sillars, A. (2014). Agreement and understanding about honesty and deception rules in romantic relationships. *Journal of Social and Personal Relationships, 31,* 178–199. doi: 10.1177/0265407513489914

Schauer, M., Neuner, F., & Elbert, T. (2011). *Narrative exposure therapy: A short term treatment for traumatic stress disorders* (2nd ed.). Cambridge, MA: Hogrefe Publishing.

Simons, J. (2013). Power, resistance, and freedom. In C. Falzon, T. O'Leary, & J. Sawicki (Eds.), *A companion to Foucault* (301–319). Malden, MA: Blackwell.

Socha, T. J. (2009). Family as agency of potential: Toward a positive ontology of applied family communication theory and research. In L. R. Frey & K. N. Cissna (Eds.), *Routledge handbook of applied communication research* (pp. 309–330). New York: Routledge.

Suter, E. A., & Faulkner, S. L. (2014, September 29). Call for papers: Special issue of the *Journal of Family Communication* on critical approaches to family communication research: Representation, critique, and praxis. Message posted to CRTNET electronic mailing list, archived at http://lists1.cac.psu.edu/cgi-bin/wa?S1=crtnet

Taylor, D. (2013). Toward a "Feminist politics of ourselves." In C. Falzon, T. O'Leary, & J. Sawicki (Eds.), *A companion to Foucault* (pp. 403–418). Malden, MA: Blackwell.

Thompson, B., Koenig Kellas, J., Soliz, J., Thompson, J., Epp, A., & Schrodt, P. (2009). Family legacies: Constructing individual and family identity through intergenerational storytelling. *Narrative Inquiry, 19*, 106–134. doi: 10.1075/ni.19.1.07tho

Trethewey, A. (2001). Reproducing and resisting the master narrative of decline: Midlife professional women's experiences of aging. *Management Communication Quarterly, 15*, 183–226. doi: 10.1177/0893318901152002

Turner, L. H., & West, R. (Eds.). (2014). *The Sage handbook of family communication.* Thousand Oaks, CA: Sage.

Vangelisti, A. L. (Ed.). (2013). *The Routledge handbook of family communication* (2nd ed.). New York: Routledge.

Vangelisti, A. L. (1994). Family secrets: Forms, functions, and correlates. *Journal of Social and Personal Relationships, 11*, 113–135. doi: 10.1177/0265407594111007

Weedon, C. (1987). *Feminist practice and poststructuralist theory.* Cambridge: Blackwell.

White, M. (2007). *Maps of narrative practice.* New York: W. W. Norton & Company.

White, M. (2011). *Narrative practice. Continuing the conversations.* New York: W. W. Norton & Company.

White, M., & Epson, D. (1990). *Narrative means to therapeutic ends.* New York: W. W. Norton & Company.

Wilson, S. R., Wilkum, K., Chernichky, S. M., MacDermid Wadsworth, S. M., & Broniarczyk, K. M. (2011). Passport toward success: Description and evaluation of a program designed to help children and families reconnect after a military deployment. *Journal of Applied Communication Research, 39*, 223–249. doi: 10.1080/00909882.2011.585399

Wood, J. T. (1994). *Who cares? Women, care and culture.* Carbondale: Southern Illinois Press.

NOTES

1. "Power in the substantive sense, *'le' pouvoir*, doesn't exist. … In reality power means relations, a more-or-less organized hierarchichal, co-ordinated cluster of relations." (Foucault, 1980b, p. 198)

2. "I think that in the public's eye I am the one who has said that knowledge has become indistinguishable from power. … I will respond with laughter. If I had said, or wanted to say, that knowledge was power, I would have said it, and having said it, I would no longer have anything to say. … I directed my attention specifically to see how certain forms of power which were of the same type could give place to forms of knowledge extremely different in their object and structure." (Foucault, 1989, p. 304)

3. In advocating a critical approach, we are reminded of Kent A. Ono's argument that "critical scholarship should include different approaches, conceptions, even ones that challenge continental thought or that provide different grounds for judgment." (Ono, 2011, p. 94)

Illuminating Darkness

An Epilogue

THOMAS J. SOCHA
Old Dominion University

Darkness and brightness are equal partners in the human condition and defining features of families of all stripes. Although darkness has come to be associated predominantly with bad things, as this volume clearly demonstrates, darkness can be illuminating insofar as we can learn about ways to counter forces of destruction and decay seeking to damage the developmental structures and accomplishments that families work hard to build.

Although often going unnoticed, good things can and do happen in darkness. Some oxygen-giving, highly resilient plants actually thrive in low- to no-light conditions: maidenhair ferns, moss, mint, Swedish ivy. Some animals have adapted to living deep underground or undersea in complete darkness. Dimmed-lights contextualize moments of intimacy and romance and of course are necessary for watching movies. Nightfall gives us a break from sunlight and signals for many of us that it is time to rest. However, for bakers, nighttime signals that it is time to head to work, so that we might enjoy breads and sweets at sunrise. Scores of other third-shift warriors labor throughout the night to keep us safe, facilitate our travel, monitor our health, move mountains of packages containing the food and goods needed for our survival, as well as maintain our standards of living, and some even watch over us while we sleep.

Of course, bad things too can grow and take place in darkness. Tumors, cancers, and hosts of pathologies grow in the darkness of our inner human biology until illuminated by the light of a surgeon's scope. Darkness cloaks crimes of violence and abuse, thievery, as well as sources that inflict pain. Feelings of despair and sadness are best suited for a dark stage. Monsters, demons, and things that go bump in the night are all woven into the cover of darkness, under which lurks nightmares and our worst of times. However, some people do like to be frightened vicariously as they view horror films, of course in the safety and comfort of their homes and theatres while accompanied by blankets, teddy bears, and loved ones.

A communication resilience framing of family life not only makes it clear that things will certainly go wrong in families, but that vigilance and ongoing care work is necessary if we are to learn how to best strengthen and fortify families for those times when things do go wrong (Beck & Socha, 2015). On this front, the current volume makes a major contribution not so much as a reminder that lots can go wrong in family life but rather by offering us hope as it illuminates the principles, processes, and practices of managing family darkness.

The chapters in this volume spotlight a wide array of obstacles and frailties, some natural and some human-made, and all chapters seek to illuminate the role of family communication as a major facilitative or inhibitive force in family growth and development. Some chapters do so by examining family communication's role in life and death itself. Miller-Day, Dorros, and Day examined family communication conditions facilitative or inhibitive of suicidality, or literally when family words can kill. Duggan and Kilmartin examined connections between family communication and eating disorders, or when words impede life-giving nourishment. Other chapters examined the role of communication in families' struggles with various conditions and circumstances including managing mental illness (Segrin & Arroyo), ADHD (Gibson, Webb, & Joseph) and temperament (Beyens & Eggermont), understanding sexual orientation (Etengoff), and managing unfavorable economics (Neppl, Senia, & Donnellan). Still other chapters examined dark family communication practices of hostility (Buehler, Weymouth, & Zhou), inflicting social pain (Vangelisti), abuse and neglect (Lin, Giles, & Soliz), and violence (Eckstein and Anderson). This latter group of chapters underscores the importance of the need for positive communication practices at home in place of practices that facilitate destruction and despair (Socha & Pitts, 2012).

Conducting research that seeks to illuminate darkness is very difficult. When marine biologists descend into the sea's depths, for example, the light cast by their submersibles into deep-sea life radically changes the conditions in which these creatures live and is undoubtedly blinding, alien, and frightening to them. However, when biologists join the darkness and turn out the light, although they do "see" many patterns of darting lights, they lose the ability to study the details of these creatures. For those that dwell above the surface, light is necessary to study that which lives in darkness.

Similarly, when family communication scholars choose to study the dark side of family life, as chapters by Afifi and Davis as well as Harter, McKerrow, and

Thompson point out, shining a light changes radically the context in which these behaviors are occurring and undoubtedly sends those engaged in family patterns fed by darkness scurrying for cover. Like the marine biologists, choosing to turn out the light and join in family darkness poses practical limitations in understanding family life but also raises significant ethical implications for family communication researchers. That is, for marine biologists, observing in darkness is a good thing for the deep-sea creatures as they go about living their natural lives. However, for family communication researchers, observing family practices that result in darkness, while illuminating, violates our human social compact of doing no harm by not helping to alleviate suffering. Yet, if we are to fully study family communication practices considered "dark," such as deception in the context of family life, we must observe and track the behaviors of liars, cheats, and cons at home, as well as those who are honest, fair, and forthright. This of course poses many methodological challenges for future studies of family communication practices that create darkness as well as those taking place in darkness, about which this volume offers some valuable guidance.

If family communication scholarship is to lead to the development of interventions and learning that contribute to the comprehensive growth and positive development of family life, it must conduct research that illuminates darkness, sheds light on dark practices, as well as seeks to understand that which is strengthening, happy, and positive, or on the bright side. Indeed, the editors and contributors of this volume have taken a major step forward in helping illuminate darkness at home.

REFERENCES

Beck, G. A. & Socha, T. J. (Eds.). (2015). *Communicating hope and resilience across the lifespan.* New York: Peter Lang.

Socha, T. J., & Pitts, M. J. (Eds.). (2012). *The positive side of interpersonal communication.* New York: Peter Lang.

List OF **Contributors**

Tamara Afifi (PhD, University of Nebraska) is a Professor in the Department of Communication Studies at the University of Iowa. Her research focuses on how people communicate in their relationships when they are stressed and its impact on health. Specifically, her research examines how parental communication patterns (e.g., conflict, avoidance, verbal rumination, social support, communal coping) during stressful times (e.g., divorce, refugee camps, natural disasters, the Great Recession, chronic illness, everyday stress) affect parents' and children's stress, adaptation, and physical/mental/relational health. Her most recent research explores the impact of parents' communication patterns on adolescents' and parents' biological stress responses (e.g., stress hormones) and resilience. Professor Afifi has received numerous research awards, including the Young Scholar Award from the International Communication Association in 2006 and the Brommel Award for a distinguished career of research in family communication in 2011. She also received a universitywide Distinguished Teaching Award from the University of California Santa Barbara in 2009.

Kristin L. Anderson (PhD, University of Texas, Austin) is Professor of Sociology at Western Washington University, where she teaches courses in domestic violence, gender, and sports. Her research examines how gender structures experiences of intimate partner violence and how partner abuse reproduces hierarchies of gender and sexuality. She authored "Conflict, Power, and Violence in Families" for the 2010 Decade in Review issue of the *Journal of Marriage and Family*. She is currently studying reproductive coercion in abusive relationships as a gendered social process, the legal response to domestic violence across different courts, and verbal aggression against women in abusive relationships and in social media such as Twitter.

Analisa Arroyo (PhD, University of Arizona) is an Assistant Professor at the University of Georgia in the Department of Communication Studies. Her primary research focuses on health and interpersonal communication in the realm of body image issues. Specifically, she explores the relationships among interpersonal dynamics (e.g., family interactions, social skills), explicit communication about weight (i.e., fat talk), and health-related outcomes (e.g., self-perceptions, psychosocial well-being). Her publications have appeared in *Communication Monograms*, *Human Communication Research*, and the *Journal of Applied Communication Research*, among others.

Ine Beyens (MA, University of Leuven, Belgium) is a PhD student in the School for Mass Communication Research at the University of Leuven, Belgium, working with Dr. Steven Eggermont. Her research focuses on the uses and effects of screen media among children and adolescents. Her most recent studies investigate the relationship between parents' decision making around children's television viewing and parents' structural circumstances, including parents' work demands, mental well-being, and time pressure. In addition, she has been studying sexual media effects among adolescents, investigating, for instance, the impact of sexually oriented television viewing on adolescents' attitudes toward uncommitted sexual exploration and the impact of sexually explicit websites on adolescent boys' academic performance.

Cheryl Buehler (PhD, University of Minnesota) is Professor in the Department of Human Development and Family Studies at the University of North Carolina at Greensboro. Her primary areas of interest and publication include family processes, including various aspects of parenting; marital conflict and early adolescent well-being; the work-family interface; adolescent close relationships; the transition into middle school; and family influences on health practices. She also has particular interest in research design, methods, and statistics.

Shardé Davis (MA, University of California Santa Barbara) is a PhD student advised by Dr. Tamara Afifi in the Department of Communication Studies at the University of Iowa. She is an alumna of UC Santa Barbara where she earned a BA in Communication and Feminist Studies in 2010 and an MA in

Communication in 2012. Her interdisciplinary research program uses theories and approaches from Communication, Feminist Studies and Ethnic Studies to investigate how ethnicity and gender shape relational dynamics and communication processes. Her most recent research focuses on the social support process among Black and White women friend circles to examine the ways Black American women uniquely bolster their strong Black womanhood.

L. Edward Day (PhD, University of Washington) is Chair of the Department of Sociology and Director of the Earl Babbie Research Center at Chapman University. He is the founding editor of *War Crimes, Genocide & Crimes against Humanity: An International Journal.* His research focuses on the prevention and consequences of risky and criminal behaviors for both perpetrators and victims and spans behaviors as diverse as delinquency, drug use, homicide, and genocide.

M. Brent Donnellan (PhD, University of California, Davis) is a Professor of Psychology at Texas A&M University. He investigates research questions at the intersections of developmental psychology, personality psychology, and psychological assessment. His current research efforts focus on theoretical models linking economic conditions to human development, personality development, and connections between individual differences and functioning in interpersonal relationships. He received his PhD in 2001 and previously worked at Michigan State University. Brent currently serves as the Senior Associate Editor for the *Journal of Research in Personality* and co-directs the Family Transitions Project with Dr. Neppl.

Sam M. Dorros (PhD, University of Arizona) is an Assistant Professor in the Department of Communication Studies at Chapman University. Her areas of interest include Interpersonal, Family, and Health Communication; and specifically how communication behaviors in relationships influence mental and physical health outcomes. She has conducted research examining the interdependence of couples coping with breast and prostate cancer and how the cancer experience affects relational well-being and mental health of dyads. She is currently conducting research on family communication patterns and health outcomes in children and adolescents. She received her MA and PhD from the Department of Communication at the University of Arizona, in Tucson, Arizona.

Ashley P. Duggan (PhD, University of California, Santa Barbara) is Associate Professor in the Communication Department at Boston College. Her research addresses the intersections of nonverbal and verbal communication processes, health, and relationships. She holds an additional appointment at Tufts University School of Medicine, and her interdisciplinary research involves integrating reflective practice in medicine, communication processes, and health outcomes. Her work addresses theoretical explanations for health as a unique context for interpersonal and relational processes. Examining communication behaviors in naturalistic interactions, she focuses on the mutual influence process of communication about health and illness and the ways health outcomes are shaped by individual and contextual behaviors. Her scholarship is regularly published in communication journals, as well as in international, interdisciplinary journals and edited volumes. She is Associate Editor for *Personal Relationships* and serves on the editorial boards for *Journal of Health Communication, Communication Yearbook*, and *Communication Research Reports.*

Jessica J. Eckstein (PhD, University of Illinois, Urbana-Champaign), Associate Professor of Communication at Western Connecticut State University, specializes in relational and health communication with a current research focus on family violence from unexplored or understudied perspectives (e.g., love, male or parent victims, masculinity norms). Emphasizing the importance of applying scholarship to people's lives, Dr. Eckstein sustains collaborations with national and community social service agencies.

Steven Eggermont (PhD, University of Leuven, Belgium) is Director of the School for Mass Communication Research and Program Director of Communication Sciences at the University of Leuven. His work, which has been recognized with several international awards, draws from literatures in communication science, developmental psychology, and social and health behavior sciences. It focuses on media use during the life course and effects of exposure to the media on perceptions and behaviors. Dr. Eggermont has published more than 70 articles and book chapters on children's and adolescents' media use, sexual media contents, media use and health behaviors, and media effects. He is principal investigator of several fundamental and applied research projects within the field of communication sciences and has a large international network.

Chana Etengoff (PhD, Graduate Center of the City University of New York) is a Term Assistant Professor at Barnard College, Columbia University and director of Barnard College's Minority Conflict & Mediation (MCM) Lab. Her scholarship is focused on understanding how cultural, gender, and sexual minority groups navigate sociorelational prejudice and discrimination. Her work is informed by a theoretical stance that human development is a constructive process embedded in relational, sociopolitical, and historical contexts. Current lines of research are focused on understanding the mediating role of transgender vlogs and how best to reduce minority prejudice on college campuses. Her publications have appeared in the *Journal of Homosexuality*,

Psychology of Religion and Spirituality, and the *Journal of GLBT Family Studies*, among others.

Danna M. Gibson (PhD, The University of Memphis) is Professor of Communication at Columbus State University in Columbus, GA, where she currently serves as chair of the Department of Communication and oversees the Non-Profit and Civic Engagement Academic Center (NPaCE). She has received numerous teaching, research, and community awards for her work with non-profits and workforce development. Her research explores ways communication can help create and maintain healthy relational communities. Dr. Gibson has written numerous literacy and workforce development grants, co-wrote the Bill and Melinda Gates Foundation Next Generation Learning Challenge Grant, has authored numerous convention presentations, co-authored an online public-speaking textbook titled *Empowering Your Public Voice*, and has published essays in *Computers in Human Behavior and Communication Law Review*. Dr. Gibson is recognized for her work with student service learning, civic leadership, and community partnership formation.

Howard Giles (PhD, University of Bristol, UK) is Professor of Communication at the University of California, Santa Barbara. He is founding Editor of the *Journal of Language and Social Psychology* and the *Journal of Asian Pacific Communication*. Giles was past President of the International Communication Association and the International Association of Language and Social Psychology. Besides being the architect of communication accommodation theory, his research interests encompass interpersonal and intergroup communication processes in intergenerational, police-civilian, and other intergroup settings, and he is the editor of the *Handbook of Intergroup Communication*.

Lynn Harter (PhD, University of Nebraska) is a Professor in the School of Communication Studies at Ohio University and Co-Director of the Barbara Geralds Schoonover Institute for Storytelling and Social Impact. Guided by narrative and feminist sensibilities, her scholarly agenda focuses on the communicative construction of *possibility* as individuals and groups organize for survival and social change amidst embodied differences. The various strands of her research are connected by a primary concern: how symbolic, material, and corporeal resources foster *resiliency* among individuals living in vulnerable bodies.

Laveda I. Joseph (MA, University of Arkansas) is a Lecturer of Communication at Columbus State University in Columbus, GA, where she teaches Public Speaking with a variety of upper-division courses in Interpersonal and Organizational communication. Her research interests include strategic communication, perception of identity through father-daughter relationships, initiation strategies used in interracial dating, and social support. She has worked in the corporate setting developing training solutions for the number 1 Fortune 500 Company. She continues her teaching outside the classroom as she develops workshops for university students focusing on enhancing their communication skills in different contexts.

Brielle Kilmartin (BA, Boston College) graduated from Boston College with a Degree in Communication in 2013, where she studied health communication and family communication processes under the direction of Ashley Duggan. Brielle is currently pursuing a JD at New York Law School with a primary focus on business and financial law. She utilizes her communication background to serve as an advocate for clients within New York Law School's Securities Arbitration Clinic. She is committed to advocacy, empowerment, and social justice within the corporate setting, promoting her belief that Communication and the Legal Ethics go hand in hand.

Mei-Chen Lin (PhD, University of Kansas) is an Associate Professor in the School of Communication Studies at Kent State University. Her current research focuses on communicative processes and issues in intergroup relationships within the family context, with an emphasis on elder abuse, aging-related discussion, and grandparent-grandchild relationships. Her research also looks at intergroup communication in the political context and the ways in which intergroup factors affect media use and effects. Her work has appeared in *International Psychogeriatrics, Handbook of Family Communication, Journal of Language and Social Psychology,* and *Journal of Aging Studies.*

Raymie E. McKerrow (PhD, University of Iowa) is Professor Emeritus, School of Communication Studies, Ohio University. His early research focused on modern rhetorical history and theory, particularly the work of Archbishop Richard Whately, as well as on argumentation theory. His more recent work has focused on contemporary rhetoric, with an emphasis on the work of Michel Foucault, as well as other continental and critical scholars.

Michelle Miller-Day (PhD, Arizona State University) is a Professor of Communication Studies and Health and Strategic Communication at Chapman University. Her research addresses human communication and health, including areas such as prevention, substance use, and suicide. Her community-embedded research has involved numerous creative projects to translate research findings into social change. For the past 25 years, she has served as the principal qualitative methodologist for a National Institute on Drug Abuse line of research. This work has developed one of the most successful evidence-based substance use prevention programs in the United States and reaches youth in 43 countries worldwide. She has lectured, conducted research, and served as a consultant at universities across the United States and internationally and has authored four books and more than 150 scholarly articles, chapters, and proceedings.

Tricia Neppl (PhD, Kansas State University) is an Assistant Professor in Human Development and Family Studies at Iowa State University, where she teaches undergraduate and graduate courses in family stress processes. She also is the co-director of the Family Transitions Project, which is a three-generation study of rural Iowa families that began in 1989. Her program of research focuses on parenting, economic adversity, family stress, and child and adolescent outcomes. Her work combines longitudinal research design with observational research methods to better understand how risk and protective factors influence child and adolescent development.

Chris Segrin (PhD, University of Wisconsin) is the Steve and Nancy Lynn Professor of Communication at the University of Arizona. His research focuses on social skills, relationship development and satisfaction, and such problems as depression, anxiety, loneliness, and marital distress. This research can be found in journals such as *Human Communication Research, Communication Monographs, Journal of Abnormal Psychology, Journal of Social and Clinical Psychology, Communication Research*, and *Journal of Social and Personal Relationships*. He is author of the books *Interpersonal Processes in Psychological Problems* and *Family Communication*. Recently he has been conducting research on the intergenerational transmission of divorce, why lonely people have more health problems, and quality of life in cancer patients and their partners. This research has been funded by the National Cancer Institute, the National Institute of Nursing Research, the Livestrong Foundation, Oncology Nursing Foundation, the American Cancer Society, and the V Foundation for Cancer Research.

Jennifer Senia (MS, Iowa State University) is a doctoral candidate in Human Development and Family Studies at Iowa State University. Her research focuses on how family stress influences family structure and individual well-being. Jennifer has served as a research assistant on the Family Transitions Project with Dr. Neppl since 2011 and currently is an instructor for the College of Human Sciences at Iowa State University.

Thomas J. Socha (PhD, University of Iowa) is Professor of Communication, Old Dominion University University Professor (of Distinguished Teaching), and Director of the Graduate Program in Lifespan and Digital Communication at Old Dominion University in Norfolk, Virginia. He has published eight co-authored/co-edited books, 38 book chapters and articles, and presented more than sixty conference papers in the areas of family communication, children's communication, lifespan communication, and positive communication. He was the founding Editor of the *Journal of Family Communication*, received the Bernard J. Brommel Award for Outstanding Scholarship and Distinguished Service in Family Communication from the National Communication Association, and is a past president of the Southern States Communication Association. He is the founding Series Editor of the Lifespan Communication: Children, Families, and Aging book series published by Peter Lang International.

Jordan Soliz (PhD, University of Kansas) is an Associate Professor in the Department of Communication Studies at the University of Nebraska-Lincoln. His current research investigates communication and intergroup processes primarily in personal and family relationships, with a current emphasis on multiethnic-racial families, interfaith families, and grandparent-grandchild relationships. In addition to scholarly chapters in various edited volumes, his work has been published in *Communication Monographs, Communication Quarterly, Journal of Family Communication, Journal of Marriage and Family*, and the *Journal of Language and Social Psychology*. Dr. Soliz is the current editor of the *Journal of Family Communication*.

Charee M. Thompson (PhD, The University of Texas at Austin) is an Assistant Professor in the School of Communication Studies at Ohio University. Her research lies at the intersection of interpersonal and health communication, with a particular focus on the individual, relational, and social factors that shape supportive interactions in health contexts. Her recent work explores how individuals make sense of and respond to another's illness based on dynamics of illness-related conversations in the relationship (e.g., disclosures, emotions), as well as their beliefs about the illness (e.g., credibility, stigma, severity). Her research also investigates the goals and barriers associated with providing and receiving social support among adolescent and young adult cancer patients and survivors. Her work appears in peer-reviewed journals such as *Human Communication Research, Health Communication, Journal of Social and Personal Relationships, Patient Education & Counseling*, and *Communication Research Reports*.

Anita L. Vangelisti (PhD, The University of Texas at Austin) is the Jesse H. Jones Centennial Professor of Communication at the University of Texas at Austin. Her work focuses on the associations between communication and emotion in the context of close, personal relationships. She has published numerous articles and chapters and has edited or authored several books, including the *The Routledge Handbook of Family Communication* and *The Cambridge Handbook of Personal Relationships*. Vangelisti was editor of the Cambridge University

Press book series on Advances in Personal Relationships, was associate editor of *Personal Relationships*, and has served on the editorial boards of more than a dozen scholarly journals. She has received recognition for her research from the National Communication Association, the International Society for the Study of Personal Relationships, and the International Association for Relationship Research and served as President of the International Association for Relationship Research.

Lynne M. Webb (PhD, University of Oregon) is Professor of Communication Arts, Florida International University. She held previous tenured appointments at the Universities of Florida, Memphis, and most recently Arkansas, where she was named a J. William Fulbright Master Researcher. Her research examines family communication, social media, and romantic communication. Dr. Webb co-edited three scholarly readers, including *Communication for Families in Crisis: Theories, Research, and Strategies*. Her 75+ published essays include multiple theories, research reports, methodological pieces, and pedagogical essays. Her work has appeared in *Journal of Applied Communication Research*, *Health Communication*, and *Journal of Family Communication* as well as important collections including the *Sage Handbook of Family Communication*, *Motherhood Online*, and *Producing Theory in a Digital World*. Dr. Webb is a past president of the Southern States Communication Association and has received a Presidential Citation for her service to the National Communication Association.

Bridget Weymouth (MS, University of North Carolina Greensboro) is a doctoral student in the department of Human Development and Family Studies at the University of North Carolina at Greensboro. Her primary interests focus on how family processes are associated with parent-adolescent relationships and adolescent well-being. Her more specific interests include parent-adolescent hostility and the development of adolescent social anxiety symptoms.

Nan Zhou (MS, Beijing Normal University) currently is a doctoral student in the Department of Human Development and Family Studies at the University of North Carolina at Greensboro. He received his bachelor's degree in special education and master's degree in developmental psychology from Beijing Normal University in China. He has conducted studies on autistic children's theory of mind as well as peer and family correlates of Internet addiction among Chinese adolescents. His current areas of interest and publication focus on influences of maternal employment on family and individual well-being, as well as the impacts of interparental conflict on children and adolescent adjustment. He has particular interests and special expertise in methodology and statistical analyses.

Index

LIFESPAN
COMMUNICATION
Children, Families, and Aging

Thomas J. Socha, *General Editor*

From first words to final conversations, communication plays an integral and significant role in all aspects of human development and everyday living. The Lifespan Communication: Children, Families, and Aging series seeks to publish authored and edited scholarly volumes that focus on relational and group communication as they develop over the lifespan (infancy through later life). The series will include volumes on the communication development of children and adolescents, family communication, peer-group communication (among age cohorts), intergenerational communication, and later-life communication, as well as longitudinal studies of lifespan communication development, communication during lifespan transitions, and lifespan communication research methods. The series includes college textbooks as well as books for use in upper-level undergraduate and graduate courses.

Thomas J. Socha, Series Editor | *tsocha@odu.edu*
Mary Savigar, Acquisitions Editor | *mary.savigar@plang.com*

To order other books in this series, please contact our Customer Service Department at:

(800) 770-LANG (within the U.S.)
(212) 647-7706 (outside the U.S.)
(212) 647-7707 FAX

Or browse online by series at www.peterlang.com

www.ingramcontent.com/pod-product-compliance
Lightning Source LLC
LaVergne TN
LVHW021120180125
801621LV00003B/160